D1563759

Worldly Stage

Theatricality in Seventeenth-Century China

Harvard East Asian Monographs 267

Worldly Stage

Theatricality in Seventeenth-Century China

SOPHIE VOLPP

Published by the Harvard University Asia Center
Distributed by Harvard University Press
Cambridge (Massachusetts) and London 2011

Printed in the United States of America

The Harvard University Asia Center publishes a monograph series and, in coordination with the Fairbank Center for Chinese Studies, the Korea Institute, the Reischauer Institute of Japanese Studies, and other faculties and institutes, administers research projects designed to further scholarly understanding of China, Japan, Vietnam, Korea, and other Asian countries. The Center also sponsors projects addressing multidisciplinary and regional issues in Asia.

Library of Congress Cataloging-in-Publication Data

Volpp, Sophie.
 Worldly stage : theatricality in seventeenth-century China / Sophie Volpp.
    p. cm.
 Includes bibliographical references and index.
 ISBN 978-0-674-02144-0
 1. Theater--China--History--17th century. 2. Chinese drama--17th century--History and criticism.
I. Title.
 PN2872.V65 2011
 792.0951'09032--dc22
                        2010045124

Index by Eileen Doherty-Sil

☉ Printed on acid-free paper

Last figure below indicates year of this printing
19 18 17 16 15 14 13 12 11

To my parents

Contents

Contents

Appendix

Reference Matter

Acknowledgments

A book whose parameters were so open necessarily drew upon my entire experience as I wrote. It gave me much pleasure as I revised to recall the friends and family who had contributed so warmly to this project. When the work was slow, the mere recollection of those whose generosity and insights found their way into this work gave me encouragement.

There is still, buried under mountains of revisions, the dissertation that Patrick Hanan and Stephen Owen advised long ago. There is not a day of teaching that I do not have occasion to cite their work or recall their example. Stephen Owen taught me to read Chinese literature, and indeed to read, beginning with a course on Tang and Song poetry that I took as an undergraduate. My interest in theatricality began as I read the work of Li Yu with Patrick Hanan, Li Yu's *zhi yin*; I am grateful to him for taking the time to teach a tutorial on Chinese drama over and above his teaching load for several years. Judith Zeitlin's work on the "Three Wives' Commentary" to *Mudan ting* fostered my interest in the questions I address in this book, and I have been extremely fortunate that in the years since, our research interests have had an uncanny resonance; she has been a wonderful teacher, mentor and friend. More recently, Susan Mann and Dorothy Ko have been mentors whose example has sustained me.

As I read over the manuscript, I recall the insights, queries and friendship of Leslie Dunton-Downer, David Eng, David Hirsch, Rania Huntingdon, Regina Llamas, Benjamin Liu, David Schaberg, Anna Shields, Shang Wei, Emma Teng and Robin Wagner, who were astute critics of

this work in its early stages. My years in graduate school now seem to be bathed in a golden glow, and it is because of these generous, witty and loving friends. I would add that it is impossible to recall those years without thinking of 36 Walker St., perhaps the most vividly felt location of my adult life.

Sandeep Baliga kept me laughing during crucial years in the gestation of this manuscript (most notably, he produced a graph of the chapter on *The Male Queen*, after arguing that he could say with one picture what it had taken me thousands of words to write). Mike Bruhn and Sheila Melvin were wonderful friends during research trips first to Shanghai and later Beijing, and to Mike and his partner Bao Yifeng I owe a special thanks for allowing me to live among "China's East Coast Glitterati." Eileen Chow, Jenny Lin, Way-don Lin, Perri Strawn and Dora Ching enlivened my trips to Taipei, and I have valued their friendship and understanding during the years that followed. My great-uncle Wu Wei-chien imparted his wisdom through many evening conversations during the period that I lived at his home in Taipei, and I shall always be grateful to him and to his daughter Wu Jia-ming for their hospitality.

I will never forget the kindness and hospitality of Chang Shu-hsiang and Ko Ch'ing-ming of National Taiwan University during my years in Taipei. Ye Changhai, Zhao Shanlin, Chen Duo and Tan Fan took the time to set me straight during my periods of research in Shanghai, and Chapters Two and Four could not have been written without them. Chapter Five, likewise, exists because of my friendship with Shang Wei; it was his suggestion that I write about the poems in tribute to Ziyun, and I consulted him regarding many of the translations I did at the time. Both Shang Wei and John Zou spent hours reviewing my translation of *The Male Queen*. Matt Sommer and Lianbin Dai were also generous in answering queries.

Various colleagues at UC Davis and Berkeley lent their wisdom to this project: Vicky Kahn, Karl Britto, Kathy McCarthy, Robert Ashmore, Beth Freeman, Andrea Goldman, Kyu-hyun Kim, Saba Mahmood, Donald Moore, Carolyn de la Pena, Karen Shimakawa, Claire Waters, Andrew Jones, and Mark Csiksentmihalyi, to name a few. My sisters Leti and Serena Volpp read the entire manuscript; I am fortunate to have sisters with whom I share books and friends. John Ziemer, who edited the manuscript before his retirement from the press, had a miraculous capability to smooth the most troubled prose, and I learned a great deal from his revisions to my work. Many thanks as well go to Kristen Wanner, who took over the project so ably when John retired. Several research assistants over the years had the honor of becoming my left brain and right arm; I am particularly indebted to Abra MacDonald, Shih-wei Ho, Brian Gotanda, Myra Sun and Shilin Jia.

I had the space and time to write four new chapters after finishing the dissertation because of the generosity of the Chiang Ching-kuo Foundation, the American Council of Learned Societies, the Center for Chinese Studies at UC Berkeley, and the University of California's President's Research Fellowship in the Humanities. I am also grateful to the Mellon Foundation (Woodrow Wilson Foundation) and to Way-don Lin for their support during graduate study. Fred Wakeman, Wen-hsin Yeh, and Steve West acted as mentors during a year of post-doctoral fellowship at Berkeley; I owe to them the excitement of finding a new community of interlocuters who pushed me to broaden the scope of the work.

Lastly, I thank my children Daniel and Julia for growing before my eyes into such interesting, engaging, and loving people. I thank my father for the special bond he has with Daniel and Julia; my husband Matt for the liveliness of his mind and the quality of his patience; and my siblings Leti, Kevin and Serena for sticking together through thick and thin.

It was not until after my mother died that I realized that I had become an academic in part to honor her. Her undergraduate thesis was published in the *Journal of the American Chemical Society*; her graduate research was written about in *The New York Times*, and she did her post-doctoral research in the labs of Nobel laureates at Oxford and Harvard. She was in the lab the day I was born, but that research was her last. Her insights continue to sustain me, and it is as though her voice and her vision have grown even more capacious. This book is dedicated to my mother, who spent all she had to raise us, and to my father, whose wisdom, patience and depth of character have left a lasting impression not only upon my generation, but upon the next.

S. V.

Note on Romanization

Romanization of Chinese names and terms originally cited in Wade-Giles or other systems have been converted to *pinyin*, with the exception of names of authors who elect not to use *pinyin* in romanizing their names.

Worldly Stage

Theatricality in Seventeenth-Century China

Introduction

The literatus Zhang Dai 張岱 (1597–1684?) composed a requiem (*jiwen* 祭文) to be read at the grave of the actor Xia Rukai 夏汝開, a member of his private acting troupe. The requiem furnishes a script for the officiants, two of Xia Rukai's fellow actors sent by Zhang Dai to sacrifice a chicken and some wine before the grave. It is written as though spoken to the deceased, following the age-old tradition of the summons to the soul. The officiants read the script written in Zhang Dai's voice, and this creates an odd sense of ventriloquism:

In 1631, the loyal actor Xia Rukai died. He was buried at Jingting 敬亭 Mountain in Shaoxing.[1] The next year, during the festival of cold food, his former master bid his fellow actors Wang Wansheng 王畹生 and Li Jiesheng 李芥生 to take a flagon of wine,[2] kill a chicken, and go to his grave, summoning his soul and making sacrifices to it; they were to call to the soul of his father Fengchuan 鳳川, who was buried with him, asking him to come eat as well.[3] They said to him: "Xia Rukai, can you still understand when I speak? You were in Yue 越 for four years,

---

1. Zhang Dai may refer to Mt. Ting 亭 in Shaoxing; Mt. Jingting 敬亭 in Anhui is about 300 kilometers away.

2. The festival of cold food (Han shijie 寒食節), during which cooking is forbidden, dates to the pre-Qin era. The Qingming 清明 festival, the day on which ancestral graves are to be visited, takes place a day or two later; during the early Tang, the practices of the two festivals were combined.

3. The earliest such instance of a summons to the soul in the literary tradition is the "Zhao hun" 招魂 (Summoning the soul) of the *Chuci* 楚辭 (Songs of the south), which David Hawkes (*Songs of the South*, p. 223) dates to the third century BCE.

and you believed that I was someone who could be relied on, so you brought your parents and your younger brother and younger sister with you—all five of you came. Half a year later, your father died. You came to me crying, and I pawned my own robe so you could bury your father. A year later, when I came back from Shandong, you were gravely ill, and were sequestered in an outer chamber; I could not see you. After seven days, you were dead as well. You were from Suzhou, and both father and son had died on this soil [far from home] within the same year; I prepared both of you for your coffins and buried you. It was not merely unusual, but heartrending. You were domineering and straightforward. Now that you are gone, we forget that you were so domineering and only remember your straightforward nature. How could I not recall this quality with affection? How could I not cherish it?"

The requiem illustrates the complex relationship that had formed between this literatus and the actor who was his servant. As the two actors ask in their master's voice, "Xia Rukai, can you still understand when I speak?," the actors literally inhabit the position of their master, prefiguring a confusion regarding the relative positions of actor and master that becomes a theme in the text. It is clear that Zhang Dai had deep affection for the actor, but we hear undercurrents of other sentiments as well. The question of whether the actor appreciated the literatus's generosity and self-sacrifice as he took care of the actor's needs resonates quietly through these first lines. Zhang notes that he pawned his own robe to raise money to bury the actor's father, and one wonders why he was not able to see the actor—who presumably was living on his property—during the week before he died. Although Zhang recalls Xia Rukai's domineering manner in a way that seems to praise his straightforwardness, we have the sense that the actor, once dead, was forgiven for not knowing his station.

As the requiem continues, we find that the actor's frankness has been invoked in part to criticize the deviousness of his family:

Before you died, you left your younger sister with me as a guarantee for forty taels of silver. After you died, I thought of you with affection, and didn't ask about any of the things you owed me; I prepared provisions, bought a boat to send your mother, brother, and sister home to their native village, and introduced your sister to a husband. Do you know all this? Or are you unaware? When your mother was on the verge of leaving, she said that once your younger sister was established, she ought to come back to gather your remains and those of your father. I have never heard from them. How could this be? When I think about the words uttered carelessly in this world, it is as though they were uncanny portents. . . .

Today, of the ten actors who arrived with you, some have fled, and some have turned to other masters; the majority are no longer here. It is unfortunate that you died young, but perhaps it is also fortunate, because it ensured that from beginning to end your character did not change. Was it because Heaven wanted you to die a good man that you died young?

The straightforwardness for which Zhang praised Xia Rukai—to which Xia Rukai's imperiousness in fact testified—is now contrasted with the glibness and lack of character of Xia's family and his fellow actors. The actors that Zhang bought at the same time as Xia Rukai have proved fickle, and the ingratitude of the actor's family has created a sense of betrayal. Zhang's aggrieved tone indicts actors as a caste: only Xia Rukai's untimely death prevented him from reverting to the faithlessness of his sort. As Zhang relates that the actor used his sister as the guarantee for a loan of forty taels of silver, his phrasing is the same as it would have been had the actor pawned an object; we are reminded that actors, like servants, were bought and sold. Zhang's mistake, it is implied, was in expecting that Xia's family would appreciate the quality of his consideration. It is almost as though Zhang had been mistaken in believing that an actor's family could have the qualities a gentleman can assume in a friend.

In the final part of the requiem, Zhang assumes a tone more conventional for a culogy, describing how Xia Rukai was beloved and feted by the gentry elite:

Back when you were alive, when you powdered your face and took the stage, you employed deep emotion as you acted serious roles and clowned around as you acted comic roles, and the spectators were bowled over. Those who heard you spat out their food laughing. All praised the wondrousness of Xia Rukai. The most splendid banquets were thought dull if you weren't there to perform. The day you died, everyone sighed, from pedestrians walking the city streets to women and children, and this can be considered an honor. Consider the many famous and important officials there are in Yue. If they don't die, people wish they'd hurry up and do so; if they do die, people celebrate that they are gone. And then there are those who are not dead yet but seem as though they were; when they die it is as though nothing had changed. When you were alive, the people of Yue took pleasure in you and praised you. Now that you have died, they sigh and miss you. And your old master misses you and makes sacrifices for you at your grave. You can close your eyes in the underworld, dry your tears and be happy, invite your father to eat and drink with you, and get falling-down drunk.

In this paragraph, Xia Rukai seems almost an honorary literatus, as the placement of this requiem among those Zhang Dai wrote for his gentry friends in his *Langhuan wenji* 瑯嬛文集 also suggests. Zhang's favorable comparison of the actor to the officials of Yue resonates with the invocation of the loyalist courtesan as a model for the literatus in the works of Zhang's contemporaries Qian Qianyi 錢謙益 and Wu Weiye 吳偉業.[4] This acceptance of the actor as a literatus in spirit should be read in the context of the easy transgression of status boundaries that was characteristic of a certain fashionable elite during the late Ming and early Qing.[5] The opening of the requiem, however, tells us that the personal costs of treating an actor as one would a literati friend have not been insignificant.

The positioning of the actor as honorary literatus paves the way for the confusion of the voices of actor and literatus in the final part of the requiem. The actor who serves as officiant, speaking in Zhang Dai's voice, introduces a song that is presented as a prototype for the dead actor's future performance in the world beyond: "I have a short song. You can beat the rhythm and sing it."

> On this mountain, you can amuse yourself;
> White bones glisten, the green grave mounds linked side by side.
> In the mournful wind and harsh rain, a crowd of chattering ghosts gathers.
> I suspect you and your father won't find anyone among them who understands
>   your own dialect.
> Seeing that you are alone, some ghosts come over to bully you.
> Today they will see that people have come to make sacrifices for you,
> and they ought no longer to tease you as a hungry ghost far from home.[6]

An odd ventriloquism is once again invoked here, as the two actors whom Zhang Dai sent to the grave presumably read and perform a song in Zhang Dai's voice, a song that, it is suggested, the ghost of the dead actor might later sing. The rhetorical peculiarity calls attention to the emo-

---

4. On the identification of the literati with the courtesan, see Chang, "The Idea of the Mask in Wu Wei-yeh"; Wai-yee Li, "The Late Ming Courtesan"; Catherine Vance Yeh, "Zeng Pu's *Niehai hua* as a Political Novel"; Hu Ying, *Tales of Translation*; and Zamperini, "Lost Bodies."

5. See, e.g., Timothy Brook, *The Confusions of Pleasure*, pp. 229–33; and Frederic Wakeman, "Romantics, Stoics and Martyrs."

6. Zhang Dai, "Ji yiling wen" 祭義伶文, *Langhuan wenji*, pp. 267–69.

tional awkwardness in Zhang's portrayal of his relationship with Xia Ru-kai. The layering of voices of literatus and actor suggests the confusion in the understanding of the actor's status that Zhang's benign treatment of the actor enabled.

The symptoms of unease regarding the transgression of boundaries of status in this requiem are reminiscent of the tensions we shall find not on-ly in the representation of the historical relations between literati and ac-tors, but also in the metaphorical likening of literati and actors as well. Such tensions derive from the profound ambiguity of the actor's status. Accusations of inconstancy and duplicity were familiar indictments of the acting profession during the late Ming and early Qing. Most actors were of base status (*jianmin* 賤民) as members of the *yuehu* 樂戶 (music households), a hereditary servile status group that included prostitutes and musicians as well as actors. Members of music households, being of hereditary base status, could not become literati; the exclusion of actors and other men of base status from the civil service examinations helped define the literati as a status group.[7] The bans against actors' participation in the examination system, which was the gateway to the civil service bu-reaucracy, originated in the Yuan, and were repeatedly reinforced; each succeeding dynasty instituted such bans early in its reign.[8] Perhaps in part

---

7. Neither the Qing nor the Ming legal code explicitly states the division of the popu-lation into different status groups, but as the historian Jing Junjian has shown, underlying the codes is a conception of the population as divided into six ranks: the emperor and im-perial family; titled officials; degreed scholars without official positions; commoners (scholars without degrees, artisans, peasants, and merchants); lowly commoners such as free servants; and base people of servile status such as actors, clerks, prostitutes, and bond-servants (Jing Junjian, "Shilun Qingdai dengji zhidu," and *Qingdai shehui de jianmin dengji*; cited in Sommer, *Sex, Law and Society in Late Imperial China*, p. 346).

8. The Yuan banned actors from taking the civil service examinations in 1313. The Ming restated the Yuan ban in 1369, the second year of its rule (Wang Liqi, *Yuan Ming Qing san-dai jinhui xiaoshuo xiqu shiliao*, pp. 6, 11). The Qing government reiterated the ban in 1652, adding a provision that anyone who had succeeded in bypassing the prohibition would be dismissed from his position. Literati adoption of members of servile classes in order to cir-cumvent the ban was forbidden by a decree in 1770 (Mackerras, *The Rise of the Peking Opera*, p. 43; Hansson, *Chinese Outcasts*, p. 42). In 1788, a statute prohibited "prostitutes and actors" as well as their sons and grandsons from taking the civil service examinations or purchasing degrees, although after three generations, descendants of actors who had reformed and en-gaged in occupations proper to commoners were permitted to take the examinations (Sommer, *Sex, Law and Society in Late Imperial China*, p. 271).

because actors were not permitted the privileges of commoners, they were often accused of seeking to acquire privileges beyond their station.[9]

The debased status of actors also meant that they were not held to the same standards of moral behavior as were commoners.[10] As we see in legal discourse, sex work was considered a normal, even normative, function of those of base status.[11] This association of actors with sex work contributed to their perception as fickle and potentially treacherous.[12] Such associations with actors and acting were common to many periods and cultures, but acquire a particular articulation in seventeenth-century China in the context of the examination system as a gateway to literati status. The literatus's fascination with the actor's ability to cast illusions (and in particular, with the erotic potential of the cross-dressed actor's illusory femininity) was accompanied by the fear that such a capacity might allow the actor to evade the hereditary restrictions on his status and infiltrate the ranks of the literatus. At the same time, as we see in Zhang Dai's requiem, the artistry of celebrated performers created a sense of exceptionalism that allowed them to mingle with literati; the actor Xu Ziyun 徐紫雲 (?–1675?), and the storyteller Liu Jingting 柳敬亭, whom I discuss in Chapters 5 and 6, furnish cases in point. It is in part by asking how texts such as Zhang Dai's "Requiem for a Righteous Actor" 祭義伶文 help us understand the historical and metaphorical relations between literati and actors that we can begin to piece together the significance of what it meant to liken a literatus to an actor during the late Ming and early Qing.[13] The literatus's fascination with actors and acting was spurred and

---

9. Although actors as an occupational group were considered to be of base status, some actors were commoners; household servants trained to perform, for example, did not lose their commoner status.

10. On the differing standards to which commoners and *jianmin* were held, see Sommer, *Sex, Law and Society in Late Imperial China*, pp. 7–8.

11. On the fungibility of the term *yuehu* with terms for prostitutes, such as *chang* 娼 and *ji* 妓, see ibid., pp. 212–15. On sex work as a normative function of base status, see ibid., pp. 4–8.

12. Many actors were also itinerant, which contributed to the deep suspicion with which they were viewed (Hansson, *Chinese Outcasts*, pp. 42–48, 55–74).

13. I do not discuss the relations between literati and actresses or courtesans in this study. In focusing on the relations between literati and actors, however, I do not mean to imply that relations between literati and actors predominated in actuality. Rather, I am

reinforced by his interest in philosophical questions about the phenomenal world and its relation to illusion.

This is a book about the emotional topography occupied by the idea of the worldly stage in seventeenth-century China. The sentiment that the world is like a stage is rarely encapsulated in neat phrases in seventeenth-century texts. The notion of the worldly stage surfaces, rather, in the parallels drawn between social roles and theatrical roles; in the sense of the self as a spectacle before others; in the stage's consciousness of itself as stage; and in the conception of the stage as a realm of illusion that enables the spectator to recognize the illusory nature of all things. These may seem rather abstract formulations, but seventeenth-century authors used them—and the notions of performance and spectatorship embedded in them—to illuminate the most pressing concerns of the period. The metaphor of world as stage thus came to elucidate phenomena as diverse as the new glamour of the mercantile, the pressure of a newly educated stratum on the traditional elite, the cultural politics of literary citation, and the need to come to terms with the significance of Confucian loyalism in the wake of the fall of the Ming.

I chose the texts presented here because they speak tellingly and directly either to the metaphorical relations between actors and literati or to the social space occupied by the stage itself, that is, to the way in which theatricals and theatricality had an enabling presence in social relations. I examine the canonical texts that book-end the seventeenth-century dramatic tradition—*Mudan ting* 牡丹亭 (The peony pavilion; preface dated 1598) and *Taohua shan* 桃花扇 (The peach blossom fan; completed in 1699)—placing them in the context of lesser-known writings that concern acting and the stage, such as Wang Jide's 王驥德 (1542?–1623) northern drama *Nan wanghou* 男王后 (The male queen), the poems of Chen Weisong's coterie in tribute to the actor Yunlang, and the anonymous tales of *Bian er chai* 弁而釵 (Hairpins beneath a cap). This book, then, is not so much a study of meta-theatricality as a consideration of the ways in which concerns regarding the relation between world and stage

---

interested in illuminating these relations because of the understudied metaphorical resonances between literati and actors.

suffused all aspects of literary culture—poetry, fiction, drama, casual essays, jokes.[14]

In the pages that follow, we will elucidate two modes of thinking about the relation between world and stage during the seventeenth century. In the first, theatrical roles are likened to social roles, and theatrical spectatorship becomes the training ground for the recognition of social imposture and inauthenticity. If the theater trains the spectator of the social realm in the art of social observation, it is because witnessing the falseness of actors and acting enables the theatrical spectator to see through social impersonation, and to acknowledge that people in society may inhabit roles for which they are not qualified. The spectator inhabits a fixed vantage point; the goal is not to participate in illusion, but to discount it. The theater then becomes a figure for the disjunction of appearance and actuality. This mode of thinking about the relation between world and stage could well be cast as anti-theatricalist.

In the second and more profound understanding of the relation between world and stage, the stage becomes a space that allows the spectator to apprehend the illusory nature of all forms. Reading drama, viewing theater, and fraternizing with actors train the social spectator to enter the spectacle and immerse himself in it, to engage with illusion even while understanding it to be such. The mobile and participatory quality of an acting culture in which boundaries of status are easily traversed is conceptually linked to a panoramic quality of perception that would allow the spectator of worldly affairs to immerse himself in the world of forms and at the same time apprehend its illusory quality. The most refined spectator—of whom Zhang Dai is the emblematic example—has a capacity for simultaneously impassioned and dispassionate observation and moves

---

14. Because my focus is the relation between the theatrical and the social, I do not include discussion of several well-known dramas that address the meta-theatrical—Li Yu's 李漁 (1611–1680?) *Bimu yu* 比目魚 (Sole mates, 1661), Hong Sheng's 洪昇 (1645–1704) *Chang shengdian* 長生殿 (The palace of eternal life, 1688), and Xu Wei's 徐渭 (1521–1593) *Kuang gushi* 狂鼓史 (The mad drummer) most prominent among them. For analyses of meta-theatricality in *Bimuyu*, *Chang shengdian*, and *Kuang gushi* respectively, see Shen Jing, "Role Types in *The Paired Fish*, a *Chuanqi* Play," *Asian Theatre Journal* 20, no. 2 (Fall 2003): 226–36; Judith Zeitlin, *The Phantom Heroine*, pp. 181–97; and He Yuming, "Productive Space," pp. 18–29.

headlong into the tangle of illusion and disillusion.[15] In this understanding of theater and theatricality, only the vulgar seek to distinguish between illusion and reality.[16] These two modes of thinking about the stage circulate in tandem through the long seventeenth century (roughly 1570–1720) and are paired in subtle and surprising ways.[17]

This book engages in conversation with (and is indebted to) a growing body of scholarship on seventeenth-century Chinese theater and, in particular, scholarship concerning the plays *Mudan ting* and *Taohua shan*.[18] I hope that my contribution to the conversation will be to elucidate conceptions of theatricality derived from writing about performance, performers, and the stage.[19] Scholars of seventeenth-century literature and

---

15. This tension between illusion and disillusion is quite similar to the trajectory of enchantment and disenchantment that Wai-yee Li has shown to be central to the classical tales of Pu Songling's 蒲松齡 *Liaozhai zhiyi* 聊齋誌異 and Cao Xueqin's 曹雪芹 *Honglou meng* 紅樓夢; see her *Enchantment and Disenchantment*. The perspectival challenge that asks the spectator to hold illusion and disillusion in tension simultaneously, however, could be considered quintessentially theatrical. Fictional narrative often posits a linear development from illusion to emptiness. Although the trajectory from illusion to disillusion is also often present in dramatic plots, particularly those of deliverance plays, the performative dimension of drama ensures that a consciousness of the illusory nature of performance is layered on top of the trajectory from illusion to disillusion within the plot of the play itself.

16. One could object to the use of the terms "theater" and "theatricality" on the grounds that most performances took part on temporary stages—a red felt carpet signified the space of the stage—rather than in theaters. If we go back to the Greek root of the word theater, *thea* (a place from which to observe or see), however, the term suggests the emphasis on spectatorship, theatrical and social, I find in these sources. Moreover, as we shall see in Chapter 2, the concept of the theater was well established during the Ming, in part because large theaters had existed during the Song, in part because fixed stages were a feature of temple architecture.

17. This periodization reflects an emphasis on social continuity from the late Ming to the early Qing despite political upheaval. For more on the significance of these dates, see Dorothy Ko, *Teachers of the Inner Chambers*, pp. 22–23.

18. See, e.g., Zeitlin's "Shared Dreams," Swatek's *"The Peony Pavilion" Onstage*; Wai-yee Li's *Enchantment and Disenchantment* and "The Representation of History in *The Peach Blossom Fan*," Tina Lu's *Persons, Roles and Minds*, and Stephen Owen's "I Don't Want to Be Emperor Anymore."

19. Several scholars of seventeenth-century literature have contributed significantly to our understanding of seventeenth-century conceptions of theatricality. Tina Lu's *Persons, Roles and Minds* draws on the work of the philosopher Stanley Cavell to discuss problems of identification and identity; in her analysis, performance is often equated with dissimu-

culture frequently note that identity had come to seem performative and
social relations theatrical, but seventeenth-century Chinese theatrical aesthetics and performance practice so differed from the practices of the
western theater that we must ask how the conceptualization of theatrical
acting and spectatorship, as well as the physical and temporal space of the
stage, might have influenced the notion that the world was like a stage. In
asking how literary and anecdotal writing about the stage can make dramatic texts newly legible, I attempt to create a bridge between two modes
of inquiry that have traditionally been segregated: the study of theatrical
culture and the close reading of literary texts.[20] By investigating the social
relations between literati and actors within the world of literati theatricals,
I show how indebted seventeenth-century literary culture was to theatrical culture and how much conceptions of social spectatorship owed to
theatrical models. In the conclusion, I show how this investigation of late-
imperial Chinese conceptions of theatricality offers a refutation to the
notion that the classical Chinese theater inherently exemplifies an alienation (Bertolt Brecht) or hollowness (Samuel Weber) that might furnish
an alternative to the western tradition's preoccupation with mimesis and

---

lation. Judith Zeitlin (*The Phantom Heroine*, pp. 131–80) investigates the phantasmic
quality of characters played by the *hun dan* 魂旦 role type (a type of female lead that specializes in ghosts), considering the theatrical representation of the divided body and soul
by examining the stage practices associated with the *hun dan*.

20. It seems particularly important to historicize conceptions of theatricality, basing
them in seventeenth-century Chinese thinking about the stage and stage practice, in that
the almost protean nature of the term has been much discussed over the past decade. As
Janelle Reinelt has remarked in an article that speaks to distinctions among notions of performance, performativity, and theatricality, theatricality has had a "more diffuse history
than performance and the performative"; although widely invoked, it has a less precise eti-
ology and is often used metaphorically, in ways that "threaten to dilute any prospective
genealogy of this discourse" (Janelle Reinelt, "The Politics of Discourse: Performativity
Meets Theatricality," *SubStance* 2002 31, no. 2&3: 205). Both the special issue of *SubStance*
in which Reinelt's article is published and Tracy Davis and Thomas Postlewait's edited
volume *Theatricality* (2003) sought to give a finer texture to usages of "theatricality" in
comparative historical context. Postlewait in particular calls for greater attention to "the
medium of theatre" in articulating historically specific notions of theatricality. Noting
that a relatively unhistoricized conceptualization of theatricality was given a great deal of
explanatory power in new historicist readings of Elizabethan state spectacle, Postlewait
suggests that "theater history is the one aspect of theatricality that gets short-changed"
(Postlewait, "Theatricality and Antitheatricality in Renaissance London," p. 115).

its epigones.[21] The spectator of the seventeenth-century Chinese theater was not estranged or alienated; rather, the culture of the theater fostered a quality of perception that was simultaneously impassioned and dispassionate, that was immersed and participatory as well as cognizant of the positive value of disillusion.

The book is organized to show the development of the metaphor of the worldly stage over the long seventeenth century. Each chapter of this book refracts a different aspect of the metaphor. My argument has three parts. The opening two chapters lay out the primary modes of thinking about theatricality in seventeenth-century China and link the preoccupation of seventeenth-century authors with the notion of the world as stage to developments in performance practice and stage architecture. Chapter 1 reads a host of sources to elucidate the two conceptions of theatricality explored in this book. As I noted above, in the first of these, the theater becomes a figure for the disjunction of appearance and actuality, so that theatrical role-playing becomes a metaphor for social imposture. This concern regarding social imposture is inspired in part by the sixteenth-century rise of the mercantile, which permitted the *nouveaux riches* to assemble the accoutrements of gentry status. As Li Yu 李漁 (1611–80?) remarks in his play *Naihetian* 奈何天 (What can you do about fate), a clown plays the role of gentleman in his play, because most "gentlemen" in society today are in fact clowns. But, as *Naihetian* reveals to us, the theater is also a figure for the conjunction of illusion and actuality, the critical element in structuring social illusion. In this model of the relation between the theatrical and the social, the social is enabled by the theatrical rather than weakened by it. The theatrical spectator's ability to keep illusion and disillusion in tension, to suspend doubt even while understanding the events on stage to be unreal, becomes a model for the social spectator's participation in the world of forms even as he understands it ultimately to be illusory. The spectator enters the spectacle, but also views it as an omniscient observer, and this gives rise to a mode of spectatorship that I suggest is participatory and panoramic. Eventually this mode of social spectatorship is trained by the literatus upon himself, so that he be-

---

21. Brecht's use of the classical Chinese theater as an example of an inherently "alienated" form of performance is well known. See Bertolt Brecht, "Alienation Effects in Chinese Acting," in John Willett, ed., *Brecht on Theater*, pp. 91–97.

comes both actor and spectator in the drama of his own literary and social aspiration. This mode of spectatorship becomes associated in the writings of partisans of the theater with the *fengliu* 風流, the nonchalant rake or romantic characterized by an insouciant disdain for careerism and social convention.

In the second chapter, the analysis of literary texts pauses as we consider performance practices and stage architecture. I argue that seventeenth-century performance practices and staging contributed to a sense that the boundaries between world and stage had become porous, and that the space of performance and spectatorship extended far beyond the stage. The practice of owning private acting troupes and sponsoring theatricals fostered an easy camaraderie between actor and spectator, and the advent in the late Ming of the new practices of performing medleys of scenes as opposed to entire texts fostered the sense that a performance should resonate thematically with its context. This sense of a soluble boundary between world and stage may have been subtly altered by the rise of the fixed stage at the end of the seventeenth century, when commercial establishments in urban centers called wine shops (*jiulou* 酒樓) began to feature fixed stages, and the professional acting troupes who performed on such stages rose to new prominence. Perhaps reflecting the increased sense of distance between spectator and spectacle on the fixed stage, the relation between world and stage is portrayed quite differently in Kong Shangren's 孔尚任 (1648–1718) *Taohua shan* than it is in texts that appear earlier in the century: the boundary between parallel ontological realms is more highly defined, and the text itself theorizes the resonance between world and stage with a degree of explicitness not found earlier.

After these introductory chapters, I move into extended analysis of dramatic texts. Chapters 3 and 4 pair Tang Xianzu's 湯顯祖 (1550–1616) *Mudan ting* and Wang Jide's *Nan wanghou* to consider the cultural politics of literary citation; in this pairing, the two conceptions of theatricality we have discussed are contrasted and further unfold. *Mudan ting* employs the first mode of theatricality, in which actors and acting are equated with social imposture and inauthenticity, to critique the overbearing use of allusion by followers of the dominant literary trend of the period, archaism. The importance attached to literary exchange on social occasions made the inappropriate use of allusion by those who were unsatisfactorily learned almost a sumptuary violation. Even as the commodification of literati culture rendered the emblems of literati cultivation available to a larger sector of society, the expansion of academies and the widespread availability of books gave a greater proportion of the populace access to the traditional canon. The *nouveaux riches* were joined by a bulging stratum we might call the newly educated. In the literature of the late Ming and early Qing, this "newly educated" stratum is represented by the pedantic schoolmaster or examination candidate anxious to display his education. *Mudan ting* exploits the potential similarities between social and theatrical roles to mock such schoolmasters and examination candidates, whose excessive use of allusion sounds scripted and staged. The members of the Gong'an school, who were among Tang Xianzu's extended circle, are well known for their anti-archaist sentiments; I show how they join Tang Xianzu in employing the figure of the theater to rail against men of insufficient culture who decorated their language with allusions, likening them to actors who declaimed words scripted by others that they did not understand. The invocation of theatricality became a means of deriding an inauthentic relation to the literary past. To say that an author sounds like an actor, in other words, was a means of decrying the shallowness of his cultural understanding.

If *Mudan ting* uses the figure of the theater to lampoon the pretensions of a would-be elite, suggesting that their relation to the cultural past is inauthentic, the next play I consider, Wang Jide's *Nan wanghou*, wittily asks whether a genuine relation to the cultural past is possible. *Nan wanghou* plays with visual and temporal perception to question the premise of authenticity and originality upon which a notion of imposture might be based. The play, which dates to the early seventeenth century, depicts an erotic liaison between a cross-dressed boy and the King of Linchuan 臨川, the future Emperor Wen 文 of the Chen dynasty. The play shares *Mudan ting*'s concern regarding the citation of allusion in the service of social aspiration, rephrasing such concerns in a ludicrously ribald fashion. The cross-dressed boy literally garbs himself in allusions to the famed consorts and courtesans of the past as he rises through the harem to become queen. The question of the spectator's susceptibility to the illusion of stage gender forms a point of departure for an exploration of the phantasmic quality of historical models. Just as *Nan wanghou* asks us to hold illusion and disillusion in tension in considering the gender of the cross-dressed actor, it asks us to simultaneously believe and disbelieve in the authenticity of historical models. If *Mudan ting* views poetic predecessors as authentic, deploring their strategic citation, *Nan wanghou* questions the authenticity of these predecessors and refuses to submit to the authority of the cultural past. The play frames its inquiry with perspectival challenges addressed to the spectator. In the opening lines, the actor teases the spectator as to his helplessness before the illusory operations of the cross-dressed actor's gender; in the closing lines, the characters taunt the audience regarding its inability to see through the illusions of presence.

In the final two chapters, we see quite concretely how the model of theatrical spectatorship articulated in *Nan wanghou* becomes a mode of social spectatorship. The poems in tribute to the boy actor that I consider in Chapter 5 emanate from the world of private theatricals. In them, a perspectival challenge similar to that elucidated in *Nan wanghou* leads the reader to question how we ought to conceptualize the literatus poet's declarations of longing for the actor. The poems I discuss were penned by some of the most prominent national figures of the mid-seventeenth century in tribute to the seventeen-year affair of the actor Xu Ziyun with the poet Chen Weisong 陳維崧 (1626–82), scion of one of the most prominent families of Jiangnan. They show how the world of private theatricals influenced the social topography of a circle of poets and statesmen affiliated with Chen Weisong and his patron, the author Mao Xiang 冒襄 (1634–1711). In examining these historical relationships between literati and actors, I want to shed light on the way in which the sexual liaisons between them were understood. As we shall see in the poems of Chen's circle, the expression of desire for the actor, nominally transgressive because of the actor's debased status, became normative in the context of the social necessity of dramatizing oneself as a man of authentic passion. Literary luminaries of the Ming-Qing transition such as Gong Dingzi 龔鼎孳 (1616–73) and Mao Xiang—and lesser-known figures such as Deng Hanyi 鄧漢儀 (1617–89), Wang Shilu 王士祿 (1626–73), and Sun Zhiwei 孫枝蔚 (1620–87)—present themselves in these poems as devoted, even besotted spectators of the actor Xu Ziyun. The authors of these poems avow a transgressive desire for the actor, declaring their rivalry with other spectators and with Chen himself. Ironically, what makes these declarations of rivalry possible is the poet's empathic identification with Chen. As the poet's *qing* (sentiment, feeling, or passion) is stirred by Chen's own, his empathy leads him to pen more poems in praise of the actor. This empathic generation renders the poems written in response to Chen's passion both mimetic and expressive, both staged and authentic; the perspectival challenge is to keep these incompatible types of utterance simultaneously in mind in considering the homoerotic sentiments expressed in these poems.

In Chapter Six, the cultivation of the ability to hold illusion and disillusion in tension furnishes a kind of consolation for those who witnessed the tragic spectacle of the fall of the Ming. Kong Shangren seeks to instruct his audience in achieving catharsis after the traumatic fall of the Ming dynasty. As the last days of the Ming are replayed on the stage, the spectator's sympathetic attachment to the events portrayed is systematically ruptured by meta-theatrical prologues and interludes that advise the spectator to watch the play—and by extension, the illusory phenomena of this world—with "clear cold eyes" (*lengyan* 冷眼). The model for this detachment is the storyteller Liu Jingting, a celebrity honored by such authors as Wu Weiye and Zhang Dai, who composed biographies for him. In *Nan wanghou*, the rhetorical pyrotechnics of the young boy who serves as a figure for the actor were depicted as dazzlingly irresponsible, a portrayal that drew on old habits of thought regarding the glibness of actors. Kong Shangren, in contrast, lauds Liu Jingting's linguistic agility, suggesting that Liu's easy movement among social strata derives in part from his jester's capacity for improvisation and his storyteller's ability to inhabit a range of discursive modes. The actor's rhetorical dexterity and command over illusionary worlds thus acquires a newly positive valence. Ultimately, the deftness with which Liu moves among disparate linguistic and social registers grants him an exemplary dispassion that translates into an understanding of the way in which illusion structures reality. Like Liu, the play itself displays an ideological versatility, in the last scene and epilogue switching rapidly between Confucian and Daoist understandings of the significance of the fall of the Ming. The play between Confucian attachment and Daoist disillusion allows the spectator to experience and be alienated from each in succession, creating the sensation of being caught within ideological illusion and then escaping its reach.

The two modes of thinking about theatricality that I discuss above— the negative charge of inauthenticity and the positive valuation of disillusion—are folded into each other through the long seventeenth century.

After the fall of the Ming dynasty in 1644, the fascination with the dialectical relation between illusion and disillusion achieved a new poignancy, as the luxurious excesses of the waning Ming came to seem but a dream. Zhang Dai, with whose recollection of Xia Rukai we began, was the scion of a gentry family whose wealth vanished with the fall of the Ming. He wrote quite touchingly in the preface of his *Tao'an mengyi* that once the polity was dissolved and his home lost, he sought refuge in a monastery in the mountains of his native Shaoxing.[22] All the splendors he had known had evaporated into emptiness. "The cock crows as I lie on my pillow; the vapors of the night are about to recede. I think upon the prosperity and luxury I have experienced in this life, and it passes before my eyes, all emptiness. The past fifty years have become merely a dream."[23] The notion that officials were but actors on a worldly stage permitted a governing class battered by political vicissitudes to cultivate a lack of attachment inflected by Buddhist and Daoist thought. The actor's plasticity of identity earlier provided a metaphor for social imposture, the urgency of this metaphor occasioned in part by the new prominence of the nouveaux riches and newly educated. After the fall of the Ming, however, the actor's privileged understanding of the illusory nature of the world of forms also came to be viewed as exemplary, a means of coming to terms with dynastic transition, as we see in Kong's *Taohua shan.*

Actors, acting, and the stage were associated with a broader crisis of representation in late Ming and early Qing China. The late sixteenth and seventeenth centuries have long been held to be the age of the literati stage, a time when private theatrical entertainments became *de rigueur* among the literati elite, and the composition of plays became fashionable among them as well. But to view this period as the age of the literati stage simply because literati engaged in private theatricals and composed plays in unprecedented numbers is to ignore the important ideological niche that the stage occupied in diverse genres of cultural production.

---

22. After Zhang fled the Manchu invasion in the summer of 1646, he shaved his head and lived in a monastery, although he never became a monk (Brook, *Praying for Power*, pp. 37–45).

23. Zhang Dai, *Langhuan wenji*, p. 9.

Scholars across the disciplines have remarked on a new sense of an "I" in seventeenth-century China, an enhanced consciousness of the multiplicity of roles available to the self.[24] This heightened awareness of the self as a spectacle visible to others is evident in an increased fascination with self-dramatization, masking, fabrication, and dissimulation. We see an interest in role-playing and self-dramatization in many genres of late Ming and early Qing literati cultural production—in Chen Hongshou's 陳洪 綬 (1598–1652) paintings, for example—but it was most felicitously expressed in plays and writing on the theater, which explored the notion that social roles might be akin to theatrical roles.[25]

The ascendance during the late Ming of drama as a performing art and literary form is typically ascribed to a trinity of factors: the expansion of the realm of print, the growth of urban centers, and the rapid development of a mercantile economy. Anthologies of dramatic texts were published in greater numbers than ever before, the development of entertainment districts in urban centers spurred competition among theatrical troupes, and the increase in commercial travelers facilitated the spread of operatic styles. However, if print, urbanization, and commercialization contributed to the development of drama as a literary and performing art, on quite another level they helped shape an increased consciousness of the potential theatricality of the literatus's sense of an "I." The print explosion rendered the author a figure on a public stage speaking to an audience of faceless readers.[26] The proximity of disparate social spheres in rap-

---

24. See, e.g., Brook, *The Confusions of Pleasure*; Cahill, *Compelling Image*, pp. 124–27; idem, *Fantastics and Eccentrics in Chinese Painting*; Hay, *Shitao*; Lu, *Persons, Roles and Minds*, and Vinograd, *Boundaries of the Self*.

25. Chen Hongshou's *A Literary Gathering*, for example, probably done in the mid-1640s, depicts the Yuan 袁 brothers Hongdao 宏道, Zhongdao 中道, and Zongdao 宗道 and several of their associates in a fashion reminiscent of a fifth-century group called the White Lotus Society. See Vinograd, *Boundaries of the Self*, pp. 30–36. On the use of gestures and props drawn from the theater in Chen Hongshou's painting, see Bentley, "Authenticity in a New Key."

26. The historian Joseph McDermott cautions that the effects of the much-vaunted print explosion should not be overstated, and must be considered in the context of the continued importance of the copying of manuscripts (*A Social History of the Chinese Book*, p. 47); this point is well taken. But however small the ratio of print to manuscript copies, print loomed large in the public imagination, and the conception of print as a desirable

idly developing urban centers fostered a heightened sense of social spectacle. As the emblems of elite culture were marketed to a wealthy but ostensibly uncultivated mercantile class, the notion of social imposture came to the fore.[27] The drama, always viewed as a genre with the potential for moral instruction, became a vehicle with which authors investigated the new fluidity of emblems of status and of social hierarchies.

In China as in the West, the notion of the world as stage originally spoke to the vanity of human achievement, the ephemerality of rank and honor. In the sub-genre of Yuan drama that Stephen H. West and Wilt Idema describe as the "deliverance play," a Daoist master converts a recalcitrant disciple, bringing him to an understanding of the vanity of worldly things and leading him to transcendence of the mundane world.[28] An example is the anonymous northern drama (*zaju* 雜劇) *Han Zhongli du tuo Lan Caihe* 漢鍾離度脫藍采和 (Zhongli of the Han leads Lan Caihe to enlightenment), which Idema and West date to the latter half of the thirteenth century.[29] This deliverance play features one of the Eight Immortals, Lan Caihe, who, previous to his enlightenment, manages a theater troupe. His experience of the stage plays a critical role in his enlightenment. Initially, Lan Caihe views his versatility in the roles he plays as a sign of his mastery of the ways of the world; he equates success on the stage with worldly success. But by play's end the significance of the stage has changed. He states in the closing lines, "In the theater I became enlightened / Never will I re-enter the actors' ranks" (构欄中得悟, 再不入

---

and ultimate destination surely occasioned fundamental changes in the conception of an author's relation to his audience.

27. The art historian Jonathan Hay has argued that the commodification of elite culture should not be blamed merely on the ability of the *nouveaux riches* to acquire the signs of elite culture; the willingness of the elite to market them was also a factor. Hay writes that "literati life was probably first made into spectacle toward the end of the fifteenth century, when literati painters in Suzhou discovered that a socially exclusionary art form originally developed for a private culture of like minds was eminently marketable" (*Shitao*, p. 53).

28. Idema and West (*Chinese Theater*, p. 305) note that two Buddhist plays of the late thirteenth century may also be considered deliverance plays.

29. The play is reprinted in *Zhongguo guben xiqu congkan*, series 4, vol. 31. See Idema and West, *Chinese Theater*, pp. 299–343, for a full translation of the play and information on its provenance; regarding the dating of the play, see ibid., pp. 308–9.

班行).[30] When he is momentarily tempted to rejoin his wife and former troupe, he lifts a curtain looking for the costumes in which he played comedy, only to find the immortals Han Zhongli and Lü Dongbin, who ask whether Lan Caihe's "worldly heart" (*fanxin* 凡心) has "not yet withdrawn" (*butui* 不退).[31] The question brings about a sudden enlightenment. The notions of acting and the stage now point implicitly to the evanescence of the affairs of this world.

The inheritance of the deliverance play can be found in such late Ming plays as Wang Heng's 王衡 (1561–1609) *Zhen kuilei* 眞傀儡 (The real puppet) and Tang Xianzu's *Handan ji* 邯鄲記 (The tale of Handan), where it underlies the notion of transcending the mundane by preserving illusion and disillusion in tension. During the late sixteenth and seventeenth centuries, however, in China as in Europe, the notion of the world as stage expanded to become a vehicle for reflecting on the complicated relations between appearance and reality in a burgeoning mercantile economy and, in particular, for critiquing the posturing and self-costuming of a rising middle elite.[32] As in the West, the figure of the theater helped articulate the sense that the increasing permeability of status hierarchies and the fluidity of emblems of status had made possible a new degree of social imposture. The self-fashioning of actors provided a metaphor for the self-fashioning of individuals. However, because of the importance of the Chinese civil service examinations rather than birth in determining gentry status, the articulation of status groups was quite different in China than it was in the West; the question of imposture in literary endeavors that we explore in Chapter 3 was thus comparatively more fraught.

As historians of the late imperial period such as Timothy Brook, Cynthia Brokaw, Kai-wing Chow, and Qitao Guo have observed, during the mid-sixteenth century, the rapid inclusion of new sectors of the economy in commercial networks set in motion a tectonic shift in traditional social

---

30. *Han Zhongli dutuo Lan Caihe*, 10b; Idema and West, *Chinese Theater*, p. 331.

31. *Han Zhongli dutuo Lan Caihe*, 15a; Idema and West, *Chinese Theater*, p. 339.

32. Jean-Christophe Agnew has examined a similar phenomenon in the literature of the Renaissance and Restoration England, arguing that "the professional theater of the English Renaissance," by "confronting the conditions of its own performance, invoked the same problematic of exchange—the same questions of authenticity, accountability and intentionality—at issue in the 'idea of the market'" (*Worlds Apart*, p. 11).

hierarchies.[33] As the status of merchants and of mercantile activity itself rose, merchants bought genealogies from bankrupt gentry families and decorated their residences with the emblems of literati culture.[34] Merchant families also began to produce degreed scholars. Qitao Guo's study of the prosperous Huizhou merchants has shown that even those unable to participate in the examination system imitated the gentry in reading Confucian texts, adopting Confucian values, and giving their sons a classical education, sometimes strategically deciding which sons would focus on classical learning and which would ensure the continuation of the family's wealth by pursuing business.[35] Richard von Glahn has stated that at no time in late imperial history were authors as vexed regarding the symbolic import of money and wealth as they were during the late Ming.[36] Seventeenth-century sources testify to increasing distress regarding the accumulation of markers of literati culture by those engaged in mercantile or other lowly pursuits.[37]

---

33. See Brook, *Confusions of Pleasure*; Brokaw, *Ledgers of Merit and Demerit*; and Qitao Guo, *Ritual Opera and Mercantile Lineage*.

34. Brokaw, *Ledgers of Merit and Demerit*, p. 5.

35. Qitao Guo's study of Huizhou merchants notes that merchant families strategically alternated from generation to generation between educating their sons to seek success in the examinations and encouraging them to pursue commercial wealth (Guo, *Ritual Opera and Mercantile Lineage*, pp. 56–69). Guo writes of a passion among Huizhou merchants to "shed their vocational skin and join the gentry class" (p. 62). Wang Daokun 汪道崑 (1525–93), a noted scholar from a mercantile family of Shexian 歙縣, noted that in Xin'an 新安, a region in which numerous gentry families chose to engage in trade, "It has been the local custom to be either Confucian scholars or merchants, alternating by generations" (Zhang Haipeng et al., *Ming Qing huishang ziliao xuanbian*, p. 438). On Wang Daokun's writings regarding the lack of contradiction between scholarship and mercantile activity, see Brook, *Confusions of Pleasure*, p. 215; and Guo, *Ritual Opera and Mercantile Lineage*, p. 67.

36. See von Glahn, "The Enchantment of Wealth," p. 651.

37. Authors of notation books (*biji* 筆記) of this period deplore the pretensions of those who seek to acquire the emblems of cultivation associated with the scholarly elite. Fan Lian's notation book *Yunjian jumu chao* (2.3b), for example, records disdainfully that even law-enforcement officials (*zao kuai* 皂快) who worked for the *yamen* 衙門 had begun to create spaces that they called studies (*haocheng shufang* 號稱書房), decorating them in the literati fashion. Fan Lian comments dryly: "I really do not know what books they studied." For another discussion of this passage, see also Wang Shixiang, *Classical Chinese Furniture*, p. 14.

Anxieties regarding social impersonation within the gentry elite surfaced in the obsession of literati authors with actors and acting. Many late Ming writers lamented the new plasticity of social identity and a lack of sincerity and accountability in human relations. Authentic passion (*zhenqing* 真情) became one of the most exalted qualities in seventeenth-century literary discourse, perhaps in part because it provided an antidote to prevailing concerns regarding social posturing and hypocrisy. Concerns about fakery and forgery in the marketplace paralleled a fear of counterfeiting, dissimulation, and forgery in social interaction.[38] The tension between seeing and knowing was expressed in the epistemological and ontological dilemmas suggested by the theater itself. The figure of the actor, then, spoke to a capacity for protean self-transformation and a lack of accountability that were seen as qualities of the *nouveaux riches* (or the newly educated). A constellation of factors—the base status of the actor, the legal restrictions that prohibited him from gaining official position, and the association of acting with prostitution—rendered the actor a potent metaphor for the appropriation of the privileges of literati by the undeserving.

If performance was the problem, discerning spectatorship was the solution. The notion of social spectatorship became a vehicle for coming to terms with the mercantile appropriation of literati cultivation. Plays such as Li Yu's *Naihetian* and essays such as those in Zhang Dai's *Tao'an mengyi/Xihu mengxun* 陶庵夢憶/西湖夢尋 (Dream recollections of Tao'an / Searching for West Lake in dreams) modeled a discreet social voyeurism by exposing the rising middle elite's appropriation of emblems of status. Such texts can be seen as countering the influence of the manuals of style so popular in the late Ming, which arbitrated questions of taste such as the proper design for a parquet floor.[39] If manuals such as Wen Zhenheng's 文震亨 (1585–1645) *Zhangwu zhi* 長物志 (Superfluous things) coached the *nouveaux riches* as to how to acquire and exhibit the

---

38. Craig Clunas has observed that the "combination of developed market structures with an enlarged but insecure body of consumers . . . made the late Ming period one of the great ages of Chinese faking" (Clunas, "Connoisseurs and Aficionados," p. 151).

39. See Li Yu's *Xianqing ouji* 閒情偶記 in *Li Yu quanji*, 11: 166–69.

decorative elements of the literatus' studio, texts such as *Naihetian* helped the literati spectator to disassemble such displays.[40]

We shall see in a host of texts that a quintessentially theatrical mode of spectatorship provided a model for the spectator of the worldly stage. Seventeenth-century authors turned to the metaphors of theatrical performance and theatrical spectatorship to suggest how a discerning spectator might evaluate the performance of status. Their exploration of theatricality provided a means to articulate the precariousness of an emerging middle elite's purchase on the symbolic capital of the inheritance of the cultural past. Theatrical metaphors thus helped parse changes in the constitution of the literary elite, and notions of performance and spectatorship became vehicles for inscribing the newly proximate relations of formerly disparate social spheres.

In its simplest form, the theatrical mode of social spectatorship encouraged the spectator of the worldly stage to see through social imposture as though it were mere costuming, to view social roles as being akin to theatrical roles. A far more complex and subtle articulation of the principles of theatrical spectatorship also circulated in seventeenth-century literary discourse, one related to the older phrasing of the world as stage, which concerned the vanity of human achievement. The drama of the late Ming often presents the implied spectator with a perspectival challenge, asking him not only to enter the enchanted realm of the theater but also to recognize its illusory quality—to hold illusion and disillusion in tension.[41] This formed a model for a simultaneous engagement and disengagement with the forms of the phenomenal world. A quatrain inscribed as a set of couplets (*duilian* 對聯) hanging from each side of a stage at the playwright Tang Xianzu's ancestral home illustrates how that simultaneous engagement and disengagement might take shape:

> Through the ages those actors who were loyal, filial, honest, and chaste simulated authenticity (*zhen* 真),
> If one thought this to be authenticity, this would be equivalent to disclosing a dream to a fool.

---

40. For a detailed discussion of these manuals of style, in particular the *Zhangwu zhi*, see Clunas, *Superfluous Things*.
41. See note 15 above.

The characters onstage are in turn delighted and mournful, reunited and separated,

If one believed their *qing* 情 [passions or emotions] to be false, this would be like a deaf-mute watching a play.[42]

As Anthony Yu has recently noted, the phrase "disclosing a dream to a fool" (*chiren shuo meng* 癡人説夢) has its origin in an anecdote concerning a monk whose efforts to stymie a would-be biographer fall upon deaf ears. When asked his name and what country he hailed from, the monk replied that his name was "what" and he originated from "what"; the replies were duly noted.[43] The reference to this anecdote suggests that theatrical spectators who believe actors on stage to be the roles they play are just as foolish as those who believe in the integrity of an "I." But, almost paradoxically, authentic spectatorship does not mean dismissing the forms of this world as mere emptiness. Rather, the spectator who can discern authenticity will be moved by the emotions of the actors on stage, even as he understands the characters they play to be false. The authentic spectator is one who simultaneously responds to the power of the actor's *qing* and grasps the falseness of theatrical verisimilitude.

The distinction drawn in the two couplets of the quatrain between a verity of feeling and superficial notions of verisimilitude points to an important difference between Platonic notions of mimesis and notions of likeness in the Chinese tradition. The distinction made between *shen si* 神似 and *xing si* 形似 in traditional Chinese aesthetics isolates a notion of internalized likeness from an artisanal notion of likeness, concerned with the mimicking of externalities. In Su Shi's 蘇軾 (1037–1101) oft-cited phrasing, a painter of bamboo would "grasp the entire bamboo in his breast before beginning to paint" rather than copy the shape of the bamboo joint by joint, leaf by leaf.[44] The quatrain draws upon this distinction,

---

42. The quatrain is attributed to Tang Yi 湯頤, a descendant of Tang Xianzu's active in the early part of the eighteenth century. See Tang Yi, *Wenchang Tangshi zong pu* 文昌湯氏宗譜, *juan* 1; cited in Mao Xiaotong, *Tang Xianzu yanjiu ziliao huibian*, p. 1384.

43. Huihong 惠洪, *Lengzhai yehua* 冷齋夜話, *juan* 9, in *Yingyin wenyuange siku quanshu*, vol. 863, p. 275. For a discussion of this anecdote, see Anthony Yu, *Rereading the Stone*, p. 142.

44. See Su Shi's account of the bamboo paintings of his friend Wen Tong 文同 in Su Shi, "Wen Yuke hua Yundang gu yanzhu ji" 文與可畫篔簹穀偃竹記, in *Su Shi wenji*, *juan* 11, p. 365.

echoing the most famous of Su Shi's pronouncements on painting, "He who uses external likeness (*xingsi*) to discuss painting should be considered a child" as it derides both those who are fooled by external likeness and those who fail to be moved by internal likeness.[45]

As the reference to the Buddhist parable in Tang Yi's quatrain might suggest, the notion of simultaneous engagement with and detachment from the events on stage finds a parallel in Buddhist notions of simultaneous immersion in and detachment from the phenomenal world. The notion that the obviously illusory realm of the theater could enlighten the spectator about the illusory quality of all sensory phenomena is given a clear articulation in the playwright Tu Long 屠龍's preface to his play *Tanhua ji* 曇花記 (The night-blooming cereus, 1598):[46]

Someone said . . . "How can writing plays be viewed as an act of Buddhist merit?" I replied: "All the myriad sensory phenomena (*yuan* 緣) of the world are false; the theater thus is falseness within falseness (*jia zhong zhi jia* 假中之假). Through experiencing this falseness within falseness, we may be enlightened that all sensory phenomena are false. Thus the theater is beneficial and not harmful. . . . If one believes the falseness within falseness of the theater to be true, then one's desires are stimulated by it and one's grief increases; this is harmful. Do you not realize that this floating world is one great stage? Birth, aging, illness, and death in this world are equivalent to separation and reunion, and sorrow and joy, on the stage."

Tu Long then describes how he uses the natural pleasure spectators take in song and dance to communicate Buddhist principles. "Although [Buddhist] principle is subtle, the lyrics of the opera are obvious, and so the audience understands. . . . If in a hundred thousand people one person repents, this may be considered an accomplishment."[47] If, he elaborates, both actors and spectators fast in the Buddhist manner, this is an act of boundless merit on their parts; if they do not fast but still believe, they al-

---

45. Su Shi, "Shu Yanling Wang zhubu suo hua zhe zhi" 書鄢陵王主簿所畫折枝, no. 1, in *Su Shi Shij, juan* 29, p. 1525. See Ronald Egan, *Word, Image and Deed in the Life of Su Shi*, p. 282.

46. The notion that the theater, as an evidently illusory realm, might enlighten the spectator as to the illusory nature of all worldly phenomena can be found in nascent form in the deliverance play; see Idema and West, *Chinese Theater*, pp. 305–8.

47. Tu Long, "*Tanhua ji* xu" 曇花記序, in Cai Yi, *Zhongguo gudian xiqu xuba huibian*, 2: 1112–13.

so have merit. But if they neither fast nor believe and simply view a play as a play, this is a sin—and a sin for which the playwright will pay a karmic price as well.

Tu Long gave an overtly Buddhist cast to the spectator's trajectory from illusion to disillusion, just as *Lan Caihe* gave a Daoist gloss to the actor's enlightenment. More frequently, authors explored the strategic rupture of illusion in a manner only indirectly influenced by Buddhist and Daoist notions of detachment.[48] Sympathetic attachment to the characters and events depicted in drama and fiction was viewed as a necessary precondition to the spectator's recognition of his entanglement in the world of forms, as the quatrain hung at Tang Xianzu's ancestral home discussed above suggested. In plays such as Kong Shangren's *Taohua shan*, the theater becomes a laboratory in which the audience experiences successive attachment to and alienation from the events depicted on stage, rehearsing the process of enchantment and disenchantment with the world of forms.

The texts that I discuss in the next chapter helped shape a discourse on spectatorship that was indebted to theatrical models. The notion that social imposture was akin to theatrical role-playing suggested the means by which a discerning spectator might evaluate the performance of status. The exploration of the model of theatrical spectatorship provided a means for seventeenth-century authors to articulate the precariousness of an emerging middle elite's grasp of the cultural inheritance of the literati, and to suggest that time spent watching theatricals might cultivate the blend of absorptive immersion and dispassion that would distinguish those with a mastery of that cultural inheritance. The notion of the vanity of reputation and achievement had long informed the Chinese conception of the worldly stage. But in the waning years of the sixteenth century and early years of the seventeenth, the notion of the vanity of all things acquired a new phrasing. Now the social spectator observed from a dis-

---

48. Wai-yee Li, who has examined in depth the trajectory from illusion to disillusion in fiction, observes that it has a literary genealogy that predates Buddhism. "The dialectics of attachment and detachment is of course a Buddhist idea, and the introduction of Buddhism had a profound influence on the rise of Chinese fiction. However, the problems of the status of illusion and of its relationship with writing and reading are already set forth in some examples of *fu* [rhymeprose] literature, especially as epitomized by the figure of the ambivalent divine woman" (*Enchantment and Disenchantment*, p. 45).

tance the alienating effects of sumptuary display. That theatrical specta-torship could provide a model for how one viewed the world was an old idea. What was new was that theatrical models of spectatorship were now applied to the fads and fashions of the urban social spectacle—in which the theater itself was deeply implicated.

ONE

The Significance of Theatricality in Seventeenth-Century China

The poet Zhu Yizun 朱彝尊 (1629–1709) wrote a letter to the scholar Tan Zuoyu 譚左羽 after hearing that Tan was thinking of quitting his post at the estate where he served as tutor in residence. Tan's frustration stemmed from his apparent lack of status; he fretted that he was less appreciated than the music master, whose table boasted an abundance of delicacies. Zhu Yizun counseled him:

So you are thinking of quitting and returning home. I think this is not worth troubling yourself over. . . . His [the master's] giving a luxurious menu to his music master is like feeding fish or meat to a pet and does not hurt you in any way. Mencius said that people who care about eating and drinking will be looked down on by others.[1] If you leave, those who do not understand the situation will think that you simply care about food and drink. How could you let them think that?[2]

Zhu Yizun's attempt to encourage Tan Zuoyu in invoking Mencius sounds almost pathetically ineffectual, for it harkens to values that now seem to be of another time. Tan Zuoyu's dilemma suggests that the fad for *Kunqu* 崑曲, the style of opera that dominated in the gentry residences of Jiangnan from the late sixteenth century to the mid-nineteenth,

---

1. Yang Bojun, *Mengzi yizhu*, p. 269.
2. Zhu Yizun, *Pushuting ji*, p. 401.

had reached such proportions that the music master of an estate was more highly esteemed than the tutor.

In this chapter, I probe the question of the relationship between theatrical spectacle and social spectacle in writings of the late Ming and early Qing, paying particular attention to how the craze for *Kunqu* might have influenced the conception of this relationship. In the first part of the chapter, I ask how seventeenth-century writers viewed the relationship between theatrical and social realms. How might notions of theatrical performance have shaped a conception of social imposture, and how might models of theatrical spectatorship have influenced social spectatorship? In the second part of the chapter, I ask how the importance of operatic performance to late Ming luxury consumption and status competition influenced the writings of both anti-theatricalists and partisans of the theater who were interested in the relation of theatrical to social spectatorship. Both sides laid claim to a transcendent spectatorship of social spectacle. What was the model of spectatorship that emerged from the writing of anti-theatricalists, and what was the rebuttal of partisans of the theater? How might the social space occupied by the theater in their writings resonate with the conceptions of theatrical and social spectatorship we examine in the chapters to follow?

The Spectacle of Status Performance

No seventeenth-century author was more concerned with the problem of the world as stage than Li Yu. Li Yu's southern drama *Naihetian*, written during the mid-1650s, offers a clear and straightforward application of the metaphor of theatrical performance to social performance. Li Yu exploits the role system of the Chinese theater to parody the acquisition of the emblems of gentry status by the *nouveaux riches*.[3] A central conceit of *Naihetian* is that the actor who typically plays slapstick clown roles (*chou* 丑) acts the role of the gentleman lead (*sheng* 生).[4] As the clown takes the stage for the first time, he explains that the reason he, rather than the

---

3. Actors were trained from a young age to play role-types that had a certain repertoire of gestures and vocal production, such as clowns or gentlemen. I discuss the role system in detail in Chapter 4.

4. On *Naihetian*, see Henry, *Chinese Amusement*, pp. 127–57, 218–45.

sheng, is playing the gentleman is that most men of elegance in contemporary society are in fact clowns.

This mismatch between character and theatrical role-type (*juese* 角色) underscores the disjunction between the *nouveaux riches'* lack of cultivation and their social status. The clown plays the role of Que Lihou 闕 裏侯, a scion of a wealthy family. Although Que's family has produced wealth for generation after generation, never once have they managed to generate a scholar, not even a licentiate. Que Lihou himself studied for over ten years, "but now, if you hung me upside down, there would not be a drop of ink in me."[5] He mocks the impotence of the scholar-gentry in the face of his own wealth:

> I often laugh at the helplessness of literati,
> In vain they have the talent of a Song Yu 宋玉[6]
>   or the handsome features of a Pan Yue 潘嶽,[7]
> They are all poor,
> But as for me,
> Though I'm foolish and thick, my allotment of wealth comes from heaven.[8]

Li Yu exaggerated the low humor typical of the clown role by endowing Que with physical defects that reflect his lack of cultivation—besides being crippled, hunchbacked, and half-blind, he emits a terrible stench.

Que is fortunate, however, to have a servant who performs acts of charity in his name and thus gains him a fine reputation (*ming* 名). This servant is played by the secondary gentleman lead, the *xiaosheng* 小生 role-type, a casting choice that suggests that the servant, rather than Que the clown, is the gentleman in this play. The servant persuades Que to donate a large sum to support soldiers at the frontier; Que agrees most reluctantly. The servant then continues doing charitable works in Que's name without Que's knowledge. Que thus acquires a *ming* that has little to do with actuality (*shi* 實).

---

5. Li Yu, *Naihetian, Li Yu quanji*, 2: 8.

6. Song Yu is traditionally supposed to have been a minister in the court of King Xiang 襄 of Chu 楚 (r. 298–263 bce) and a distinguished orator; a number of *fu* 賦 (rhymeprose) are attributed to him.

7. Pan Yue (247–300) was a Jin 晉 dynasty author renowned both for his writing and for his exceptional handsomeness.

8. Li Yu, *Naihetian, Li Yu quanji*, 2: 8.

Because of these good deeds, Que is awarded the title Lord of Righteousness. An angel of transformation then descends from Heaven and bathes Que in a magical solution that washes away his deformities, so that his physical appearance matches his newly ennobled rank—in short, so that he resembles a *sheng* rather than a *chou*. Li Yu exploited this scene for all its slapstick potential. Que tells the maid preparing to bathe him, "This bath needn't be the usual one. I want to be like a pig or sheep prepared for slaughter. You can rake my skin to scrape away the dirt as you wash me— even if I have to endure some pain, the important thing is to get clean."[9] At this point the angel appears on stage and announces to the audience that he will impersonate Que's maid and bathe Que. "But," he says, "wait until I transform myself," adding the adage, "If you want to change others, you'd best change yourself first." He then goes to the stage entrance (*guimen* 鬼門) and makes gestures indicating that he has changed himself into a woman.

When the angel addresses the audience and then transforms himself in full view of the audience, the play ruptures the illusory self-sufficiency of the theatrical realm. More important, it simultaneously ruptures the illusory self-sufficiency of the social realm by showing that the social needs the theatrical in order to make actuality conform to appearance. In this play, the theater is a figure for the disjunction between appearance and actuality; the gentleman is played by the clown. But at the same time, the theater is a figure for the *conjunction* of appearance and actuality. Just as the theatrical spectator suspends disbelief before theatrical illusion, the social spectator closes the gap between appearance and actuality by suspending disbelief in the face of social illusion. He ignores the fact that the clown is no gentleman.

Li Yu suggests that the discriminating spectator perceives the disjunction between appearance and actuality, and identifies it as theatrical. As a case in point, Que hires an actor who plays leading gentlemen to impersonate him in an arranged encounter with a prospective second wife from a gentry family. Que delights over the actor's looks and bearing and gives the actor his fine clothing to costume himself for the occasion. However, the prospective bride perceptively remarks of the actor, "His figure and face are fine, but it's a shame that he seems somewhat superficial (*qingfu*

---

9. Ibid., 2: 91.

輕浮). In the end, he seems like an actor."[10] The superficial actor is associated with a certain weightlessness—the moral weightlessness of one who habitually impersonates. This, in turn, comments on the moral weightlessness of wealthy but uncultivated men such as Que, who mistakenly believe that others will not see through their performance of status.

Indeed, Que's first wife, who is of a gentry family, similarly remarks on the sense of staginess and superficiality she feels on seeing Que's study for the first time, "The study is clean and quiet, but it bothers me that it is somewhat ostentatious. Look at how the rafters are carved, the walls painted with pictures. The railings, of course, had to be decorated with the *wan zi* (卍 字); the paintings in his chambers naturally had to feature birds and animals. When you see how meticulously wrought it is, you know its inhabitant is not a man of elegance. From the looks of it, his [literary] talent is limited." The gentry bride's aesthetic values are those of the literatus; she expects understatement and simplicity, aesthetic qualities associated with depth of character and contemplation. The style of decor she finds, however, is radically inappropriate to the literatus's study.[11] The birds and animals are popular subject matter, reflecting a level of taste associated with the market. According to Wen Zhenheng, the author of the treatise on interior decoration *Superfluous Things* (ca. 1615–20), the *wan zi*, a decorative motif that resembles a reverse swastika, was suitable only for the women's quarters, being "not very antique or ele-

---

10. Li Yu, *Naihetian*, *Li Yu quanji*, 2: 31.

11. Writing in another genre, the manual of taste, Li Yu instructed would-be gentlemen as to how properly to decorate a study. His *Xianqing ouji* 閒情偶寄 (Casual expressions of idle feeling) made recommendations that could be derived from his depiction of Que's study. Paint on the walls is vulgar; and walls should simply be polished, left a natural color. Of course, one needs a few paintings and pieces of calligraphy, but to display them in such profusion that there is no space left on the walls is a kind of vulgar posturing to which, Li Yu says, "we" literati are susceptible. There is very little about books in Li Yu's remarks on decorating the study, except a warning that they should not be placed within cubbies in the walls according to the "ancient" fashion, because that makes them liable to moisture and encourages insects and rot. Li Yu's repeated injunctions against vulgarity, his warnings against profuse display, and his expectation that his readers need to learn how to store books suggests that although he may have had a diverse audience in mind, one sector of his readers was likely a middle elite whose experience of owning books was fairly recent. Li Yu, *Xianqing ouji*, in *Li Yu quanji*, vol. 11, *juan* 4, p. 185.

gant."[12] It is precisely because such a high degree of attention has been paid to surface ornamentation that the bride knows that the owner of this study is not a man of depth. Her discriminating spectatorship foils Que's attempt to pose as a man of cultivation. The gentry bride, like the prospective second wife who saw through the social impersonation of the actor, is a discriminating spectator of status performance. Such scenes suggest that the refined spectator has the crucial task of limiting the power of the theatrical to transform the social.

Li Yu suggests that if theatrical performance could become a metaphor for social performance, notions of social spectatorship could also be informed by the model of theatrical spectatorship. Two different models of the relationship between theatrical and social spectatorship are at play in the examples above. The gentry women who see through the imposture of the actor, and of Que himself, employ a social spectatorship that is modeled on the notion of the theater as a figure for the disjunction of appearance and actuality (the role of the gentleman is played by the clown). In this model, the theater is in excess of the social; strip away the (unnecessary) costuming and posturing, and one will find the genuine intact beneath. We might remember, however, that in the scene where Que, the clown-like figure, magically comes to resemble a gentleman, the theater was also a figure for the conjunction of appearance and actuality. In this second model of the relationship between the theatrical and the social, the two realms are mutually imbricated, precisely because the social spectator suspends disbelief, keeping illusion and disillusion in tension. As we will see in Zhang Dai's classic essay "Xihu qiyue ban" 西湖七月半 (West Lake on the fifteenth day of the seventh month), this suspension of disbelief paves the way for a visual and social aesthetic that is panoramic, mobile, and participatory.

Refined Spectatorship and Social Distinction

In this essay, Zhang Dai depicted himself as a connoisseur of the urban social spectacle. He ridiculed the boorish consumption patterns of the urban middle elite even as he displayed a connoisseurship, indeed, a refined consumption of social spectacle. If the mercantile appropriation of literati

---

12. Clunas, *Superfluous Things*, p. 54.

emblems of cultivation fostered an interest in discerning spectatorship, the new proximity of disparate social spheres in the burgeoning urban centers of the late Ming also fostered a sense of social voyeurism, which often manifested itself as an interest in classifying status groups according to hierarchies of taste. Zhang Dai began by ranking the urbanity of the various merrymakers viewing the full moon on Hangzhou's West Lake. There is little to capture the connoisseur's gaze but the spectacle of others amusing themselves: "On the fifteenth day of the seventh month, there is not a lot to see; one can only observe the people who come out that day."[13] But not all those merrymakers were alike: "one could view them as five types."[14] By not presenting the five types in ascending or descending order, Zhang focused the reader's attention on the elements that govern the ranking as much as the ranking itself. Zhang lauded those with the capacity to observe and derided those who desire to be seen. The word *kan* 看, which I translate below as "see," "observe," "regard," "look," or "watch," is repeated obsessively throughout the text.

Those of the first type, who dress sumptuously and arrive on large boats filled with musicians, are less interested in seeing than in being seen, which immediately places them in an inferior position. "They make a pretense (*ming* 名) of looking at the moon, but actually (*shi* 實) they don't look at it." The members of the second group, accompanied by famed beauties and pretty boys, betray their self-consciousness by "gazing to left and right; their bodies are right there beneath the moon, but they actually don't look at the moon." A third sort includes in its retinue noted courtesans and Buddhist monks. They sing softly, their voices accompanied by the quiet music of pipes and strings. More refined than the first two groups, they do observe the moon, but not without purpose: "They, too, were beneath the moon; they also looked at the moon and wanted people to see them looking at the moon." A fourth party is composed of rowdies who drunkenly sing out of tune; they "look at the moon, at those looking at the moon, and at those not looking at the moon, but in actuality (*shi*) they don't see a single thing." Those in the fifth class, the most elegant, arrive in small boats with "good friends and beautiful women. They sit and brew tea and invite the moon to sit with them. . . . They regard the moon,

---

13. The Ghost Festival occurs on the fifteenth of the seventh month.
14. Zhang Dai, "Xihu qiyue ban," in *Tao'an mengyi / Xihu mengxun*, p. 62.

and no one sees what they look like as they watch the moon; nor do they make a point of looking at the moon." All five types are characterized in part by their capacity for spectatorship. Those who claim to view the moon but "don't see a single thing" receive the greatest scorn. The most refined set is defined by the disinterestedness of its appreciation of the moon; because it does not see in order to be seen, it transcends any suspicion of self-consciousness or self-dramatization. Zhang explicitly positioned himself as omniscient observer, ending his thumbnail sketch of each class of merrymakers with the words *kan zhi* 看之 (I observed them).[15]

In its final lines, the essay takes a surprising turn: Zhang himself enters the spectacle. He notes that it is only after the rank and file of Hangzhou have left that "people of our sort (*wubei* 吾輩) move their boats closer to the shore." (There is no elaboration as to whom "our sort" might be; it is simply a pluralization of Zhang Dai's omniscient eye.) At this point the landscape is suddenly cleansed of the degrading regard of the vulgar: "The moon was like a newly polished mirror, the mountains seem to have gained a new aspect, and the river to have washed its face." Those of the third and fifth groups—"those who self-consciously regard the moon" as well as those who made no special point of viewing the moon—emerge from the shadows to join Zhang Dai and his party, "and those of our sort go toward them and drag them over to sit with us." Suddenly, Zhang Dai mingles with those whom he has dispassionately classed as beneath him, and this is the gesture that bears Zhang Dai's signature. The essay, which had relentlessly segregated the pleasure-seekers into distinct classes, ends by partially erasing such distinctions. Zhang, who played the distant observer, now mingles with the others. The spectator has entered the spectacle. The tension this gesture creates between dispassionate observation and participation illustrates Zhang's refined vision, effortlessly justifying his claim to be the most distinguished observer of the urban spectacle.

That such a tension between observation and participation is characteristic of a superior level of perception is even more apparent in Zhang Dai's description of a fireworks display at the court of the Prince of Lu 魯,

---

15. As Wai-yee Li has noted, Zhang's repetition of the phrase *kan zhi* "carries a faint suggestion of superciliousness," for "to be on the outermost ring in this 'hierarchy of seeing' is to establish some sort of superiority" (*Enchantment and Disenchantment*, p. 48).

where Zhang's father served. Zhang lauds the heightened quality of perception that characterizes the spectators of the fireworks at court:

The fireworks of the Prince of Lu at Yanzhou 兗州 would make the whole world marvel. For fireworks, one must first set out lanterns. The lanterns at the Prince of Lu's palace illuminate the palace, the walls, the columns, the screens, and his throne, as well as the fans, parasols, and canopies of the palace. The prince and his sons, palace women and servants, dancers and musicians—all are absorbed into the lanterns, becoming objects in the lantern's scenes. When they set off fireworks, the objects in the lantern's scenes are gathered into the firework's scenes. Everywhere else in the world, people look at lanterns from their exterior, and watch fireworks from *their* exterior. They have never entered the lanterns, the illuminations, the shadows, the mists, the flames—all of which flicker and become illusions, so that one does not know whether one sees the fireworks of the prince's palace, or the prince's palace within the fireworks.[16]

Only the most sophisticated spectator perceives the ontological questions behind the aesthetic display. Zhang Dai distinguished the mundane sensibility of those unable to enter illusion—who simply look at the lanterns and fireworks from the exterior—from that of the most discerning viewers, who have the capacity to enter illusion. The question of authenticity is no longer framed in terms of the relation of the scenes on the lanterns to their referents; rather, it is a matter of the sophistication of the spectator's capacity for perception. Taken together, Zhang Dai's two essays suggest that the most refined observer has the capacity to participate in social spectacle even after cataloguing its vulgarities, and that this is similar to entering illusion even after recognizing it to be such. The trajectory from disillusion to illusion inverts and supersedes the conventional trajectory from illusion to disillusion. It is the reversal of this trajectory that distinguishes the refined from the mundane spectator.

The sophistication of the spectator, then, is defined in part by a capacity for deft inversions that suggest the capacity to keep illusion and disillusion in tension. Zhang Dai, himself a playwright, employed the tension between dispassionate observation and passionate engagement character-

---

16. Zhang Dai, *Tao'an mengyi / Xihu mengxun*, pp. 12–13.

istic of theatrical spectatorship.[17] This tension was hinted at in the quatrain that hung from the stage at Tang Xianzu's ancestral home, which (as I mentioned in the previous chapter) urged the spectator to engage with the characters on stage even while recognizing that the stage was, in Tu Long's words, a realm of "falseness within falseness." If Li Yu's *Naihetian* articulated the conventional formula of acting as a metaphor for social imposture, Zhang Dai took the notion that only the vulgar would mistake illusion for actuality and turned it on its head: only the vulgar would seek to differentiate illusion and actuality.

Li Yu and Zhang Dai both sought to distinguish the sophisticated spectator from the mundane viewer. They introduced refined perception as a sign of social distinction to replace conventional emblems of social distinction that could be purchased and displayed. Quality of perception, then, became a means of distinguishing the genuinely cultivated.

Spectator of the Self

What if such sophisticated capacities of perception were trained on the spectacle of one's own social aspiration? In Pu Songling's classical tale "Senior Licentiate Zhang" ("Zhang gongshi" 張貢士), the dialectics of interiors and exteriors, representations and simulacra, are grafted on to the tale of a licentiate named Zhang, who sees his own life acted before him as though it were a spectacle on a stage.[18] A scholar stymied in his quest for official position, Zhang is lying ill in bed when suddenly he sees a tiny man climb out of his heart. Dressed in the cap and robes of a man of cultivation (*ru* 儒), he strikes the pose of an actor and begins to sing in the *Kunshan* 崑山 style. As the tiny man introduces the role he is about to play, he gives his name and place of origin, as is conventional in the Chinese opera. Not only are his name and ancestral home the same as Zhang's, but the plot of the play he narrates tells the story of Zhang's life. When the fourth and final act is finished, the actor chants a poem and disappears.

---

17. Zhang Dai is best known for his essays on the theater, but he also wrote an opera entitled *Bing shan* 冰山 (Ice mountain), which concerned the fall of the eunuch Wei Zhongxian 魏忠賢 (1568–1627).

18. Pu Songling, *Liaozhai zhiyi*, ed. Ren Duxing, pp. 1740–42.

This extremely compressed anecdote speaks to a number of seven-teenth-century concerns that fall under the rubric of theatricality—the metaphorical resonance between literati and actors; the sense of the self as a spectacle on a public stage; the notion that the realm of illusion is po-tentially a sphere of deeper authenticity. It complicates the argument that the figure of the theater elucidates the shifting relationships among vari-ous social spheres. If Zhang Dai argued that sophisticated plays on per-ception allowed a certain type of elite to distinguish himself from those who engage in social imposture, here the licentiate himself is caught in such a play on perception. If Li Yu and Zhang Dai posed as distant ob-servers of the spectacle of social aspiration, licentiate Zhang is both actor and spectator in the drama of his own failed social aspirations. Of particu-lar note is that the text signals the crossing of ontological status with the crossing of genre; as this prose account of a strange event invokes a play, its literati protagonist is figured as an actor.[19]

Pu Songling's friend Gao Fenghan 高鳳翰 (1683–1748) notes in a comment attached to the anecdote that after reading it, he wondered if the Zhang in question were related to his friend Zhang Maojun 張卯君 of Anqiu 安丘.[20] When he next saw Zhang Maojun, he brought up this episode and found that, indeed, the story concerned his friend. Zhang told him that after recovering from his illness, he had remembered the lyr-ics the actor had sung perfectly and had written them all down. But his wife, believing them to be inauspicious, had burned them. Just as the actor sung his songs and disappeared, the physical manifestation of the actor's song vanished in flames. After the story of his life was consigned to the flames, Zhang Maojun could remember no more than the coda, and when he had friends over for wine or tea, he would sing the coda for them. The ephemerality of the text that contained the story of Zhang Maojun's life points to the fleeting quality of life itself, which is further underscored by Zhang's illness. The fragility of the text also speaks to the wasted dreams of a literatus who never found a position equal to his education.

---

19. I am indebted to Robert Ashmore for this insight.

20. The edition of *Liaozhai zhiyi* by Zhang Youhe, long considered the standard, mis-takenly includes the comment by Gao Fenghan as part of the tale. In Ren Duxing's more recent edition (pp. 1740–42), the comment rightfully appears as commentary and not as part of the story.

Pu Songling's anecdote duplicates nearly exactly an account found in Wang Shizhen's 王世禎 (1634–1711) collection *Chibei outan* 池北偶談 (Random conversations north of the pond), but contains an additional and telling detail: whereas in Wang Shizhen's text, the protagonist is simply "a certain Zhang" (Zhang mou 張某), Pu describes Zhang as a licentiate.[21] It is this detail and its elaboration in Gao's commentary that lends the anecdote an entirely different quality from that we find in Wang Shizhen's simple recording of a strange event (*zhi guai* 志怪), for the mention of Zhang's status as licentiate transforms Pu Songling's anecdote into a comment on the way in which the disjunction between social aspiration and social status renders the world a stage. The figure of the actor and the notion of performance of status here speak to the plight of the lower reaches of the literati, the licentiates who pursued a traditional means of advancement, study of the classics, only to find themselves left out in the cold.[22]

Gao Fenghan's commentary includes a few lines from the coda that the actor sang: "No need to know what the *Classic of Poetry* or the philosophers said, it's no more than *doudou pingzhang*." As Gao explained: "It is said that a village schoolmaster taught boys to read the *Analects*, and their characters were often mistaken. One of the funniest mistakes was that they read *yuyu hu wen zai* 郁郁乎文哉 as *doudou pingzhang wo* 都都平丈我."[23] The punch line depends upon a semiliterate misreading of a line from the *Analects* of Confucius, *yuyu huwen zai* (How complete were the rites [of the Zhou dynasty]).[24] The misreading substitutes more common

---

21. Wang Shizhen, *Chibei outan*, p. 625. Since we do not know the dates of the addition of either Pu Songling or Wang Shizhen's versions of the anecdote to their respective collections, we cannot state which version of the anecdote is earlier; although Pu Songling's preface is dated 1679 and Wang Shizhen's 1691, both authors continued to add material to their collections during the 1690s. Alan Barr ("Pu Songling and *Liaozhai*," p. 260) has suggested that narrative variants would indicate that both authors drew on a third source; Judith Zeitlin (*Historian of the Strange*, p. 275) has noted that since the 24-*juan* manuscript of *Liaozhai* contains a comment on this story by Wang Shizhen, it would seem that Wang took the account from Pu Songling. Oddly, Wang Shizhen's version feels earlier, since it is the more spare account.

22. Pu Songling was famously one such licentiate, forced to earn a living as a tutor after repeatedly failing the provincial exams.

23. *Liaozhai zhiyi*, pp. 1740–41.

24. *Lunyu zhushu* 論語注疏, in *Shisan jing zhushu*, p. 2467.

characters, rendering the classical phrase as a line of untranslatable vernacular doggerel.[25] The coda continues, "All depends on the 120 lines of the Buddha." Pu Songling glossed this line: "In the village schools there was a primer called *Miscellaneous Characters for Farmers*. Its opening stanza ran, 'The Buddha left 120 lines, but farmers are the best of all the rest.' This is the height of boorishness." Gao concluded, "If you play with the meaning of this, it's as though Zhang were saying that his life were a disappointment. In the end he was a schoolmaster on a farm, and the head of the family scorned him, and so he composed this tune." The actor's song, then, seems an externalization of Zhang's innermost thoughts, expressing his great disappointment at having wasted his life attempting to teach rustic schoolboys the Confucian classics. The actor mocks the failed aspirations of the senior licentiate, but his emergence from Zhang's heart also suggests that Zhang's failure to realize his aspirations is a matter of self-reproach and is in that sense heart wrenching. The plight of Zhang Maojun, a schoolmaster scorned by the head of the family who employed him, recalls that of the scholar Tan Zuoyu, whose host treated his music master better than his tutor. If Tan Zuoyu was overshadowed by a music master whose skills were valued more highly than Tan's learning, senior licentiate Zhang was haunted by a ghostly actor whose arias held a mirror to his failure.

Senior licentiate Zhang is both the actor and the spectator of the story of his life. The figure of the actor who emerges from Zhang Maojun's heart to sing the story of his life suggests that the failed literatus has become the passive spectator of his own downward mobility. At the same time, we recall Zhang Dai's signature mode of perception, in which the spectator both enters the spectacle and views it as an omniscient observer. In Pu Songling's tale, the two versions of social spectatorship we discussed in the context of Li Yu's *Naihetian* are layered on each other, and the licentiate whose failed aspirations expose him to ridicule as no more than

---

25. These lines also appear in a joke collected by Feng Menglong 馮夢龍 in his *Gujin xiao* 古今笑 (Jokes old and new) that appears under the heading "Wuzi jiecuo" 五字皆錯 (All five characters are wrong). A scholar of the classics was passing by a village school and heard the teacher drilling the students with *doudou pingzhang wo*. Realizing the error, he corrected the teacher. The students left in shock. People of the time made up a saying about this: "*Doudou pingzhang wo*, students fill the hall; *yuyu huwen zai*, the students no longer stop by" (Feng Menglong, *Gujin xiao*, 1: 162).

an actor is consoled by the notion that the world is but a stage. For Zhang Dai, panoramic and participatory spectatorship had been a signature of refinement; here it affords instead an occasion for critical self-reflection as well as consolation.

A quality of social perception that mirrored the engagement and disengagement of the spectator before theatrical illusion, then, became a means of distancing oneself from the vulgarity of social spectacle, and of addressing the complexity of one's implication in and participation in social spectacle. At this point, it may be instructive to step back and ask, how did the analogy between theatrical and social spectacle function in the most concrete sense—how did authors who commented on the fashion for theatricals relate theatrical performance and social spectacle? How was actual theatrical spectatorship (rather than a theatrical mode of seeing) implicated in the arbitration of social status? As we consider the writings of anti-theatricalists as well as partisans of the theater, it will be instructive to ask how various configurations of the trajectory from illusion to disillusion might lie behind seemingly simple claims as to the vulgarity of the theater or its transformative powers. At first glance, the texts I discuss below are more straightforward than the ones I have just examined; they seem either to dismiss or to promote the theater with arguments that are not unexpected. But when we examine these arguments in the context of the complicated configurations of illusion and disillusion outlined above, an underlying complexity begins to emerge.

Anti-theatricalist Diatribes: Fashion and Theater

The ideological niche occupied by the figure of the theater can be understood in part through scrutiny of entries in *biji* that show the reader how to interpret the urban social spectacle. *Biji* are often not so much documentary sources as miscellanies that record trends and events in a manner that seems not far removed from omenology. Entries in *biji* such as Lu Rong's 陸容 (1436–94) *Shuyuan zaji* 菽園雜記 (Miscellaneous notes of the bean garden), Zhang Han's 張瀚 (1510–93) *Songchuang mengyu* 松窗夢語 (Dream conversations by the pine window), Gu Qiyuan's 顧起元 (1565–1628) *Kezuo zhuiyu* 客座贅語 (Trivial remarks from the guest's seat), Fan Lian's 范濂 (fl. 1602) *Yunjian jumu chao* 雲間據目鈔 (Witnessed by my eyes in Yunjian), Shen Defu's 沈德符 (1578–1642) *Wanli yehuo bian* 萬歷野獲編 (Unofficial harvest of the Wanli years), and

Xu Shupi's 徐樹丕 (fl. seventeenth century) *Shixiao lu* 識小錄 (Little record of my knowledge) lament the susceptibility of gentry and commoners alike to the allure of boy actors or theatrical entertainments.[26] Such entries disdain the atmosphere of licentiousness surrounding the theater and disparage the opportunism, untrustworthiness, promiscuity, and vulgarity of actors. Condemning the detrimental effect of the theater on social mores, these authors criticized the role of theatricals in fueling the conspicuous consumption and slavishness to fashion they found so characteristic of their age.[27]

The theater became a vexed figure in late sixteenth- and seventeenth-century literature in part because the social contradictions of a rapidly commercializing economy were displaced upon it. Successive entries in Fan Lian's *Yunjian jumu chao* (preface dated 1602), for example, deplore a trio of social trends: an upsurge in the counterfeiting of silver, the use of inflated titles of address, and a heightened interest in theatrical entertainments. Although these three entries seem to be unrelated, the conventions of reading *biji* remind us to seek the underlying resemblance of items placed next to one another:

The practice of circulating and using counterfeit silver is of great harm to the people. And it has never been as severe a problem as in recent years. The counterfeit silver of the past could be distinguished from real silver. That of today cannot. In the past, those who circulated and used counterfeit silver were still few. Today they are everywhere. In the past one had to hide one's tracks. These days they counterfeit money recklessly without a sense of taboo. In addition they rely upon the might of local strongmen to open currency stores everywhere. Locals do not dare raise the issue and the official *yamen* cannot prohibit it. For this reason, the people gnash their teeth.

When the gentry address one another, they always say "venerable" (*lao* 老) this and "venerable" that. This is the form of address used by the gentry. Since the Longqing 隆慶 [1567–73] and Wanli [1573–1620] reign periods, all men of culti-

---

26. Some notation books, such as Shen Defu's, contain entries that are rabidly anti-theatrical and others that are far more neutral; rather than considering an author like Shen to be an anti-theatricalist, we ought to conceive of him as writing comments that reflect various modes of thought.

27. For a discussion of diatribes against the vulgarity of theatrical texts and the licentiousness of the stage, see Dolby, *Chinese Drama*, pp. 106–9; and West, "Text and Ideology."

vation with white beards have allowed themselves to be called "venerable," for example, "Venerable Zhao" and "Venerable Quan," without any sense of taboo or embarrassment at all. It is to the point that when people of that class meet for the first time, they say *dalaoguan* 大老官 or *erlaoguan* 二老官 and don't feel as though they have said anything odd.[28] Prostitutes, actors, lictors, and soldiers address one another in even stranger ways.

Songs, folk tune lyrics, and opera (*geyao ciqu* 歌謠詞曲) have been around since ancient times, but only in recent times have they been particularly prevalent in our Hangzhou. Groups of friends amuse themselves in this way, and if the gentry of the district or commandery engage in the least bit of unworthy behavior, it immediately becomes fodder for a ditty of some sort and circulates from person to person. Items with lines of seven characters are the most prevalent. They go so far as to deceive people with these songs. One must say it's the fashion. At the banquets of the base people of the villages, they must have crowds of singers singing to the tune of *Yin jiaosi* 銀絞絲, *Gan heye* 乾荷葉, and *Da zaogan* 打棗竿.[29] In the end, I don't know where these fashions came from.[30]

The juxtaposition of these three paragraphs hints at the ways in which the theater was implicated in status competition during the late Ming. Underlying all three entries is a concern for a misalignment between nominal and real, which results not only in false valuation but also in false devaluation. The counterfeiting of silver is associated with the counterfeiting of social status by those who allow the use of inflated titles of address. The fashions of the gentry are aped and exaggerated by those of lower social station, so that "prostitutes, actors, lictors, and soldiers address one another in even stranger ways" than do officials, and the absurdity of the "base people of the villages" hiring "crowds of singers" mirrors the folly of the gentry's indulgence in theatricals.

---

28. *Dalaoguan* is a term akin to "Boss" that is used to address a wealthy man. *Erlaoguan* would refer to the junior of two such men.

29. *Yin jiaosi*, *Gan heye*, and *Da zaogan* were popular tunes (*xiao qu* 小曲) that the late Ming author Shen Defu described as having achieved widespread circulation during the Jiajing (1522–67) and Longqing (1567–72) reigns. Like Fan Lian, Shen Defu expressed incomprehension at the popularity of these tunes and finds their indeterminate origin troubling; Shen also condemned their licentiousness (Shen Defu, *Wanli yehuo bian*, p. 647).

30. Fan Lian, *Yunjian jumu chao*, 2.6a.

Fan Lian registered his disapproval of these trends with the words, "I don't know where these fashions came from."[31] As Timothy Brook has stated, the late Ming economy was characterized by factors that facilitated conspicuous consumption and quick changes in fashion: the greater availability of goods of all sorts, an increase in the manufacture of luxury goods, and anxiety over the continuing significance of traditional markers of status.[32] Late Ming observers such as Gu Qiyuan, Li Yue, and Fan Lian saw the very existence of fashions as a clear sign of the corruption of the social fabric.[33] Fashion was blamed for the inversion of high and low—for the fact that old hierarchies no longer prevailed and new sources of authority had sprung up.[34]

The airs of actors (who, according to these authors, were encouraged by gentry who fawned upon them) spoke to the association between fashion and social aspiration. As is apparent in Fan Lian's grouping of "prostitutes, actors, lictors, and soldiers," actors and others of base status were perpetually under suspicion of desiring to exceed the limitations placed on them. Gentry aficionados of the theater may well have contributed to

---

31. Elsewhere, Fan provided a long list of items in vogue during his youth that had fallen out of fashion by the early seventeenth century, including hats in the *zhongjing* 忠靜 (loyalty and tranquility) style, ostensibly the privilege of those who had passed the second level of the examinations. His tone makes clear that this sort of change in fashions felt new (Fan Lian, *Yunjian jumu chao*, 2.1a). Li Yue 李樂 (1532–1618) wrote in his notation book, *Jianwen zaji* 見聞雜記 (Miscellaneous records of things seen and heard; 2.60a–b), that whereas sumptuary laws had previously been effective, by the 1560s, there was no way to control what people wore. For another discussion of this passage, see Brook, *Confusions of Pleasure*, p. 219.

32. Brook, *Confusions of Pleasure*, p. 218.

33. See Ko, "Bondage in Time," p. 204.

34. The rapidity with which custom in dress changed was equated with political instability. Frederic Wakeman writes: "The association of gaudy clothing with political and social decadence has venerable antecedents in China. Xunzi 荀子 (c. 300–238 bc) wrote: 'The signs of a disorderly age are that [men's] clothes are gaily coloured, men are made up to look like women, customs are lewd, minds are set on profit, conduct is filthy, music is deviant, and ornamentation is vile and variegated'" (Wakeman, *The Great Enterprise*, 1: 95, *n*24). Ko observes, "Although Chinese official clothing did change over time—by means of dynastic decrees and adaptation to new habitats—there is no denying that the classical ideal of stability had continued to shape the discourse on fashion and change in China. According to the *Yijing* 易經, the mythical Yellow Emperor and sage kings 'draped their upper and lower garments, and heaven and earth was put to order'" (Ko, "Bondage in Time," p. 204).

the association of actors with social aspiration by rewarding them with fine clothing and other luxuries considered beyond their station. Tang Xianzu's warning to the actor Luo Zhang'er 羅章二 against presuming on his success indicates that actors expected to receive such gifts as gratuities: "When you go to people's homes to perform, take what is suitable and no more," he wrote in a letter to the actor. "Do not, because people love my plays, seek to receive more than your due of wine, food, money, or things."[35]

Authors often decried the affectations of actors in the same breath that they mocked the airs of the lower classes that put on theatricals. Xu Shupi warned in *Shixiao lu* (preface dated 1641) that the vogue for theatrical spectacle had corrupted the social fabric of Suzhou. Performers were demanding perquisites beyond their station, encouraged by gentry who pandered to actors' pretensions in order to be sure of their services:

Superficially, Suzhou has become more and more beautiful over the past few decades, but on the inside it is in fact rotten. Now, after the unusual drought we have had for the past few years, even from the outside Suzhou is not a pretty sight. Actors wear fine clothes and eat sumptuous food and swagger through the streets. When people engage them for a theatrical performance, even if they are paid over ten taels, the actors still are resentful, looking down on it as being too little. There are even some who ride horses or travel in sedan chairs, ask for ginseng soup backstage, and engage in all sorts of unseemly behavior. But yet there are still those among the gentry who wait on these actors diligently. If a day passes without incident, they reward them even more handsomely. Butchers and wine sellers pride themselves on sponsoring dramatic performances, and when actors come to put on plays in the alleys and villages, spirits are high. These types are even more licentious and have no taboos or fears. People say the inhabitants of Suzhou are fools. Is this not the truth?[36]

The fashion for theatrical entertainments has effected such a reversal between high and low that elites fawn upon actors, who in turn no longer know their place. In a further deterioration of the social fabric, "butchers and wine sellers" now ape the gentry in putting on theatricals; sponsoring

35. Tang Xianzu, "Yu yi ling Luo Zhang'er" 與宜伶羅章二, in *Tang Xianzu quanji*, p. 1519.

36. Xu Shupi, *Shixiao lu*; cited in Liao Ben, *Zhongguo gudai juchang shi*, p. 71; Lu Eting, *Kunju yanchu shigao*, p. 93; and Zhang Faying, *Zhongguo xiban shi*, pp. 99–100.

theatricals has become an easy route to the acquisition of markers of gentry status.

In *Songchuang mengyu*, Zhang Han lamented the expenditures of gentry families on theatrical entertainments, suggesting that they were abandoning such core obligations as providing relief for the poor.

During the past two or three decades, wealthy gentry families have used gold and expensive cloth to make costumes, ornaments, instruments, and props. They array musicians and summon ten actors to come and form a troupe to perform *chuanqi*. Aficionados compete to compose lascivious and beautiful lyrics, passing them around and singing them together. Who knows how many thousands of people in a single prefectural city could be fed and clothed for the same sum of money? The fashion is to take pleasure in lax morals and to compete to see who can enjoy greater luxuries. Although these people trespass all prohibitions, they do not know how to restrain themselves. I respect my ancestral teachings and do not dare disobey them.[37]

By invoking his ancestral teachings as he criticizes the fad for private theatricals, Zhang Han positions himself as a member of a traditional elite, differentiating himself from those families who attempt to gain social position with sumptuary display.

Fan Lian deplored the fact that the gentry spared no expense on theatricals, and noted that the extravagant theatrical costumes used in temple festivals in 1590 in his native Huating were unconscionable given that the region had experienced famine for years on end. Of the actors, who wore brightly colored clothing and leather boots, as well as gauze caps adorned with gold, pearls, kingfisher feathers, and flowers, he remarked caustically: "It was as though they were costumed as *zhuangyuan* 狀元 [the top graduate in the civil service examinations] parading the streets. They used three whips adorned with jewels, whose value was over a 100 taels."[38] Each

---

37. Zhang Han, *Songchuang mengyu, juan* 7, p. 139.

38. Fan Lian, *Yunjian jumu chao*, 2.6b. Also see Dolby, *Chinese Drama*, p. 106. The playwright Li Yu noted the desire of the gentry for sumptuary display as he caustically skewered the fashion for luxurious costumes and props in his *Xianqing ouji*, published in 1671: "These days, the costumes of entertainers can be said to be luxurious in the extreme. It could not be otherwise in things that are meant to amuse wealthy aristocrats; one cannot blame them for not displaying frugality and thrift. But what one cannot understand is that although women's clothing should prize lightness and softness, today's dancing costumes are as hard and unyielding as coats of armor. Not only do they have broad, thick

day of the productions, which supposedly lasted for four or five days, cost
a thousand taels. In 1592, he wrote, such displays were severely prohibited,
and "men of discernment were made happy by this."[39] From Fan Lian's
point of view, those who spend vast sums on theatricals contribute to the
effacement of the gentry as it has been traditionally constituted. The actors costumed as *zhuangyuan* speak to the moral vacuity of the gentry
who neglect their traditional obligations.

The Neo-Confucian philosopher Liu Zongzhou 劉宗周 (1578–1645),
a fellow townsman and mentor of the connoisseur of the theater Qi Biaojia 祁彪佳 (1602–45), also registered outrage at the expenditure of the
gentry on such amusements.[40] The city of Shaoxing, he noted, was given
to such frivolities; several thousand people would gather at night, not dis-
persing until dawn. For Liu, conspicuous consumption is clearly associated with moral laxity: "In a day, they would waste a thousand gold to
support these thieves who teach immorality. . . . The social disorder of
Shaoxing must originate in this."[41] Recent efforts by officials to prohibit
public performances had not been successful because they had made an
exception for their own banquets. Liu argued that the gentry had to set an
example and illuminate a path for the rest of society; only then, "if you set
out a rule in the morning, will people follow it by night." He suggested
that officials prohibit not only performances but also banquets if they
wished to rid the populace of theatrical entertainments.[42] Liu's need to

---

shoulders, but besides the outer layer and the lining, they feature overlays of gold embroi-
dery and silk brocade. The back and front panels of the skirts are called 'modesty shields.'
These must be made of stiff cloth stretched over bone. These are things to be worn on the
battlefield . . . how can they have entered the realm of the stage?" *Li Yu quanji*, II: 103. For
a translation of the passage from which this quotation is drawn, see Faye Chunfang Fei,
Chinese Theories of Theater and Performance from Confucius to the Present, p. 85. As Ann
Jones and Peter Stallybrass (*Renaissance Clothing and the Materials of Memory*, p. 175–206)
have argued in the context of the English Renaissance theater, the sumptuousness of costume was likely one of the primary attractions for a premodern theatrical audience. Since
theatrical troupes depended on the display of excess to attract audiences, they could hardly
have been expected to engage in restraint.

39. Fan Lian, *Yunjian jumu chao*, 2.6b.
40. On Liu Zongzhou's relation to Qi Biaojia, see Smith, "Gardens in Ch'i Piao-chia's
Social World," p. 59.
41. Liu Zongzhou, *Liuzi quanshu*, 20.7b.
42. Ibid.

advocate such a radical solution testified to a sense that the theater was highly infectious. It was seemingly impossible to vaccinate against this plague; one had to eradicate the host.

All the authors writing in this vein spoke as though a fascination with the dazzling spectacle of the theater had robbed the gentry of their powers of judgment. This becomes particularly apparent when authors allude to the vogue for *Kunqu*. Xie Zhaozhe 謝肇淛 (1567–1624) lamented that "the whole country seems to have gone crazy" as he deplored the gentry's contention for the favors of the best male singers from the southeast, the region where *Kunqu* originated:

This all began in the Ningshao 寧紹 [Ningbo and Shaoxing] region of Zhejiang, but today half of them [male singers] come from Linqing 臨清 [in present day Shandong]. For this reason, nowadays we distinguish between northern and southern male singers. Although there are multitudes of them, seldom are they exquisite. If there is one among them who is exquisite, then all the rakes among the gentry do their utmost to engage him to entertain them. The whole country seems to have gone crazy. It is a most ridiculous situation. . . . As for their prettiness and wiliness, those [singers] of the northwest are no match for those of the southeast.[43]

Xie wrote as though he could safeguard the reader against such excesses by labeling them a mere vogue. Xie's contemporary Shen Defu similarly sought to warn the reader that the fad for southern actors encouraged deceit. Although most "singing boys," Shen noted, came from the north, all of them claimed to be from Zhejiang. He once asked an actor from the north from whence he hailed. The boy pretended to be a southerner, answering, "Cixi 慈溪 in Zhejiang." Shen quizzed him further and found that although he had clearly never been to Zhejiang, he cleverly peppered his speech with Zhejiang dialect, which Shen suspected that he had learned from his peers.[44] Several decades later, Li Yu commented caustically: "What is remarkable is that in theater troupes these days every actor speaks with a Suzhou accent, wherever they are from—north, south, east or west—and without any regard to where the characters in the play were born. Does this mean that all the people of Suzhou are actors?"[45] All these

---

43. Xie Zhaozhe, *Wuzazu*, pp. 304–5.
44. Shen Defu, *Wanli yehuo bian*, p. 621.
45. Li Yu, *Li Yu quanji*, II: 104.

authors noted that as *Kunqu*, a local form of opera, achieved a national following, its popularity encouraged false claims to authenticity.

Those who criticized the vogue for southern opera clearly believed themselves to be impartial observers beyond the influence of fashion, writing as transcendent spectators who stood outside the illusion of social spectacle. The discriminating social spectator would see through the vagaries of fashion, detect imposture, and understand that the frivolous interest in theatricals disconnected the gentry from the deeper mission of providing for the poor; only he truly understood the timeless mission and authentic constitution of the gentry, in part because he was impervious to the charms of the theater.

The Theater as Refuge from Convention

What is interesting is that the claim to a transcendent social spectatorship free of the blinders of fashion informs the writings of *partisans* of the theater as well as those of its detractors. Partisans of the theater laid claim to a superior level of discernment as social spectators precisely because of their relationship to the theater, which they believed afforded them a freedom from conventional modes of thought. Rather than asserting that they could see through social imposture in the anti-theatricalist vein, they drew upon the mobile and participatory form of social spectatorship that we noticed in Zhang Dai's essay on watching the moon at West Lake. They invoked a different model of *seeing*, postulating a more complicated relationship between illusion and disillusion than the anti-theatricalists who claimed simply to see through or discredit pretense and masquerade. Partisans of the theater accused the anti-theatricalists of a stunted adherence to commonplace notions of the acceptable and professed a disdain for the narrow-mindedness of those with a conventional understanding of the distinction between vulgarity and refinement. Such pro-theatrical arguments often engaged simply in an iconoclastic inversion of commonplaces. If anti-theatricalists feared that literati would be mesmerized by actors and spellbound by the lascivious tunes of the southern opera, devotees of the theater (even those who were high-ranking officials) viewed it as an antidote to the crass superficiality of officialdom. In rebuttal to those who argued that sons of the gentry would become wastrels under the influence of the theater, connoisseurs claimed that indulging an interest in the theater did not hinder examination success; rather, because the theater unfettered the imagination and freed one from social convention, it enabled the examination candidate to compose more interesting essays. The fad for theatricals clearly benefited from the cachet afforded the transgression of conventional hierarchies of value among the late Ming elite.

These arguments must be read in the context of a more general effort to elevate the status of the theater that began during the mid-Ming. Before the mid-Ming, literati conceived of the composition of plays as not only a trivial art but a vulgar one. The drama of the Yuan was largely authored by commoners and men of uncertain status; we know of only two literati authors, Ma Zhiyuan 馬致遠 (fl. ca. 1280) and Bai Pu 白樸 (1226–?). Opera had a tertiary status in the hierarchy of *shi* 詩 (poetry), *ci* 詞 (song lyric), and *qu* 曲, and the low status of dramatic texts was closely linked to the vulgarity of actors in the literati imagination.[46] However, during the mid-Ming, literati aficionados of the theater began to elevate the status of northern drama (*zaju*), appropriating it as a literati art.[47] As Stephen West and Patricia Sieber have documented, this process reached its zenith during the Wanli era, when literati compilation and publication of anthologies of northern drama reached their height.[48] Literati aficionados of northern opera (*beiqu* 北曲) and, to a lesser degree, of southern opera (*nanxi* 南戲) employed a number of strategies to raise the status of dramatic texts: they attempted to distance the texts from the licentiousness of the world of the theater, argued for them as a vernacular literature imbued with the particular vibrancy of "popular" forms, and, beginning in the Wanli era, published such plays in luxury editions.[49]

The arguments that engagement in the theater aided examination success, then, occurred in the context of a larger effort to raise the status of

---

46. See West, "Text and Ideology," p. 276.

47. For the ways in which the Yuan playwright Guan Hanqing's 關漢卿 oeuvre was appropriated and transformed as literati editors of the Ming sought to claim art song and opera as literati forms, see Sieber, *Theaters of Desire*, pp. 45–80.

48. West, "Text and Ideology," p. 238; and Sieber, *Theaters of Desire*, pp. 83–161. West notes that literati editing and collation of dramatic texts was extraordinarily concentrated between 1570 and 1630; ten major editions appeared then, as opposed to only two in the preceding two hundred years.

49. West, "Text and Ideology," p. 279. On Ming editions of Yuan drama, see Sieber, *Theaters of Desire*, pp. 83–161.

dramatic texts vis-à-vis literary genres. This elevation of the status of the theater has been well discussed elsewhere; what I focus on below is the subtle way in which the arguments of partisans of the theater resonate with the notion of preserving a tension between illusion and disillusion that we identified in Zhang Dai's writing above. Disparaging the mundane mentality of those who viewed the theater as a distraction from the all-consuming goal of examination success, partisans of the theater argued instead that reading or watching plays opened the wells of inspiration and enlivened even the most turgid prose. They suggested that reading, writing, and watching plays freed the mind to write lively and original *baguwen* 八股文 (eight-legged essays) in preparation for the civil service examinations. Ni Yuanlu 倪元璐 (1594–1644), a friend of the connoisseurs of the theater Zhang Dai and Qi Biaojia, argued that contemporary examination essays and Yuan drama were similar in their methods of composition. It was commonly held that the writer of examination essays must allow the words of the sages to flow through him; Ni pointed out that the Yuan playwrights had similarly channeled the voices of their characters. Reading Yuan drama thus enabled one to write better *baguwen*:

> From the classics and histories to the poems and songs, all come from the same embryo, as though they had the same mother but suckled at different breasts. . . . The plays of the Yuan and the *baguwen* of today are twins, their features alike in every respect. It is probably because their method of writing is to use one's own intelligence to express the spirits of others, which is the same as using human speech to substitute for the language of ghosts.[50]

Jin Shengtan 金聖嘆 (1608–61) argued that the northern drama *Xixiang ji* 西廂記 (The western chamber) would shake the mind free of conventional habits of perception, and that one ought to give it to sons of good family to read, just as one would the writings of the iconoclastic philosopher Zhuangzi 莊子 or the *Shi ji* 史記 (Historical records) of Sima Qian

---

50. Ni Yuanlu, "*Mengzi ruo taohua ju xu*" 孟子若桃花劇序; cited in Zhao Shanlin, *Zhongguo xiqu guanzhong xue*, p. 48. Although *baguwen* now has a reputation as a stultifying genre in which formal constraints were paramount, it is important to remember that during the seventeenth century, *baguwen* were read as entertainment and, in this respect as well, could have been considered similar to dramatic texts.

司馬遷.[51] Tang Shunzhi 唐順之 (1507–60) declared that his essays were composed half drunk, and that in preparation for writing them, he would sing at the top of his voice the section of the *Xixiang ji* in which the character Huiming declares that he is ready to leave the monastery and engage in battle.[52] Tang claimed that as his hands and feet danced, he would let his brush play until it filled the page, and an essay would be finished.[53] Such anecdotes suggest that the iconoclastic promotion of theatricals allowed the literatus to claim freedom from social convention and, implicitly, freedom from social aspiration, while maintaining examination success as a goal.

This pairing of an iconoclastic disdain for careerism with presumably effortless examination success is exemplified in an anecdote recorded by Tang Xianzu's contemporary Dong Qichang 董其昌 (1555–1636), who was well known for his interest in vernacular forms and his disdain for conventional literary valuations. He wrote that when a *juren* from Qi'nan named Liao Tongye 廖同野 came to see Lu Shen 陸深 (1477–1544) of Shanghai in order to promote his essays, Lu began with the question, "Have you read the plays *Xixiang ji* or *Bojie ji* 伯喈記?" Liao, who never allowed himself to read texts that were not "composed by the sages," thought this question quite odd. After another month or so had passed, he again sent his essays to Lu and went to call on him. After reading his work, Lu said to him, "You still have not read the two plays. Why is that?" This time Liao took him seriously and, when he went home, began to read them. After another month, Lu read his compositions again, and said, "It's a shame; you'll place second in the examinations. If you had read the plays earlier, you could have placed first."[54] Lu's preternatural discernment, which allowed him to ascertain from the texture of Liao's writing that he had not yet read the plays, gives credibility to his prediction.

The notion of drama as a remedy for turgid prose applied not merely to reading plays but to watching performances. Wu Weiye 吳偉業 (1609–72) ostensibly urged a student to watch a professional troupe per-

---

51. Jin Shengtan, *Jin Shengtan quanji* (Di liu caizi shu 第六才子書, "Du fa 讀法"), in Chen Duo and Ye Changhai, *Zhongguo lidai julun xuanzhu*, pp. 276–86.
52. *Xixiang ji*, ed. Wang Jisi, pp. 54–55.
53. *Cao gu shiliu guan* 操觚十六觀; cited in Jiao Xun, *Jushuo*, p. 111.
54. Dong Qichang, *Rongtai ji* 容臺集, 2.7a.

forming on a temple stage (a far more déclassé environment than the private salon). The student thought Wu was joking and did not dare go, only succumbing after Wu urged him repeatedly. After a month of watching such performances, it was "as though the brush and ink were singing and dancing before him" and his "thoughts were riding the wind, his words flowing out of a spring."[55] The student's reluctance underscores Wu's iconoclasm.[56] Engagement in the theater encouraged fluidity of thought precisely because the social world of the theatrical fostered a disdain for careerism.

Such anecdotes, which contrasted the aesthetic of pleasure and *savoir vivre* associated with the theater to the dullard's emphasis on studies alone, promoted the nonchalant wit characteristic of the "rake" or *fengliu* 風流. The common translation of *fengliu* as "rake" or "romantic" does not reflect the insouciant disdain for careerism central to the term. Indeed, what emerges most clearly in all these anecdotes is that it is a disdain for careerism that will give one's essays an unnamable quality that insures examination success.

As He Yuming has noted, the social space of the private theatrical afforded the *fengliu* the perfect opportunity to display his freedom from social convention.[57] Zhou Shi 周詩 was only 21 when he took first place in the provincial examinations of Zhejiang in 1549. It was said that while his fellow candidates jockeyed for position before the *yamen* gates, waiting for the list of successful graduates to be posted, Zhou spent the night at

---

55. Qian Yuanxi 錢元熙, *Guoting jiwen* 過庭記聞; cited in Cheng Zai 承載 and Qian Hang 錢杭, *Shiqi shiji Jiangnan shehui shenghuo*, p. 232.

56. That such iconoclasm had a self-dramatizing quality is clear in the following anecdote: Huang Junfu 黃君輔 sought to gain approval of his essays from Tang Xianzu. Tang threw them on the floor crying, "You can burn these essays. Have you read my plays?" Tang then gave Huang a copy of *Mudan ting*, and Huang's creativity gushed forth after reading it (He Yisun 賀貽孫, *Ji shu* 激書; cited in Zhao Shanlin, *Zhongguo xiqu guanzhong xue*, p. 48).

57. Yuming He has discussed this point, noting that the social space of private theatricals during the late Ming was associated with freedom from social convention, providing a "fertile ground for self-fashioning" that allowed individuals to create alternative personalities within a temporary and provisional space that "walled off public expectation and monitoring of what was speakable or doable and encompassed instead uncensored linguistic and social acts" (Yuming He, "Productive Space," p. 7).

the opera.[58] When the crowds came looking for him with the news that he was the top graduate, he was on stage performing the opera about Fan Li searching for spring (*Fan Li xunchun* 范蠡尋春) and seemed not to hear them calling "Top graduate Zhou!" Not until the song was over did he descend the stage and return with them.[59] Zhou's affected absorption in the world on stage highlighted the seeming effortlessness of his examination success.

A pair of anecdotes related by Xu Fuzuo 徐復祚 (1560–1629 or after) suggests that immersion in opera fortified one against the pressure to perform well in the examinations (and thus also contributed to success). The prefect of Hengzhou, Feng Guan 馮冠, excelled at playing the lute and singing the lyrics of the Jin and Yuan from a young age (by the mid- to late sixteenth century, the music of the Jin and the Yuan was already quite specialized knowledge, the province of connoisseurs). Feng Guan attended the examinations five times, bringing with him only the text of the southern drama *Pipa ji* 琵琶記 (The lute). He was so enamored of the opera that even if he were alone in a room, he would sing it without ceasing (*ming ming bu jue kou* 鳴鳴不絕口), underscoring the fact that he performed not for others, in accord with social convention, but to please himself. Xu's friend Qin Silin 秦四麟 of Changshu, who also excelled at singing the lyrics of the Jin and Yuan, went to take the examinations bringing nothing but his copies of the *Pipa ji* and *Xixiang ji*. Someone reproved him, asking Qin whether he was not anxious about the exams. He smiled and said, "I am anxious that my singing is not good. How could I worry about my essays?" Xu concluded, "He was *fengliu* to that degree."[60] The scorn in Qin's answer is evident. One who specializes in the lyrics of the Jin and Yuan cannot worry about something so trivial as examination essays.

The relationship between engagement in theatricals and success in the examinations in the anecdotes above recalls Zhang Dai's logic of the pan-

---

58. It is unclear from the wording of the text whether the setting was private or public.

59. Wu Chenyan 吳陳琰, *Kuangyuan zazhi* 曠園雜志; cited in Jiao Xun, *Jushuo*, p. 100. For another discussion of this passage, see Zhao Shanlin, *Zhongguo xiqu guanzhong xue*, p. 51.

60. Xu Fuzuo, "*Qu lun fu lu*" 曲論附錄, in *Sanjia cunlao qu tan* 三家村老曲談, 10a. For another discussion of this passage, see Zhao Shanlin, *Zhongguo xiqu guanzhong xue*, p. 51.

oramic and participatory. The immersion of the *fengliu* in the illusions of the stage gives them the perspective necessary to achieve an unconventional quality of vision. Although they disdain careerism, they do not shun participation in the exams. Just as Zhang Dai, having classified the five types of participants viewing the moon on West Lake, leaves his perch of observation to join the festivities, Zhou Shi leaves the stage to accept the honors of a top graduate.

Extreme devotion to the pleasures of theatrical connoisseurship offered a haven from the assumption of social ambition. In its most exaggerated form, such devotion was cast as obsession, as we see in an account of the career of Wu Zhensuo 吳珍所. As the diarist Li Rihua 李日華 (1565–1635) noted in 1612, Wu suddenly left his post as district magistrate of Lanyang in Henan, wanting nothing more to do with the vulgar and vile. He built a yacht (*loufang* 樓舫) and housed a number of singers and beauties on it, amusing himself among them all day. Every year when the peach trees blossomed, he would head toward the Sixth Bridge on West Lake, taste the newly harvested tea, and then proceed to the famed sites of Suzhou and Yangxian.[61] The yacht allowed the connoisseur to travel freely to sample the delights of each season, even as its self-contained quality clearly segregated him from the mundane.

Absorption in the theater protects the connoisseur from encounter with the mundane; this is clearly illustrated in Zhang Dai's unforgettable portrait of a beloved friend haunted by a passion for the theater. Zhang Dai's requiem for Qin Yisheng 秦一生 (who died suddenly at the age of fifty-five in the eighth month of 1638) describes Qin's daily habit of infiltrating the private performances of the gentry:

Whenever the landowners of Shaoxing had great feasts for officials and aristocrats, whether in the renowned gardens of famous sites or in remote residences in secluded alleyways, there was not a day that he did not disguise himself to attend. When the night grew still and the lamps began to flicker, when all the wine was gone and the guests had scattered, then from among the columns and pillars two eyes would burn like lightning shooting down from a cliff. It would be none other than Yisheng. . . . Several days before he died, he was still at someone's residence watching opera. He spoke of it to me, mumbling and muttering.

---

61. Li Rihua, *Weishuixuan riji* 味水軒日記, p. 221. The entry is for the twenty-second day of the first month of Wanli 40 (1612).

Qin Yisheng embodies the disinterestedness of the elite connoisseur perfectly. His attendance at the theatricals held by the landowners of Shaoxing is not a social act; he not only attends in disguise but hides behind a pillar to observe the performances. He is completely defined by spectatorship; it is not incidental that his eyes, which "burn like lightning," are all that is visible at banquet's end.

Zhang Dai contrasted the purity of Qin's obsession with the theater with the coarseness of the mundane spectator:

The people of the world spend their days seeking renown and profit. They are like maggots eating dung, or flies following goats. They run back and forth without cease. They don't know what landscape or opera are. Yisheng reviled them and thought them despicable. The world also has coarse bullies who are careless and haphazard. The stench of their wine and meat reeks in the garden pavilions of famous landscapes. The space before them is filled with actors. They are dull-witted and uncomprehending. But Yisheng was as though he lived in a world beyond all this.[62]

The mundane mentality of those who seek only profit and fame, who view the actors before them in a coarse and sensual fashion, contrasts pointedly with the purity of Qin's appreciation. Qin's refinement as a spectator is a function of his freedom from social aspiration.[63]

Of all the texts discussed above, Zhang Dai's requiem for Qin Yisheng at first seems to represent the sole attempt to divorce theatrical spectacle from social spectacle, for "Yisheng was as though he lived in a world beyond all this." However, as Zhang Dai contrasts Qin to the mundane

---

62. Zhang Dai, *Langhuan wenji*, p. 266.

63. The all-absorbing passion of the connoisseur was associated with a realm of refinement far removed from the vanity of ambition as early as the ninth century. Judith Zeitlin quotes the Tang dynasty art historian Zhang Yanyuan: "Only in calligraphy and painting have I not yet forgotten emotion. Intoxicated by them I forget all speech. . . . Does this not seem wiser, after all, than all that burning ambition and ceaseless toil when fame and profit war within one's breast?" (Zhang Yanyuan 張彥遠, *Lidai minghua ji* 歷代名畫記, p. 25, translated in Zeitlin, *Historian of the Strange*, p. 65). By the seventeenth century, as Zeitlin observes, obsession had become a vogue, and the connoisseur's indifference to worldly affairs potentially a pose (Zeitlin, *Historian of the Strange*, p. 69). That one had the social latitude to be indifferent simply signified one's elevated status. Nearly all the anecdotes cited above carefully attest to the examination honors and high rank of the *fengliu* who disdained worldly success.

spectator, he condemns those "dull-witted and uncomprehending" social boors for whom the theater is a sensual, rather than an aesthetic, pleasure. Zhang's remarks remind us that the social space of the private theatrical has its own aesthetic, and that this aesthetic is firmly tied to questions of social distinction. Zhang's portrait of Qin Yisheng shares with his two essays we discussed earlier the conviction that it is refined spectatorship that sets one apart, but it draws on a different notion of the relation between the spectator and his or her social context than prevailed in "West Lake on the Fifteenth Day of the Seventh Month." Zhang's requiem for Qin Yisheng, with the complexity that is Zhang Dai's signature, invokes both the anti-theatricalist notion that the theater is a decadent realm whose denizens are slaves to fashion, and the pro-theatricalist idea that connoisseurship of the theater elevates one above mundane concerns.

Conclusion

We began with the question, how did seventeenth-century authors conceive of the relationship between theatrical and social spectacle—in other words, how might notions of theatrical performance and spectatorship have colored conceptions of social performance and spectatorship? The texts we examined above led us to two models of theatrical performance and spectatorship. In the first, social roles were analogous to theatrical roles; acting became a metaphor for social imposture, and the theater a figure for the disjunction of illusion and actuality. The refined spectator has the task of limiting the power of the theatrical to transform the social. In the second model, the theater became a figure for the conjunction of illusion and actuality; the social spectator suspends disbelief in the face of social illusion just as the theatrical spectator suspends disbelief in the face of theatrical illusion. The social is enabled by the theatrical rather than weakened by it. Refined social spectatorship is characterized by an understanding of the ontological questions behind aesthetic display, by the tension between dispassionate observation and immersion quintessential to theatrical spectatorship, and by a desire to engage with the social realm even after having identified it as illusory. The most refined spectators have the capacity to enter the "lanterns, the illuminations, the shadows, the mists, the flames," that is, to move headlong into the tangle of illusion and disillusion.

When we turned to examine how these notions of theatricality might have applied to writing about the stage itself, we saw that anti-theatricalist writings depended exclusively on the first of these conceptions of theatricality, whereas that of partisans of the theater adopted the second. The anti-theatricalists who criticized the vogue for *Kunqu* believed themselves to be transcendent spectators standing outside the illusion of social spectacle. They aimed to see through the pervasive imposture that weakened the gentry; not surprisingly, anti-theatricalists railed about the social airs of actors (and of the gentry themselves) as they lamented the expenses of the gentry on theatricals. In the writings of partisans of the theater, we see that the *fengliu*—the rake or romantic free of the constraints of social convention—offers a more complex model of a social spectator whose perspective is informed by theater. The *fengliu* eludes conventional habits of perception in part because he adopts a mobile and participatory, yet panoramic aesthetic equal to the task of preserving the conjunction of illusion and disillusion.

These conceptions of theatrical performance and spectatorship will be a compass that will guide us through the chapters that follow. In Chapter 3, the analysis of Tang Xianzu's *Mudan ting* shows how the first of these conceptions of theatricality is employed to explore the cultural politics of citation. *Mudan ting* critiques the social imposture ostensibly made possible by the allusive practices of archaism, the dominant school of literary thought during the late sixteenth-century; the task of the social spectator is to see through the superficial literary adornments of archaism. The play seems to adapt a position aligned with that of anti-archaist advocates of the vernacular among Tang Xianzu's extended circle, but in fact, slyly exposes the vernacular to be as scripted and staged as archaist literary practice. In Chapter 4, the play *Nan wanghou* will, as though in rebuttal to *Mudan ting*, consider the practice of allusive citation from the viewpoint of the second of these conceptions of theatrical spectatorship, drawing on the notion that the social is enabled by the theatrical. The play opens by asking us to hold illusion and disillusion in tension as spectators of the "stage gender" of the cross-dressed actor; by play's end, it has become clear that that ability to hold illusion and disillusion in tension enables the literary practice of allusive citation.

Chapter 5 revisits the figure of the *fengliu*. Inspired by the world of private theatricals to affect an ignorance of convention, the coterie of the mid-seventeenth-century poet Chen Weisong cast him as the last of the romantics, celebrating his abandoned devotion to the young actor Xu Zi-yun and positioning themselves as his rivals in their poems. The poems written by Chen Weisong's circle in response to his own passion for the actor are simultaneously expressive and mimetic, authentic and staged. The poems, then, suggest a conflict as to how we are to understand the homoerotic sentiments inscribed therein; the impossible necessity of preserving both polarities of understanding recalls the challenge issued to the spectator by *Nan wanghou* to preserve illusion and disillusion in tension. Lastly, in Chapter 6, the storyteller Liu Jingting adopts the panoramic and participatory aesthetic of the *fengliu*, but does so in order to model the dispassion of this aesthetic for the literatus coming to terms with the fall of the Ming.

In the next chapter, to appreciate the potential influence of late Ming trends in performance practice on the metaphorical relation between theatrical and social spectacle, I ask how the seventeenth-century problematization of the boundaries between theatrical illusion and reality might have been influenced by stage practice itself.

TWO

Performance Practice and
Stage Architecture

In this chapter, I examine the potential influence of performance practices and stage architecture on the notion of the "world as stage" in seventeenth-century China, paying special attention to how performance practice and stage architecture might have developed over the course of the century. I draw on the research of a number of Chinese scholars of performance—most notably Lu Eting, Liao Ben, Sun Chongtao, Zhao Shanlin, and Wang An-Chi—to argue that practices that became fashionable toward the beginning of the seventeenth century—such as the performance of selected scenes rather than entire plays, the housing of private troupes, and the privately hosted theatrical—fostered a sense of resonance between a play text and its performance context, a sense that the boundaries between world and stage were "soluble" and could be readily dissolved.[1] Longstanding features of seventeenth-century staging, such as abstract set design and the use of temporary, provisional performance spaces, suggested that any space could easily be transformed into theatrical space, and that the spectator did not inhabit a fixed vantage point. These characteristics of performance practice and stage architecture fostered the mo-

---

1. See Lu Eting, *Kunju yanchu shigao*; Liao Ben, *Zhongguo xiju tushi*; idem, *Zhongguo gudai juchang shi*; Sun Chongtao and Xu Hongtu, *Xiqu youling shi*; Wang An-Chi, *Mingdai xiqu wulun*; idem, *Mingdai chuanqi zhi juchang ji qi yishu*; and Zhao Shanlin, *Zhongguo xiqu guanzhong xue*.

bile and participatory quality that we argued in the previous chapter was characteristic of seventeenth-century theatrical spectatorship. By the end of the century, by contrast, commercial playhouses with fixed stages on which professional troupes performed had become popular in the capital, Beijing. This development in part fostered a greater sense of an ontological division between worlds on- and offstage than that which prevailed at the beginning of the century. Such a division informs the late seventeenth-century play *Taohua shan* (completed in 1699), which has the most highly developed conception of audience and spectatorship and most sophisticated articulation of meta-theatricality in the seventeenth-century repertoire.

Carlo Ginzburg has written that sixteenth-century Italian art traveled two "iconic circuits," one "public, widespread and socially undifferentiated, and the other private, circumscribed, and socially elevated."[2] This distinction is quite useful for thinking about seventeenth-century Chinese theater. There were roughly four types of settings for performances during the Ming and Qing: (1) palace stages; (2) commercial establishments such as restaurants, inns, and wine shops; (3) open-air settings such as temples and markets; and (4) the private *tanghui* 堂會 (opera salons), which took place in restricted spaces such as the residences of the wealthy, government offices (*yamen* 衙門), and *huiguan* 會館 (halls and compounds for members of guilds and officials from a particular locale). Public arenas such as markets and temples were open to all sectors of society; such socially undifferentiated venues were typically considered déclassé. By contrast, attendance was circumscribed at salon-style performances (*tanghui yanchu* 堂會演出); such gatherings were considered socially elevated.[3] In effect, men of means encountered a far greater variety of performance contexts than other members of society, for they had access both to private theatricals and to public areas such as markets, temples, and wine shops (*jiulou* 酒樓). Since certain types of plays tended to be

---

2. Ginzburg, *Myths, Emblems and Clues*, p. 79.

3. The notion that performances at banquets, brothels, and the *yamen* might be linked because they were private and circumscribed in attendance is of modern coinage. As Yuming He ("Productive Space," p. 37) notes, *tanghui* is not a seventeenth-century locution; Ming performances were described in terms of the specific setting, as in the term *yanyue* 宴樂, "banquet music."

performed on public, open-air stages and others only in the more intimate space of salon-style performances, only the relatively wealthy had access to the full seventeenth-century repertoire.[4]

This schema of public and private iconic circuits, however, is complicated by the fact that individual actors moved back and forth between public and private arenas of performance, between markets and temples and brothels and gentry homes. The plays that they learned in one realm, they brought to the other. Actors might move from professional to private troupes or vice versa, taking their knowledge with them; professional troupes were coached in private households to perform the latest plays and then took the plays to public spaces such as markets and temples. Tang Xianzu taught a troupe of actors from Yihuang 宜黃 in Jiangxi to perform his *Handan ji* so that they could perform it at his banquets, but they later performed portions of it at a funeral.[5] They could easily have performed it on temple stages, where its theme of the evanescent and illusory nature of worldly success would have been quite appropriate.

Moreover, a single text might circulate in various manifestations: plays appeared as reading and performance texts; they might be performed in full or as part of a medley of selected scenes (*zhezi xi* 折子戲); and they might be sung without gesture or dialogue or acted with full costumes and sets. The textual permutations of Tang Xianzu's *Mudan ting* furnish a case in point. When first published, the play caused a sensation; its heroine Du Liniang quickly became a cultural icon, her name synonymous

---

4. To examine the variations in repertoire performed in different types of performance spaces, Cheng Zai and Qian Hang (*Shiqi shiji Jiangnan shehui shenghuo*, pp. 234–35) compare two compilations of dramatic texts: a miscellany entitled *Yuefu hongshan* 樂府紅珊 (Red coral ballads) containing plays commonly performed in the pleasure quarters of the Qinhuai, and a record of plays performed at a temple in Shanxi province entitled *Yingshen saishe lijie chuanpu sishi qu gongdiao* 迎神賽社禮節傳譜四十曲宮調 (Register for posterity of forty melodies used in rituals to welcome the spirits on festival days). As one might expect, in the rustic setting of the temple in Shanxi, over 52 of the 103 plays or scenes listed concerned military campaigns and acts of heroism, whereas only 5 of the plays listed in the *Yuefu hongshan* featured such themes. The largest category of plays in *Yuefu hongshan* is romance and parting, with 26 plays; stories of the achievement of renown through deeds of merit, which provided material for banquets and celebratory occasions, were also popular. The list of plays performed at the temple included slapstick plays making fun of literati; none of these were included in the *Yuefu hongshan*.

5. Yung, Sai-shing, "A Critical Study of the *Han-tan chi*," pp. 140–45.

with the all-important term in seventeenth-century literary culture, passion (*qing* 情).[6] Yet the play was criticized by some as unperformable.
Taking advantage of the fact that the performance text was a publishing
niche distinct from that of the reading text, the dramatists Shen Jing 沈
璟 (1553–1610), Feng Menglong 馮夢龍 (1574–1646), and Zang Maoxun
臧懋循 (1550–1620) later published revisions that they claimed rendered
the play more performable, to Tang Xianzu's great resentment.[7] Selected
highlights of the text were also performed, as their publication in miscellanies of commonly performed scenes attests.[8] Although we have no record of a full performance of *Mudan ting*, the existence of a full eighteenth-century score suggests that the play also was performed in its
entirety. A single text, then, might be shaped and manipulated to suit all
these performance contexts.

The ease with which texts were adapted to performance belies the
common notion that the seventeenth century was the age of the closet
drama (*antou xi* 案頭戲), an anachronistic term that refers to plays believed to have been read more than performed.[9] It is more accurate to
think of closet drama as a way station that a text might inhabit at some
point as it traveled the iconic circuits outlined above. Some *chuanqi*, such
as Kong Shangren's *Taohua shan*, fell out of the repertoire after enjoying a
period of popularity on the stage and became *antou xi*. Likewise, by the
mid-Ming many Jin and Yuan *zaju* likely were read far more often than
they were performed; these texts, although not written as closet dramas,
had achieved that status. Labeling specific texts as closet dramas never intended to be performed ignores the extreme flexibility of performance
contexts and styles.

Most plays were probably performed in the *qingchang* 清唱, or pure
singing, style—accompanied by instruments but presented without costume or gesture—before they began to circulate in manuscript. This style
of singing can be construed as an intermediate realm between reading and

---

6. See Zeitlin, "Shared Dreams," p. 128.

7. See Swatek, *"Peony Pavilion" Onstage*, esp. pp. 10, 25–68.

8. Swatek (ibid., pp. 101–57) also analyzes the circulation of scenes from *Mudan ting* as
zhezi xi by examining performance miscellanies.

9. The scholar Liao Ben has suggested that the notion of the closet drama is an anachronistic concept; all seventeenth-century playwrights hoped to have their work performed
on the stage. Liao Ben, private conversation, Berkeley, spring 2004.

performance. Wang Jide, whose *Nan wanghou* is the subject of Chapter 4, wrote that as soon as his teacher Xu Wei 徐渭 (1521–93) finished a play for his *zaju* collection *Sisheng yuan* 四聲猿 (Four cries of a gibbon), he would call Wang over, and they would sing it together.[10] In the historical play *Taohua shan*, the literatus Yang Wencong 楊文驄 (1597–1646) pays a call on the playwright Ruan Dacheng 阮大鋮 (1587–1646) just as he happens to be proofreading his play *Yanzi jian* 燕子箋 (The swallow letter), and on the spur of the moment, they sing lyrics from the play together.[11] This type of performance took place in the literatus's study or at the banquet table; it could be conducted anywhere, at any time, and at any point in the various stages of the play's circulation.

Qingchang was a literati art suited to informal gatherings of friends, but professional troupes also might be invited to perform without costumes or gestures, simply singing along with a script; this was called *zuochang* 座唱 (singing in one's seat). *Zuochang* was a specialized niche for professional troupes; the expectation was that the musical standards of these troupes would be especially high, since there were no visuals to distract the audience. Invited to the homes of literati, the actors would sit around a table in a circle, the various musical instruments on the table to be picked up as needed. *Zuochang* was closely associated with salon-style performance. When private theatricals eventually diminished in popularity, the number of troupes specializing in this type of performance dwindled.[12]

The Flexibility of Performance Practice and Participatory Spectatorship

The practice of performing selected scenes from plays (*zhezi xi*) rather than plays in their entirety gained currency during the late Ming.[13] Nearly

---

10. Wang Jide, *Qulü* 曲律, in *Zhongguo gudian xiqu lunzhu jicheng*, 4: 167.

11. Kong Shangren, *Taohua shan*, p. 32.

12. This practice of performing selected highlights should be distinguished from that of singing only the lyrics to an opera (Luo Di 洛地, *Xiqu yu Zhejiang*, pp. 315–16).

13. On *zhezi xi*, see Lu Eting, *Kunju yanchu shigao*, pp. 170–202; Qi Senhua 齊森華, "Shilun Mingdai jiayue" 試論明代家樂, in Hua Wei and Wang Ayling, *Ming Qing xiqu guoji yantaohui lunwenji*, pp. 305–27; and Wang An-Chi, *Mingdai xiqu wulun*, pp. 1–81. Lu Eting (*Kunju yanchu shigao*, p. 126) believes that *zhezi xi* gained currency during the late Ming and early Qing, arguing that *zhezi xi* was likely first restricted to salon-style per-

all information regarding *zhezi xi* in salon-style performance derives from records left by the connoisseurs Zhang Dai, Qi Biaojia, Feng Mengzhen 馮夢禎 (1546–1605), and Pan Fangbo 潘方伯 (1525–1601). Their diaries and recollections furnish persuasive evidence that *zhezi xi* was a common feature of private theatricals during the Wanli period. Feng Mengzhen recorded inviting the courtesan Ma Xiangjun 馬湘君 and her "sisters" (most likely other prostitutes) in the sixth month of 1591 to perform two acts of the northern drama *Xixiang ji* at the home of the aficionado Bao Hansuo 包涵所, who, according to Zhang Dai, was one of the early owners of a private acting troupe.[14] The diary of Pan Fangbo, a *jinshi* of 1563 who left office in 1580 to devote himself to his garden and theatricals, mentions *zhezi xi* four times. He noted, for example, that he had attended a banquet at the residence of an acquaintance surnamed Guo 郭, where a professional troupe had been invited to perform. They did not act well and were told to leave the stage. Then the servants were summoned, and

---

formance arranged by connoisseurs who were less interested in the plot than in showcasing the artistry of a particular actor. The performance of entire plays, he believes, was more common at public performances by professional troupes. His conclusions have been severely criticized by Wang An-Chi (*Mingdai xiqu wulun*, pp. 1–49), who states that *zhezi xi* was a feature not only of private but of palace and public performances as early as the Jiajing (1522–67) reign period. The controversy derives in part from the paucity and brevity of the records, which enable the two scholars to read the same sources in support of opposing points. See, e.g., the discussion of the significance of the use of the term *zaju* to describe *zhezi xi* (the term *zhezi xi* was not used during the late Ming or early Qing) in a scene from Meng Chengshun's 孟稱舜 *Ying wu mu zhen wen ji* 鸚鵡墓貞文記 (preface dated 1644) in Lu Eting, *Kunju yanchu shigao*, p. 177; and Wang An-Chi, *Mingdai xiqu wulun*, p. 3. Wang's arguments take advantage of the discovery of the *Yingshen saishe lijie chuanpu sishi qu gongdiao* in 1986, six years after Lu's work was published (see note 4 to this chapter). The *Register* suggests that *zhezi xi* was performed on a temple stage in the Shanxi countryside during the Jiajing period. The text preserves a list of plays commonly performed at temple festivals and records the music performed on seven occasions. A number of the entries are scenes excerpted from plays. One could, of course, argue that these scenes were probably interspersed with sacrifices and rites and that their presence does not indicate that during the Jiajing, *zhezi xi* was a common feature of public theatricals beyond the temple stage; nor is this evidence relevant to the question of whether *zhezi xi* were a feature of private theatricals as early as the Jiajing.

14. Feng Mengzhen, *Kuaixue tang riji* 快雪堂日記, sixth month of 1605, sixth day; cited in Wang An-Chi, *Mingdai xiqu wulun*, p. 10. On Bao Hansuo's troupe, see Zhang Dai, *Tao'an mengyi / Xihu mengxun*, p. 37.

they performed several acts.[15] A number of Qi Biaojia's diary entries mention seeing excerpts from plays.[16] For example, the entry for the fourteenth day of the tenth month of 1639 mentions that he went to a banquet at the home of Qian Deyu 錢德輿, at which numerous friends were in attendance. "Deyu brought out his entire acting troupe, and they exerted themselves in performing the act 'Picking Lotuses' from *Huansha ji* [Washing gauze]."

Typically, scholars explain the ascendance of *zhezi xi* by pointing to the unwieldy length of *chuanqi* plays, which often totaled fifty-odd acts. Only a few records explicitly mention the full performance of a *chuanqi*, and those records suggest that it might take several days. Zhang Dai described a performance of the Mulian 目蓮 opera by a troupe of actors from Anhui commissioned by his uncle that lasted three days and three nights.[17] Similarly, when Hong Sheng, the author of the *chuanqi* drama *Changsheng dian* (The palace of eternal life), went to Nanjing in 1704, the textile commissioner of Nanjing, Cao Yin 曹寅 (1658–1712), held a banquet at his residence at which *Changsheng dian* was performed in its entirety; the performance spanned three days and three nights.[18]

---

15. Cited in Wang An-Chi, *Mingdai xiqu wulun*, pp. 12–13. Pan Fangbo's diary exists only in manuscript and is held in the collection of the Shanghai Art Museum. For more on the representation of Ming performance contexts in this diary, see Zhu Jianming 朱建明, "Cong Yuhuatang riji kan Mingdai Shanghai de xiqu yanchu" 從玉華堂日記看明代上海的戲曲演出, in Zhao Jingshen, *Xiqu luncong* 戲曲論叢.

16. Qi Biaojia, *Qi Zhongmin gong riji*. Since some editions of the diary are unpaginated, I give the dates of entry: Chongzhen fifth year (1632), fifth month, twentieth day; Chongzhen ninth year (1636), eleventh month, twenty-second day; Chongzhen tenth year (1637), ninth month, ninth day; Chongzhen eleventh year (1639), second month, fourteenth day. For another discussion of these entries, see Lu Eting, *Kunju yanchu shigao*, pp. 176–77.

17. Zhang Dai, *Tao'an mengyi / Xihu mengxun*, p. 52. Qi Biaojia noted that when the Mulian opera was performed in Jiangnan, the 109 scenes lasted three days and three nights (Qi Biaojia, *Yuanshantang Ming qupin jupin jiaolu* 遠山堂明曲品劇品校錄, pp. 134–35; cited in Qitao Guo, *Ritual Opera and Mercantile Lineage*, p. 11). Guo notes that Qi may have been mistaken regarding the number of scenes, but that the number would likely have been between 100 and 110.

18. Zhang Peiheng, *Hong Sheng nianpu*, pp. 365–66. The performance of Tang Xianzu's *Mudan ting* at Lincoln Center in 1999 used an eighteenth-century score (the earliest still extant) and lasted eighteen hours, broken into six three-hour segments.

We cannot attribute the rise of *zhezi xi* solely to the length of *chuanqi*, however, for *zaju* plays, which were typically only four acts long, were also excerpted in this manner.[19] It may be that *chuanqi* were first excerpted because of their length, and that the practice was later extended to *zaju*. It is also possible that the practice of performing *zhezi xi* arose from the habit of performing suites of arias (*santao* 散套) drawn from *zaju* or *chuanqi*; since each act of a play consists of such a suite, it would have been a short step from the performance of *santao* to the performance of *zhezi xi*.

Clearly, there were aesthetic valuations attached to the performance of *zhezi xi*. The juxtaposition of scenes as well as their pairing with a performance context was an art. Just as dishes in a banquet menu were to be properly paired, scenes from different operas were expected to achieve a certain resonance with one another. More important, they were also expected to resonate with the performance context. *Zhezi xi* were chosen from a "menu" (*xidan* 戲單) or playlist that the actors presented to the host or guest of honor. The term "selecting plays" (*dianxi* 點戲) is related to the term "ordering food" (*diancai* 點菜) and refers to the patron's selection of plays from this proffered menu. The same term was used for selecting plays at both public and private performances. In wine shops, the patrons who paid for the performance would order a sequence of scenes.[20] In private performance, scenes would be selected by the host or guest of honor.

Scenes might be selected because they showcased the skills of particular actors or the specialties of a troupe. But they also were chosen to suit the occasion. A performance at a birthday celebration, for example, might feature a scene that augured long life. The mid-seventeenth-century poet Chen Weisong described the pressures on the guests given the privilege of selecting scenes. In a preface to a lyric, he quoted his friend Du Jun 杜濬 (z. Du Yuhuang 杜于皇, 1611–87) as saying, "Among our friends, Weisong and I are the most clumsy [at this]."[21] Du Yuhuang related that on

---

19. For example, the last two acts of *Nan wanghou* appear in a miscellany of dramatic selections to be performed in the *yiyang* style, *Zhaijin qiyin* 摘錦奇音 (Rare notes plucked from brocade), compiled by Gong Zhengwo 龔正我 and published in Anhui during 1611. This excerpt provides a *terminus ad quem* for the composition of the play.

20. See Liao Ben, *Zhongguo gudai juchang shi*, pp. 84–85.

21. Chen Weisong, "He xinlang, zi chao yong zeng Su Kunsheng yun tong Du Yuhuang fu" 賀新郎, 自嘲用贈蘇崑生韻同杜于皇賦, in *Huhailou ciji*, p. 340.

one rainy afternoon, he and Weisong were drinking wine and chatting at an inn. "I mentioned [to Weisong] that we ought not to take the seat of honor at banquets, for choosing from the menu of plays is a painful affair." Once, as the guest of honor at a birthday banquet, he saw a new play with an auspicious-sounding name, *Shouchun tu* 壽春圖 (Picture of youthful longevity), and so he requested it. "I didn't know that it was thoroughly morbid; the whole audience squirmed in their seats." Chen described a similar experience of ordering an unfamiliar play with the title *Shou ronghua* 壽榮華 (Longevity, honor, and prosperity), thinking that the title sounded auspicious; to the horror of Chen and the other guests, the play was most unsuitable. "I didn't know that it would be nothing but crying and weeping; the whole hall was unhappy." The two of them shared a good laugh that their gaffes had been so similar. [22]

In that a "theater menu" allowed spectators to piece together a medley of songs and scenes from different plays that suited their mood and the occasion, *zhezi xi*, as a development in performance practice, enhanced the potential resonance between a performance and its context. Because *zhezi xi* were more easily paired to particular occasions than were full-length texts, the advent of this performance practice had the potential to enhance a sense of permeability between world and stage.[23] A scene in Chapter 63 of the novel *Jin Ping Mei* plays with this sense of permeability, as the lesser and female characters rupture the social space of the theatrical by commenting on the homologous relationship between world and stage. The merchant Ximen Qing 西門慶 hires a Haiyan acting troupe to entertain the guests who have come to his home to offer condolences on the death of his beloved concubine Li Ping'er[24] 李瓶儿 (see Fig. 1). The coffin is placed at one end of the hall, a screen in front of it. In front of the screen sits Ximen Qing, the actors performing before him. On the other side of the stage, across from Ximen Qing, sit a row of guests. Behind

---

22. Lu Eting (*Kunju yanchu shigao*, p. 123) speculates that such embarrassing situations could only have occurred when a professional troupe entertained; a private troupe would have been apprised ahead of time by the host as to what scenes would be suitable to the occasion. Lu Eting also observes that the pressure to select auspicious—or at least inoffensive plays—likely meant that satirical or dark texts more easily dropped out of the performance repertoire.

23. Wang An-Chi, *Mingdai xiqu wulun*, pp. 40–42.

24. *Jin Ping Mei cihua*, 63.9a–11b.

Fig. 1.   Ximen Qing watches a Haiyan troupe perform.

curtains hung to the left and right of the stage, the women of the house and their guests watch. The female servants occupy one side, Ximen Qing's principal wife and concubines and other female mourners the other.[25]

The architecture of this arrangement divides this space into a number of parallel ontological worlds: the world of the dead behind one screen, wives and female servants behind screens to the left and right of it, the stage in the center, the host and his guests hemming in the stage from either side. The text seems less interested in the relationships between these realms, however, than in illustrating the parallels between the brothel that

---

25. On the stages of salon-style performance, see Liao Ben, *Zhongguo gudai juchang shi,* pp. 61–74.

is the play's setting and the brothel-like atmosphere of Ximen Qing's mourning banquet. Ximen Qing in fact has hired musicians and actors associated with his favorite brothel to serve wine to his guests; the actors circulate easily on- and offstage.

The play being performed is *Yuhuan ji* 玉環記 (The jade bracelet); the plot is suited to the occasion in that it relates a tale of karmic affinity through death and life.[26] The play is cited or performed numerous times during the course of the novel; Li Kaixian's 李開先 (1502–68) *Baojian ji* 寶劍記 (The double-edged sword) is the only play more often quoted. (Chapter 4 of this book opens with an episode from chapter 36 of the novel in which Ximen Qing's servant Shutong 書童 sings some arias from *Yuhuan ji*, playing the role of the chaste bride.) The novel quotes the play to comment ironically on the disjunction between the fidelity of the characters of the play and the faithlessness of the characters of the novel.[27] The plot concerns an examination candidate named Wei Gao 韋臬, who upon failing the examinations descends into the world of the brothels, where he meets the courtesan Yuxiao 玉蕭. They fall in love and are betrothed. When Wei Gao's money is exhausted, the madam of the brothel expels him, and he decides to try his luck at the examinations a second time. Wei Gao and Yuxiao exchange love tokens, the jade bracelet of the title and a fan. Unfortunately, Wei Gao mistakes the date of the examination and misses his chance once more. Ashamed to return to Yuxiao, he goes home. Yuxiao remains loyal, refusing to see all other customers. Ill with longing, she has a portrait painted of herself as she looked in her prime and sends it to him. She then commits suicide by swallowing the jade bracelet. Wei at first refuses his family's attempts to find him a wife, but then agrees to wed the daughter of a friend of his father's. Yuxiao's reincarnated soul is ultimately reunited with Wei Gao, when she is reborn as a girl who becomes Wei Gao's second wife.

---

26. According to Mao Jin's 毛晉 *Liushi zhong qu* 六十種曲 (Sixty plays), the southern drama *Yuhuan ji* was written by the Wanli playwright Yang Rousheng 楊柔勝 (Mao Jin, *Liushi zhongqu*, vol. 8, "Xiukan Yuhuan ji ding ben," p. 5). It is an expansion of a northern drama entitled *Liangshi yinyuan* 兩世姻緣, which according to Katherine Carlitz, was "revised in an increasingly didactic fashion over the course of the Ming" (Carlitz, *The Rhetoric of the "Chin P'ing-mei,"* p. 115). For more on the citation of *Yuhuan ji* in *Jin Ping Mei*, see Carlitz, pp. 109, 115–16.

27. Carlitz, *The Rhetoric of the "Chin P'ing-mei,"* p. 116.

The anonymous author of *Jin Ping Mei* typically quotes *Yuhuan ji* to develop ironic contrasts between novel and play. In chapter 11, for example, as the faithless prostitute Li Guijie 李桂姐, a favorite of Ximen Qing's, sings Yuxiao's arias, Yuxiao's loyalty implicitly critiques Li Guijie's infidelity. In chapter 63, the text pays very little attention to the performance itself, which is described in the baldest terms: "The actor who played the *sheng* 生 (gentleman lead) and was costumed as Wei Gao sang for a while and left the stage; the actor who played the *tiedan* 貼旦 [auxiliary female lead], costumed as Yuxiao, sang for a while and left the stage, and the cooks brought soup, rice, and goose."[28]

Rather than describing the performance, the text focuses on slapstick exchanges among members of the audience regarding the parallels between events on- and offstage. One of the maids standing behind a screen watching the play happens to have the same name as the play's heroine, Yuxiao. When the Yuxiao of the play is called to entertain customers in the brothel, another servant, Xiaoyu 小玉, pushes the servant named Yuxiao out from behind the curtain saying, "Slut, your man is here!" Similarly, the prostitutes who have come to mourn Li Ping'er exploit the potential similarity between events onstage and off to tease and curse Ximen Qing's friend Ying Bojue 應伯爵. Ying Bojue suggests that the singing girls who have come to mourn Li Ping'er be brought out from behind the curtain to serve them. Another of Ximen Qing's friends protests that it is unseemly to ask mourners to serve. The scene performed directly after this exchange presents Wei Gao and his associate Bao Zhishui 包知水 arriving at the brothel and asking the madam to allow Yuxiao to come out. The madam retorts, "You don't know how to ask for someone. My girl won't just come out for someone who comes by on a whim. You'd best say please." One of the entertainers among the audience, the prostitute Li Guijie, looks toward the tables, coughs, and says, "This Bao is like Ying Huazi 應花子 [Ying Bojue], a maladroit ass (*bu zhi qu de jian wei er* 不知趣的蹇味兒*)."[29]

As Yuming He has observed, it is a common feature of illustrations of private theatricals in Wanli editions that there be a voyeur beyond the audience whose presence makes the social space surrounding the stage

---

28. *Jin Ping Mei cihua*, 63.10a.
29. Ibid., 10b.

seem part of the spectacle. [30] In this episode, the serving women and prostitutes behind the screen seem to fulfill this function. If the novel holds up the protagonists of the play to suggest that its own protagonists fail in comparison, the maid Xiaoyu and the prostitute Li Guijie compare the lesser characters of the novel to the lesser characters of the play to suggest that they are similarly deficient. It is ironic that rather than finding Ying Bojue wanting in constancy or fidelity, Li Guijie faults his lack of understanding of the proper conduct in a brothel. The minor characters of the novel—female servants and prostitutes—work to redefine the resonance between performance and context that the master of the house, who selected the play to commemorate his deceased wife's loyalty, had intended. As Xiaoyu pushes Yuxiao out into the audience from behind the screen, her abrupt entrance into the space of nested theatrical and social performance ruptures the boundary between the outermost rung of spectators (the women offstage) and the inner rung of spectators (the male host and guests) and revises the intended social significance of the performance.

The Provisional Stage and the Mobile Perspective

Even after the establishment of the professional theater as an architectural space in its own right during the early to mid-Qing, most of the spaces in which theatrical performances were held primarily served other purposes. Until the late seventeenth century, most stages other than those in palace and temple compounds were provisional and temporary. [31] Typically, private residences did not boast fixed stages. Rather, the red felt carpet that

---

30. Yuming He ("Productive Space," p. 145) demonstrates this point convincingly by analyzing a number of illustrations in late Ming drama miscellanies and anthologies.

31. The earliest evidence of a fixed stage is a stele dated 1020 at a temple to the god of the earth in Shanxi province (Mackerras, *Chinese Drama*, p. 82). Liao Ben notes that one of the most important architectural features of temples was the stage. Temple stages were originally open air, but later roofs and back walls were added, so that the stage evolved from a four-sided to a three-sided stage. Typically, the stage faced north, toward the hall of the god housed in the temple, so that the audience would stand between the hall of the spirit and the stage. Sacrifices to spirits often included musical performances. During festival days, extended families would meet at the temple for several days of feasting and performances. In small towns and villages, the only experience of the stage was at the temple. The temple stage was thus akin to a community center. On temple stages, see Liao Ben, *Zhongguo gudai juchang shi*, pp. 111–31; and Sun Minji, *Youling kaoshu*, pp. 249–50.

transformed ordinary space into theatrical space could be laid anywhere, in a garden, courtyard, or residential hall. A few gentry devotees of the theater did have rooms reserved for theatricals, which could be considered fixed stages. The residence of the dramatist Ruan Dacheng, notorious for his political intrigues and abuse of power in high posts, had such a hall. It was lined with thick curtains and illuminated by flares in bejeweled candlesticks.[32] However, even if the stage was fixed, seldom was it raised; a simple red carpet still designated the stage, and a portable screen might serve as a divide between the stage and the greenroom, if a greenroom were necessary.

The space occupied by the stage was opportunistic, its boundaries open. Temporary stages (*xi peng* 戲棚 or *cao tai* 草台) would be built in the streets on festival days. Wealthy families might celebrate the birth of a son by erecting a stage in front of their gate and hiring an acting troupe to perform there. The spatial reach of the stage might increase or decrease freely as passersby might stop to watch a performance taking place on a boat across a lake or customers in a restaurant might eavesdrop on a performance at another table. Thus there was no fixed or established distance between spectator and spectacle, as there is in the modern theater, where members of the audience are immobilized in seats before a fixed stage.

If, in the modern theater, each spectator has access only to a singular perspective, sitting before only one of the four sides of the stage, spectators in the premodern Chinese theater could roam around three, and sometimes four, sides of the stage (see Fig. 1). In a residence, seats were placed on three sides of the carpet that formed the stage; the unoccupied side was typically at the entrance of the room. There is no evidence that plays were staged differently on three-sided as opposed to four-sided stages. Zhang Dai described a stage an uncle built for a performance of a Mulian opera. Over ten thousand spectators were seated on all four sides, and his uncle inscribed couplets for the calligraphic banners that hung vertically from both sides of the front of the stage.[33]

The flexibility of theatrical space was made possible in part by the fact that traditional Chinese theater made no inherent demands regarding stage design or decor. It was customary to use only a few props, often sim-

---

32. Jiao Xun, *Jushuo*, p. 100.
33. See Zhang Dai, *Tao'an mengyi / Xihu mengxun*, pp. 52–53.

ply a table and chairs that could have various functions from scene to scene: what in one scene was a dressing table in a lady's boudoir could, in another, become an official's desk. The sparseness of props on the Chinese stage and their flexibility have often been attributed to the supposedly abstract and symbolic nature of the Chinese theater.[34] This line of thinking, however, may well confuse cause and effect, making virtue out of necessity. Before the advent of permanent, fixed stages, the inconvenience for itinerant troupes of carrying large inventories of elaborate props and stage settings from place to place may have led to the development of a more abstract system of representation.[35]

Not only was the spatial reach of the stage flexible, but the distance between spectator and spectacle was unfixed and ever-shifting. The best illustration of the "fluidity" of the distance between spectator and spectacle on the provisional stage is waterborne entertainment, for which Nanjing, Hangzhou, and Suzhou were well known.[36] Suzhou, a city of canals, was a busy hub of commerce that became a center of theatrical entertainment.

---

34. The notion that a relatively bare stage with few props was quintessential to the premodern Chinese theater was propagated by early twentieth-century aficionados of the theater such as Qi Rushan and practitioners such as Mei Lanfang in an effort to position it as "abstract" in relation to Western theater. As Wilt Idema (*The Red Brush*, p. 715) has observed, however, there was no inherent distaste for elaborate scenery and props; some popular forms of drama had elaborate costumes and props, as did palace productions as well.

35. As Idema and West have noted, "The stage and the performance exist in a kind of dialectical relationship. The shape of the stage may dictate many elements of the performance itself, and the evolution of stage design may reflect changes in the modes of performance" (Idema and West, *Chinese Theater*, p. 185).

36. For aquatic performances, see Liao Ben, *Zhongguo gudai juchang shi*, pp. 153–54; Wang An-Chi, *Mingdai chuanqi juchang ji qi yishu*, pp. 171–72; and Zhao Shanlin, *Zhongguo xiqu guanzhong xue*, pp. 79, 89–90. In Hangzhou, waterborne theatricals took place on West Lake. Zhang Dai (*Tao'an mengyi / Xihu mengxun*, p. 27) writes of three-storied boats built for theatrical entertainments by a literatus named Bao Hansuo, whom he mentions elsewhere as a pioneer in the housing of private troupes. The largest was set up for banquets with opera music, at which singing boys would serve. Yu Huai's 余懷 *Ban qiao zaji* 板橋雜記 (Miscellaneous records of the warden bridge) describes an extravaganza held by a literatus named Yao Zhuangruo of Jiaxing on the Qinhuai of Nanjing. Yao invited over a hundred renowned officials and examination candidates to a river excursion, dividing the guests among twelve boats. Each boat was provided with four courtesans to serve wine. A theater troupe performed at night on each boat beneath the illumination of lanterns and flares (Yu Huai, *Banqiao zaji*; cited in Jiao Xun, *Jushuo*, p. 109).

Merchants routinely entertained customers with theatrical performances on large barges (*louchuan* 樓船); the audience would assemble in smaller skiffs. Passersby could simply row their boats toward the stage and enjoy the spectacle, coming and going as they pleased. The theater boats of Suzhou had their own lexicon; the large boat that held the stage was called the "curled oar," and the small boats in which the audience sat had names such as "ox tongue" and "flying sand."[37] The Qing author Gu Gongxie 顧公燮 noted that when the gentry of Suzhou wished to entertain at Suzhou's Tiger Hill (Huqiu 虎丘), the play would be performed at the front of the "Curled Oar" boat, and the middle portion of the boat would hold the greenroom.[38] Skiffs ferried the audience from the banks to small boats that encircled the stage. Those without the money to pay for seats in these boats watched for free from the banks.

The duration of aquatic performances was uncertain; they were susceptible to interruption, especially by foul weather. Zhang Dai wrote of a tempest that threatened a stage that his family built on a barge:

> The elders in my family built a tower and made a boat of it. They built a boat and made a tower of it. So the people in the village called it *chuan lou* 船樓 [boat tower] or *lou chuan* [tower boat]; it does not matter how one puts it. On the day it was finished, it was the fifteenth day of the seventh month, and from my father on down, men and women, old and young, everyone was gathered to watch. They used a number of wooden timbers to make a stage, and all those from the neighboring city and villages came to watch, so that there were over a thousand boats large and small. After noon a great wind arose, giant waves crashed against the boat, and the rain came pouring down. [Among the boats] only the *louchuan* was threatened. The wind pressed against it so hard that it almost capsized. They used thousands of ropes and wooden timbers to lash the boat down, so many that it was as if there were a woven net, and then the wind could not disturb the boat. After a while, the wind calmed, the play finished, and all dispersed.[39]

This passage is beautifully reminiscent of Zhang Dai's other writing in part because of the sense of the precariousness of aesthetic pleasures. Of

---

37. Zhao Shanlin, *Zhongguo xiqu guanzhong xue*, p. 89.

38. Gu Gongxie, *Xiao xia xianji zhai chao* 消夏閑記摘鈔, 卷下 20b, cited in Liao Ben, *Zhongguo gudai juchang shi*, pp. 153–54, and Zhao Shanlin, *Zhongguo xiqu guanzhong xue*, p. 89.

39. Zhang Dai, *Tao'an mengyi / Xihu mengxun*, p. 73.

the many boats on the water, only the one that was critical to aesthetic pleasure was, to Zhang Dai's mind, threatened by the waves. Aquatic performances serve beautifully as a metaphor for the flexible parameters of the seventeenth-century stage. The spectator's vantage point was quite literally mobile, and encompassed a series of disparate perspectives. Thus it could be linked to the quality of vision that we identified in Chapter 1 as mobile and participatory, a quality of vision that we isolated as characteristic of the writing of partisans of the theater who advocated a social spectatorship modeled on theatrical spectatorship.

The use of the temporary, provisional stage meant that any space could be transformed into theatrical space at any time. Zhang Dai wrote in his memoir *Tao'an mengyi* of impulsively stopping his boat at the celebrated Jinshan 金山 (Gold mountain) monastery in the middle of the night and, on a whim, ordering the main hall to be lit so that his servants might perform. Zhang's description of this performance illustrates the ways in which the makeshift nature of theatrical space rendered the boundaries between world and stage more permeable, allowing the spectator an unbroken passage to the alternative ontological realms suggested by the stage:

On the day after the Mid-Autumn festival in the year 1629, I was traveling through Zhenjiang 鎮江 on the way to Yanzhou. As the sun set, we arrived at Beigu 北固, and we anchored our boat at the river's mouth. The moonlight entered the water as if spilled from a bag. The billows on the river made as if to swallow and spit it out, and the air, heavy with dew, sucked in the moonlight so that the sky grew white. I was surprised and delighted and steered the boat so that we passed Jinshan temple. It was already past the second drum roll of the night watch. Coming to the Longwang tang 龍王堂 (Dragon King's chamber), we entered the great hall. Everything was as still as though it had been lacquered. Moonlight filtered through the trees; here and there on the ground were patches of moonlight that looked like leftover snow.

I called my servants to bring the theatrical props, and we lit up the great hall with many lanterns, and sang *Han Qi Wang Jinshan* 韓蘄王金山 [Han Shizhong 韓世忠, Prince of Qi, at Jinshan] and *Chang jiang da zhan* 長江大戰 [Great battle on the Yangzi River].[40] The cymbals and drums made a great noise,

---

40. Both pieces refer to the victories of the famed Southern Song general Han Shizhong (1089–1151), who took 8,000 soldiers on boats to this spot at Zhenjiang 鎮江 to cut off the route of the invading Jin general Wuzhu 兀術 (?–1148); Wuzhu was defeated and held captive for forty-eight days before escaping.

and everyone in the temple got up to watch. There was an old monk who rubbed his eyes with the back of his hands, his mouth open, sneezes and laughs issuing from his mouth all at once. He slowly fixed his gaze, staring at us as though wondering from whence we had come, when we had arrived, and for what purpose, daring not to ask us a single question. When the play was over, dawn was nigh, and we untied the boat and crossed the river. The monks of the mountain went as far as the foot of the mountain, their eyes following us for a long time. They did not know whether we were men, ghouls, or ghosts.[41]

Zhang Dai's representation of this whimsical moment draws on the fluidity of the relationship between the space of performance and the space beyond. The metaphysical boundaries between world and stage on this moonlit night seem uniquely open, as befits a temple setting. To the dazed monks roused from sleep by the drums and cymbals, the nighttime guests seem akin to "ghouls" or "ghosts"—their theatricals resemble a dream vision. The dazed monks are indeed the ideal audience, for before their mute wonder, even the leavetaking of Zhang's entourage as it crosses the river is a theatrical exit. The guests depart as playfully as they have come, giving no explanation to their confused spectators. It is this irreverence that testifies to the insouciant disregard for convention characteristic of the *fengliu*. Indeed, Zhang Dai makes of his caprice a public spectacle, and in this sense, the theatrical performance he puts on is nested within a social performance. That the monks are the presumed sole witnesses of this social performance heightens the sense of its irrelevance and thus aestheticizes it.[42]

Clearly, little preparation was needed for Zhang to enjoy a theatrical performance on a moment's notice. Since his servants doubled as actors, his troupe in essence traveled with him. Before the eyes of Zhang, the aficionado of the theater, any space could become theatrical space. The natural setting that Zhang Dai described is itself so dramatic that it seems to inspire his desire for theatricals—and the space of the performance he set into motion seems to extend to the natural world. The moonlight not on-

---

41. Zhang Dai, *Tao'an mengyi / Xihu mengxun*, p. 11. For translations of this passage and comments on it, see Brook, *Praying for Power*, pp. 37–38; Wai-yee Li, *Enchantment and Disenchantment*, pp. 47–50; and Owen, *Anthology of Traditional Chinese Literature*, pp. 815–16.

42. I am reminded here of Yuming He's insight that the social space of private theatricals allows whimsy to be publicly performed ("Productive Space," p. 3).

ly acts as stage lighting but also itself takes center stage, engaged in a dynamic play with the waves on the river, which make as if to "swallow" the moonlight and "spit it out." The silence of the night, "still as though it had been lacquered," creates the perfect backdrop for the hubbub that Zhang and his entourage create as they play their drums and cymbals.

In the case of performances on provisional stages such as these, the boundaries between world and stage were not so much spatial as temporal. The great hall of the temple became a theatrical space because a performance was taking place in it.[43] Once the performance was over, the space reverted to its original function. The temporal duration of performance, rather than the spatial demarcation of the walls of the theater, created a particular kind of separation between world and stage that helped enhance the sense that the world beyond the stage was an extension of the stage itself.

The text is ambiguously worded, and it is unclear whether Zhang himself performed, or whether his servants simply performed for his amusement. This is quite fitting, in that it incorporates the subtlety of the participatory relationship between spectator and spectacle. As the anecdote about Chen Weisong and Du Yuhuang's embarrassments might suggest, it was in part when social gaffes were made that the resonance between world and stage felt most palpable. The lack of fixed distance between spectator and spectacle imbued theatrical vision with a "mobile" quality; the understanding of theatrical space as provisional, and the ensuing spontaneity of theatrical performance helped to create a sense of participatory spectatorship.

Public Stages: Wine Shops

This portrait is complicated by the murky history of the fixed stage, which disappeared and then reappeared during the Ming. The written records regarding the development of the fixed stage are extremely sketchy, and scholars have more questions than answers. One conundrum is that fixed stages were already in existence during the Song but mysteriously disap-

---

43. Although this performance takes place in a temple, I would view the nocturnal performance at Jinshan temple as an example of salon-style performance rather than of temple performance.

peared after the early Ming. Tellingly, the term *goulan* (balustrade) 勾 欄, which in the Song and early Ming referred to large theaters that could seat thousands of customers, meant "brothels" by the mid-Ming.[44] The most interesting suggestion regarding the disappearance of the *goulan* and the rise of the private theatrical is Yuming He's linkage of the Ming founder's severe regulation of the public theater to the sponsorship of private theatricals among the aristocracy. Most scholars simply state that as private theatricals became more important, salon-style performance replaced the *goulan* theaters. Although this is precisely what we see in the historical record—notation books and other sources stop mentioning the *goulan* and speak primarily of the private stage—it is hard to believe that the clientele for the two types of performances could have been the same. The private stage was a luxury only the elite could afford; the *goulan* theater of the Song had been available to the urban masses.

The wine shop (*jiulou* or *jiuguan* 酒館), which dates to the Song, offers an intermediary space between the *goulan* and the private theatrical.[45] Zhou Mi's 周密 (1232–98) *Wu lin jiu shi* 武林舊事 lists two types of wine shops in the Southern Song capital of Lin'an. The first list consists of wine shops run especially for officials and managed by the government, in which prostitutes of a less refined sort roamed from table to table, singing for the guests. Wu Zimu's 吳自牧 (*ca.* 1270) *Meng liang lu* 夢梁錄 (Record of the yellow millet dream) speaks of officials holding entertainments in wine shops where official prostitutes registered and taxed by the government (*guanji* 官妓) were invited to perform. Popular troupes also performed in wine shops. During the Song and Yuan, wine shops were viewed as more refined venues than the *goulan* theaters, where townspeople went to view performances. By the mid-Ming, wine shops had replaced the *goulan* as one of the primary venues of theatrical entertainment for people of all classes. Such wine shops were not theaters in the modern sense of the word, but restaurants in which one could eat and be entertained by actors and musicians. The terms *jiulou* and *jiuguan* referred to any establishment in which drink was served with food; a tavern, a restau-

---

44. As Yuming He observes (Productive Space, pp. 37–41), the two royal theaters built during the reign of the Ming founders were called *yu goulan* 御构欄 (royal balustrades); several early Ming playwrights also use the term *goulan* to describe theaters.

45. Zhou Mi, *Wu lin jiu shi*, pp. 406–80; Wu Zimu, *Meng liang lu*, pp. 255–56.

rant, a hostel or an inn could be referred to as a *jiulou* or *jiuguan*. (As a case in point, the Yueminglou 月明樓, a famous *jiulou* in Beijing during the early Qing, was also called a restaurant [*fan pu* 飯鋪].)

A gazetteer of Cixi 慈溪 district compiled during the Tianqi reign period (1621–28) describes an intermediary step between the mobile and the fixed stage, a raised stage with wine shops surrounding it on four sides. The walls on the sides of the wine shops that faced the stage were likely open to some degree, so that patrons of all four establishments could lean over the railings and view the stage. This arrangement presages the configuration of the modern theater, as the scholar Liao Ben has observed.[46] And yet, the configuration suggests that the performance was no more than a sideshow, an attraction certainly, but unworthy of the audience's undivided attention.

We know from the diaries of late Ming connoisseurs of the theater that wine shops were frequented not only by commoners but also by the elite. Qi Biaojia wrote in his diary of visiting a *jiuguan* of Beijing in 1632 with a friend named Yang Yuyuan 羊羽源, where he watched a play performed by a troupe using limited costume and props (*banban zaju* 半班雜劇), and of going to a *jiulou* in 1633 to have a drink and watch a performance of *Guanyuan ji* 灌園記 (Watering the garden).[47] Hu Yinglin 胡應麟 (1551–1602) wrote three poems that record his attendance at performances of plays composed by the literati authors Wang Jiusi 王九思 (1468–1551), Wang Daokun 汪道崑 (1525–93), and Zhang Fengyi 張鳳翼 (1527–1613) at a wine shop near Hangzhou's West Lake. From the title of this sequence of poems, "At a wine shop on the lake, listening to Examining Editor Wang Jingfu 王敬夫 [i.e., Wang Jiusi] and Vice Prefect Wang Boyu's 汪伯玉 [Wang Daokun] *yuefu* [*zaju*] and Zhang Boqi's 張伯起 [Zhang Fengyi] *chuanqi*," we may infer not only that literati went to wine shops to listen to theater during the late Ming but that the works of eminent literati were performed in them.[48] A performance of Hong

---

46. Liao Ben, *Zhongguo gudai juchang shi*, p. 78.

47. See *Qi Zhongmin gong riji*, Chongzhen fifth year (1632), fifth month, twentieth day, as well as Chongzhen sixth year, first month, twelfth day. For another discussion of these entries, see Liao Ben, *Zhongguo gudai juchang shi*, p. 77.

48. Hu Yinglin, *Shaoshi shanfang leigao* 少室山房類稿; cited in Zhao Shanlin, *Zhongguo xiqu guanzhong xue*, p. 86.

Sheng's *Changsheng dian* in 1698 that caused a public scandal was rumored to have taken place in one of Beijing's famed *jiulou*, the Guanghe 廣和; it was performed by the professional Juhe 聚和 troupe and attended by many Hanlin Academy scholars.[49]

Theatrical entertainments provided proprietors of wine shops with a means of enticing and detaining customers. Sun Zhiwei wrote of a wine shop in Zhenjiang, "In the suburbs are wine sellers who have brought in actresses to attract guests. . . . They seat a thousand people in rows. . . . I estimate that in one day they could take in hundreds of thousands of cash (*qian* 錢), which probably has not been done in any wine shop before."[50] As the historian of the theater Zhao Shanlin has pointed out, the stages at such wine shops were probably open air, perhaps covered by tents; covered structures of a more permanent nature were likely not large enough to accommodate such crowds.[51]

The rise of the wine shop as a site of theatrical performance is as shrouded in mystery as the demise of the *goulan*, but by the Kangxi reign period (1662–1723), wine shops that featured theatrical performances had achieved prominence in Beijing. Both Liao Ben and Zhao Shanlin give the names of six of these; however, their lists are overlapping but not identical.[52] That these were establishments specifically devoted to theatrical en-

---

49. There are different accounts of the controversy, some claiming that the performance took place at another of the six *jiulou* in Beijing with a fixed stage, the Taiping yuan 太平園. One version states that a district magistrate surnamed Huang 黃, believing himself to have been insulted by a friend of Hong Sheng's, claimed that the play had been performed during a period of national mourning (the Emperor Kangxi's consort had died in the seventh month of that year); Hong Sheng and all the guests at the performance were dismissed from office. Another version of the story suggests that one of Hong Sheng's friends, the poet Zhao Zhixin 趙執信 (1662–1744), insulted a censorial minister. See Dolby, *Chinese Drama*, p. 118.

50. Sun Zhiwei, *Gaitang qian ji*, 7.14a. For another discussion of this passage, see Zhao Shanlin, *Zhongguo xiqu guanzhong xue*, p. 87.

51. Zhao Shanlin, *Zhongguo xiqu guanzhong xue*, p. 87.

52. According to Liao Ben (*Zhongguo gudai juchang shi*, p. 80), the six were the Taiping yuan 太平園, Siyi yuan 四宜園, Yueming lou 月明樓, Bishan tang 碧山堂, Baiyun lou 白雲樓, and Zha jia lou 查家樓. Zhao Shanlin (*Zhongguo xiqu guanzhong xue*, p. 87) lists the Taiping yuan 太平園, Siyi yuan 四宜園, Yueming lou 月明樓, Zha jia lou 查家樓, Zhongchun yuan 眾春園, and the Guangde lou 廣德樓. The last of these was said to have been opened during the Ming; Wu Weiye had supposedly inscribed *duilian* on its columns.

tertainments distinguished them from restaurants or inns at which actors stood before tables. Zhang Dai's description of an inn in Tai'an 泰安 prefecture that he visited while making a pilgrimage to Mount Tai 泰 provides an illustration of the latter. Zhang wrote that for pilgrims who had returned from the summit, there were three gradations of increasingly elaborate feasts:

The highest had private tables, at which they were served sweet cakes, five sorts of fruit, ten types of meat and nuts, and were regaled with theatrical performances. In the second class, two parties were seated at a table. They also had sweet cakes, meats, and nuts and were treated to theatrical performances. In the lowest class, three to four parties sat at a table, and they also had sweet cakes and meats and nuts but were not provided with theatrical performance. They were entertained with singing to the accompaniment of stringed instruments instead. I'd reckon that in this inn, there were over twenty performances taking place as well as countless ballad singers performing.[53]

Because performances took place before individual tables, it was possible to offer theatrical entertainments to some guests and not to others. In the *jiu-lou* of early Qing Beijing, by contrast, all patrons were expected to watch a performance that took place in a central arena, and performances occurred at regular times arranged by the establishments; such performances were as important to the conception of the space as food and drink.[54]

However, even if such spaces were dedicated to theatrical entertainment, customers were not expected to pay rapt attention. In the Wuliang 無量 temple of Hohhot, capital of modern Inner Mongolia, there is a

---

53. Zhang Dai, *Tao'an mengyi / Xihu mengxun*, p. 73.

54. Beijing was half a century earlier in the development of a significant number of permanent stages than Suzhou; Suzhou was relatively late in the development of public theaters on land, in part because waterborne stages had such a long history there. After the first permanent stage on land in Suzhou (named the Guo Gardens [*Guo yuan* 郭園]) opened during the Yongzheng 雍正 reign period (1723–35), others quickly followed suit. By the Qianlong 乾隆 reign period (1736–96), there were several dozen permanent stages in Suzhou, most of them in wine shops. A New Year's painting that dates to the Qianlong reign illustrates the facade of the Qingchun lou 慶春樓 in Suzhou. The dedication of the structure to performance is evident in the placement of *duilian* (calligraphic couplets on either side of the gate) posting the names of the plays to be performed that week; see Liao Ben, *Zhongguo gudai juchang shi*, Appendix, p. 24.

mural of a wine shop with a stage called the Yueminglou (see Fig. 2).[55] Whether this is the same Yueminglou wine shop that existed in Beijing during the latter half of the seventeenth century is uncertain. The painting illustrates a fracas during a theatrical performance in the wine shop. The stage is not on a raised platform. Nor are the observers tidily arrayed around it. Guests sit at tables on two sides of a hall lit by lanterns. Some are seated with their backs to the fight, simply talking, paying no more attention to the rumble at the center than modern customers in a bar might to a jazz pianist playing in the background. As is evident in the mural, at both privately sponsored and commercial performances, there was no expectation that the spectator would pay attention in silence for any length of time. Spectators would gossip, play cards, tell jokes, call for wine, crack melon seeds, and eat nuts.[56] Customers sitting in the balcony, however, where seats were likely more expensive, are portrayed as though they were riveted on the play. The place of honor appears to be in the center of the balcony, where officials distinguished by their pheasant-feather caps are seated.

As noted above, the early Qing witnessed the ascendance of commercial theatrical spaces with fixed stages. The substitution of commercial public stages for private theatrical space, a trend that theater historians view as increasing throughout the Qing, is exemplified by the widespread speculation that the famous Beijing theater Guanghe xiyuan 廣和戲院 was originally the private theater of the late Ming magnate Zha Riqian 查日乾 (1667–1741) and was converted from a private stage to a public thea-

---

55. Liao Ben, *Zhongguo gudai juchang shi*, p. 85. A drum song (*guci* 鼓詞) narrates the story of the Emperor Kangxi's visit to the Yueming lou in Beijing. The emperor left the palace in plainclothes, traveling incognito. Tradition has it that he stopped for a drink at the Yueming lou and was treated with so little respect by the local ruffians he encountered there that he consequently engaged in a campaign to purge the capital of such "negative elements." For the illustration of the mural in Hohhot, see ibid., Appendix, p. 25.

56. Martha Feldman has described a similar scenario with regard to the eighteenth-century Italian opera. The Milanese Pietro Verri wrote in 1778: "It is necessary that the spectacle divert, for there are 'as many conversational groups as there are [theater] boxes.' The audience 'seeks to pass the evening in [reading] novels or gambling, enjoying inter-rupting these diversions with a brief and restricted attention to some piece [of music] which interest it'" (Feldman, "Magic Mirrors and the *Seria* Stage," p. 452).

Fig. 2. The mural of the Yueminglou in Hohhot. Photo courtesy of Liao Ben.

ter during the Kangxi reign period.[57] As in the European theater, improvised and occasional theatrical space had a far longer history than permanent theatrical space, but, after a temporary coexistence, the fixed stage came to dominate over the temporary stage, the temporary stage becoming associated primarily with popular theatrical venues, such as marketplaces, that were viewed by the gentry as déclassé.

By the mid-Qing, observers were describing raised stages with carved prosceniums, surrounded by tiers on three sides.[58] Before, the audience as well as the actors had been relatively mobile. Now, they were given fixed seats and separated from the actors by railings. Yet still, as Stephen Greenblatt has said in distinguishing the English Renaissance stage from the modern playhouse, there was "no dimming of lights, no attempt to isolate and awaken the sensibilities of each individual member of the audience, no sense of the disappearance of the crowd."[59] The modern theater hall with tiered seating and dimmed lights did not appear until the end of the Qing.[60]

---

57. In 1780, it was destroyed by a fire, and when rebuilt it was named the Guanghe Theater (Guanghe xiyuan). See Zhao Shanlin, *Zhongguo xiqu guanzhong xue*, p. 87.

58. Ibid.

59. Greenblatt, *Shakespearean Negotiations*, p. 5.

60. The way in which the physical properties of the stage affect the relationship between actor and audience can be seen in changes deliberately made to the London stage in the mid-eighteenth century. In 1762, the actor and impresario David Garrick banished spectators from the stage at Drury Lane, one of the two public theaters in London at the time. Garrick's intention was to prevent spectators from participating in the spectacle.

The new prominence toward the end of the seventeenth century of commercial theaters with fixed stages in Beijing presumably fostered a sense that the space of performance was more highly demarcated and that the social space of the audience was now less integrated with the space of performance. Similarly, the increased dominance of professional troupes (as opposed to privately housed actors) toward the end of the century likely helped to solidify the sense of a boundary between world and stage. As commercial theaters grew in number during the Qing, the professional troupes associated with them rose to prominence as well. Professional troupes had always performed for literati at their homes and in other private venues, as well as in commercial spaces. Qi Biaojia, for example, wrote in his diary of summoning actors to perform at his home to celebrate his mother's birthday in 1638.[61] The difference in the ways professional actors are described in early and late seventeenth-century records, however, suggests that the status of professional actors rose over the century. Early to mid-seventeenth-century sources generally speak of professional actors in quite general terms, complaining, for example, that the actors had arrived late. It is the privately housed actor who is the celebrity, as we see in the poems in tribute to the actor discussed in Chapter 5.[62] Late seventeenth-century authors, however, mention particular profes-

---

Prior to the mid-seventeenth century, it was customary for spectators to sit on the stage, where they often disrupted the performance. If displeased, they might force the performers to repeat songs or speeches until they got them right; if pleased, they demanded that actors sing favorite lines again. Garrick darkened the auditorium and increased the number of footlights, further enhancing the distinction between audience and stage by ensuring that the auditorium was dimmed and the stage brightly lit. The point of creating this division between stage and audience was to create an atmosphere in which the audience would passively and silently appreciate the performer's art. See Brewer, *The Pleasures of the Imagination*, pp. 331, 335.

61. Qi Biaojia, *Qi Zhongmin gong riji*, 5.26a (Chongzhen 11 [1638], eighth month, ninth day).

62. The actors of private troupes were often cherished by their owners and served as servants and traveling companions. As we saw in Zhang Dai's account of the performance at Jinshan temple, they could leave their everyday duties and put on a performance in a matter of seconds. Yet, while they were performing, their personal identity beyond the world of the stage lay just underneath the surface. With the greater prominence of professional troupes and commercial stages, gentry audiences more frequently saw actors perform with whom they had no relation offstage. What they knew of those actors' personal lives was largely rumor, adding to the glamour of their personae on stage.

sional troupes by name as though there were a cachet attached to having them perform. Kong Shangren stated, for example, that the Jingyun 景雲 troupe performed his first play, *Xiao hulei* 小忽雷 (Little thunderclap).[63] Two professional troupes were called in to perform his *Taohua shan* in Beijing; the better troupe provided the principal roles, the lesser troupe acted the secondary parts. Kong also noted that the Xiao nanya 小南雅 troupe admired his friend Gu Cai's 顧彩 *Lisao pu* 離騷譜 (Songs of the South) so much that the troupe staged it in 1694. Such phrasing is unthinkable earlier in the century; it suggests that the actors' praise validated the literatus's texts.

The effect of the new prominence of professional troupes and of commercial theaters with permanent stages on the conceptualization of the relation between world and stage must to some degree remain ineffable. Yet, I would contend that the new importance of the permanent stage in Beijing at the end of the seventeenth century should be taken into account as we consider the conceptualization of the relation between world and stage in Kong Shangren's *Taohua shan*. We know that Kong Shangren frequented several of the wine shops of Beijing, and he mentioned the Taiping yuan 太平園, Bishan tang 碧山堂, and Baiyun lou 白雲樓 in his poems.[64] Although it would be foolhardy to suggest that Kong had one type of stage as opposed to another in mind as he wrote, I would argue that the new prominence of the fixed stage partially influenced the conception of the stage even in works that would never be performed on a fixed stage, just as the print explosion influenced the relation between author and reader even in works that circulated only in manuscript.[65]

Consider the different relationships between spectator and spectacle in the opening lines of *Nan wanghou*, composed early in the seventeenth

---

63. See Zhao Shanlin, *Lidai yongju shige xuanzhu*, p. 371.

64. Kong Shangren, *Kong Shangren shiwen ji* 孔尚任詩文集, *juan* 4, pp. 351, 369, 374-75 and 379-83; reprinted in Zhao Shanlin, *Lidai yongju shige xuanzhu*, p. 370.

65. An example of the latter would be the extensive discussion of the potential publication of the manuscript *Honglou meng* in its prefatory chapter. We have no indication that Cao Xueqin ever intended to circulate *Honglou meng* more widely than among his friends, and it was not published until twenty-nine years after the author's death. Yet, in the first chapter, the manuscript (personified as a stone) famously discusses its possible publication. See Cao Xueqin, *Honglou meng*, pp. 2–3; and Hawkes, *The Story of the Stone*, vol. 1, *The Golden Days*, p. 15.

century, and *Taohua shan*.[66] In the opening lyrics of *Nan wanghou*, the actor banters with the spectator, challenging him to solve the tantalizing mystery of his illusory femininity: "Iridescent clouds of hair, black sleeves so graceful that I myself am surprised / I fear you will not be able to distinguish when you cast your eyes."[67] As the character whom this actor plays, the young boy Zigao 子高, describes his feminine charms and the erotic positions he can assume, the spectator is reminded of the sexual availability of the actor. *Nan wanghou* seems ideally suited to the intimacies of salon-style performance. The boundary between actor and audience seems highly permeable; the distance between spectator and performer unfixed. One could imagine an actor singing the lyrics before a banquet table and ending up sitting in a spectator's lap. The lack of a significant physical boundary between spectator and spectacle, the expectation that actors would double as servants to pour wine, and the presumed resonance between text and performance context contribute to the nonchalance with which the boundaries between world and stage are crossed in the world of the private theatrical.

In *Taohua shan*, by contrast, spectator and spectacle inhabit two distinct realms. It is as though the physical separation of spectator from spectacle in the commercial theaters of Beijing had resulted in the severing of the world onstage from that offstage. In the opening prologue, the implied spectator of *Nan wanghou* has been replaced by a virtual audience whose voices are heard from backstage. They engage in dialogue with a character, the Keeper of Rites (*lao zanli* 老贊禮), who once witnessed the events portrayed on stage firsthand, and in that capacity is himself a character in the play. The audience has become as though it were composed of invisible characters, and the stage has become hermetically sealed.

The Keeper of Rites models spectatorship for the audience whom he addresses, presumed to be backstage. Each half of the play opens with a soliloquy by the Keeper of Rites, whose sole purpose is to mediate between past and present, and between worlds onstage and off. He describes his own rapt investment in the events on stage and the necessity of tempering this attachment with detachment, of watching the stage (and by implica-

---

66. Xu Shuofang (*Xu Shuofang ji*, p. 269) speculates that *Nan wanghou* was composed in 1604 and shows conclusively that it was composed before 1611.

67. Wang Jide, *Nan wanghou*, 1a.

tion, the debacle of the fall of the Ming) with "clear cold eyes" (*lengyan* 冷眼). Although such remarks are clearly meant for the readers and spectators of the play, they are addressed to the "voices from backstage" that ask his opinion of the performance; the actual spectator's engagement with the figure onstage who addresses him is only virtual. The stage has become sufficient unto itself, ontologically at a remove from the spectators offstage.

The Keeper of Rites and his onstage audience are segregated from the spectators (or readers) offstage temporally as well as spatially. The historical drama is set in the late Ming, but the prologues in which the Keeper of Rites purportedly addresses us are set in the year 1684; the play was first performed in 1698. Because of the temporal distance between the prologues and the events of the play proper, the audience experiences in miniature the Keeper of Rites' own sense of loss as it emerges from the world of the late Ming into the year 1684. He instructs the spectator as to the benefit of a detached perspective: "Back then reality was a play, / A play is reality today. / Twice a spectator, / Heaven preserves those with clear cold eyes."[68] To have been "twice a spectator," to have lived through the fall of the Ming and then to see the events of that period acted on stage, enables one to understand the role of illusion in structuring historical reality and thus promotes the cultivation of dispassion. *Taohua shan* eulogizes the late Ming literatus; it also eulogizes the mobile and participatory quality of late-Ming theatrical spectatorship. The segregation of the space of the spectator from that of performance in *Taohua shan* is in stark contrast to the integration of the spectator into the space of performance earlier in the seventeenth century.[69]

---

68. Kong Shangren, *Taohua shan*, p. 139.

69. As we shall see in the succeeding chapters, *Nan wanghou*'s and *Taohua shan*'s representations of actors and acting also differ significantly. In Wang Jide's *Nan wanghou*, the actor is portrayed as sensual, a wayward force who seems to challenge and seduce the spectators individually with his dazzling performance. In *Taohua shan* by contrast, the entertainer—as represented by the courtesan Li Xiangjun and the storyteller Liu Jingting—has become a moral character, an exemplar of loyalty. Thus the status of the actor, and of the theater itself, is elevated in the work of a playwright who was himself at a greater remove from the world of the stage. Ironically, Kong Shangren's prefaces show that he was absolutely removed from contact with actual actors and considered them vulgar and unreliable, a necessary evil; see Kong Shangren, *Taohua shan*, "Fan li" 凡例, p. 12.

During the late Ming and early decades of the Qing, the performance practices we have examined enhanced a sense that the spectator inhabited a mobile vantage point and held a participatory relationship to the spectacle. The boundaries between world and stage were permeable, allowing the spectator to gain a panoramic quality of vision as he moved from an immersion in the world of the stage to a recognition of its illusory quality. The popularity of salon-style performance rendered the performance space intimate; the custom of owning private troupes ensured that the world beyond the stage was explicitly present. The performance of clusters of scenes as opposed to entire operas allowed for resonance between text and social context. During the late seventeenth century, however, the private salon-style performance did not so much give way to, as it was joined by, the fixed stage of the *jiulou*, a form of theater that could not maintain the intimacy of the private theatrical. We can see the potential influence of that nascent division between stage and spectator in *Taohua shan*, which in its portrayal of Liu Jingting eulogizes a mobile, panoramic, and participatory quality of theatrical and social spectatorship, even as the play's structure heralds newly articulated boundaries between world and stage.

THREE

Pedagogy and Pedants
in Tang Xianzu's Mudan ting

Pu Songling's anecdote about a literatus who sees an actor emerge from his heart to tell the story of his life spoke to the failed aspirations of a licentiate condemned to teach schoolboys who reduce classical Chinese to vernacular doggerel. That anecdote was likely written some hundred years after the impassioned heroine of Tang Xianzu's *Mudan ting* (completed in 1598) became an overnight sensation, a figure for the power of dream and desire to overcome the mundane. At first glance, the notion of a relation between *Mudan ting* and Pu Songling's anecdote might seem counterintuitive.[1] In the reading of *Mudan ting* below, however, I show that the actor who emerges from the licentiate's heart points backward to a concern that gains urgency during the late sixteenth century and could be considered critical to a full understanding of Tang Xianzu's play: the cultural politics of the practice of literary citation.

The plot of *Mudan ting* is well known: the education of its heroine, Du Liniang, the only child of an official, goes awry on her first day of lessons. Her tutor's exposition of "Guanguan jujiu" 關關雎鳩 (Fishhawk), the first poem in the *Shi jing* 詩經 (Classic of poetry), sets Du Liniang on

---

1. For descriptions of the public frenzy that followed the publication of *The Peony Pavilion*, see Ko, *Teachers of the Inner Chamber*; Xu Fuming, *"Mudan ting" yanjiu ziliao kaoshi*, pp. 213–25; and Zeitlin, "Shared Dreams."

a path of desire that leads to her death and resurrection. The poem inspires her to dream of being ravished in a garden by a scholar named Liu Mengmei 柳夢梅. Upon awakening, she falls ill with longing and ultimately dies. However, her love is such that her ghost finds the young man and engages in a passionate reunion. She begs Liu to excavate her remains. When he complies, the strength of her passion returns her to life.

In this chapter, I argue that Tang Xianzu's late sixteenth-century drama critiques the dominant literary school of his time, archaism. Tang portrays archaism as a vehicle for social aspirants—would-be officials whose invocations of the literary past inadvertently reveal the shallowness of their learning.[2] A number of studies of *Mudan ting* have discussed the heroine's status as an icon of authentic passion (*zhenqing*) in late imperial literary culture. In focusing rather on the minor characters, I suggest that Tang Xianzu underscores the genuineness of Du Liniang's passion by contrasting it with the inauthenticity of a social discourse influenced by archaism. Tang Xianzu mocks the pedantry and scholasticism of archaism by criticizing its use of citation as theatrical and thus inauthentic, in contrast to the "vernacular."[3] Yet ultimately, he shows that the vernacular, which had seemed a firm ground from which to fault archaism, can itself be as staged and as allusive as the refined language of the elite.

In *Mudan ting*, the notion of theatricality is invoked to criticize sumptuary violation in the literary realm. Du Liniang's tutor, Chen Zuiliang

---

2. The date of the first printing of *Mudan ting* is unclear. Xu Shuofang (*Xu Shuofang ji*, 3: 485) believes it to have been close to 1605. For recent studies of *Mudan ting*, see Wai-yee Li, *Enchantment and Disenchantment*, pp. 50–64; Lu, *Persons, Roles and Minds*; Swatek, "The Peony Pavilion"; and Zeitlin, "Shared Dreams."

3. In recent years, scholars have questioned the anachronistic application of the May Fourth opposition of *baihua* 白話 (vernacular language) and *guwen* 古文 (classical literature) to the study of premodern literature, suggesting that it obscures the way in which linguistic register was linked to genre in late imperial texts. See, e.g., Owen, "The End of the Past," p. 172. The use of the term "vernacular" in a late imperial literary context has itself been questioned, for the term belies the fact that there was no cluster of premodern genres thought of as "vernacular." Given these caveats, I use the term to describe the sense that certain genres (drama, the novel, and folk song, for example) were allied in their use of a language that sounded like speech, whether local dialect or *guanhua* 官話, the *lingua franca* of the literati elite. We see this presumed sense of likeness, for example, in the exclusion of writings in such genres from authors' collected works.

陳最良 (Tutor Chen), is widely recognized as an incarnation of the stock figure of the pedant. But pedantry infects nearly all the officials and aspirants to officialdom in the opening chapters of *Mudan ting*. Du Bao 杜寶, Du Liniang's father, has an unfortunate tendency to speak in quotation and boasts that the ivory tags labeling his books number 30,000. Liu Mengmei, an impoverished licentiate (*xiucai* 秀才), cites Li Bai and Du Fu in an attempt to impress an innkeeper into giving him a meal. Their quotation of the ancients seems stagey, an aid to their social aspirations. *Mudan ting* opposes this inauthentic relation to literary texts with the instinctive and practical understanding of literature modeled by Du Liniang's maid, Chunxiang 春香. In the schoolroom scenes, in which Tutor Chen expands on "Guanguan jujiu," the maid hears the classical phrases of the poem as though they were spoken in the vernacular; her understanding of the poem paves the way for Du Liniang's later initiation into the sensual world of the garden.

Tang Xianzu does not, however, romanticize a vernacular mode of reading. In later scenes, the maid's vernacular reception of classical texts infects both the Daoist nun Shi Daogu (dubbed Sister Stone in Cyril Birch's translation) and Tutor Chen. Shi Daogu engages in a hilarious disquisition on her sexual history (or lack thereof) as a "stone maiden," in which she imbues the four-character phrases of the classical primer *Qian zi jing* 千字經 (Thousand-character text) with unintentionally obscene overtones. Tutor Chen subsequently doctors the languishing Du Liniang with prescriptions derived from reading the *Shi jing* as though it had been written in the demotic, with disastrous results. Their slapstick quotation of the classics further mocks the allusiveness of archaism by transposing it to the vernacular. Ultimately, *Mudan ting* reveals the literary employment of the vernacular to be as staged as archaist citation, as we see in Du Bao's visit to a farming village in Scene 8.

I preface this discussion of *Mudan ting* by placing its concern with the theatricality of refined registers of speech in the context of late Ming jokes about pedants (*yu fu*) 迂腐. Late Ming and Qing compendia of humor are littered with jokes about dogmatic Confucian scholars and dimwitted officials. The first section of Feng Menglong's *Gu jin xiao* 古今笑 (Jokes old and new), for example, is dedicated to such gibes, with over sixty entries.[4] These jokes testify to concerns regarding impersonation and imposture within the world of officialdom. They satirize the pedant's use of the classical language as a badge of distinction and locate authenticity in the sounds and sights of the natural world—the cries of a bird or the speech of a farmer.

These jokes share with *Mudan ting* an interest in the interplay of different sociolinguistic registers. One of their most prominent rhetorical features is the mutual illumination—or dialogization, to use Bakhtin's term—of such registers.[5] The puns in these jokes juxtapose two parallel linguistic worlds, a refined register and a vulgar register that mirrors and mocks it, by playing on the different significances of an ideograph in classical and vernacular Chinese. The effort of aspiring scholars to engage in linguistic self-discipline and self-improvement is contrasted with the simple and unmannered speech of the unlettered, who do not compromise themselves to achieve social status. Elite speech seems self-conscious and labored; the vernacular, because it is both more explicit and more easily understood, seems more genuine.

In the final part of this chapter, I consider *Mudan ting*'s mockery of the theatricality of allusive citation in relation to late Ming debates on literary composition. Tang Xianzu left few theoretical statements, but I would argue that *Mudan ting* itself stakes out a position opposed to archaism.[6] *Mudan ting*'s use of the notion of theatricality to critique archaism is echoed in the writings of the famed opponents of archaism among

---

4. These jokes are not necessarily of late Ming origin; many were drawn from earlier compendia, including Liu Yiqing's 劉義慶 Six Dynasties collection *Shishuo xinyu* 世説新語, the seventh-century *Qiyan lu* 啓顏錄, and Li Fang's 李昉 Song dynasty compilation *Taiping guangji* 太平廣記. Many of the jokes also were recycled among various late Ming anthologies. Feng Menglong's *Xiaofu* 笑府, for example, drew heavily on other late Ming joke books, including Li Zhi's 李贄 *Shan zhong yixihua* 山中一夕話 and Jiang Yingke's 江盈科 three collections, *Xue Tao xiaoshuo* 雪濤笑説, *Xue Tao xieshi* 雪濤諧史, and *Tan yan* 談言; see Pi-ching Hsu, "Feng Meng-long's *Treasury of Laughs*." Three members of Tang Xianzu's extended literary network, Xu Wei 徐渭, Li Zhi, and Jiang Yingke, compiled such compendia, but since many of these jokes were recycled from previous anthologies or simply in the common domain, one cannot strictly argue that the jokes reflected the viewpoint of the compilers.

5. See Bakhtin, *The Dialogic Imagination*, pp. 411–12.

6. Xu Shuofang (*Xu Shuofang ji*, 3: 370–71) asserts that Tang Xianzu's play *Zixiao ji* 紫簫記 (The jade flute) was censured because it obliquely criticized archaism.

Tang Xianzu's extended network, such as Xu Wei, Li Zhi, and the various members of the Gong'an School, who included the brothers Yuan Hongdao 袁宏道 (1568–1610), Zongdao 宗道 (1560–1600), and Zhongdao 中道 (1570–1624), and their associate Jiang Yingke 江盈科 (1556–1605).[7] Archaism and anti-archaism alike are typically viewed as purely literary positions.[8] My discussion of the figure of the theater in the writings of these anti-archaists elucidates the cultural politics that lay behind their disparagement of the "theatricality" of a literary style. As Jonathan Chaves and Chou Chih-p'ing have shown, anti-archaists such as the Yuan brothers did not aim their criticisms at the primary architects of archaism, all of whom were men of high official position respected for their literary prowess.[9] Rather, they reserved their ire for men of shallow learning who sought to distinguish their prose by taking advantage of the clear guidelines offered by the archaists and embellishing their texts with Han dynasty place-names and official titles and with diction imitative of the Tang poetic masters. In part, the anti-archaist disparagement of imitation seems motivated by the anxiety that imitation of the ancients would allow lesser talents to gain recognition simply by following archaist prescriptions. The ease with which archaist formulations can be adopted permitted a transgression of status hierarchies in the literary realm that was akin to the more material forms of sumptuary violation lamented by Tang Xianzu's contemporaries.

The Formation of a New Middle Elite

The concern over an imitative poetics became common as access to education increased during the mid- to late Ming. The spread of cultural literacy was accompanied by a process of canon formation heavily influenced by anthologies compiled by archaists. Stephen Owen observes that

---

7. Guo Shaoyu 郭紹虞 suggests that Tang Xianzu was one of the three most salient influences on the Yuan brothers' anti-archaism; see Guo Shaoyu, *Zhongguo wenxue piping shi* 中國文學批評史, p. 348; cited in Lynn, "Alternate Routes to Self-Realization in Ming Theories of Poetry," pp. 317–41.

8. An exception is the writing of Xu Shuofang on Tang Xianzu's struggles with archaists; see *Xu Shuofang ji*, 1: 365–82.

9. Chaves, "A Panoply of Images," p. 342; Chou Chih-p'ing, *Yüan Hung-tao and the Kung-an School*, p. 32.

because of "the archaists and their ubiquitous textbooks" even the "newly educated" stratum of the elite "knew the norms of Tang poetry and had the techniques of *guwen* 古文 explained in excruciating pedagogic detail."[10] Portions of the canon, once the province of the pedigreed elite, became widely available. It is in this context that we begin to hear diatribes against men of shallow education who believe they can compose passable poetry by following the dictates of archaism. As the expansion of academies and the increasing availability of printed materials rendered the traditional canon accessible to a larger section of the populace, the figure of the pedant became increasingly prominent. In the derision of pedantry in late Ming literature, we hear the protest of the old cultural elite that a "newly educated" stratum—the educational counterpart of the *nouveau riche*—has not internalized the cultural canon but simply displays its acquisition of learning.

With greater access to education, the number of men participating in the examination system rose dramatically. As a percentage of the total population, licentiates (*shengyuan* 生員 or, more commonly, *xiucai*), men who had passed the local level of the civil service examinations, increased sevenfold between 1500 and 1700.[11] For these *xiucai*, opportunities for employment were meager. Reduced to finding a livelihood outside the official bureaucracy, *xiucai* served as private tutors and village schoolmasters or eked a living from writing and publishing. Official positions were awarded only to those who succeeded at the provincial and metropolitan levels of the examinations. Despite the surfeit of candidates, the Ming government did not increase the quotas for provincial and metropolitan graduates or the number of bureaucratic positions. Thus the chances of succeeding at the provincial and metropolitan levels became more daunting than ever.[12] Under the Ming, those who failed at the pro-

---

10. Stephen Owen, "Seventeenth-Century Introductory Lecture," unpublished paper, p. 15.

11. In 1500, there were around 30,000 licentiates in a population of about 65 million, a ratio of 1 to 2,200. In 1700, there were 500,000 in a population of 150 million, about 1 in 300 (Elman, *A Cultural History*, pp. 140–41).

12. By the late Ming, the ratio of *xiucai* to *jinshi* 進士 (metropolitan graduates) was 21 to 1. The ratio was even more distorted for candidates hailing from provinces that were cultural centers (ibid., p. 141, quoting Wada Masahiro, "Mindai kyojinzō no keisei katei ni kansuru ichi kōsatsu," in *Shigaku zasshi* 83, no. 1, pp. 36–71).

vincial level had to retake the local examinations every two years to maintain their status as *xiucai*.[13] Condemned to sitting the lowest level of the examinations for years on end, they endured because participation in the examinations in itself conferred gentry status.[14]

The frustration of such *xiucai* with their dim prospects registers in the complaint of Du Liniang's intended, Liu Mengmei, to his friend Han Zicai 韓子才: "Men like us have read myriad books; might we obtain half a piece of land?"[15] Although Liu has trusted in his studies to gain him entry to the ruling caste, they have not brought him the wealth he believes he deserves. Liu eventually obtains an interview with an imperial inspector of jewels, Miao Shunbin 苗舜賓, whom he importunes to fund his travel to take the examinations. Commenting on the jewels Miao has collected from tributary countries, Liu states, "Sir, even though these jewels are authentic (*zhen*), they cannot feed the hungry or clothe those who suffer cold. I view them as empty boats (*xu zhou* 虛舟) or fallen tiles (*piao wa* 飄瓦)."[16] Miao belittles Liu's bravado: "According to you, *xiucai*, what would be an authentic jewel?" Liu replies, "I cheat you not, I myself am a true and rare jewel. If I can take this jewel to the imperial court, it will be considered without price." Miao laughs, "I'm just afraid that at court, this

---

13. Elman, *A Cultural History*, p. 137.

14. Given the quotas, repeated failures at the provincial level were in a sense institutionalized. Yet, motivated by the desire to maintain their status as a member of the local elite, candidates spent years preparing for examinations that they were nearly certain to fail. As Elman (ibid., p. 298) notes, "Enough local social prestige, legal privileges, and corvée labor exemptions continued to accrue to both *sheng-yuan* and *chü-jen* 舉人 to keep both young and old men from elite families competing in the examination market."

15. Tang Xianzu, *Mudan ting*, p. 23. The edition of *Mudan ting* quoted here is Xu Shuofang's modern reprinting (with commentary) of the *Huaide tang* 懷德堂 edition, which dates to the Wanli period; Xu uses this edition because it seems to have undergone the fewest emendations. I cite Cyril Birch's translation, *The Peony Pavilion*, unless I translate passages myself to highlight a particular point, as in the quotation above. I have in some cases changed the names of characters in Birch's translation to *pinyin* romanization, so that Birch's "Spring Fragrance" here is "Chunxiang," and his "Bridal Du" has become "Du Liniang."

16. Tang, *Mudan ting*, p. 115. The phrases "empty boats" and "fallen tiles" are drawn from Zhuangzi's "Shanmu dasheng" 山木達生, although their significance in this context differs from that in Zhuangzi (see *Zhuangzi jishi* 莊子集釋, pp. 636, 674).

kind of jewel is quite common!"[17] *Xiucai* such as Liu are now a dime a dozen, and only connections will secure them wealth and position.

Refinement and Vulgarity

The proliferation of *xiucai* such as Liu Mengmei, stragglers seeking to gain the benefits of membership in the bureaucracy, created a need to distinguish the various strata of the educated elite. Late Ming and early Qing texts satirize the social imposture inherent in the newly educated's adoption of refined diction and deride the inauthenticity and theatrical hollowness of their rhetorical manipulation. The concern to separate the "truly cultured" from the "newly educated" can be related to the ubiquitous play on refinement (*ya* 雅) and vulgarity (*su* 俗) in the literary culture of the late Ming and early Qing. The significance of the Chinese terms is more capacious than that of the English terms; *ya* and *su* describe not merely the social standing of individuals and the sociolinguistic registers they consequently inhabit but also the directness with which they express their thoughts.[18] Although *su* is associated with crass mercantilism and low social standing, it also connotes unhesitating emotional expression. It is allied with the earthy, practical, material and somatic, and in this wise comes to represent authenticity (*zhen*).

It is the particular task of the *chuanqi* among late imperial literary genres to contrast the points of view of different social strata. (The late imperial novel also engages in this sort of productive juxtaposition, but seems less single-mindedly devoted to it.) The formal properties of *chuanqi* suit it to the mutual contextualization of *ya* and *su*.[19] Its large cast of characters, sprawling length, and numerous subplots give ample room for the comparison of refined and ordinary linguistic registers in linked charac-

---

17. Tang, *Mudan ting*, p. 111.

18. Du Liniang, for example, is *ya* not only because she is of high social standing and speaks in a refined register of speech, but also because she indicates her thoughts indirectly, whether verbally or through gesture (Swatek, *"Peony Pavilion" Onstage*, p. 265).

19. Stephen Owen discusses this mutual "contextualization" of *ya* and *su* in "Salvaging the Poetic in the Qing," in which he argues that the great *chuanqi* of the seventeenth century—in particular, *Changsheng dian*—can be read in terms of a desire to preserve a space for the poetic (defined as the realm of lyrical self-expression, or *qing*), a space that is constantly eroded as it is contextualized by the juxtaposition of social hierarchies and levels of language.

ters such as mistress and maid or in twinned scenes that contrast court and countryside. The alternation between the elevated register of the lyrics and the colloquial speech of the dialogue permits constant opportunity for the ironic parataxis of high and low.

It may be impossible to know just how the fascination in late Ming literature with relativizing the points of view of different social strata was related to the cataclysmic social and economic changes taking place from the sixteenth century on. But we can speculate that it may have been related to the growth of urban centers, in which members of vastly different social strata as well as people from disparate geographical regions congregated. The dialogic relation between *ya* and *su* in *chuanqi* reveals how different social strata view the same phenomena through different lenses, creating a linguistic and ideological versatility particular to this genre.[20] In the context of *chuanqi*, language that is *su* is not simply colloquial speech, but colloquial speech employed with a slapstick humor; it often reveals the hypocrisy and pretensions of the elite. As the refinement of the linguistic register of the social elite is exposed as artificial, the effort with which the baser appetites are ignored becomes obvious. In Bakhtinian terms, the elite characters speak undialogized language; the "low" characters' interpretation of elite speech dialogizes it.[21]

In *Mudan ting*, Tang Xianzu exploits to its fullest the dialogic interaction of *ya* and *su* characteristic of the *chuanqi* as a genre. Both the literariness of his lyrics and the "vulgarity" of the speech of his comic characters far surpass the norms established by his contemporaries.[22] With this dia-

---

20. I should note that the discussion of *ya* and *su* in *chuanqi* has a different cast in American academic discourse than it does in Chinese scholarship on the theater. In Chinese scholarship, it refers to the contrast between staging that supports subtlety of gesture and voice and staging that seeks to provide visual spectacle; the latter is often a feature of modern interpretations that aim to please a relatively uninformed audience. See Swatek, *Peony Pavilion Onstage*, pp. 158–59.

21. The ironic juxtaposition of *ya* and *su* in *chuanqi* bears a striking resemblance to the phenomenon Bakhtin (*The Dialogic Imagination*, pp. 261–63) described as heteroglossia, the mutual "illumination" of languages (discourses appropriate to social station, profession, or literary genre) through a reciprocal contextualization. Swatek discusses this briefly in *Peony Pavilion Onstage*, pp. 177–78.

22. Swatek (*"Peony Pavilion" Onstage*, pp. 25–67) has shown that Tang Xianzu's contemporaries Zang Maoxun and Feng Menglong toned down Tang Xianzu's excesses of literariness and vulgarity in their revisions of *Mudan ting*. In making Tang's highly allusive

logic play of refined and vulgar discourses, Tang Xianzu explores the cultural politics of authenticity. The quick shifts in perspective between *ya* and *su* serve to alienate the spectator from his or her identification with an individual character's perspective. The movement from identification to alienation invokes the dialectics of illusion and disillusion (or attachment and detachment) that are integral to the genre's exploration of the theatricality of social relations and the hollow, ephemeral nature of the phenomenal world.

Late Ming Jokes Regarding Pedants

The preposterously elevated diction of the *xiucai* is a standard feature of late Ming jokes. The pedant's pretended ignorance of the vulgar registers of language is in itself vulgar, for it betrays an aspiration to enter a higher social stratum. His unnecessary allusions and arcane diction reveal a worldly concern with sumptuary display. Zhao Nanxing's 趙南星 (1550–1627) *Xiao zan* 笑贊 (Commentary on jokes) records a joke about a *xiucai* who goes to buy firewood. Mixing classical Chinese with the demotic, he states: "He who beareth firewood, come over here" (*he xin zhe guo lai* 荷薪者過來). The firewood vendor, because he understands the words "come over here," carries the firewood over to him. Then, using classical syntax, the *xiucai* asks: "Its price; how much?" (*qi jia ji he* 其價幾何). The vendor grasps only the word "price" and gives the price. The *xiucai* says: "Solid externally and empty internally (*wai shi er nei xu* 外實而内虛), much smoke and little flame. I request that you lower the price." The firewood seller does not understand and carries his goods away.[23]

Determined to employ the phrase "solid externally and empty internally" despite its tangential relevance, the *xiucai* cares more about the dignity of his diction than the quality of his communication. Zhao comments, "*Xiucai* such as these chew on texts and chomp at words. What are they trying to accomplish? Studying leads people astray in this way." Zhao continues: "There was an official who went to the countryside. He asked

---

language more accessible and in minimizing the "vulgarity" of the low characters, Zang and Feng muted the dialogic interplay between high and low, flattening out the rich ironies created by Tang Xianzu's productive juxtaposition of *ya* and *su*.

23. Zhao Nanxing, *Xiao zan*, p. 14.

an old man, 'How are the common folk (*li shu* 黎庶) doing this year?'
The old man said, 'This year the pear trees (*li shu* 梨樹) are doing well,
it's just that the insects have eaten some of them.'" Like the *xiucai*, this official values classical diction over communication. Zhao's comment puns
on two different sets of characters pronounced *li shu*; the joke depends in
part on the assumption that the farmer is illiterate in classical Chinese
and has a functional rather than a decorative vocabulary. If Bourdieu has
described an "official language" as one that "imposes itself upon the whole
population as the only legitimate language," the joke here is that the language of officialdom, although it may conceive of itself as the only legitimate language, is irrelevant to the larger part of the population. [24]

A similar sort of pun plays on the fact that a single character may have
different meanings in classical and demotic Chinese, even though it is
pronounced the same way in both. Du Liniang's tutor, for example, instructs her that the *guan* 關 in "Guanguan jujiu" signifies the cry of an os-
prey. But the maid Chunxiang assumes that *guan* means "shut in," as it
does in the demotic. These puns invoke the vernacular significances of
ideographs to suggest a parallel discourse that shadows the language of officialdom; the vulgar significance of a term trails after its refined counterpart like a piece of toilet paper caught on a debutante's heel.

In a joke from Jiang Yingke's *Xuetao xieshi* 雪濤諧史 (Xuetao's History of jests), Confucius asks his disciple Gongye Chang 公冶長, who excels at interpreting the sounds of birds, to translate bird calls for him: [25]

Once Confucius heard a pigeon calling and asked, "What is it saying?" Gongye
Chang answered, "A goblet that does not resemble a goblet" (觚不觚 *gu bu gu*).
Then Confucius heard a swallow calling and asked, "What is it saying?" He replied, "It is saying, 'To know what you know and do not know, this is knowledge'" (知之爲知之，不知爲不知，是知也 *zhi zhi wei zhizhi, bu zhi wei bu zhi,
shi zhi ye*). Then they heard a donkey bray, and Confucius said, "What is this
sound?" Gongye Chang said, "This cannot be understood; it is speaking in local
dialect."[26]

---

24. Bourdieu, *Language and Symbolic Power*, p. 45.

25. Confucius supposedly gave Gongye Chang his daughter in marriage. See *Lunyu jishi*, p. 285.

26. Jiang Yingke, *Xuetao xieshi*, p. 29. The prevalence of jokes on pedantic Confucians
points to the status of Cheng-Zhu Neo-Confucianism as state orthodoxy. On Neo-

In interpreting the birds' cries in this manner, Gongye Chang imputes
to these birds the words of his master, Confucius; both phrases appear in
the *Lun yu* 論語 (Analects).[27] Confucius's cryptic phrase *gu bu gu* was interpreted by later commentators to signify "a goblet that does not resemble a goblet" and consequently to be a veiled reference to a "name without
reality," appearance with nothing substantive behind it.[28] Gongye Chang's
misguided translations form an apt example of "name without reality";
the dictum "to know what you know and do not know, this is knowledge"
similarly spoofs Gongye Chang's claim that he knows the classical speech
of the birds but not the local dialect employed in the donkey's bray.

Many jokes involving pedants pun on types of heteronyms relatively
specific to Chinese—not only the common mispronunciations of written
characters but also the mistaken substitutions of similar-sounding characters known as *baizi* 白字 (an English equivalent would be the substitution of "hear" for "here"). Feng Menglong cites a joke about two Confucian scholars who battle over the pronunciation of Taihang 太行
mountain (*tai* can be read as *dai*, and *hang* as *xing*, making multiple com-
binations possible).[29] One scholar claims that he knows the correct pronunciation because he has been to the mountain and seen the stele on
which the characters are engraved. This of course proves nothing; that the
characters can be read in multiple ways is, after all, the source of the dispute. The humor lies in the scholar's attempts to bolster his case by privileging the engraved version of the characters rather than appealing to the
local pronunciation. Unable to resolve the issue, the two scholars agree to
visit a senior scholar to settle the matter. The senior scholar misleadingly
states that the name should be pronounced *dai xing*. Privately, he tells the
scholar who lost the bet that the joke is on the winner, who will now mis-
pronounce the characters for the rest of his life. The joke makes fun of the
newly educated stratum's privileging of authority: the two junior scholars
appeal to the senior to settle a dispute that should have been resolved by

---

Confucianism as state orthodoxy, see Elman, "The Formation of 'Dao Learning' as Imperial Ideology."

27. "A goblet that does not resemble a goblet—can this be considered a goblet?"
(*Lunyu jishi*, p. 412). Confucius said to his disciple Zilu, "Do you understand what I have
taught you? To know what you know and do not know, this is knowledge" (ibid., p. 110).

28. Ibid., p. 412.

29. Zhao Nanxing, *Xiao zan*, p. 3.

an appeal to local pronunciation, only to be ridiculed by him as he deliberately furnishes the wrong answer.

In a joke cited by Jiang Yingke, a member of the "true elite" similarly ridicules a junior scholar who seeks his approval:

A Confucian scholar (*ru sheng* 儒生) would pay a call on his elders every time he completed a repulsive composition. One of his elders commented upon his writing: "When Ouyang Xiu 歐陽修 in days of old composed essays, he said that he often drew inspiration from the "three Tops" (*san shang* 三上). Your composition seems so excellent that it resembles the third of Ouyang Xiu's Tops."[30] The Confucian scholar was extremely pleased. A friend saw him and said, "That gentleman is making fun of you." The Confucian scholar said, "He compared me to Ouyang Xiu. How could that be said to be making fun of me?" His friend replied: "The Three 'Tops' of Ouyang Xiu were 'atop' his pillow, 'atop' his horse, and 'atop' his toilet.' The third 'Top' is the toilet." The Confucian scholar then understood that he had been made to look a fool.[31]

The narrow band of understanding of the newly educated will never permit them the fluidity and ease of the true elite in the realm of high culture. Only the true elite have a native's sense of *habitus*, to use Bourdieu's term, in the land of classical allusion.

The obsequiousness of such junior scholars before their seniors was common fodder for jokes. Zhao Nanxing records a joke about a *xiucai* who dies and has an audience with Yama, the King of Hell. When Yama accidentally farts, the *xiucai* presents him with a laud:

The golden buttocks were lifted high
and spread the precious air.
It resembled the music of strings and bamboo,
was redolent of the scent of musk and orchid.
I stood downwind
and was overcome by its far-reaching fragrance. [32]

---

30. See Ouyang Xiu, "Zuowen duo zai san shang" 作文多在三上, in *Tang Song ba da jia wenzhang jinghua*, p. 483.

31. Jiang Yingke, *Xuetao xieshi*, p. 43.

32. Zhao Nanxing, *Xiao zan*, p. 4–5.

Yama is greatly pleased and extends his lifespan by ten years. Zhao comments that the *xiucai*'s obsequiousness leaves a stench that will last 10,000 years.

These jokes subject the instrumental and inauthentic application of the classical language to ridicule, whether in the case of a scholar who pretends to be more at home in classical Chinese than the demotic or a *xiucai* willing to call farts fragrant in order to flatter the King of Hell. They scoff at scholars who perpetuate the representational hegemony of a classical language in which they themselves are not fully at ease. In their concern with authenticity, the jokes share a common ground with Tang Xianzu's ridicule of the pedant who believes that literary allusion itself has value, even if such reference has little currency outside the narrow purview of officialdom.

Mudan ting

The ridicule of pedantry is most apparent in the early scenes of the play. Each of the male characters in the first scenes claims to be a descendant of one of the great poets of the Tang: Du Bao asserts a connection to Du Fu 杜甫, acclaimed by the Ming archaist Gao Bing 高棅 (1350–1423) as the greatest of the High Tang poets; Liu Mengmei to Liu Zongyuan 柳宗元, whom Gao Bing promoted as one of the dozen-odd poets who best represented the High Tang style;[33] and Han Zicai to Han Yu 韓愈, whom Gao Bing also praised.[34] Even the humble characters echo these claims, making them seem all the more preposterous. A gardener who supports Liu Mengmei states that he is a descendant of "Camel Guo" (Guo Tuotuo 郭橐駝), the gardener immortalized by Liu's purported ancestor Liu Zongyuan.[35]

---

33. Gao Bing, *Wuyan gushi xumu* 五言古詩序目 (Introduction to pentasyllabic ancient-style verse), quoted in Lynn, "Alternate Routes to Self-Realization," p. 321.

34. See Lynn, "Alternate Routes to Self-Realization," p. 322. The archaists were not, however, unanimous in their appraisal of Han Yu; Li Mengyang 李夢陽 (1472–1529) disparaged his mannerism, considering him too late to be worthy of praise (Li Mengyang, *Yu xu shi lun wen shuo*, quoted in Guo Shaoyu, *Zhongguo wenxue piping shi*, p. 614; see Lynn, "Alternate Routes to Self-Realization," p. 324).

35. Liu Zongyuan, "Zhong shu Guo Tuotuo zhuan" 種樹郭橐駝傳 (Biography of the gardener Camel Guo), in *Liu Zongyuan quanji*, p. 145. See also Cyril Birch's translation in *Anthology of Chinese Literature*.

Such exaggerated claims to literary ancestry are made even more tenuous by these scholars' lack of literary sensitivity. Du Bao's poetic sensibilities are limited to the instrumental use of books to signal educational pedigree and membership in the ruling elite. He confides, "You see how my regulation of the nation and ordering of my family are all just many volumes of books":

> Through two score years and ten,
> books have been my delight;
> "My shelves hold thirty thousand ivory tallies"
> (He sighs)
> Like Cai Yong lacking sons, to whom shall I pass
> this rich inheritance of learning?[36]

Although Du Bao states that "books have been my delight," his boast incorporates an allusion that suggests that these books have never been read. Han Yu poked fun at the Marquis of Ye 鄴, famed for his collection of 30,000 volumes:

> The family of the Marquis of Ye owns many books,
> Thirty thousand volumes are tucked on their shelves.
> From each dangles an ivory tally,
> new as though never touched.[37]

Tang Xianzu's sly reference to Han Yu's poem suggests that the 30,000 books on Du Bao's shelves represent not his delight in literature but his accumulation of cultural capital, to use Bourdieu's term.[38] The books on Du Bao's shelves signal his social position and his right to rule. They literally form an inheritance. Classical texts have been reduced to the stage props of the ruling elite.

If books resemble stage props, poetic allusions provide a social script, as we see in Du Bao's interview of Chen Zuiliang for the post of tutor to Du Liniang. Both Du Bao and Chen Zuiliang speak in a pastiche of allusions. In their first exchange, which clearly marks an initiation of sorts, they take

---

36. Tang, *Mudan ting*, p. 19; Birch, *The Peony Pavilion*, p. 17.
37. Han Yu, *Han Changli quanji*, p. 251.
38. Bourdieu, *Distinction*, p. 12.

turns reciting lines from a poem by the Tang emperor Xuanzong 玄宗.[39]
Employing the classical language as though it should supplant the vernacular on the most mundane occasions, they seek to lift daily exchanges
out of the realm of the vulgar. Chen bows before Du and says: "Let
learned discourse lighten library." Du replies, "Exalted scholar, gem of our
assembly." To which Chen responds, "Be trencher and flagon readied for
exchange." Du caps the last couplet, "and seats for guest and host drawn
in due order."[40] After Chen and Du recite the poem, stage directions direct the chorus to "assent and withdraw." The presence and then disappearance of the chorus highlights the histrionic quality of their citation.

Although Du Liniang's all-absorbing passion provides a foil for the
staginess of archaist citation, Tang Xianzu shows us that Du Liniang herself is not immune to narcissistic self-observation or archaist emulation.
She introduces herself as "the scion of a scholar's line":

> Brows limned black with emerald sheen,
> pendants swaying at waist,
> pictured beauty steps as from broidered screen.
> Lotus feet in tripping measure
> set long ago as mark of reverence
> by the son of the Master, Confucius himself,
> scion of scholars' line I now appear.[41]

Hastening to heed her parents' summons, Du Liniang preposterously
compares herself to Confucius's son, who rushed to his father's side
whenever called.[42] She, too, has been infected by the pedantry of the men
of officialdom. Her phrase "pictured beauty steps as from broidered
screen" underscores the narcissism inherent in the emulation of historical
models. Envisioning herself as a mirror of antiquity, Du Liniang instructs

---

39. See Emperor Xuanzong, "Jixian shuyuan cheng song Zhang Shuo shang jixian xue-
shi ci yan de zhenzi" 集賢書院成送張説上集賢學士賜宴得珍字 (On the establish-
ment of the Academy of Assembled Worthies, I sent Zhang Shuo to head the academy; at
the congratulatory banquet I drew the character *zhen* as the rhyme word for a poem),
Quan Tang shi 全唐詩, 1: 35.

40. Tang, *Mudan ting*, p. 16; Birch, *The Peony Pavilion*, p. 15.

41. Tang, *Mudan ting*, p. 18; Birch, *The Peony Pavilion*, p. 16.

42. *Lunyu jishi*, p. 1169.

Chunxiang that she also must discipline herself according to the models of the past: "Maid, wise and accomplished ladies are all models mirrored on antiquity. You also must gain some knowledge of books, in order to become a good servant." Chunxiang, however, mocks such pretensions and later notes the uselessness of book learning for a maid:

Wise Words of the Ancients—
what a deadly thought—
but when I'm through,
I'll be able to teach the parrot to order tea.[43]

It is the task of the low characters associated with colloquial language to expose the abstraction of literary language and the distancing of the elite from the material world. It is not just the classical language that exists at a remove from practical, everyday concerns; the elite themselves are distanced from practical concerns, dangerously so. It is quite conventional in *chuanqi* that elite characters often depend on their servants for advice and support, but the world portrayed in *Mudan ting* takes that phenomenon to an extreme. Liu Mengmei is supported by the gardener; the gatekeeper at the prefectural school gains Tutor Chen an interview with Du Bao for the post of Du Liniang's tutor. When the gatekeeper congratulates Chen on his success, Chen demurs, quoting Mencius, "The human vice is the urge to teach others." "What about human rice?" counters the gatekeeper. "At least you'll be fed."[44] Tutor Chen, whose proper name is Chen Zuiliang (Chen the best) is nicknamed among the locals "Chen Jueliang" (Chen the foodless). In this context, Du Bao's conventional phrase of flattery, "I have long heard that you are one who has filled his belly with books" (*jiu wen xiansheng bao xue*) 久聞先生飽學, seems to hold a special irony.[45]

Toward the end of the play, Liu Mengmei, at Du Liniang's request, undertakes a journey to ascertain Du Bao's welfare after the siege of

---

43. Tang, *Mudan ting*, p. 28; Birch, *The Peony Pavilion*, p. 25.
44. Tang, *Mudan ting*, p. 15; Birch, *The Peony Pavilion*, p. 12.
45. Tang, *Mudan ting*, p. 18 (my translation).

Huai'an. Impoverished *xiucai* that he is, he must sell the objects Du Bao buried with Du Liniang in the tomb to finance his trip. Liu proudly describes himself as "a scholar by training and quite ignorant of the marks of the merchant's scale."[46] Indeed he is; Liu's attempt to use his cultural capital as financial currency ends in disaster as he tries to trade his scholarly implements and, failing that, scholarly allusions, for food:

> Liu: This book here is one I am constantly reading; it's worth a jug of wine.
> Innkeeper: Book looks pretty worn.
> Liu: I'll add a brush to go with it.
> Innkeeper: Brush looks pretty fuzzy.
> Liu: With all the customers passing this way, you must have heard Du Fu's line about "scholarship that wears out ten thousand books?"[47]
> Innkeeper: Can't say I have . . .
> Liu laughs: "My mistake—these are not things one buys wine with."

The innkeeper rejoins: "Fairies have given their pendants of jade, ministers of state their gold and sable."[48] Here the clown, playing the role of the innkeeper, mocks Liu's pedantry by trading allusions with him; Ruan Fu 阮孚, according to the *Jin shu* 晉書 (History of the Jin), was so enamored of his wine that he traded gold and sables to obtain it.[49] Liu parries with such clichés as "The brush of a man of true learning / Can restore peace to the empire." Seeing that references to his learning fail to impress the innkeeper, he asks, "You won't take my book, you won't take my brush—how about this umbrella?" The innkeeper replies drolly, "It's going to rain." Liu says, "Then I won't go out tomorrow." To which the innkeeper responds, "Then you'll die here—of starvation."[50] Liu clearly believes that cultural capital should translate not only into symbolic but also into financial capital. A few lines from Du Fu or Li Bai should be worth a meal. But classical allusion, the common currency of officials, is mere pedantry outside the seemingly narrow purview of officialdom.

---

46. Tang, *Mudan ting*, p. 251; Birch, *The Peony Pavilion*, p. 282.

47. Du Fu, "Feng zeng Wei zuocheng zhang ershier yun" 奉贈韋左丞丈二十二韻 (Twenty-two poems presented to Vice Minister Wei), in *Du shi xiang zhu*, p. 74.

48. Tang Xianzu, *Mudan ting*, p. 252; Birch, *The Peony Pavilion*, p. 284.

49. *Jin shu* 晉書, 5: 1364.

50. Tang, *Mudan ting*, p. 252; Birch, *The Peony Pavilion*, p. 284–85.

The Schoolroom Scenes

Du Liniang's fervent, somatic response to her introduction to the poem "Guanguan jujiu" is an implicit foil to the archaist pedantry of Liu Mengmei and Chen Zuiliang. In the schoolroom scenes, Tang Xianzu exposes the shallow pedantry of Du Liniang's tutor Chen Zuiliang by contrasting his exposition of "Guanguan jujiu" with Chunxiang's vernacular reading and Du Liniang's physical response. Her parents decide that her education should begin with this poem because (in the then-orthodox interpretation) it describes the virtue of the consort of the Duke of Zhou 周公.[51] They hope that the comportment she learns in the classroom will serve as the female equivalent of archaist citation. But her education goes awry when the poem inspires Du Liniang and her maid to leave the schoolroom, the realm of inculcated norms of behavior, for the natural idyll of the garden, where she experiences a sensual awakening. The maid hears "Guanguan jujiu" as though it were written in the vernacular. Du Liniang, as though inspired by her maid's reading of the poem, dreams of an erotic encounter with Liu Mengmei, a response to the poem that is "vernacular" in that it is somatic, spontaneous, and outside the norms of propriety.

While waiting for the first lesson to start, Tutor Chen recites the poem. "*Guanguan* cry the ospreys / On the islet in the river / So delicate the virtuous maiden, / a fit mate for our prince." He goes on to gloss it in an unwitting parody of a traditional commentary: "'Fit,' that is to say, 'fit'; 'mate,' that is to say, 'seeking.'"[52] Tutor Chen's commentary offers the most accurate gloss possible—a nearly precise repetition of the words themselves. The use of other words to define the original would open the dan-

---

51. As the first poem in the *Shi jing*, the founding text of the literary canon, "Guanguan jujiu" is an irreproachably authoritative text. According to the Mao commentary, one of the earliest and most influential commentarial traditions, as the first poem in the *Shi jing*, "Guanguan jujiu" must be the earliest. Even by the time of Mao commentary, the poem was seen as an artifact of a lost period of wholeness. Yet at the same time, "Guanguan jujiu" and the section of the *Shi jing* in which it appears, the *Guo feng* 國風 (Airs of the States), were frequently cited in prefaces of late imperial literary texts that dealt with romance to defend against charges of obscenity. Thus the invocation of "Guanguan jujiu" already carries an unintended doubleness that portends Du Liniang's journey into the sensual world of the garden.

52. Tang, *Mudan ting*, p. 27; Birch, *The Peony Pavilion*, p. 24.

gerous possibility of interpretation. The repetition enshrouds the words, robbing them of vitality. The pedant's insecurity vis-à-vis the text leads him to embalm it.

The maid distrusts this veneration of classical texts. Seeing a book entitled *Wise Words of the Ancients*, the maid remarks, "They'll shackle and kill a person."[53] She hears "Guanguan jujiu" as though it were written in the vernacular; to her ears, the line glossed by countless commentators as "the islet in the river" (*zai he zhi zhou* 在河之洲) becomes "at the house of Assistant Magistrate He" (*zai he zhi zhou* 在何知州).[54] Chunxiang understands the poem as a comment on lived reality, not as a cultural artifact; she is a vernacular reader.

In response, Tutor Chen immediately elevates the debate by appealing to literary terminology: "That's ridiculous. This is a stimulus (*xing* 興)." When the maid asks what a "stimulus" is, Tutor Chen defines it as a phrase that introduces thoughts of something: "To 'image,' that is to say, to introduce thoughts of. It introduces the thought of the 'delicate virtuous maiden,' who is a nice, quiet girl waiting for the prince to come seeking her." The maid then asks, "What's he seeking from her?"[55] As Chunxiang's question suggests, Tutor Chen's "stimulus" is more stimulating than he thinks. The literary-critical term *xing* signifies sexual arousal in colloquial speech. The maid's question brings out the double entendre. "Guanguan jujiu" is no longer an ode to the virtue of the royal consort but a mating call. The maid restores the sensual overtones that classical commentary excludes. When Chunxiang tells Tutor Chen that he is to blame for Du Liniang's erotic longings, he responds, "I only spoke of 'Guanguan jujiu.'"[56] The maid replies that that is precisely the problem:

"That's just it. The mistress said, 'Even if the fishhawk is shut in (*guan*), it still has the stimulus (*xing*) of being on the isle in the river, how can a person not be better off than a bird?'

---

53. Tang, *Mudan ting*, p. 27.
54. Stephen Owen's translation of the schoolroom scenes vividly brings out these puns; see *Anthology of Traditional Chinese Literature*, pp. 71–74. Owen also discusses Chunxiang's exposure of Chen's scholasticism and "high-cultural blindness" in "Salvaging the Poetic," p. 110.
55. Tang, *Mudan ting*, p. 27; Birch, *The Peony Pavilion*, p. 26.
56. Tang, *Mudan ting*, p. 43.

To read you must bury your head in a book,
but to taste the world around you,
you lift your head and look."[57]

Chunxiang argues that the type of reading Tutor Chen teaches is deadening. One has a choice: either bury one's head in the vestiges of a dead world or taste and look, experiencing the world in a way that is material and physical.

Du Liniang's response to "Guanguan jujiu"—in which the poem literally becomes an erotic stimulus (*xing*)—shows that a vernacular response to canonical texts renders them dangerous in precisely the way the gentry assumed vernacular texts to be. Tang Xianzu not only proposes a vernacular style of "reading" but also points out that if this style of reading gains currency, vernacular texts will no longer be singled out as sensual or obscene; classical texts may fall under that rubric as well. Moreover, although the elite of *Mudan ting* bases its claim to rule on its familiarity with a select body of texts, it refuses to confront the fact that a contemporary context can radically alter a classical text's significance. Placing these canonical texts in contemporary context, as Chunxiang does in her interpretation of "Guanguan jujiu," reveals secondary and subversive significances. With the revelation of their polyvalence, the power of these texts to establish norms of propriety dissolves.

Tang Xianzu treats us to just such an obscenely "vernacular" reading of a classical text in the Daoist nun Shi Daogu's racy narrative of her sexual history as a "stone maiden," which is studded with four-character phrases from the *Qian zi jing*. Just as Tutor Chen's pedantry provides a foil for that of his elite counterpart, Du Bao, Shi Daogu's frank and ironic discussion of sex underscores the unstated but obvious presence of frustrated sexual desire at the root of Du Liniang's illness. In contrast to the social impediments faced by Du Liniang and Liu Mengmei, Shi Daogu's bridegroom meets with a physical obstacle, her closed hymen.

The most salacious parts of Shi Daogu's narrative appear in the quotations from the *Qian zi jing*, which are taken ludicrously out of context. This classical primer was a gateway to the language of officialdom. No character is repeated in its verses, which thus grant the student a mne-

---

57. Tang, *Mudan ting*, p. 43; Owen, *Anthology of Chinese Literature*, p. 75.

monic device for memorizing 1,000 characters. In the following passage,
lines from the *Qian zi jing* (indented below) acquire new overtones:

> Down he goes to look
>> two vast saloons lie left and right
>> the "spacious hall," the "mansion bright"
> and there he's gazing
>> o'er many a gorgeous ivory bed.
> I lay there without a word, but I had a good grin to myself, aha,
> mister bridegroom, this thing I've got here
>> for private as for public wear
>> but don't start thinking you can have it
>> and eaten with a keener zest.
> A few more bouts, and him panting away
>> thus men in every age have shown
>> those virtues that support a throne.
> But I was made all wrong; he just couldn't get through
>> dark skies above a yellow earth.[58]

Set in a vernacular matrix, the language of the classic seems at once exces-
sively literary and debauched and defiled. The aspirations it propagates
are now polluted by the sexual overtones that the classical language typically elides.[59] In this pastiche, Tang Xianzu displays the brilliant linguistic
play we see elsewhere in his *jiju* 集句, the quatrains composed of pastiches
of lines from Tang dynasty poems with which he ends each scene.

Tang Xianzu further complicates the relation between the classical and
the vernacular in the next scene, as Tutor Chen attempts to ease Du
Liniang's lovesickness with prescriptions drawn from the poems of the
Shi jing. Tutor Chen, like Shi Daogu, seems to have been infected by
Chunxiang's mode of vernacular reading, and he and Chunxiang engage
in a slapstick interchange as he conjures up prescriptions based on vernacular readings of the *Shi*. When Tutor Chen asks Du Liniang the reason for her sickness, Chunxiang answers for her: "Why need you ask?
It's those *Songs* you were expounding, 'So delicate the virtuous maiden, /

---

58. Tang, *Mudan ting*, p. 85; Birch, *The Peony Pavilion*, p. 83.

59. The performance tradition has amplified the vulgarization of the *Qian zi jing* in
this scene by rendering the entire scene in dialect. In Chen Shizhen's 1999 version performed at Lincoln Center, the scene was performed in Sichuan dialect by a male actor.

A fit mate for our Prince'—no wonder she's delicate!" Tutor Chen replies, "This being the case, since it's a *Songs* sickness we'll use a *Songs* cure. Right in the first section there's a Sacred Simple for the treatment of feminine disorders. We may prescribe accordingly."[60] Tutor Chen's ludicrous prescription derives its ingredients from poems of the *Shi jing* traditionally read as courting songs. Tang Xianzu fashions a series of puns in which individual ideographs from lines of the *Shi* bring to mind medicinal herbs whose names contain the same characters: "The young lady's sickness was caused by a prince (*junzi* 君子), so we'll use the Envoy Prince" [*shi jun zi* 使君子, the herb *Fructus quisqualis*].[61] Recalling the poem "Piao you mei" 摽有梅 (Plums are falling),[62] Tutor Chen decides that his prescription must include ten sour plums.[63] His treatment inadvertently incorporates the name of Du Liniang's dream lover, Liu Mengmei, whose given name is "Dreaming of the Plum." The prescription unwittingly uses the logic of the rebus so often found in dreams, providing a symbolic materialization of Liu Mengmei to heal Du Liniang's love-sickness. Tutor Chen then pilfers various sounds and characters from the line "zhizi yugui, yan mo qi ju" 之子于歸，言秣其駒 from the poem "Han guang" 漢廣 (The river is broad), directing Chunxiang to wipe out (*mo* 抹) a large chamber pot (*ma tong* 馬桶), in preparation for the "flushing out" of excess heat he will do with *zhi ziren* 梔子仁 (*Fructus gardaniae*) and *dang gui* 當歸 (angelica).[64] At this point, Chunxiang protests against this equation of the classical and vernacular readings of ideographs, "Tutor, that 'horse' isn't the same as the other 'horse.'" Tutor Chen retorts with an appeal to the somatic that levels all sociolinguistic distinctions, "It'll all come out the same fart-hole."[65]

Tutor Chen's "vernacular" readings drive home the point that in teaching the *Shi*, he reinforces the hegemony of symbols he himself does not understand. His puns, which are based on his ignorance of the dis-

---

60. Tang, *Mudan ting*, p. 92: Birch, *The Peony Pavilion*, p. 91.

61. Tang, *Mudan ting*, p. 92; Birch, *The Peony Pavilion*, p. 91.

62. Plums are falling / seven are the fruits / many men visit me / let me have a fine one. // Plums are falling / three are the fruits / many men want me / let me have a steady one" ("Piao youmei," *Shi jing zhuxi*, 1: 47–48; Owen, *Anthology of Chinese Literature*, p. 36).

63. Tang, *Mudan ting*, p. 92; Birch, *The Peony Pavilion*, p. 91.

64. *Shi jing zhuxi*, p. 24.

65. Tang, *Mudan ting*, p. 92 (my translation).

tinction between the literary (*ya*) and vernacular (*su*) significances of characters, seem an involuntary tic of speech, and point to Tutor Chen's inability to maneuver fluently in the language of distinction.[66] With each such pun, his speech stutters, and his language drops precipitously from the heights of the *Shi* to a bawdy vernacular. If, in the schoolroom scenes, Chunxiang mocked Tutor Chen's scholasticism with a reading of the *Shi* that seemed contemporary, practical, and indeed, more relevant to Du Liniang's situation than his deadening commentary, here the "vernacular" reading is wildly inappropriate. The elevated linguistic register from which he derives his legitimacy has no practical application, much as he tries to force one on it. Struggling to maintain a consistently elevated distinction, Tutor Chen is at home neither in the literary nor the vernacular, a man without a country.

"Encouraging the Farmers": The Theatricality of the Vernacular

Immediately following Tutor Chen's battle with Chunxiang over the significance of "Guanguan jujiu," Du Bao travels to a farming village in his capacity as an official to participate in a ritual entitled *quan nong* 勸農 (encouraging the farmers). The scene begins by mocking the aspiring bureaucrat's use of archaist allusion. But ultimately, it subverts the opposition between the theatricality of archaist citation and the material grounding of the vernacular language by showing that the vernacular language may also be invoked theatrically to signal social distinction.[67]

---

66. Although the notion of a language of social distinction is clearly derived from Pierre Bourdieu's *Distinction*, there are some important differences between Bourdieu's approach and that of the sources I consider here. For Bourdieu, the working class forms a touchstone of authenticity that reproaches the pretensions of the aspiring middle class, and the dialects of France are natural and authentic in contrast to the acquired language of the mandarinate. See, e.g., *Distinction* (p. 179) and *Language and Symbolic Power* (pp. 46–49). As we shall see, *Mudan ting* anticipates and refutes such sentiments regarding the authenticity of the vernacular, showing instead that the vernacular is as allusive as the language of the elite.

67. This scene slyly refers to a literary predecessor text that mocks the pomposity and irrelevance of such official visits. Liu Zongyuan's essay lauding Camel Guo, the "ancestor" of Liu's Mengmei's gardener, likens a gardener who harms his trees by shaking the roots to see if they are still planted firmly to an official who increases the burden of his people with

On taking the stage, Du Bao announces that he has come to collect the *Bin feng* 豳風 (Airs of Bin), the earliest songs among the *Guofeng*. His statement refers to the traditional notion that officials journeyed to the countryside to collect folk songs (*cai shi* 采詩) in order to discern the concerns of the people.[68] Du Bao's excursion offers him an opportunity to create an allusive tableau in which he envisions himself as an incarnation of the ancients. Referring to an anecdote from the *Han Shu* 漢書 (History of the Han), Du Bao reveals that he sees himself as a latter-day Zheng Hong 鄭弘, who on just such a visit to encourage the farmers spotted a white deer that portended his ascent to prime minister:[69]

From eave of thatch comes call of dove
my crimson carriage draws forth the stag
as once the white deer, happy omen
followed the good Zheng Hong
and I shall rest "beneath the sweet apple's shade."[70]

The elders of the village mock the social scripting of such meetings between prefect and people: "The prefect in his tour of inspection / Riding in benevolent state / No doubt will proclaim the virtues of toil in the fields?"[71] Du Bao catechizes the farmers: "Uncles, do you understand the reasons for my spring excursion?"[72] The farming scene begins to echo the schoolroom scene. Unlike Chunxiang, however, the farmers speak from the same script as Du Bao. Their responses are properly schooled and seem generated through a rote mimicry of phrases.

"In the past we had official messengers all day long and watches to stand against thieves at night. But when Your Honor came to us:

---

frequent visitations to give unnecessary orders such as "Name your children!" and "Feed your animals!" (Liu Zongyuan, *Liu Zongyuan quanji*, p. 145).

68. On the mythologization of the Han dynasty Music Bureau's collection of local songs, see Egan, "Reconsidering the Role of Folk Songs."

69. See "Zheng Hong zhuan" (The biography of Zheng Hong) in Fan Ye, *Hou Han shu*, 4: 1154.

70. Tang, *Mudan ting*, p. 35; Birch, *The Peony Pavilion*, p. 31. In using the phrase "sweet apple's shade," Du Bao likens himself to the Earl of Zhao (召伯) Ji Hu 姬虎 of the Zhou dynasty; the phrase is an allusion to the *Shi jing* poem "Gan tang" 甘棠 (sweet apple), which commemorates a tree beloved of the earl (*Shi jing zhuxi*, p. 38–40).

71. Tang, *Mudan ting*, p. 36; Birch, *The Peony Pavilion*, p. 32.

72. Tang, *Mudan ting*, p. 37; Birch, *The Peony Pavilion*, p. 33.

[*sing*] In a thousand hamlets harvests flourished.
As reverence was shown in ancient days, so now
we elders 'carry incense bowls on our heads'
while children 'ride on hobbyhorse to hail you.'
Like a 'two-legged summer sun'
you warm our humble homes.
'By moonlight no dog yaps at chrysanthemums,
when rain is past men go to plough fresh fields.'
Truly welcome you are as rain and dew
To hemp and mulberry."[73]

As low characters, the village elders not only mirror but mock the pretensions of the elite. Their excessive quotation mimics the scholasticism of Du Bao and Tutor Chen in a more vernacular register. In their lyrics, the elders employ a more familiar sort of allusion than the literary references Du Bao employs, adorning their speech with proverbs (*cheng yu*) 成 語 and literary allusions to other vernacular texts. The lines "By moonlight no dog yaps at chrysanthemums / when rain is past men go to plough fresh fields" are drawn from the opening lines of the Yuan *zaju* (northern drama) *Qu jiang chi* 曲江池 (Tunes of rivers and ponds), in which they are spoken to set the scene by the first actor to appear on stage.[74] Thus in describing their own village, the elders allude to a theatrical text and to the invocation of a setting within that text.

Du Bao and his retinue soon form the audience for a literal performance of rusticity. When a farmer singing offstage (*nei ge*) 內歌 is heard, Du Bao hushes everyone on stage: "We ought to listen to the folk song of this village." The farmer sings:

Slippery mud,
Sloppery thud,
Short rake, long plough, catch 'em as they slide.
After rainy night sow rice and hemp,
When sky clears fetch out the muck,
Then a stink like long-pickled fish floats on the breeze.[75]

---

73. Tang, *Mudan ting*, p. 37; Birch, *The Peony Pavilion*, pp. 33–34.
74. *Qu jiangchi*, in *Yuan qu xuan*, p. 263.
75. Tang, *Mudan ting*, p. 37; Birch, *The Peony Pavilion*, p. 34.

Du Bao applauds the performance with a "well sung." He then subjects the folk song to exegesis as though it were a classical poem: "'Then a stink like long-pickled fish floats on the breeze'—that would be referring to the stench of manure." "But uncles," Du Bao protests, "he doesn't realize that manure is really fragrant. There is a poem to prove it." Du Bao then quotes a poem in the classical style that he misreads to insist that manure is more fragrant than ambergris:

> Incense burns, cauldrons
>   are heaped high to honor the prince,
> foods costly as gold or jade
>   plied for his delectation.
> But when to a starving stomach
>   comes a whiff of plain boiled rice
> then ambergris itself fails to match
>   the fragrance of manure.[76]

Du Bao's misguided pedantry forms an apt parallel to Tutor Chen's. Although he comes to gather folk songs in order to understand the sentiments of the people, he woefully misunderstands their songs and comically insists on the primacy of classical text over contemporary experience. According to his classical lexicon, shit smells good. His faith in the universal applicability of randomly selected classical models leads him to ignore empirical circumstances, not to mention the evidence of his senses.

The schoolroom scenes oppose the authenticity of the vernacular to the theatricality of the pedant's relation to the classical past. The farming scenes elaborate on that opposition. The simplicity of the farmers' song contrasts with the excessive claims of the court poem that Du Bao quotes, and the song's presumed spontaneity underscores the self-consciousness of Du Bao's exegesis in the classical style. In the farming community, there is no literary past. In Du Bao's world, the burden of the past is an obstacle to perception.

Du Bao and Tutor Chen's relation to poetry is false in that it is always mediated. They view contemporary circumstances through the prism of literary allusion, and classical texts through the prism of commentary.

---

76. Tang, *Mudan ting*, p. 37; Birch, *The Peony Pavilion*, p. 34.

Canonical texts are invoked as the authoritative discourse of officialdom
and are used to signal social position. Once allusions to canonical texts
have been dragged into contexts far removed from their originals, however, they point to the act of alluding itself rather than to the sources from
which they were drawn. Yet despite the contrast between the spontaneity
of vernacular orality and the self-consciousness of classical exegesis, we
find that the language of the "low" characters echoes the theatricality and
even the allusivity of the elite. The lyricism of the elders' allusions to
agrarian life and the farmer's opportune performance of a rustic song
points to the dubiousness of the equation of the vernacular with authenticity.[77]

The association of the vernacular language with authenticity depends
on its alignment not only with the local but with the somatic. Yet, just as
the farming scene proves the local and agrarian to be a literary fantasy, so
the somatic is often aligned with the phantasmic in this play. It is only in
her dreams or as a ghost, for example, that Du Liniang can act spontaneously on her passion. Once Du Liniang comes back to life, she can no
longer act artlessly and is no longer guided by desire. If the play is populated by phantasms—ghosts that wander out of place—so, too, is its vision of the vernacular language. The vernacular joins Du Liniang's ghost
and her portrait as a simulacrum that becomes, almost paradoxically, the
locus of the somatic and the authentic. Rather like the farming village, the
"vernacular" is a performative space that portrays itself as the locus of authenticity.

---

77. Indeed, this is a point that can be made not just with reference to *Mudan ting* but
to the *chuanqi* itself. Although in performance, the dialogue of the low characters might
well have been spoken in local dialect, the vernacular language employed in the dialogue of
chuanqi is in fact not the local dialect that farmers or maids would speak in real life, but
guanhua (literally, "official's language"), the *lingua franca* of officialdom. Ironically, the
plain language of the locals is voiced in a "dialect" of the elite that is explicitly supralocal.
Patrick Hanan defines *guanhua* as a "semi-standardized version of the Northern dialect
groups. He notes that "some version of [the] Northern [dialect group] had been used, at
least since the Tang dynasty, even for writers who lived . . . outside the area. . . . Vernacular
authors took some pains to avoid words and idioms with too narrow a currency and tended to choose a vocabulary intelligible within the whole Northern area" (Hanan, *The Chinese Short Story*, p. 2).

Tang Xianzu and Anti-archaism

The satirization of pedantry as theatrical in *Mudan ting* illuminates the use of the figure of the theater in the anti-archaist writings of Tang Xianzu's extended literary network. The scholar Xu Shuofang has discussed Tang Xianzu's anti-archaism in detail, and Cheng Pei-kai and David T. Roy have documented the friendship of Tang Xianzu with a number of cultural luminaries who voiced anti-archaist sentiments.[78] Tang Xianzu hailed as his teacher the playwright Xu Wei, who encouraged him in his anti-archaism. Similarly, Tang Xianzu had a deep sense of intellectual kinship with the Yuan brothers Hongdao, Zongdao, and Zhongdao.[79] Although there is no record of Tang's having met the famed iconoclast Li Zhi, the two shared a teacher, Luo Rufang 羅汝芳, and Xu Shuofang believes Li to have been a major influence on Tang Xianzu.[80]

Tang Xianzu's limited prose writing that touches on the subject of archaism anticipates the later writings of the Yuan brothers.[81] In his preface for a volume entitled *He qi* 合奇 (Compilation of the strange) compiled by his acquaintance Qiu Zhaolin 丘兆麟 (1572–1629), he disparages pedantry and inauthenticity in literary composition and links it to archaist citation: "The world is dominated by old Confucian scholars with whom it is impossible to discuss literary art. Their ears have not heard much, and their eyes have not seen much, yet they spew forth their superficial and

---

78. See Cheng, "Tang Hsien-tsu, Tung Chi-ch'ang, and the Search for Cultural Aesthetics in the Late Ming"; and idem, "Reality and Imagination." See also David T. Roy, "The Case for T'ang Hsien-tsu's Authorship of the *Jin Ping Mei*."

79. Tang met frequently with them in Beijing in the winter of 1594; see Cheng, "T'ang Hsien-tsu, Tung Ch'i-ch'ang and the Search for Cultural Aesthetics in the Late Ming."

80. Xu Shuofang (*Xu Shuofang ji*, 4: 205) notes that Tang was an avid reader of Li Zhi's work; he tried, for example, to procure a copy of Li Zhi's *Fen shu* 焚書 (A book to burn) from friends as soon as it was published.

81. Xu, *Xu Shuofang ji*, 4: 211–12. Xu notes that although Tang anticipates the sentiments of the Gong'an, he also seems to engage in a veiled criticism of them. Xu views the poems of the archaists as "fake antiques" (*jia gudong* 假古董) and the writing of the Gong'an as too slick (*you hua* 油滑), praising Tang's individualism in both poetic practice and theory (see ibid., 4: 212).

prejudiced opinions. . . . I say that the miraculous qualities of prose do not result from following another's example and becoming exactly like him."[82]

Xu Shuofang argues that Tang Xianzu's career suffered because he refused to espouse archaism: social relations with the dominant advocate of archaism, Wang Shizhen 王世貞 (1526–90), and his brother, Wang Shimou 王世懋 (1536–88), who happened to be Tang's direct superior in the Bureau of Rites of Nanjing, became difficult and strained.[83] Wang Shizhen advocated the Western Han as a model for prose and the High Tang as a model for poetry.[84] In contrast, Tang took the Six Dynasties as his poetic model and favored the Song essayists. Thus it was difficult for Tang to rhyme poems with Wang's clique at banquets.[85] Archaism or anti-archaism were not purely literary theoretical views but were imbricated in the politics of the day.[86] Xu Shuofang observes that Xu Wei objected

---

82. Tang Xianzu, "He qi xu" 合奇序, in *Tang Xianzu quan ji*, p. 1138, translated in Lynn, "Alternate Routes to Self-Realization," p. 335. Also see Xu Shuofang's discussion of this letter in *Xu Shuofang ji*, 1: 370.

83. Xu Shuofang, *Xu Shuofang ji*, 4: 211.

84. Ibid.

85. Ibid., 1: 371. In a letter to Wang Shizhen's eldest son, Zhansheng, Tang Xianzu confessed that in his youth, he had criticized the compositions of Wang and the other leaders of the archaist school with his friends. Commenting on the archaists' dependence on quotations from the Han histories and Tang poetry, Tang Xianzu and his friends concluded that despite the great accomplishments of the archaists, an archaist poetics could never explain in any depth even the most basic fundamentals of the literary spirit. This letter was probably written in 1594, four years before the completion of *The Peony Pavilion*. At the time, someone told Wang Shizhen of Tang's daring critique. Wang merely smiled and said, "Tang is editing my writing, and there will come a day when others edit his writing." Tang concluded his anecdote by telling Wang's son, "When I heard of this, I was chagrinned and said, 'I am ashamed before his generosity.'" ("Da Wang Zhansheng," in *Tang Xianzu quanji*, p. 1303). The incident is also mentioned in Qian Qianyi's biography of Tang Xianzu in his *Liechao shiji xiaozhuan*, pp. 562–64. Although Tang's letter to Wang Zhansheng sounds apologetic, Xu Shuofang characterizes Tang Xianzu's attitude toward Wang Shizhen and his clique as embittered. Tu Long, considered one of the Latter Five Masters of the archaist school, wrote a letter to Tang begging him to have more respect for Wang Shizhen. Tu Long flattered him, saying that Tang and Wang Shizhen were "two sages" "perched on the same branch," who should "join shoulders." Tang's reply was curt; see Xu Shuofang, *Xu Shuofang ji*, 1: 373.

86. For example, Xu Shuofang notes that before Wang Shizhen and Li Panlong 李攀龍 achieved high official rank, they flattered the scholar Xie Zhen 謝榛, one of the elders among the Latter Seven Masters of the archaist school. Later, when they were sufficiently secure in their careers, they turned against him. Li Panlong insultingly compared Xie Zhen

not so much to the archaists' mimetic poetics as to their monopoly over the making or breaking of literary reputations. It was not merely the archaists' practice of imitative citation that irked the anti-archaists; their dominance of officialdom proved vexing as well.

Because the anti-archaism of Li Zhi, Xu Wei, and the Gong'an School have been amply discussed elsewhere, here I will merely explore the cultural politics that underlie their critique of the theatricality of archaist citation.[87] A number of the passages cited below are well known, but it is worth re-examining them to underscore the significance of the figure of the theater. Li Zhi's essay "Tongxin shuo" 童心説 (The childlike mind), considered one of the first sallies against archaism, railed against the inauthenticity that archaism had brought to literary discourse. Li Zhi contrasted the childlike mind, unsullied by social aspiration or cramped by the burden of literary tradition, to the theatricality of a literary world populated by social aspirants. "When false literature is spoken of with false people, then false people delight. There is nothing that is not false, and nothing that does not delight them. The whole theater is false, and how can the dwarves argue?"[88] Li Zhi portrays a literary arena that feeds on spectacle and is populated by mental dwarves who applaud whether or not they comprehend what is taking place on stage. Not only authors but those who constitute their audiences, it seems, are actors on a public stage.

Li Zhi places the blame for the theatricality of literary culture on the imitative poetics of the literary archaists, who take the words of the ancients as "absolute truths that can be applied to the problems of all eternity." Li Zhi's disciple Yuan Zongdao stated even more clearly that the archaists had introduced a new theatricality (and inauthenticity) to literary

---

to the famous catamite of the duke of Wei, who cried at the thought of how he would be abandoned once the duke found a new favorite. In an inconceivable affront, Li compared himself to the duke. See Xu Shuofang, *Xu Shuofang ji*, 1: 368.

87. Billeter, *Li Zhi*; Chou Chih-p'ing, *Yüan Hung-tao and the Kung-an School*; Chaves, *Pilgrim of the Clouds*; idem, "A Panoply of Images"; Hung, "Yüan Hung-tao and the Late Ming Literary and Intellectual Movement"; Levy, "Un document sur la querelle des anciens et des modernes more sinico"; and John Wang, *Chin Sheng-t'an*.

88. Li Zhi, "Tongxin shuo," in *Li Shi fen shu / Xu fen shu*, p. 117. Chaves (*Pilgrim of the Clouds*, p. 347) notes that although Li Zhi does not specifically mention the archaist school in this essay, "there can be little doubt that he has in mind" the archaist "masters and their followers."

discourse. Authors who use trite archaic expressions, Yuan claimed, are like "actors on a stage. Although there is no happiness in their hearts, they must force themselves to smile; although there is nothing to inspire sorrow, they must force themselves to cry; under these circumstances, they have no option but to borrow models falsely."[89] In an essay entitled "Gui zhen" 貴眞 (Valuing authenticity), Jiang Yingke, a friend of the Yuan brothers, compared the archaist to an actor costumed as an official:

> Now as for composing poetry, if poems derive from what is authentic (*zhen* 眞), even if they are not exquisite in every regard, they will definitely be interesting (*qu* 趣). If their origin is in falseness (*jia* 假), they will not necessarily lack for the exquisite, but even so, they will not have *qu*. Consider a scholar-official of our sort, in an official's robe and wide sash. Even if his countenance is unimpressive and his physique unprepossessing, people will definitely respect him, impressed by his authenticity. If there were an actor of heroic countenance and imposing stature, and one gave him an official's robes and caps, he might seem dignified, but still people would look down upon him, scorning his falseness. I remember that once someone sent a composition to Wang Yangming asking for his tutelage. Wang commented, "This paragraph is like the Zuo 左 commentary, this paragraph resembles the work of Ban Gu 班固, and these paragraphs resemble the writing of Han Yu and Liu Zongyuan." The person was greatly pleased. Someone asked Wang Yangming about it, and he replied, "In commenting on those authors he resembles, I meant precisely to say that he does not compose on his own, but seeks to be like others. It's as though a boy did up his hair in child's fashion and straightened his clothes to greet guests, solemnly believing himself to be worthy of respect. If you made a child wear a mask and a false beard, and had him hunch his back and cough, people would only laugh. What would there be to respect?" In light of this, we know that compositions that resemble others' are never the best compositions, and poems are an example of this. [90]

As Li Zhi did in "Tongxin shuo," Jiang Yingke derides the inauthenticity of archaist imitation by contrasting the falseness of stage acting with the innocence and authenticity of the child. A child is worthy of respect in his own right; it is not necessary to costume him as an elder for him to gain respect. Similarly, literary composition should be innocent and uninhibi-

---

89. Yuan Zongdao, "Lun wenxia," in Kong Decheng, *Ming Qing sanwen xuan zhu*, p. 93.

90. Jiang Yingke, *Jiang Yingke ji*, 1: 807.

ted. A composition that strives to resemble the ancients is as false as a child costumed as an old man or an actor costumed as an official.

Jiang's metaphor of the actor, whose impersonation of the official fools no one despite his apparently imposing nature, ties the problem of inauthenticity in literary composition to the problem of impersonation within the scholar-official class. It is almost as if archaist imitation permitted a kind of sumptuary violation. For if imitation were all that were required, anyone could be a poet. Just as an actor's donning of an official's robes marked a sumptuary transgression that, Jiang insisted, was readily apparent to the spectator, the poorly educated use allusions that should be reserved for those with a distinguished educational pedigree. Jiang's use of the telltale phrase "our sort" (*wo bei* 我輩) to describe the ruggedly honest official who is the antithesis of the actor suggests that he distinguishes an elite whose authenticity is unquestionable from the "actors" who have apparently entered officialdom.

Jiang, of course, was not worried about stage actors becoming officials.[91] The metaphor merely speaks to his concern regarding imposture and impersonation in the realms of officialdom. The archaists' promotion of an imitative poetics, the anti-archaists feared, allowed men without deep learning to seem cultivated. Yuan Hongdao likened those who superficially cite the ancients to acquire social prestige to the sons of wealthy families who "depend upon their family's might" to impose their will on others:

The people of today take delight in the Tang; I say the Tang had no poetry; they take delight in the [prose of the] Qin and Han, but I say they had no essays. . . . The people of today . . . smack their lips at little pieces of shit and take advantage of the opportunity to hold their mouths open to catch farts. They use their power to cheat the good, just like those sons of Suzhou nowadays who depend on their family's might. They remember a few well-known stories and call that erudition; they use a few commonly seen phrases and call themselves poets. . . . If we call this poetry, then one can find poetry anywhere. I hate them so deeply that my censure of them is sometimes rather extreme.[92]

---

91. Numerous prohibitions barred actors from participating in the examination system; see, e.g., *Da Ming huidian* 大明匯典, 77.25a, cited in Hansson, *Chinese Outcasts*, p. 42.

92. Yuan Hongdao, "Zhang Youyu" 張幼于, in *Yuan Zhonglang suibi*, pp. 99–101.

Like the *xiucai* who claimed to delight in Yama's fart, the "people of to-day" (*shi ren* 世人, a phrase that also suggests contamination by worldly concerns) "hold their mouths open to catch farts," pandering to current poetic fashion as they profess delight in the poets of the Tang. The Yuan brothers' ire was not directed at the archaists' poetics but at a type of person who expected to gain social recognition for compositions that substituted allusive citation for true learning. Although the Yuan brothers protested that they were criticizing not the most prominent proponents of archaism but their derivative followers, inevitably both groups were tarred by the same brush.

This concern that allusive citation had come to function as a false sign of literary learning, that hollow imitation was allowing the insufficiently cultivated to engage in sumptuary violation of a literary nature, should be considered in the context of more general anxieties regarding the gullibility of social spectators.[93] Since literary renown was one of the primary means of social advancement in seventeenth-century China, concerns about sumptuary violation easily spilled over into this arena. Jean-Christophe Agnew, in a discussion of the interplay of the discursive worlds of the theater and the marketplace in early modern England, suggests that the development of a mercantile economy in England introduced an anxiety regarding the mercurial, unsteady quality of social relations.[94] The seventeenth-century English poet John Hall observed, for example, that "man in business is but a Theatricall person, and in a manner but personates himself . . . in his retired and hid actions, he pulls off his disguise and acts openly."[95] Agnew points to a sense of looming crisis in representation in seventeenth-century England, a concern that "traditional signs and symbols had metamorphosed into detached and manipulable commodities."[96]

The emergence of a mercantile class in China created, as it did in Europe, a new anxiety. With the ability to purchase signs of distinction previously associated with talent or birth, scholarship itself was becoming

---

93. See Brook, *Confusions of Pleasure*, pp. 219–22.

94. J Agnew, *Worlds Apart*, pp. 59–61.

95. Hall, *The Advancement of Learning*, pp. 36–38; quoted in Agnew, *Worlds Apart*, p. 97.

96. Agnew, *Worlds Apart*, p. 97.

commodified as the purchase of the *shengyuan* or *jiansheng* 監生 degrees became more common.[97] The concern about the commodification of literary learning extended to the critique of the archaist practice of citation. For if the words of the ancients are not internalized but simply external symbols, they become a kind of currency. Just as money has the potential to become a floating signifier detached from gold, the citations of the archaists have the potential to be floating signifiers detached from the original words of the ancients.

What would prevent the words of the ancients from becoming a floating currency? The anti-archaists argued that literary expression must be internally anchored in *qing* (passion). (As Richard Lynn has shown, the archaists in fact did not dispute this, a fact that their opponents conveniently ignored.) *Qing*, the most important term in seventeenth-century literary discourse, is variously translated as "passion," "emotion," "feeling," and "sentiment," but it refers to the possession of feeling as much as feeling itself. In an oft-cited passage, the playwright Xu Wei argued that *qing* was precisely the quality the archaists lacked:

If a person imitates a bird's voice, even if his voice is that of a bird, his nature is still that of a man. If a bird imitates a person, even if it does sound like a person, its nature is still that of a bird. How are those who write poems today different from this? They do not write from what they know and simply steal things people once said, saying that such and such a piece is in such and such a style, and such and such a piece is not, that such and such a phrase is like that of such and such an author, and such and such a phrase is not. Although their works are crafted and refined, they cannot avoid seeming like birds imitating the speech of men. Now my friend Zisu's poems are not of that sort. His passion (*qing*) is frank and straightforward.[98]

Xu Wei then describes the quality of Zisu's *qing* in great detail and concludes that those who write with passion will "speak from what they know, rather than resorting to what people once said." In other words, only those with no *qing* resort to citing the ancients. The issue is not education but ontology. A bird cannot become a man. At best it can learn to

---

97. See Brokaw, *The Ledgers of Merit and Demerit*, p. 5.

98. Xu Wei, "Ye Zisu shixu" 葉子肅詩序, in Liu Shide, *Mingdai sanwen xuanzhu*, pp. 102–3.

speak and become a parrot. It is passion that distinguishes people from parrots, and *qing* cannot be learned.

Xu Wei's invocation of passion is both elitist and populist. If passion is what the archaist pedant lacks, it is something that even the untutored may have. The straightforward expression so valued by the anti-archaists could not be learned, acquired, or imitated. At the same time, there were no objective criteria by which *qing* might be measured. Rather, it was the special prerogative of the anti-archaists to detect it in the writings of others. In promoting such nebulous values, the anti-archaists appealed to an "ideology of innate tastes," to use Bourdieu's phrase, that could easily be used "to distinguish those who had inherited cultural capital from those who had more recently acquired it."[99] The archaists' prescriptions for poetic form were arguably less elitist; any educated person could follow them.

The poetics of the anti-archaists, their valuation of the spontaneity and simplicity of the untutored, has been characterized as radical and subversive in comparison with that of the archaists. Yet, as Chou Chih-p'ing has argued, the notion that archaism is inherently conservative is mistaken.[100] Moreover, as Chou has shown, it was the archaist poets who first promoted the simple language of the common folk and opposed an imitative poetics.[101] Ironically, the archaists were the first to criticize the shallow imitations of the insufficiently learned and to use the figure of the theater to deride the instrumental use of allusion by the socially aspiring poet.[102] The cultural politics of the anti-archaists were ultimately no less exclusive and no less complex than those of the archaists themselves.

A caveat is in order: the attacks of the advocates of vernacular literature were so witty and so abusive that they have determined the terms of the debate. But not only were many of their arguments borrowed from

---

99. Bourdieu, *Distinction*, p. 74.

100. Chou Chih-p'ing, *Yüan Hung-tao and the Kung-an School*, p. 4.

101. Ibid., p. 8.

102. Li Mengyang, the most prominent of the early archaists, derided the mannerism of poetry after the High Tang: "How is this any different from going into the marketplace and clawing for gold or getting up on stage and posturing a role! Are there such who, when they see someone wearing a scholar's cap and jade pendants at his waist, do not grow timid, cast down their pens and run away? Why is this so? It is because they are ashamed at not being *junzi* 君子 (true gentleman)" (Guo Shaoyu, *Zhongguo wenxue piping shi*, p. 614, translated in Lynn, "Alternate Routes to Self-Realization," p. 324).

the archaists, but Li Zhi and the Yuan brothers were far from immune to imitation of the ancients.[103] During the late Ming, re-enactments of famed literary gatherings of the past were in vogue.[104] Yuan Zhongdao published a dialogue between Li Zhi and the Yuan brothers in which they re-enacted Confucius's dialogue with his disciples regarding their aims.[105] As the dialogue begins, Li Zhi suggests: "Why doesn't each of us name a great master who resembles himself?" Li Zhi's question inverts the relation between ancients and moderns—the simplest form of iconoclasm. But the effort required to maintain such iconoclastic inversions becomes clear by the end of the dialogue, in which the precedence of the ancients is ultimately reasserted.

Each member of the party seeks to model himself on someone who acknowledges no master: all the disciples cite predecessors famed for their spontaneity, eccentricity, and iconoclasm. Surprisingly, Li Zhi cuts all of them down, telling them that their aims are too high. The dialogue clearly reveals that they *have* a master: Li Zhi, who artfully plays on the power relations between master and disciple. The disciples choose Laozi as a fitting predecessor for Li Zhi. As Yuan Hongdao's letter to Zhang Youyu tells us, it was the rhetorical abusiveness of Laozi and Zhuangzi and the iconoclasm of Xunzi that the Yuan brothers admired.[106] Yet even though these comparisons explicitly reject Confucius and the normativity he represents, this dialogue is implicitly modeled after Confucius's famous dialogue with his disciples.[107] As the dialogue ends, Li Zhi rummages for the appropriate epithets to bestow on his disciples. Yuan Zongdao, he states, resembles

---

103. For the term *qu* and its history in archaist writing before the anti-archaists adopted it, see Chaves, *Pilgrim of the Clouds*, p. 346.

104. See, e.g., James Cahill's discussion of a painting in the archaist style by Chen Hongshou that portrays the Yuan brothers at a meeting of their literary club, the Grape Society. Cahill notes that the depiction echoes Li Gonglin's earlier portrayal of the White Lotus Society. "The implication is not that the Grape Society was a recreation of the White Lotus Society, but only that to portray the Grape Society meeting as though it were merely a modern, unprecedented event would somehow demean it" (Cahill, *Compelling Image*, pp. 129–31).

105. *Ke xue zhai waiji* 柯雪齋外集, 15.7b; reprinted in Aying 阿英, *Hai shi ji* 海市集, pp. 175–78; cited in Hung, "Yuan Hongdao," p. 81.

106. Yuan Hongdao, *Yuan Zhonglang suibi*, pp. 99–101. See also Hung, "Yuan Hongdao," p. 104.

107. See *Lunyu jishi*, pp. 797–807.

Huang Xian 黄憲 in his talent and Guan Ning 管寧 in his insight.[108] Ultimately, Li Zhi's original iconoclastic question, "Which of the ancients resemble us?" turns into a more familiar question: "Which of the ancients do we resemble?"

We find a similar amnesia in the relation of the twentieth-century vernacular movement to that of the seventeenth century. The seventeenth-century advocates of the vernacular claimed that the folk songs of their day would become the classics of tomorrow. Little did they suspect that they would, three centuries later, become the ancients upon whose words the twentieth-century vernacular movement would draw. In 1917, the primary architect of the vernacular movement, Hu Shi 胡適 (1891–1962), espoused a program of "Eight Don'ts"—practices to avoid in literary composition. Blaming the inferiority of modern Chinese literature on the archaist practice of citation, Hu Shi wrote, "As a result of my study . . . I have come to the conclusion that we must start with the following eight principles if we want to achieve a literary revolution."[109] His pronouncements sound startlingly familiar. "Avoid using allusions to classical texts"; "Do not copy the writings of those of ages past"; "Do not write about being happy or sad when you are not happy or sad."[110] In the last of these, we see a surreptitious allusion to Yuan Zongdao's disparagement of the archaists as actors who pretend to be happy or sad when they are not happy or sad. These "Eight Don'ts" are no more than a baldly reductive restatement of Yuan Zongdao's "Lun wen" 論文 (Essay on literature). Hu Shi's eight points became the battle cry of the New Literature movement. Yet, no one remarked on Hu Shi's imitative citation until Zhou Zuoren noted it fifteen years later, in 1932.[111] It is the ultimate irony that Hu Shi was himself an archaist of the stripe that his seventeenth-century predecessors derided.

---

108. Huang Xian (75–122) was a scholar of the Latter Han; Guan Ning (158–241), a recluse of the Three Kingdoms period.

109. Hu Shi, *Hu Shi wencun*, 1: 5–17. See also Chow Tse-tung, *The May Fourth Movement*, pp. 29–30, 274; and Hung, "Yuan Hongdao," pp. 172–73.

110. See Hung, "Yuan Hongdao," pp. 172–73.

111. Zhou Zuoren spoke about the debt of Hu Shi to the Yuan brothers in his lectures at Furen University in Beijing in 1932; see ibid., p. 281; and Pollard, *A Chinese Look at Literature*, p. 158.

Conclusion

In this chapter, I have argued that Du Liniang's authentic passion (*zhenqing*), for which *Mudan ting* is so famed, must be understood against the backdrop of Tang Xianzu's criticism of the highly theatrical social discourse of the followers of archaism. The staginess of the archaists' allusive discourse provides a foil for the "vernacular" reception of literary texts first modeled by Du Liniang's maid, Chunxiang. Chunxiang's vernacular rereading of classical texts inspires Du Liniang's tour of the garden, and at first seems refreshingly unpretentious in contrast to the utilitarian employment of classical texts by Du Bao, Liu Mengmei, and Tutor Chen. However, Tang Xianzu quickly reveals that a "vernacular" reading of texts is not necessarily any more authentic than archaist allusion, as Shi Daogu's and Chen Zuiliang's ludicrous misreadings of the *Qianzi jing* and *Shi jing* attest. Indeed, in the farming scenes we see that the vernacular can be slyly allusive, that it forms not so much a counterpart to archaism as a parody of it.

I framed my discussion of *Mudan ting* with late Ming jokes regarding pedantry as well as the Gong'an's anti-archaist writings in order to show how Tang Xianzu drew from both these sources in mocking the pedantry of those who employ archaist citation as a kind of social credential. The Gong'an used the simple equation of social and theatrical roles—and the accompanying notion of seeing through imposture—to engage in a socially conservative and somewhat elitist critique of a stratum of society anxious to demonstrate its learning but unable to do so in a socially appropriate fashion. Tang Xianzu invoked the cultural politics of authenticity laid out by the Gong'an but never fully aligned himself with the Gong'an critique. *Mudan ting*'s own position is more elegant and nuanced. In *Mudan ting*, the vernacular does not form a locus of authenticity as it does for the Gong'an. The vernacular, instead, forms a kind of false bottom. It, too, is staged and thus is an unstable source of authority. Rather than suggesting that authenticity lies in the impassioned or straightforward literary expression one might associate with the vernacular, the play locates authenticity entirely outside literary expression, restricting it to the passion of Du Liniang.

Few texts could seem as disparate from *Mudan ting* as the play that is the subject of our next chapter, *Nan wanghou* (The male queen). Roughly contemporaneous with *Mudan ting* but nearly forgotten, *Nan wanghou* is a campy farce that features a young boy who seduces the future Emperor Qian of the Chen dynasty. The emperor has him adopt women's clothes and crowns him queen. As the cross-dressed boy engages in a sort of allusive investiture of gender, claiming his right to rule by cloaking himself in a series of historical allusions to the most famed consorts and concubines of the past, this play takes *Mudan ting*'s concerns regarding the instrumental use of allusion to a ludicrous conclusion. Ultimately, *Nan wanghou* moves beyond *Mudan ting*'s concern that allusive reference might aid in a kind of social costuming, and questions not only the authority of the cultural past, but the very structure of allusive reference itself.

FOUR

Illusion and Allusion in Nan wanghou

In Chapter 36 of the late sixteenth-century novel *Jin Ping Mei*, the wealthy merchant Ximen Qing hires an acting troupe to entertain the first- and second-place graduates of the most recent palace examinations. Ximen Qing's personal servant Shutong dresses as a woman and performs with the actors of the troupe.[1] The second-place graduate, surnamed An 安, initially mistakes Shutong for one of the actors and is much taken with him. He asks for a song from the play *Yuhuan ji* 玉環記.[2] Shutong complies, singing the part of the chaste bride:

> From the time I was young to the time I was fifteen,
> The grace of my mother and father was as profound and vast as the sky.
> I am ashamed that there is nothing that I can do to repay them,
> This is something that troubles my heart.
> My husband and I have deeply absorbed my parents' favor,
> And I hope that my husband will be honored and distinguished.

The narrative continues:

An, the graduate of the palace examinations, was originally from Hangzhou, and his preference leaned toward the "Southern Mode" (*nan feng* 南風). When he saw that Shutong sang well, he took his hand, and the two of them drank one af-

---

1. "Shutong" means "servant in the study," but in the novel it is used as though it were a proper name.

2. Katherine Carlitz discusses this scene with reference to the play's didacticism in *The Rhetoric of "Chin P'ing Mei,"* pp. 115–16.

ter the other in turn. . . . [An and the top graduate, Cai 蔡,] played two games of chess underneath an awning while the actors sang two acts. Fearing that it was growing late, Ximen Qing gave the actors their fee and bade them leave. Only Shutong was left, and he waited on them and poured the wine. . . . Shutong was wearing a jade-colored jacket over a red skirt and a gold band round his waist. Holding the jade cup high, he lifted his wine and sang again. . . . That day they drank until night and then stopped to rest. Ximen Qing had beds spread with embroidered quilts of fine silk set up in the Hidden Spring Grotto and the Emerald Jade Dais, and sent Shutong and Dai'an 玳安 [his page] to wait on the guests.[3]

Shutong is expected not only to serve the guests wine but to serve them sexually after the performance ends, and this reinforces the sense of a solubility of the boundaries between the performance context and the performance itself.[4] At the same time, Shutong's erotic allure is enhanced by the incongruities between performance and performance context: between the bride's chastity and his promiscuity, between her feminine sentiments and his male body. Ximen Qing's friend Ying Bojue alludes to these incongruities when he exclaims after an earlier performance by Shutong: "The sound that issues from his throat is that of a flute. Why talk of those women of the bawdy houses. . . . We've heard all their songs! How could theirs be as luscious as his!"[5] Ying Bojue's remarks refer to Shutong's lusciousness both onstage and off, to his performance at the banquet as well as in the bedroom. His reference to Shutong's "flute" calls attention to the fact that Shutong has an instrument that the women of the bawdy houses do not have.[6] Shutong's performance of the role of the

---

3. *Jin Ping Mei cihua*, 36.6a–7b.

4. It was not uncommon for actors to perform at a banquet and then make themselves available for guests to fondle. We read about this practice, for example, in the notation book *Zhishi yuwen* 治世餘聞 (Sundry things I have heard about governing the realm), whose preface is dated 1521 (Chen Hongmo 陳洪謨, *Zhishi yuwen*, p. 53; cited in Brook, *Confusions of Pleasure*, p. 231).

5. *Jin Ping Mei cihua*, 35.14b.

6. The practice of fellatio is referred to as "playing the flute." Ying Bojue's words recall the recurrent debates as to the relative merits of women and boys in the vernacular literature of the late Ming and Qing. Such debates were possible precisely because it was presumed that the elite male might choose to have sexual relations with either sex. Even though the debates were partisan in the sense that they seem to describe sexual preferences that are exclusive, the underlying assumption was that the reader of the debate had a

chaste bride is in fact a seduction of An, a seduction set in motion by Ximen Qing, for whom Shutong is an object of exchange.

Such discussions of the erotic appeal of the cross-dressed actor's illusory stage gender might be viewed as far indeed from the anti-archaist's
concern with the deracinated quality of citation discussed in Chapter 3.
Yet they are conjoined in a relatively unknown play likely written not
long after *Jin Ping Mei*, Wang Jide's[7] northern drama *Nan wanghou* (The
male queen).[8] *Nan wanghou* is the only premodern Chinese play known
to me that takes a man who cross-dresses as a woman as its theme.[9] The
implied analogy between the cross-dressed boy who is the play's protagonist and the cross-dressed actor who plays him suggestively illuminates the
literati spectator's susceptibility to the charms of the cross-dressed male
actor. The social havoc that might ensue from the actor's manipulation of
the literati spectator becomes a subtext of the play. But more importantly,

----

choice. (Regarding such debates in ancient Greece, see David Halperin, "Historicizing the
Subject of Desire"; for such debates in premodern Japan, see Pflugfelder, *Cartographies of
Desire*, pp. 59–63).

7. Wang's date of birth is unknown, but Xu Shuofang suggests a date around 1542
based on the comment made by Xu Wei that Wang suggested the theme of Xu's play *Nü
zhuangyuan* 女狀元 (The female scholar). *Nü zhuangyuan* was finished in 1558, and Xu
postulates that Wang would probably have been at least sixteen at the time. See Wang Jide,
Qulü, in *Zhongguo gudian xiqu lunzhu jicheng*, 4:168; and Xu Shuofang, "Wang Jide
nianpu" 王驥德年譜, in *Xu Shuofang ji*, 3: 237–89.

8. A full translation of the play is provided in the Appendix, pp. 261–312. The play was
anthologized in *Sheng Ming zaju* 盛明雜劇 (Northern drama of the high Ming), an anthology whose preface dates to 1629, six years after Wang's death; see Shen Tai 沈泰, ed.
Sheng Ming zaju, 1: 1–29b (facsimile edition of an illustrated edition published by the
Song Fen studio). As mentioned in Chapter 2, note 19, we know that the play was composed before 1611 because the last two acts were compiled in the miscellany *Zhaijin qiyin*
published in 1611.

9. The singularity of *Nan wanghou* as a play about a male who cross-dresses as a woman
contrasts with the popularity of plays about women cross-dressing as men. Wang Jide's
teacher Xu Wei, for example, wrote two plays on the topic, *Nü zhuangyuan* and *Hua Mulan* 花木蘭 (The woman warrior). *Hua Mulan* has been one of the most popular plots in
Peking Opera; in regional theater the stories of the cross-dressed women Zhu Yingtai 祝
英台 and Meng Lijun 孟麗君 have also been popular. See Siu Leung Li, *Cross-Dressing in
Chinese Opera*, pp. 83–136. Shen Jing's *Bo xiao ji* 博笑記 (Tales to incite laughter) and Wu
Bing's 吳炳 (1595–1648) *Huazhong ren* 畫中人 (The person in the painting) include skits
that feature a cross-dressed actor; these plays, however, do not take this conceit as their
theme.

the play uses the illusoriness of the actor's stage gender as a point of departure to remark on the illusoriness of the literatus's primary inheritance,
the models of the cultural past. If *Mudan ting* mocked those who had an
unauthentic relation to the cultural past, *Nan wanghou* laughingly questions whether an authentic relation to the cultural past is possible. By
play's end, this exploration of the illusory quality of the historical also becomes an investigation of the rules that govern the relationships between
historical and dramatic (or fictional) texts.

The author of *Nan wanghou* was an aficionado of the theater who
composed the first full-length theoretical treatise on drama, the *Qulü* 曲
律 (Rules of drama).[10] Although as many as six *chuanqi* have been attributed to Wang Jide, all his plays have been lost save *Nan wanghou* and
Tihong ji 題紅記 (Poems written on red leaves), a drama authored by
Wang Jide's grandfather that Wang Jide revised during a childhood illness.[11] Wang was the son of a wealthy gentry family from Kuaiji 會稽
who had been connoisseurs of opera for several generations.[12] A bon vi-
vant who never served as an official and devoted himself to the theater,

---

10. Perhaps because Wang Jide seems not to have taken his *zaju* seriously, there seems
little relation between his *Qulü* and the themes of *Nan wanghou*. For scholarship on *Qulü*,
see Li Huimian, "Wang Jide qulun yanjiu"; Ye Changhai and Chen Duo's annotated edition of Wang's *Qulü*; and Ye Changhai's *Wang Jide "Qulü" yanjiu*. The most complete biographical information regarding Wang Jide is in "Wang Jide nianpu," in Xu Shuofang,
Xu Shuofang ji, 3: 237–89.

11. Although Fu Xihua (*Mingdai chuanqi quanmu*, pp. 164–67) attributes six southern
dramas to Wang, the authorship of all of them save for *Tihong ji* is uncertain. In two in-
stances, Wang's northern dramas seem to have been mistakenly listed as southern dramas
by collectors. All the northern dramas except for *Nan wanghou* have been lost.

12. A substantial proportion of Wang's works no longer survive. There were a collection of poems, *Fang zhu guan ji* 方諸館集 (The works of the Moondew Basin Retreat),
mentioned in the preface to *Qulü* and a collection of arias, *Fang zhu guan yuefu* 方諸館樂
府 (Ballads from the Moondew Basin Retreat). Besides *Qulü*, Wang penned two other
works that were guides for lyricists, the *Nanci zhengyun* 南詞正韻 (Correct rhymes for
southern lyrics) and *Shengyun fenhe tu* 聲韻分合圖 (A diagram of matching and un-
matching rhymes), neither of which is extant. His editions of plays have fared better. Although his edition of *Pipa ji* is no longer extant, his commentary to *Xixiang ji* survives. See
Wang Jide, "Xin jiaozhu guben *Xixiang ji* zixu" 新校注古本西廂記自序, in Cai Yi,
Zhongguo guben xiqu xuba huibian, 2: 656–57. An anthology edited by Wang of twenty
well-known Yuan plays was collected in the 1958 reprinting of premodern editions of dramatic texts *Guben xiqu congkan* 古本戲曲叢刊.

Wang had the means and the leisure to travel to Beijing to research the local dialect for his compilation of Yuan *zaju* (northern drama of the Yuan dynasty).[13] Wang was much acclaimed for his arias (*sanqu*), as well as his editions of *Xixiang ji* and *Pipa ji*. He seems to have considered his *zaju* trivial; *Nan wanghou* receives only a single mention in his *Qulü*.[14]

Wang Jide based *Nan wanghou* on two source narratives. The first is a biography of the general Han Zigao 韓子高, which appears in the dynastic histories of the Chen and of the Southern Dynasties.[15] The second is a vernacular tale of the late Ming based on the earlier biography.[16] At the

---

13. For a treatment of Wang's editions of Yuan drama, and in particular, his edition of the *Xixiang ji*, see Patricia Sieber, *Theaters of Desire*, pp. 137–161.

14. Because Wang Jide used a pseudonym in writing *Nan wanghou* that he used nowhere else, Qin lou waishi 秦樓外史 (The unofficial historian of the towers of Qin), the play was believed an anonymous work until Huang Wenyang, the compiler of the *Quhai zongmu tiyao*, noticed Wang's self-identification as the author of *Nan wanghou* in his *Qulü* (*Quhai zongmu tiyao*, 2: 589).

15. The biography of the Chen dynasty general Han Zigao appears in the *Chen shu* 陳書 (History of the Chen) and in the *Nan shi* 南史 (History of the Southern Dynasties). Focusing on Han Zigao's military exploits rather than his personal traits, it betrays no consciousness of a sexual liaison between Han Zigao and the Emperor Wen. However, in hindsight, it paves the way for the vernacular tale's suggestion of such a liaison. The physical description of Zigao, for example, emphasizes youth, beauty, and effeminacy, stating that at age sixteen his hair was still done in child's fashion, and his build was that of a woman. The biography also stresses the intimacy of the relationship between Zigao and Emperor Wen, particularly Zigao's ability to anticipate the emperor's needs. See Yao Silian, *Chen shu*, 20: 269–75; and Li Yanshou, *Nan shi*, 68: 1664.

16. The Ming compendium *Lüchuang nüshi* 綠窗女史 (History of women of the green windows) cites the Ming author Li Xu 李詡 as the author of its "Biography of Chen Zigao," on which *Nan wanghou* is based. This clears up a longstanding confusion over the story's authorship. A number of sources have inaccurately identified the author of the tale. The Qing catalogue of dramatic works *Quhai zongmu tiyao* declares the tale to have been the work of an otherwise unknown Li Yi 李翊 (Huang Wenyang, *Quhai zongmu tiyao*, p. 589). This attribution probably led Koake Takeshi (*Zhongguo tongxingai shilu*, p. 85) to mistakenly identify the story as the work of the Tang dynasty poet Li Yi 李翊, who was a friend of Han Yu's. The language of the story certainly does not indicate Tang authorship; were the tale by the Tang poet Li Yi, it would have had to have been rewritten by a late imperial author to reach its present form. Since the character *xu* 詡 differs from the character *yi* 翊 by only a few strokes, it seems likely that a mistake in transcription led to the false identification of the Tang author Li Yi as the author of the vernacular story. Like many other authors of the late Ming, Li Xu sat the civil service examinations repeatedly but never passed. Only one work of his is extant, *Jie'an laoren manbi*

opening of the play, a penniless young boy named Chen Zigao is seized by two soldiers of the King of Linchuan (the future Emperor Wen of the Chen dynasty [r. 560–66]).[17] Initially they plan to kill him, but noting his good looks, they decide to offer him to their king. The king, observing that Zigao is more seductive than any of the women in his harem, has the boy dress as a woman and crowns him queen. The boy's successful impersonation of a woman gives rise to an unusual comedy of errors. Soon the king's sister, Princess Yuhua 玉華, is after the queen. Not knowing that Zigao is a boy, the sister declares that this new queen is the most seductive woman she has ever seen. "Forget about my brother, a man, falling in love with her. I am a girl, and I wouldn't mind swallowing her down like a drink of cold water." Her maid offers to find her a "husband like that," but the princess insists that no man could compare. Thereupon, the princess's maid reveals to her that the object of her affections is, in fact, a boy. The princess is undeterred by this revelation and simply uses her privileged knowledge of the boy's true sex to blackmail him into marrying her. But her maid, who has had an interest in Zigao herself, exposes the marriage to the king. The king initially decides to behead both Zigao and the princess, but hesitates, unwilling to sacrifice his unique partner. Finally, the king reasons that if he allows his sister to formalize her marriage to Zigao, he and his sister can share the boy.[18]

My reading of *Nan wanghou* explores the ways in which the figure of the cross-dressed boy issues an optical and hermeneutical challenge to the

---

戒庵老人漫筆 (The casual notes from the cloister of renunciation of an old man) in eight *juan*, published by his grandson.

17. Zigao's name has been changed from Han to Chen, so that the King can joke that they have the same surname (*tong xing* 同姓).

18. The neat inversions that structure *Nan wanghou*'s plot can be attributed in part to the properties of *zaju* as a genre. The conventions of the *zaju* are quite different from those of *chuanqi*. Zaju are far shorter in length, conventionally four acts (although one to three acts are also possible). Partly for this reason, significance is produced differently in the *zaju* than in the *chuanqi*. The length of *chuanqi*, normally some fifty-odd acts, allows the juxtaposition of diverse modalities of speech. As noted in the previous chapter, in *chuanqi*, significance is produced through contrast: elite and rustic characters, classical and vernacular language, are compared to ironic effect. Any character in a *chuanqi* drama may sing, whereas in *zaju*, only one character per act has a singing role. Zaju are thus far more tightly constructed and tend to be more singleminded in their concerns than *chuanqi*. The tautness of the plot of a *zaju* allows for neat inversions impossible in the sprawling *chuanqi*.

spectator. Plays on perspective and perception are ubiquitous in late Ming and early Qing art and writing—in the paintings of Wu Bin 吳彬 (ca. 1543–ca. 1626) and Dong Qichang, in the classical tales of Pu Songling's *Liaozhai*, and in vernacular fiction such as the *Xiyou bu* 西遊補 (Sequel to the *Journey to the West*). In seventeenth-century writing about the theater, this interest in paradoxes of perception led to a privileging of indeterminacy that was, in turn, informed by Buddhist concerns regarding the evanescence of the world of forms. Wang Jide himself described the quality of "wondrous art" in his *Qulü* as "what Buddhism calls 'not arriving at and not departing from' (*bu ji bu li* 不即不離), having the appearance of being and yet not being there (*shi xiang fei xiang* 是相非相) . . . like a shadow cast by a lamp in a mirror."[19]

In Chinese aesthetics, this ethereal sense of indeterminacy is often described by the term *xu* 虛.[20] Like the term *qing*, the definition of *xu* is so inclusive that it may be used in a number of different ways by the same author. Because it embodies the principle of constant mutation, *xu* is even harder to define.[21] *Xu* designates ethereality and plasticity; it would describe, for example, the ability of mist or water to fill the shape of any container. Often translated as "empty," it "combines the notions of insubstantiality, elusiveness, and otherworldliness," as Stephen Owen has

---

19. Wang Jide, "Lun yongwu" 論詠物, in *Qulü, Zhongguo gudian xiqu lunzhu ji cheng*, 4: 134.

20. Although the term *xu* has a long history in criticism of painting and poetry, it was Wang Jide who incorporated the terms *xu* and *shi* into drama criticism and gave them a new significance in that context, applying them to the verifiability of historical material when used in allusion. (Wang was referring to a specific type of allusion, *yong shi* 用事, the employment of stories from official and unofficial histories in fictionalized treatments.) See Wang Jide, *Qulü*, in *Zhongguo gudian xiqu lunzhu jicheng*, 4: 154. Wang argued that verisimilitude in the theater need not be based on an artisanal conception of external likeness (*xingsi* 形似); rather, it should rest on an understanding of the internal qualities of the object imitated (*shensi* 神似). As we discussed in the Introduction, the distinction follows Su Shi's famous dictum that in painting bamboo, one should attempt not to achieve literal verisimilitude but rather to internalize the spirit of the bamboo.

21. A word is considered *xu* if its meaning cannot be fully defined or pinned down (the term *qing* is an excellent case in point), and for this reason words that have an emotive, subjective context are considered *xu*. As a linguistic term, "*xu* characters" (*xuzi* 虛字) are those that impart modality or indicate sentiment, such as the exclamatory *yi* 矣 or the declarative *ye* 也.

written.[22] This quality would seem uniquely appropriate to the theater and to performance; an actor, for example, must shift shape as he fills a succession of roles.

In Wang Jide's dramatic criticism, *xu* has a meaning similar to that it has in late Ming commentary on fiction: it designates the addition of fictional elements to the historical event that serves as a basis for a play.[23] In modern criticism, by contrast, the notion that *xu* substitutes for *shi* 實 (the solid, concrete, and actual) commonly refers to the use of gestures to indicate concrete forms. An actor, for example, employs a certain kind of gait to indicate that he is a horse or crossing a bridge, so that his movements create illusions that substitute for concrete props.[24] The primary aspiration of Chinese theatrical aesthetics is the synthesis of *xu* and *shi* (*xu shi jie he* 虛實結合). Like other dyads in traditional Chinese thought, *xu* and *shi* are thought to be generated from each other, so that *shi* takes form in the extremes of *xu*. In the words of Ye Xie 葉燮 (1627–1703), as *xu* and *shi* mutually take shape, presence and absence are mutually established (*xu shi xiang cheng, you wu hu li* 虛實相成,有無互立).[25]

This waxing and waning of the plastic and concrete, and of illusion and actuality, underlies the provocative indeterminacy of the cross-dressed actor's gender. In *Nan wanghou*, the illusory quality of the male actor's femininity points to that of the stage. The actor's femininity plays with the boundaries between illusion and reality, and this, in turn, becomes an essential component of his eroticism. The spectator, fascinated with this indeterminacy, desires to maintain a simultaneous belief and disbelief in the actor's transformation, to be taken in by the performance of female gender even while cognizant that it is a performance. Thus, the uncertainty of the actor's gender resonates with and enhances the challenges of the stage itself.[26]

---

22. Owen, *Readings in Chinese Literary Thought*, p. 161.

23. Wang wrote: "In choosing a subject one prizes *shi* [historical validity]; in treating it one prizes *xu* [the creative additions of the author]" (Wang Jide, *Qulü*, in *Zhongguo gudian xiqu lunzhu jicheng*, 4: 154).

24. See Lu Eting, *Kunju yanchu shigao*, p. 71.

25. Ye Xie, *Yuan shi* 原詩, cited in Owen, *Readings in Chinese Literary Thought*, p. 532.

26. Although there is no equivalent in the western critical tradition for the term *xu*, the sense of simultaneous presence and absence invoked by the term (the sense of both "being and not being there," in Wang Jide's words) recalls the optical paradoxes associated

In the pages that follow, I examine the ways in which *Nan wanghou*'s representation of the illusory qualities of gender influences its commentary on the illusory nature of historical allusion. A play between avowal and disavowal characterizes the spectator's relation not only to the actor's gender but to the historical past. *Nan wanghou* attempts to unsettle habits of seeing by forcing the spectator to rid himself of the visual blindspots that would have allowed him to achieve a singular perspective, requiring instead that he hold seemingly incommensurable possibilities in tension—for example, that he understand both masculinity and femininity to be immanent in the body of the cross-dressed actor. Refusing to submit to the spectator's gaze, the cross-dressed actor issues a hermeneutical challenge that exploits the indeterminacy of his gender and amplifies the spectator's potential for misrecognition. The actor insists that the viewer both subscribe to the illusion he casts and understand it to be an illusion.

This challenge to the spectator is not only visual but verbal. If the first two acts of *Nan wanghou* focus on the actor's visual plasticity, the second half of the play casts a spotlight on the actor's rhetorical plasticity, drawing a parallel between the actor's abilities to create visual and verbal illusions. Indeed, the boy Zigao claims for himself the role of author, ending his succession of poses by claiming to be the rhetorician Song Yu. Although the play initially seems to focus on the delightful malleability of the boy's gender, ultimately the actor's more threatening rhetorical dexterity takes pride of place, and fittingly so, in that his stage gender is encoded through a series of speech acts. Ultimately, the play extends its con-

---

in the western theoretical tradition with fetishism in the Freudian sense. A number of critics of Elizabethan theater have employed the notion of fetishism to illuminate the optical effects of theatrical cross-dressing. See, e.g., Stallybrass, "Transvestism and the 'Body Beneath'"; Garber, "The Logic of the Transvestite: The Roaring Girl"; *idem, Vested Interests*, and Phelan, *Unmarked: The Politics of Performance*. I would argue, however, that there is a signal difference between the Freudian notion of fetishism and classical Chinese notions of simultaneous presence and absence. In the Chinese theatrical tradition, which is influenced by Buddhist-Daoist notions of transcendence, the spectator of the theater is meant not to compensate for lack but to engage in a simultaneous immersion in and recognition of theatrical illusion, which parallels the ideal of simultaneous immersion in and disenchantment from the world of forms. In such a system, the fetishist's compensation for a lack that he or she refuses to acknowledge would be disparaged as reliance on a secondary level of illusion.

sideration of the illusory qualities of gender to comment on the illusory nature of the referents of literary and historical allusion.

The play explores both the positive and the negative resonances of the illusory stage gender of the boy actor. The king, the onstage spectator of the boy's performance, delights in the protean flexibility of the boy's gender, eroticizing his pleasure in being challenged by the actor. But the anxieties of anti-theatricalists regarding the actor's social aspirations also form a subtext of the play. The moralists who fretted over the association of literati with actors viewed actors as *femmes fatales* bent on social advancement. It was feared that actors would use their feminine wiles to ingratiate themselves with officials and then, taking advantage of these liaisons to enter the world of officialdom themselves, ultimately assume a masculine and empowered position.

Intimacy of association between literati and actors, then, was particularly threatening given the actor's pliant gender. Shen Defu, the author of the commonplace book *Wanli yehuo bian*, claimed that professional actors (*xiao chang* 小娼) spied for the government, eavesdropping in order to gain information about confidential matters, and hence should be viewed with mistrust and apprehension:

This type of false person knows how to cater to others' whims. Every time these actors entertain guests at a party, they will be entrusted with hundreds of warmers of wine. By the time the party is over, they have sold them all, so that not a drop is left. People like these slave boys have agreements to help one another so as to avoid censure. . . . They spread rumors, have been hired by the *yamen* as spies, and serve as the eyes and ears of the *yamen*. For this reason, in recent years people have come to fear and despise them. Those among them who are glamorous and smart are hired by people in important positions. When they are on the verge of sexual relations with a man, they receive wine and money and a license to be a low-ranking official. Suddenly, they wear an official's cap. Once they are appointed as low-level officials, they say farewell to their lovers. I've seen this with my own eyes, dozens of times.[27]

Shen assumed that any association between an actor and a literatus would inevitably lead to sexual relations and that the goal of any actor in engaging in such a relationship was to gain an official position himself.

---

27. Shen Defu, *Wanli yehuo bian*, 2: 621.

Shen emphasized that actors were professionally trained to simulate and deceive.[28] Of course, it was precisely the actor's ability to cast illusion—his power over representation—in which the literati aficionado of the theater delighted. The source of the literatus's pleasure was also the source of danger.

The fear of authors such as Shen Defu that actors might obtain official positions through their feminine wiles finds an echo in the cross-dressed boy's quick ascension as the king's favorite. Their warnings regarding the actor's corruption of public morals through his promiscuity resonate with the uneasiness of Zigao's clandestine affair with the princess. Ultimately, however, *Nan wanghou* underscores the fact that it is the actor's facility with words that truly threatens the literatus, for the literatus's own stock in trade is his capability with words.

Immanent Genders

The putative performance context of *Nan wanghou* is important for our understanding of the play. By "performance context," I am not referring to actual incidences of performance; no record of a performance of *Nan wanghou* has been found. This does not mean, however, that it was not performed. As I discussed in Chapter 2, late Ming conceptions of performance, audience, and text were quite different from their modern western counterparts. Performance of a play did not necessarily imply that the whole text was performed; parts of a text were often excerpted. Actors were frequently asked to sing favorite scenes or lyrics, as we saw in the scene from *Jin Ping Mei* mentioned above. This text, then, was not a play in the modern sense of the word.

Scholars often try to determine the frequency with which dramatic texts were performed by examining their publishing history. Some anthologies are known to have been compilations of performance texts; others were published as reading editions. In the case of *Nan wanghou*, the evidence is scant and inconclusive. The full text was published in *Sheng Ming zaju* 盛明雜劇 (Northern drama of the high Ming), a luxury edition of texts composed for the most part in the northern musical style (*beiqu*), which most scholars believe was seldom performed by the early

---

28. Ibid.

seventeenth century.[29] This suggests that *Nan wanghou* was not in the performance repertoire. However, Acts 3 and 4 were also published in a miscellany of dramatic texts entitled *Zhaijin qiyin* 摘錦奇音 (Rare sounds plucked from brocade), which is considered a compilation of performance texts in the Yiyang musical style; the excerpting of only two acts suggests that the plot was well known and that the two final acts were either performed more frequently or viewed as more suited to performance.[30] In other words, the play appears both in an anthology of texts that scholars believe were not performed and in a performance miscellany. The inconclusiveness of the evidence points to the dangers of labeling some texts "closet dramas" and others "performance texts" as well as to the difficulty of judging whether a text was performed by appealing to its publication history.[31]

How do the performative possibilities of *Nan wanghou* themselves become a subtext of the text? The play takes the social space of performance, in which the cross-dressed boy actor's play with gender is assumed to appeal to the literati spectator, and inscribes it in the cross-dressed boy Zigao's relations with the king. That *Nan wanghou* takes the cross-dressing of the boy actor as a subtext is apparent in the way in which the stage di-

---

29. He Liangjun 何良俊 (1506–1573), for example, boasted in his *Siyou zhai congshu* 四友齋叢書 (1569) that his private troupe, composed of female servants, knew over fifty plays. The greater part were lyrics of the Jin and Yuan in the northern style, which even the court musicians of Nanjing no longer knew (*Siyou zhai congshu*, p. 340).

30. As mentioned in note 8 to this chapter, the miscellany was in circulation by 1611, eighteen years before *Sheng Ming zaju*. Contrary to what we might expect, then, the performance text was not a redaction of the reading text now extant, although, of course, it might well have been a redaction of another, unknown edition of *Nan wanghou*.

31. There are indications that *Zhaijin qiyin* was not just a compilation of performance texts but was intended for reading pleasure as well; the two need not, of course, be mutually exclusive. The text is accompanied by three illustrations that do not appear in the later facsimile edition of *Sheng Ming zaju*. Two of these illustrations depict the cross-dressed boy and the princess in garden settings and are markedly pornographic, featuring large phallic-shaped rocks entangled in vegetation. The two acts of *Nan wanghou* published in *Zhaijin qiyin* are also festooned in the top register of each page with a list of geographical place-names beginning with the two capitals of the Ming, Beijing and Nanjing, and continuing with the various provinces, districts and so forth; such lists were considered a kind of leisure reading (*Zhaijin qiyin*, pp. 189–205). For more on the significance of the inclusion of geographical names in drama miscellanies, see Yuming He, "Productive Space," pp. 117–30.

rections inscribe gender-crossing; they assign the role of Zigao, which would normally be played by an actor or actress specializing in principal male (*sheng*) roles, to the female lead (*dan* 旦). The primary distinction between cross-dressing in Chinese opera and western theater is that Chinese opera has the added variable of the system of role-types.[32] Actors of both sexes were trained to play either male or female role-types from a young age. Each role-type had a certain style of movement, vocal production, makeup, and costume. The number of role-types increased through the Ming.[33] By Wang Jide's time, they had proliferated to accommodate the large cast of characters typical of the sprawling *chuanqi*.[34] Actors usually specialized in only one role-type or often even a subset of a role-type.

In the study of premodern performance, much is of necessity extrapolation. We have numerous instructions for playwrights, but the actor's art was transmitted orally. There is no seventeenth-century text akin to the Japanese author Zeami's (ca. 1363–ca. 1443) manual of the actor's art, in which he wrote that "the performance by a man of a woman's posture is the most difficult accomplishment of all," and that actors must internalize a "woman's figure" rather than engage in "mere imitation" that results in a "surface copy."[35] Reflecting the interests of literati connoisseurs, premodern Chinese sources simply mention anecdotally the qualifications of those who trained the actors. The decision to train a child as an actor of a particular role-type was probably made on the basis of height, vocal range, physical strength, and facial features. A particular family's lineage of expertise would also have been a consideration. Given the young age at which professional training began, the movements and mannerisms suit-

---

32. For discussion of the theatrical role system in the late Ming, see Dolby, *Chinese Drama*, pp. 105–6.

33. Different sources give different accounts of the number of role-types in *Kunqu*; the variation in numbers depends in large part on the fineness of the subdivision of the primary role-types, *sheng* and *dan*.

34. In his *Qulü*, Wang Jide listed eleven role-types: primary male lead (*zhengsheng* 正生), auxiliary male lead (*tiesheng* 貼生), primary female lead (*zhengdan* 正旦), auxiliary female lead (*tiedan* 貼旦), older female character (*laodan* 老旦), lesser female character (*xiaodan* 小旦; often interchangeable with the *tiedan*), the "extra," who played a lesser male character (*wai* 外), secondary male lead (*mo* 末), martial or villainous character (*jing* 淨), clown (*chou* 丑), and lesser clown (*xiaochou* 小丑). Wang Jide, "Lun buse" 論部色, *Qulü*, in *Zhongguo gudian xiqu lunzhu jicheng*, 4: 143.

35. Brown, *Theatricalities of Power*, p. 24.

able to the actor's role-type was ideally meant to become innate, to form a sort of *habitus* for the actor.[36]

It was virtually unheard of for the actor or actress who played the female lead to play a male character. But that is precisely what the stage directions of *Nan wanghou* request when they state that the character of Chen Zigao is to be played by the female lead. Because the female lead could be played by either men or women, this stage direction inscribes the sex of the character, not that of the actor. In western theater, an actor's gender is presumed to be aligned to that of the character he or she plays; if the actor is in drag, this is assumed to serve an interpretation of the play. In Chinese opera, the cross-dressing of actors is so common as to have no particular significance for the presentation or interpretation of a particular play. The norms of gesture, vocal production, and costume are the same for both male and female actors playing a certain role-type; women training to play the female lead, for example, might be instructed by a male performer of female lead roles.

The *dan* who acted the part of Chen Zigao, then, could have been male or female. However, a reader of the text would probably have imagined a male actor in the role of the female lead, not only because of the putative parallel between the cross-dressed actor and the cross-dressed young boy but also because the overwhelming number of performers were male. Indeed, not only were there fewer actresses than actors, but they were far less visible. They seldom performed in public venues such as the temple or market fair; rather, they appeared in salon-style performance in more restricted venues, such as private residences, brothels, the official *yamen*, and guild halls.[37] Because most actresses were either courtesans trained in

---

36. As Saba Mahmood (*Politics of Piety*, p. 136) notes, Pierre Bourdieu's contemporary use of the word *habitus* has obscured the significance of the term in the Aristotelian tradition. In Bourdieu's use of the term, *habitus* is a sense of the rules of the game that is acquired largely unconsciously (see Bourdieu, *Outline of a Theory of Practice*). In the Aristotelian tradition, by contrast, *habitus* is defined in terms of "excellence at either a moral or a practical craft, learned through repeated practice until that practice leaves a permanent mark on the character of a person." Bourdieu does not retain the Aristotelian emphasis on the repeated self-disciplining of a subject through training and practice, an aspect that is useful in thinking about how actors of the traditional theater acquired their sense of the "rules of the game."

37. The actresses of palace troupes most commonly were *yuehu*, but could be disgraced gentry women. The founder of the Ming as well as the Yongle emperor 永樂 (r. 1403–25)

the musical arts or servants kept in private households, they were a luxury available only to the privileged few. The notation book *Qiang'an suibi* 蕆庵隨筆 (Casually noted by the Qiang studio) mentions a male troupe that would on request and for an extra fee add a few actresses.[38]

It is commonly held that because the preponderance of acting troupes were single-sex and male, the cross-dressing of actors to play female roles originated out of necessity. However, sources suggest that male actors played the female lead even when actresses were available, an indication that the cross-dressing of actors was not a simple matter of necessity. The seventeenth-century critic Pan Zhiheng 潘之恒 mentions a famed male actor of *dan* roles, Xu Pian 徐翩, whose actress daughters Pianpian 翩翩 and Tingting 聽聽 were "capable" and resembled their father.[39] It seems clear from his phrasing that it was the father who excelled with regard to the particular requirements of creating the illusion of femininity on stage.

The feminized mannerisms of the actors who played *dan* seem to have fascinated literati aficionados of the theater, perhaps in part because the uniqueness of such mannerisms offstage called attention to the oddity of their normalization onstage. Within the two contexts, these mannerisms had radically different significances. Onstage, the mannerisms of the *dan* simply signaled stage gender; offstage, they signaled an excess of femininity and thus the potential sexual availability of the actor. Notation books depict *dan* actors as having exaggeratedly sensual feminine names such as Peach Blossom Rain (Taohua yu 桃花雨) and Crossed Branches of Jade (Yu jiaozhi 玉交枝) and describe them using feminine kinship terms, such as "big aunt" (*da gugu* 大姑姑), "little aunt" (*xiao gugu* 小姑姑), and "sister number six" (*liu jie* 六姐).[40] An anecdote in Jiao Xun's *Jushuo* tells of a male actor whose belly grew increasingly large. From time to time movement was discernible in his belly, as though he were pregnant. One day, as he was performing, he gave birth onstage to a piece of flesh three to

---

humiliated the wives and daughters of disgraced officials by forcing them to serve as actresses within the palace. In fact, the wife and daughters of the disgraced official Yan Shifan 嚴世蕃 were subjected to this punishment during the Jiajing period (Zeng Yongyi, *Shuo xiqu* 説戲曲, p. 43).

38. Cited in Sun Chongtao and Xu Hongtu, *Xiqu youling shi*, p. 175.

39. Pan Zhiheng, *Pan Zhiheng quhua*, p. 51.

40. Huang An, *Xijin shixiao lu*, 9b.

four *cun* 寸[41] in length enclosed in a sac. He died because he could not stand the labor pains.[42] That the actor gave birth while performing suggests that the stage was necessary to accomplishing this gender inversion. One wonders, however, if the actor's death from labor pains is meant to remind us that although the actor's stage gender could bestow femininity on him, it could not make him a woman.

Cross-dressing was by no means unusual on the Chinese stage, but crossing role-types was highly unusual. In other words, although actors commonly crossed biological gender to play a certain role-type, they rarely strayed from the role-type that they were trained to play.[43] The stage directions of *Nan wanghou* are, to my knowledge, nearly unique among traditional Chinese plays in specifying that the role of a young boy is to be played by the *dan*. The only other example known to me is a skit from the late sixteenth-century playwright Shen Jing's *Bo xiao ji* 博笑記 (Tales to incite laughter; see below).[44] In both *Nan wanghou* and *Bo xiao ji*, the confusion that ensues from the crossing of genders is strategic. Having the female lead play a male character immediately disrupts the sedimented

---

41. Three to four *cun* was roughly 10.2–13.6 centimeters.

42. Jiao Xun cited the notation book *Jianwen lu* as his source. He continued: "During the years 1774 to 1775, in my city, there was an actor surnamed Fan 範. He also had such an experience, but he did not die" (Jiao Xun, *Jushuo*, p. 108).

43. The term *fanchuan* 反串, now used to describe cross-dressing on the stage, originally meant playing a role-type other than the one an actor normally played. See Wang An-Chi 王安祈, "Jianban, shuangyan, daijue, fanchuan: guanyu yanyuan, juese he juzhongren sanzhe guanxi de jidian kaocha" 兼扮，雙演，代角，反串—關於演員，腳色和劇中人三者關係的幾點考察, in Hua Wei and Wang Ayling, *Ming Qing xiqu guoji yantaohui lunwenji*, pp. 625–69.

44. A similar case is the mid-nineteenth-century woman playwright Wu Zao's 吳藻 play *Yinjiu du "Li sao" tu: Qiao ying* 飲酒讀離騷圖喬影 (Encountering Sorrow: A reflection in disguise), pp. 287–310, in which the stage directions request the female protagonist be played by the male lead (the *sheng*); the play is a soliloquy spoken and sung by a woman who cross-dresses in official's robes to show her frustration that her talents are unused. Theatrically, the play shares little in common with *Nan wanghou*, though interestingly, the speaker, like Chen Zigao, cross-dresses verbally as much as visually, in a torrent of allusions posing as Du Fu, Li Bo, and Su Shi in rapid succession. See my analysis and translation in Susan Mann and Yu-Yin Cheng, ed., *Under Confucian Eyes*: pp. 238–50. Wilt Idema translates this play under the title *The Fake Image*; see his biography of Wu Zao and translations of her work in Wilt Idema and Beata Grant, *The Red Brush*, pp. 685–702.

norms with which the spectator perceives the actor's stage gender and leads the spectator to interpret rather than merely accept the actor's performance of gender. One can imagine various ways in which a spectator might be cued as to the crossing of role types. For example, the actor's carriage might be that of a *dan*, while his gestures were that of a *sheng*. Most likely, the spectator would know which actors in a troupe were *dan*, so that from the actor's first lines, the conceit would be evident.

As discussed above, it is likely that readers of the play would have imagined a male actor in the role of Chen Zigao, in part because of the obvious parallel between the cross-dressed boy and the actor who plays him, and in part because the preponderance of actors were male. If a male actor played the role of the female lead, the audience would witness a male actor dressed as the female lead playing the part of a young boy who cross-dresses as a woman. In this set of nested spheres of gender-crossing, the queen would be the outermost sphere, the boy the next. Inside the boy is the female lead, and inside the female lead, the male actor. These nested gender-crossings ensure that both genders are immanent in the body of the actor.

A cross-section of these spheres would reveal two sets of parallels in this series of concentric circles: between the actor and the boy Zigao on one hand, and between the cross-dressed female lead and the cross-dressed male queen on the other. The play teases us by jumping from one of these concentric circles to the next, from actor to boy and back again; not only are both genders immanent in the actor, but both actor and character are present for the spectator. The parallel between the cross-dressed actor and the cross-dressed character frustrates any dissolution of actor into character. Instead, it fosters a repeated rupturing of the identification between actor and character.

Indeed, the oscillation between actor and character occasioned by this crossing of role-types calls attention to the artifice of the stage itself. Shen Jing's *Bo xiao ji*, in which the female lead plays the part of a male actor (as in *Nan wanghou*, crossing not genders but gendered role-types) illustrates this reverberation between the illusory quality of the actor's stage gender and the illusions and epiphenomena of the worldly stage. *Bo xiao ji* is composed of a series of skits, each comprising from one to several acts. In one such skit, the junior female lead (*xiaodan*) plays a young boy who has gained renown as an actor of women's roles.[45] As this segment opens, he bemoans the fact that he has been reduced to acting for a living. Several rakes of the pleasure quarters (played by the various clown role-types) appear on stage on their way to visiting this actor. As they stroll along, they discuss the hard life of an actor. One says, referring to the expectation that the *xiaodan* is a sexual plaything: "Even when his 'awning' is pounded open, it's nothing extraordinary." Another concurs: "Although he has to get used to having his awning pounded, it's just part and parcel of being an actor."[46] When the *xiaodan* answers the door, the clowns note with surprise that even at home, he speaks in a woman's voice; they had expected him to talk in a man's voice offstage. Of course, the actors are still "onstage"; were the female lead to speak in a man's voice, it would constitute a grave rupture of stage convention. The illusory self-sufficiency of the onstage world is ruptured as the exigencies of the plot, which presume that the character should speak in a masculine voice "offstage," come into conflict with theatrical conventions.

These explorations of the artifice of stage gender are coupled with jokes about the play's presumed ignorance of its status as theater. The clowns begin a conversation with the *xiaodan* about the plays in his repertory. After he mentions a number of standard works, they ask if he knows any new plays, and in particular, whether he knows *Bo xiao ji*, the script that they are at that moment performing. The *xiaodan* claims not to have heard of it. The clowns tell him that it is quite an interesting play and reproach him for not having learned it. Similarly, when one of the clowns cracks a joke, the female lead complains, "There you go, joking again." The clown's retort, "That's a clown's natural capacity," again calls attention to the play's conditions of production and ruptures the normalization of stage convention. As the skit ends, the clowns and the female lead decide to perform together elsewhere. The clowns stipulate that the female lead must wear women's stockings and put his hair in a bun; he replies: "I'll take some women's clothes from my costume trunk," a statement that once again points to the way in which the stage gender of the cross-dressed actor troubles the fiction that the world onstage constitutes

---

45. The skit is equivalent to the sixteenth act of *Bo xiao ji*.
46. Shen Jing, *Bo xiao ji, juan xia*, 4a.

reality. Although this skit is little more than a series of one-liners, it offers an encapsulated version of the concerns of *Nan wanghou* and illustrates the ways in which highlighting the artifice of stage gender simultaneously points to the sexual availability of the *dan* and calls into question the relationship between the world and stage.

The question of the sexual availability of the cross-dressed actor, then, draws attention to the permeability of the boundaries between the world and stage, as we saw in Shutong's performance of the role of chaste bride. The following poems by Wu Weiye describe a boy prostitute cross-dressed as a bride for the first time.[47] Read in tandem, these poems suggest that just as the gender of the cross-dressed actor is a potential site of misrecognition, so is the expectation of subservience to the literati spectator. Both types of misrecognition translate into a sensuous incongruity between expectation and actuality.

I

Close-fitting sleeves, a light gauze bodice suitable for the wedding chamber,
He Sui 何綏 is costumed as a woman for the first time.[48]
Scented sachet and blossoms tied in a lover's knot,
His clothes fragrant even from ten leagues away.[49]

II

Jade hairpins still in place, he has not removed the palace yellow.[50]
I laugh at this boy whose words are so crazed.
To my surprise he says that the jade one is languid and weary,
Unwilling to serve King Xiang of Chu with clouds and rain.[51]

---

47. From Wu Weiye, "Xizeng shi shou" 戲贈十首, in *Wu Meicun quanji*, 1: 204.

48. He Sui was a man of the Jin dynasty famous for his extravagant tastes in clothing; see Fang Xuanling, *Jin shu*, *juan* 33, p. 1000.

49. The term used for the boy's clothes (*kuzhe* 袴褶) may suggest androgyny; it designates a kind of uniform worn primarily by men, but in the Northern Dynasties, by women as well. The phrase I have translated as "even from ten leagues away" alludes to Du Mu's 杜牧 poem "Zeng bie" 贈別 (Given on parting), which includes the line "Spring breeze along ten leagues of the road to Yangzhou" 春風十里揚州路 (Du Mu 杜牧, *Fanchuan shi jizhu* 樊川詩集注, ed. Feng Jiwu, p. 311).

50. Palace women used a cosmetic that was a particular shade of yellow.

In these poems, it is not merely the incongruity of the boy's femininity but its transience that fascinates. The first lyric shows the speaker enjoying the spectacle of the boy costumed as a woman "for the first time"; the second describes him in the process of removing his toilette. The boy prostitute carries "the scent of the pleasure quarters," yet is not of them; he is suited to the "wedding chamber," yet not in one. It is when the boy is newly dressed or half-undressed that the literatus most deeply senses the ephemeral and thus the illusory nature of the boy's femininity.

In the second poem, the boy subverts the speaker's expectations by refusing to serve him sexually, inverting the conventional power relations between literatus and prostitute. In the first poem, our eyes followed the speaker's gaze, concentrating on the spectacle of the boy. Now the boy reverses the gaze, making the original spectator, the poet, into a spectacle of discombobulation. The audience for that spectacle is not the boy, of whom we are permitted to see only clothes and a voice, but the reader. As the boy frustrates the speaker's expectations, the position of the privileged voyeur shifts from speaker to reader. If the indeterminate quality of the boy's gender captivates the literatus, the boy's refusal to serve also fascinates him. As the boy actor reverses the gaze, and the power relations inherent in the gaze, he thwarts the literatus's expectation of subservience.[52]

Nan wanghou similarly calls attention to the reversal of the anticipated power relations between actor and spectator. The repeated emphasis on the conditions of its performance represents the stage as a site of misrecognition. The play thematizes the constraints of spectatorship by challenging the spectator with paradoxes of perception. In particular, it links the visual indeterminacy of the gender of the cross-dressed actor with the historical indeterminacy of allusive reference, which the play reveals to be as staged and fetishized as the gender of the actor.

---

51. The allusion to King Xiang of Chu and "clouds and rain" refers to a sexual tryst between the king's ancestor and the goddess of Chu described in Song Yu's *Gaotang fu* 高唐賦 (Rhapsody on Gaotang); see Xiao Tong, *Wen xuan*, pp. 875–86.

52. The word "boy" in my usage does not indicate so much age as junior socioeconomic status.

Nan wanghou

In the opening lyric of *Nan wanghou*, the actor praises his success at creating the illusion of femininity:

> Luscious clouds of hair, black tunic so feminine that I myself am surprised,
> I fear that you won't be able to distinguish when you cast your eyes.
> In the East the sun shines, in the West the rain falls.
> People say they have no feelings, but surely they do.[53]

The actor represents the stage as a site of misrecognition. As he twits the spectators for their inability to discern his gender, the actor points to the "prosthetic devices," to use Peter Stallybrass's term, that signal stage gender: the wig of the female lead and the long, fluttering sleeves whose manipulation is an integral part of the actor's art.[54] Advertising his ability to dupe the spectator, he questions whether the spectators' connoisseurship is equal to his artistry.

The cross-dressed actor's special ability is to keep the mutually opposed poles of masculine and feminine in tension. This yoking of incompatible states is thematized in these opening lines. The line "People say they have no feelings, but surely they do" puns on two characters pronounced *qing*: 晴 "clear" and 情 "feeling" (although the two characters have different tonal inflections, the difference would be masked as the actor sang the lines). The character for "feeling" is used here, but in the context of the previous line, "In the East the sun shines, in the West, the rain falls," the audience would presumably hear not "feeling," but "clear," so that the last line would be understood as, "People say the skies are not clear, but surely they are."[55] The pun provides an aural equivalent to the

---

53. *Nan wanghou*, 1a. Subsequent references to the play are cited in the text.

54. Peter Stallybrass uses the term "prosthetic" to "suggest the attempt to supply an imagined deficiency by the exchange of male clothes for female clothes or of female clothes for male clothes; by displacement from male to female space or from female to male space; by the replacement of male with female tasks or of female with male tasks" (Stallybrass, "Transvestism and the 'Body Beneath,'" p. 77).

55. The couplet alludes to one of the Tang poet Liu Yuxi's 劉禹錫 "Zhuzhi ci" 竹枝詞 (Bamboo Branch poems): "Green the willows, level the river waters / I hear the sound of my love singing above the waters / In the East the sun rises, in the West the rain falls / People say they have no feelings, but surely they do" (Guo Maoqian, *Yuefu shiji*, 4: 1141).

visual pun inherent in the actor's cross-dressing. It is through this sort of oscillation between two poles of meaning that significance is produced in this play. The very term *qing* points to the ultimate significance of such punning—in combining the notions of clarity and sympathetic attachment, the pun points to the fact that the spectator's enlightenment is dependent on the rupturing of sympathetic identification.

The performance of the play becomes a subtext that itself provides a kind of punning and doubling. Although the *dan* actor challenges us to "distinguish" (*fenming* 分明) between actor and character, and masculine and feminine, he also challenges the spectator to keep both terms present. Complicitly, he reminds the spectator not to disavow his knowledge of the actor's costuming. In this sense, he demands that the spectator appreciate the tension between illusion and disillusion instead of naïvely entering the world of the play.

As the actor issues this challenge to the spectator, he advertises not merely his ability to create the successful illusion of femininity, but his—and the boy Zigao's—erotic charms. As Zigao's self-introduction continues, he points to the source of the actor's erotic allure, his resistance to being reduced to a single gender:

Even though my body is that of a man, my features are like those of a woman. I was born with a beauty most tempting. A painting could not capture the beauty of my face when my makeup is freshly applied. Come to think of it, if I am not the Dragon Girl who scatters flowers before the throne of the bodhisattva Guanyin, mistakenly reincarnated on Earth, then I must be a reincarnation of the Golden Boy clasping a tray from the Jade Emperor's palace, now descended to Earth.[56] Yesterday a physiognomer told me that I had the face of a dragon and the neck of a phoenix.

Zigao argues that, ironically, it is the overdetermined plenitude of both genders that renders him "natural." He has a quality that is beyond repre-

---

56. The Dragon Girl is a servant of the bodhisattva Guanyin 觀音 and is said to be responsible for bringing the flowers of spring. The Jade Emperor is the head of the Taoist pantheon; the Golden Boy and the Jade Maiden are two scribes of the Jade Emperor. According to legend, the Golden Boy and the Jade Maiden had a secret affair, and the Jade Emperor punished them by sending them to Earth. They needed to go through seven generations of marriage before they could return to Heaven. Here Zigao is probably suggesting that he is a doomed lover of one of those generations.

sentation in that it resists portrayal; it defies verisimilitude. Cross-dressing is usually held to be artifice, a falling away from nature, but here the cross-dresser implies that his gender cannot be seen as imitative or derivative because he offers a plenitude not usually found in nature. He is a figure for overdetermination; he cannot be subsumed under the rubrics "masculine" or "feminine."[57]

As we shall see, this plenitude allows Zigao to supersede not only the women who will assist him in his initial transformation but also his historical predecessors. Moreover, it allows Zigao to resist the spectator's definition and limitation of his gender. Zigao amplifies his illegibility by issuing an invitation to interpretation—the same gesture that the actor made as he dared the spectator, "I fear that you won't be able to distinguish when you cast your eyes":

If I were a woman, I could certainly make a match with a king. [Sighs.] Had I only been born a girl, I could depend on my talent and beauty. I wouldn't need to be competitive with others in the harem. I'd be so foxy, I would bewitch the king. Even if he were a man of iron, I could make half his body go so limp it couldn't move. What a pity I was made a boy by mistake! (1b–2a)[58]

Even as this speech introduces us to the primary concern of the play, the erotic relationship between the boy and the king, it invites the audience to consider the actor as an erotic spectacle. Zigao's fantasy paradoxically suggests that the spectator's arousal will paralyze him. "Half" the body of the "man of iron" will go limp; the spectator will be partially emasculated. The actor, then, has mastery not only over his own gender but also over that of the spectator. However, in keeping with the play's demand that the spectator both enter the enchanted realm of the stage and remain detached from it, it is only "half" the spectator's body that

---

57. In the premodern writing system, the universal third-person pronoun *ta* 他 designates both "she" and "he," and is, moreover, often elided; having to make a choice in English between "she" and "he," I have chosen "he" in part because the arc of the play is toward a re-assumption of masculinity on the part of the cross-dresser.

58. These lines allude to the description of the future Empress Wu Zetian by Luo Binwang 駱賓王 (ca. 640–84), "Entering the harem, she feels jealous; being a beauty she is unwilling to yield to another / She hides her face with her sleeves, and excels at flattery; so foxy she can bewitch an Emperor." 入門見嫉, 娥眉不肯讓人; 掩袖工讒, 狐媚偏能惑主" (see Liu Xu, 劉昫, *Jiu Tang shu* 舊唐書, *juan* 67, pp. 2490–91).

goes limp, the half that responds to the actor's illusion. Like the boy, the spectator will become half-this and half-that.

The king later asks, "What abilities have you?" As Zigao entices the king with a list of erotic positions, the actor advertises his own body before the audience:

> (Zigao sings:) My charming figure is used to straddling a horse.
> My soft waist knows how to pull a bow of the most flexible wood.[59]
> I can with great care hold your precious sword.
> With patience I'll accompany you as you drink from your jade cup.
> And when you are bored,
> I'll be the puppet with which you play.

(He speaks:) My lord, I don't dare tell you that I am the most delightful little lover.

Zigao speaks of himself as a puppet, as a malleable figure devoid of agency. The speech lures the king—and the audience—into believing in the empowerment of the spectator. Yet although the actor promises to be the puppet of the spectator, the spectator is also the actor's plaything. Thus the spectator simultaneously inhabits both a hypermasculine and an emasculated position, positions that might seem as incongruous as Zigao's masculinity and femininity.

Zigao's self-introduction recalls the rhetoric of *sanqu* (aria) in its combination of comic titillation and flagrant self-promotion. Indeed, Wang Jide was well known as an author of *sanqu*. As the scholar Xu Shuofang notes, he recycled lines between his *zaju* and *sanqu*; several lines from *Nan wanghou* appear in a *sanqu* dedicated to a courtesan surnamed Hu 胡.[60] *Sanqu* is an urban genre, aggressively vernacular, often given to a witty but cartoonish sort of declamation, in which rhetorical dexterity is it-

---

59. *Wu hao jia* 烏號架: the *wu hao* is a kind of bird that makes its nest in a tree of very flexible wood.

60. In a poem to the courtesan Hu, Wang Jide wrote, "Even though your peony is gorgeous, it needs green leaves by its side to complement it." In Act II of *Nan wanghou*, as the cross-dressed Zigao lords it over the ladies of the harem, he assures them he has not displaced them entirely: "This is what is meant when it is said that a gorgeous peony / Still requires green leaves to complement it." We do not know which was composed first, the *sanqu* or *Nan wanghou*. We know that the *sanqu* was composed in 1604, and the appearance of the line in both texts led Xu Shuofang ("Wang Jide nianpu," in *Xu Shuofang ji*, 3: 269) to suggest that *Nan wanghou* was also written in 1604.

self eroticized. It is the speaker's capacity for braggadocio as much as any concrete quality he might have that renders him captivating. This eroticized rhetorical dexterity is at the crux of *Nan wanghou*'s representation of illusory stage gender—and, by extension, of the play's representation of the relation between world and stage.

Act II: Dressing Up for a Dressing Down

Cross-dressing in this play is at least as much a verbal as a visual act, and Zigao's linguistic dexterity at least as important as his cross-dressing in creating an erotic potential between the king and the boy (the implied spectator and the spectacle). Impressed with Zigao's quick wit, the king asks Zigao to enter his harem, saying that none of the many women in his harem has the charms of Zigao's figure. The king then orders the women of the palace to help Zigao dress as a woman. As Zigao is being dressed, we can see that the femininity that is his currency is created rhetorically as much as visually. At first he literally repeats the women's words. He mimics their speech and actions as though taking dictation from them:

Second Palace Woman: Your highness, wear these two hairpins.
Zigao sings: Two gold hairpins.
First Palace Woman: Mistress, weave these flower blossoms in your hair.
Zigao sings: I take tender flower blossoms, and stick them charmingly in the dark clouds of my hair.
Second Palace Woman: Your highness, fasten these jade pendants at your waist so that they chime.
Zigao sings: Listen to the sound of these jade pendants, chiming as they hang.
(9a–9b)

Although Zigao adopts the women's words and garments, he soon declares his femininity to be independent of these signs of gender. As his transformation proceeds, he moves from obedient mimicry to self-creation, declaring himself independent of the "real women" on stage, of their tutelage, and even of the rouge and powder that they have applied to his face.

(Sings:) You women just streak on some rouge to mimic sweet blossoms,
If you don't use cosmetics, you don't stand out.
I, however, just lightly apply powder and kohl, thinly brush on yellow.
I need only glance flirtatiously,
And I become more charming than women in rouge. (9b–10a)

Zigao turns the gaze that has been directed at him back at the palace women. Although the cross-dressed boy, whose gendering has become a theatrical spectacle, is to be prized because of his artifice, the women who form his model are denigrated for their reliance on imitation. His claim that the palace women inhabit a baser femininity enables him to lay claim to a superior femininity. Of course, the "real women" on stage to whom Zigao addresses these scathing comments would likely have been played by men. By alluding obliquely to its performance context, the play draws attention to the fact that the female body is absent precisely where the cross-dresser has located it.

In accusing the palace women of a dependence on artifice and imitation, Zigao reverses the quite legitimate assumption that he is dressed in imitation of them. As his abuse of the palace women continues, he claims that when they fall out of favor, all they can do is intensify their artifice. He, by contrast, can always re-assume a masculine role:

> Were I one of those ladies who trails silk in the royal consort's chambers,
> Or one who has been stripped of her jewelry, having lost the king's favor.
> I would still assume women's garb.
> But if I were to change my clothes and alter my voice,
> I would be suited to a warrior's magnificent helmet. (12b)

The palace women may "assume women's garb" when they fall out of favor, but women's clothing cannot make up for, or even cover, what the female body truly lacks. Women must resort to artifice because they cannot fall back on masculinity. Zigao reminds the spectators onstage and off that simply by acquiring the prostheses of masculinity, by "chang[ing] his clothes" and "alter[ing] his voice," he can play male instead of female roles, becoming "suited to a warrior's magnificent helmet." This is perilously close to what Shen Defu and other authors who warned against the actor's seduction of the literatus feared: that the actor, after securing the literatus's favor, would through his feminine wiles acquire the emblems of elite masculinity and wear an official's cap and robes. If earlier, femininity was Zigao's currency, now he vaunts his mobility—his ability to alter his voice. His exposure of the artifice of the femininity of the female sex was always a foil for a more pressing concern: his declaration of his control over the illusory oppositions of gender. As he shifts positions in relation to his context, his mutations prevent the spectator from placing him within a specific visual or interpretive frame of reference.

Zigao alternates between imitation and aggression as he accepts the directions of the palace women and then rejects them as models. He has a similar relationship with the icons of femininity—both male and female—of the historical past. Just as he will later prove sexually unfaithful to the king, he is determinedly unfaithful to the "originals"—the women on stage and the historical models of the past—that ostensibly inscribe him with meaning. Zigao next declares himself a superior incarnation of the archetypal *femme fatale*, the Tang dynasty consort Yang (Yang Guifei 楊貴妃), who was popularly blamed for the An Lushan 安祿山 rebellion and the subsequent crumbling of the Tang empire. In a satire of the court's corruption, the Tang author Chen Hong 陳鴻 (*jinshi* 805) quoted a popular ditty that suggested that as Yang Guifei gained political power, families began to wish for girls instead of boys in hopes of duplicating her success. In Chen's words, daughters began to "bring honor to a family" (literally, became "the lintel of the family's gate"), creating an inversion of the normal valuation of the sexes.[61] Zigao promises to position a male body in Yang Guifei's place: "Who says that daughters bring honor to a family? I tell you, a boy now rides in the chariot of the monarch's first wife!"(7a).

Zigao argues that his femininity is superior to that of the palace women not only because he has mastery over his gender but also because as a male *femme fatale* he prevents women from wrongfully achieving political power. Correcting the inversion inherent in Yang Guifei's acquisition of political power, he imagines himself to be, like Yang Guifei, one whose rise to power creates a model for imitation. Now that Zigao has replaced Yang Guifei as an icon for future generations—now that a male body has taken the consort's position in the inner palace—families will wish for boys again.

Referring to the female consorts and male favorites of past emperors, Zigao sets a standard by which he will be judged and then immediately declares himself to have surpassed it: "When it comes to shedding tears for cast-off fish, I will make Longyang 龍陽 astonished / When it comes to holding golden pellets I'll leave Han Yan 韓嫣 to gape in

---

61. Chen Hong, "Changhen ge"; cited in Bai Juyi, *Bai Juyi ji jianjiao*, 2: 656–59. When a girl received imperial favor, the characters inscribed on the lintel of her family's gate would change.

surprise."(7a)[62] Zigao claims that he is the male favorite who renders all predecessors superfluous. Even Han Yan, a male favorite of Emperor Wu 武 of the Han 漢 (r. 140–87 BCE) who was so spoiled by the emperor that he had golden pellets for his slingshot, cannot compare.[63] When the palace women helping Zigao with his toilette attempt to flatter him by asking, "Which of the ancients could compare to you?" Zigao replies:

> There was only Dongxian 董賢 of the Han, who once because of the
>   emperor's favor of the cut sleeve could lord it over grandees and ministers.
> But even he did not have the primary position in the harem.
> Today I will be crowned and receive an official status that tops all other con-
>   sorts and women of the court.
> To have such high position and power as a woman,
> Will render my name praised for a thousand years. (10a)

The male favorite Dongxian was so beloved by the Emperor Ai 哀 (r. 7 BCE–1 BCE) that the emperor reportedly had his own sleeve cut off rather than disturb Dongxian as he lay napping upon it.[64] This anecdote gave rise to a common classical epithet for male homoerotic desire, the "passion of the cut sleeve" (*duanxiu zhi ai* 斷袖之愛). Until the late sixteenth century, when terms such as "male love" (*nan se* 男色) and the "southern mode" (*nan feng* 南風) became more common, allusions to Han Yan, Dongxian, and other male favorites formed the primary means of referring to homoerotic desire. Dongxian's name was virtually synonymous with male love. Yet Zigao claims that he trumps even Dongxian, for Dongxian did not have the "primary position in the harem" (10a). "For a

---

62. Zigao's pity for the cast-off fish refers to a story in the *Zhanguo ce* 戰國策 (Stratagems of the Warring States) about the lord of Longyang 龍陽, a male favorite of the king of Wei 魏. Fishing one day in the company of the king, he suddenly realized that his position as the king's current favorite was as precarious as that of a fish, which would be thrown back into the water as soon as a bigger fish were caught (Liu Xiang, *Zhanguo ce*, Wei 4, *juan* 25, p. 917).

63. Han Yan's biography in the *Shi ji* (*juan* 125, 10: 3194) describes his abuses of the privileges the emperor's favor brought but does not include the story of the golden pellets, which is a later interpolation that appears in sources such as Feng Menglong's *Qingshi leilüe*, vol. 12, 22.15b–16b.

64. "Once they took a nap together during the day, and Dongxian lay on the emperor's sleeve. The emperor wanted to get up, and since Dongxian had not woken, he did not want to disturb him, so he had his sleeve cut and rose. Such was his love and favor for Dongxian" (Ban Gu, *Han shu, juan* 93, p. 3733).

thousand years" Zigao's name will be praised, precisely because his acquisition of the "primary position in the harem" renders the female sex unnecessary. Once again, Zigao effects the erasure of the originals that he ostensibly imitates, employing the indeterminacy of his gender to suggest an omnipotentiality with which no male or female predecessor can compete.

Just as Zigao claimed that crossing genders allows him to occupy a space beyond representation, he claims that his capacity to switch genders permits him to trump all historical predecessors. There is no hierarchy or historicity among the allusions Zigao employs: they become prostheses of gender like his wig and hair, tacked on and then discarded. Just as he can change his clothes and switch his tune, donning a warrior's helmet, he crosses genders with ease in his adoption of allusive camouflage. Indeed, Zigao overfills the space created by the absence of past models for himself as a cross-dressed male favorite. His quick substitution of one allusion for another suggests that no one allusion suffices. Each of his references points to a lost totality. But the rapidity of his shifts from one index to another changes the emphasis from a lost historical totality to the fractured present created by this pastiche. Zigao's imitation of historical predecessors, like his imitation of the palace women, invokes the ostensibly concrete or actualized (*shi*) to show that it is "empty" (*xu*). It is this exposure of the *shi* as *xu* that allows Zigao not only to supersede any model he invokes but to declare his independence from it.

By now, Zigao's transvestitism has become a matter of verbal rather than visual illusion. Ostensibly, he cloaks himself in allusion, filiating himself to the famed consorts and male favorites of the past. He does not cite predecessors to bask in their cultural authority so much as to trump them—but once he has trumped them, he robes himself in the mantle of their authority. Zigao begins by describing himself as resembling "Dongxian of the Han," but just as quickly he erases Dongxian as his predecessor, claiming that even he did not have the primary position in the harem. Almost paradoxically, he manages to insert himself in the tradition by declaring himself superior to it.

In the context of a high literary tradition in which the past is always presumed superior to the present, in which allusion is often used in order to suggest that the work of one's predecessors is immanent in one's own, Zigao's use of citation is markedly iconoclastic. If Zigao exposes the artifice inherent in insignia of gender, he similarly reveals the self-costuming inherent in the employment of allusion. As we saw in the previous chapter, *Mudan ting* faults archaism for encouraging individuals to cite allusions detached from their original contexts. *Nan wanghou* also plays with this concern regarding unmoored rhetoric. The cross-dressed young boy of *Nan wanghou* bewitches the onstage spectators with incantatory rhetoric, dazzling them with pyrotechnic displays of allusion to historical models. The play cartoonishly mocks the facile deployment of allusion in the service of social aspiration. As the new queen vaunts his superiority over the models of the past, the cross-dressed boy seems an archaist gone mad.

Zigao's defiant trumping of his predecessors is a farcical version of the more refined arguments against imitative copying that circulated among literary men during the late Ming and early Qing. The painter Dong Qichang, perhaps the most famed artist of the age, wrote: "If one copies closely without rest, and labors unsparingly, regrettably it won't be complete in terms of nature, but only like slavish writing; how could it be worth propagating distantly? Those who study the ancients don't go beyond the ancients' words, and don't attain the intent of the ancients."[65] Dong's words suggest that the declaration of independence from cultural models vests the self with sociocultural authority; autonomy lies in the aggressive creation of difference. *Nan wanghou* argues that cultural authority resides in the copy, which supersedes the original. The play takes the arguments regarding imitation in poetic composition at the center of the anti-archaist diatribes and reverses the valuations associated with original and copy: if anti-archaism viewed imitation to be false (*jia* 假) and so coded it as theatrical, *Nan wanghou* engages in a mimetic performance that calls into question the authenticity (*zhen* 眞) of originals.

Zigao's refusal to kowtow to the icons of the cultural tradition paves the way for his claim to authorship of its feminine icons. Zigao begins by complaining that the king has mistaken the creator for his creation:

> You have mistaken Song Yu 宋玉, whom women peeped at over his eastern wall,
> For the goddess of Gaotang.

---

65. Written on an inscription for his "Eight Views of Yen and Wu," an album from 1596 painted in the Southern Song mode. Translation from Vinograd, "Vision and Revision in Seventeenth-Century Painting," p. 18-7.

I have been forced to become the consort Zhao Feiyan 趙飛燕 in the Zhao-yang 昭陽 palace. [66]

I am about to enter the wedding chamber, be regarded as a woman, and follow my wifely duties.

I only hope that I may bring you happiness and pleasure, and that I will be forever free from harm. (11a)

Although the goddess of Gaotang is a standard in the inventory of allusions typically used to describe courtesans and other women defined by their eroticism, Zigao resists assimilation to that category, claiming that he is not the goddess but the author who created the goddess, Song Yu.[67] By adopting the position of Song Yu, Zigao takes an active role with regard to the literary canon, a role that the literatus, not the actor, has traditionally played. Zigao's claim to authorship is the verbal equivalent of the actor's visual challenge to the spectator; he reveals his control over representation. Language has nearly replaced the body as the site of inversion.

The allusion to Song Yu is the only reference Zigao makes that functions in the customary manner, that he allows to encode him without attempting to surpass it. It is fitting that Zigao ends his allusive tour de force by claiming to be the author of the *fu* on the divine woman Song Yu, for the way in which Zigao strings together allusions recalls the enumerative syntax characteristic of *fu*.[68] Zigao's assumption of Song Yu's mantle also neatly fits the exigencies of *Nan wanghou*'s plot. Song Yu, in his *Deng tuzi haose fu* 登徒子好色賦 (Rhapsody on licentious master Deng), defended himself from the accusation that he could not be trusted around the royal harem, given his astounding good looks and persuasive wit.[69] (He argued that despite the fact that a comely neighbor had often peeped

---

66. Zhao Feiyan was the consort of Emperor Cheng 成 of the Han (r. 33–7 bce).

67. See footnote 51.

68. The origin of *fu* in court oration also resonates with Zigao's rhetorical display before the king. Typically, the *fu* opens with a frame in which an aristocrat asks a question that allows the orator to describe exhaustively the properties of some phenomenon, for example, the divine woman of Gaotang. The ruler's simplemindedness often contrasts with the orator's spellbinding rhetoric; his question often seems a foil that permits the orator to display his vertiginous dexterity with words. The king's earlier question to Zigao, "What abilities have you?," which was followed by Zigao's clever rhymed response, could be read in this light.

69. Song Yu, *Deng tuzi hao se fu*, in Xiao Tong, *Wen xuan, juan* 19, pp. 892–95.

at him over the eastern wall of his garden, he had remained faithful to his ugly wife.) By analogy, Zigao implies that he, too, may be trusted around the king's harem. Ironically, it is immediately afterward that Zigao succumbs to the desire of the princess, who robs Zigao of his power of self-improvisation and forces him to accept her redefinition of his gender. Zigao's transition from the plaything of the king to the illicit bedfellow of the princess encapsulates the contradictions inherent in the literati fetishization of the actor. On one hand, it is feared that the actor will seduce the literatus with his feminine wiles and, on the other, that the actor will usurp the role of the literati male and seduce the gentry woman.

Act III: The Female Spectator

Although most writing about the actor's wayward sexuality concerns the literatus's susceptibility to the actor, there is also an undercurrent of concern about the actor's potential fascination for female audiences.[70] It was not uncommon for household regulations written by patriarchs for their descendants to contain prohibitions against women watching theater. The Qing dynasty literatus Zhou Tanran 周坦然, in a set of clan rules prefaced in 1662 and recorded by his son Zhou Lianggong 周亮工, stated that "one of the forty auspicious signs" (觀宅四十吉祥相) for a household would be that "women do not watch plays from behind a curtain":

---

70. For example, Tao Shiling 陶奭齡, the author of the Ming notation book *Nannan lu* 喃喃錄 (Recorded mutterings),wrote:

Of the plays that are composed these days, most are about clandestine romance. A thousand texts are guided by this same principle, and this is deeply to be regretted. People always have these plays performed at home, gathering fathers, sons, and brothers, and putting the womenfolk behind a curtain to watch them. All of them witness the licentiousness and degeneracy of these plays, which contain every kind of unseemly behavior. How is this different from the ancients who chased naked women around? A hall full of people acting like animals—how is this not tragic? (Tao Shiling, *Nan nan lu, juan shang* 卷上, 65b.)

For another discussion of this passage, see Zhao Shanlin, *Zhongguo xiqu guanzhong xue*, p. 100. "The ancients who chased naked women around" is a reference to King Zhou 紂 of the Shang 商, at whose banquets there were "lakes of wine and meat hung as though a forest of trees. Women and boys were made to strip naked as the king chased after them, drinking the whole night long" (Sima Qian, *Shiji, juan* 3, p. 105).

When you invite actors to perform plays, it should only be to amuse guests. If women watch from behind a curtain, the fragrance of their powder wafts from behind it. As they lean against the curtain, their gauze tunics and crescent shoes are discreetly visible behind the screen, and they comment on and judge the assembled guests, chatting away in high voices and laughing with delight. The gazes of the actors penetrate directly into their midst, and the minds of the guests turn to the women behind them. The dangers are manifold: it is not merely that women should not be allowed to watch actors but that spectatorship itself spreads to the assembly of male guests.[71]

A similar concern regarding actors' seduction of gentry women can be found in an anecdote regarding the playwright Tu Long related in Shen Defu's early seventeenth-century notation book *Wanli yehuo bian*. Shen Defu commented: "The wife of the marquis of Xining was a talented woman, good at composing music. Tu Long also excelled at composing new tunes and was quite proud of himself in this regard. Every time a play was put on, he would stroll onto the stage among the actors and take a role. The wife of the marquis saw him from behind a curtain and rewarded him with fragrant tea, and this story got around."[72] Pan Zhiheng describes a female lead (*dan*) named He Shaoying 何少英, who "trilled in his throat and pursed his lips to make a strange sound; all the gentry women thought him bewitching."[73] The seductiveness of actors endangered gentry women as well as gentry men; the cross-dressed *dan*, in particular, charmed both sexes.

In the first act of *Nan wanghou*, Zigao enhances his eroticism by pointing to the indeterminacy of his gender. In a sense, what makes the cross-dressed actor's performance successful is that the question of his gender is unresolvable. In this regard, it is allied with the natural, closer to the

---

71. Zhou Lianggong, *Laigu tang cangshu*, 1.1b. For another discussion of this passage, see Zhao Shanlin, *Zhongguo xiqu guanzhong xue*, p. 100. Qian Decang 錢德蒼, the editor of the massive compilation of performance texts of the Qianlong period, *Zhui baiqiu* 綴白裘 (A cloak of patchworked white fur) struck a similarly severe note, using much the same language as had Zhou Tanran, adding: "And this is not the worst! Plays that are about loyalty, filiality, chastity, and righteousness are few, whereas plays about clandestine romance are many. When women watch them, they become aroused and their hearts stray; these concerns are not to be minimized. One must not be careless" (*Xinding jie ren yi guang ji* 新訂解人頤廣集, quoted in Zhao Shanlin, *Zhongguo xiqu guanzhong xue*, p. 100).

72. Shen Defu, *Wanli yehuo bian*, 2: 644–45.

73. Pan Zhiheng, *Pan Zhiheng quhua*, p. 52.

omnipotentiality of nature than to the flatness of mere representation. In the second act, Zigao exploits the indeterminacy of his gender, trumping his female models by invoking his masculinity and his male predecessors by evoking his femininity. In the third act, Zigao is stripped of that omnipotentiality and indeterminacy by the king's sister, the Princess Yuhua, who employs those qualities to beat Zigao at his own game. The princess proves a far less passive spectator than her brother and quickly moves to take charge both of the play of gender and of the play.

In *zaju*, typically only one actor has a singing role in each act. Wang Jide gave the singing role in each act to the character who has mastery over allusion, and consequently the capacity to define gender. In the first two acts it is Zigao; in the third act, it becomes the princess. If Zigao defines his gender in large part through the invocation of models from the cultural past, the princess uses allusive reference to redefine him.

Unlike her brother the king, the princess did not witness Zigao's transformation at the hands of the palace women. She falls in love with Zigao believing he is female:

I am the younger sister of the king of Linchuan, Princess Yuhua. I'm just sixteen years old and have not yet been matched with a husband. My brother yesterday crowned a queen. She has such a countenance that fish would dive to the bottom of the stream when they saw her and geese would alight from the sky; the moon would hide itself and flowers would feel ashamed.[74] With such a heavenly figure, she is the most attractive woman in the kingdom. In this generation she has no peer. Forget about my brother, a man, falling in love with her. I am a girl, and I wouldn't mind swallowing her down with a drink of cold water. Oh, that there are such women in the world!

Her maid, overhearing this soliloquy, asks, "Does her ladyship admire the beauty of her highness? It would be so nice if you could marry a husband of that sort tomorrow." The princess replies in no uncertain terms that she is completely uninterested in finding a husband:

You silly wench, she is a woman! How can a man compare to her?

---

74. See note 81 in the Appendix for an explanation of this passage.

(Sings)

She is a sprite on the riverbanks picking kingfisher feathers.[75]
An immortal beauty from Shao Shi gathering pine nuts.[76]
Pendants chiming, the goddess of the mountains of Chu.
How can you take some outsider, a *man*,
And compare him to this charming consort of the king's inner palace?
Don't mention that idea again!   (16a)

Describing Zigao as "the goddess of the mountains of Chu," the princess employs the same allusion to describe Zigao as did the king, creating a parallel between the king's desire for Zigao and her own. Zigao chastised the king for mistaking him for the goddess of Chu, declaring that he was the poet who created the goddess. The princess repeats the same error, and her desire is at first glance an imitation and inversion of the king's.

In describing Zigao's sexual affiliations, the plot embarks on the same pattern of imitation and inversion that Zigao used to encode his gender. The portrayal of the princess's desire for the boy as a replication and an inversion plays with a commonplace of seventeenth-century Chinese conceptions of sexuality, that homoerotic desire is but a substitute for or an imitation of heteroerotic desire. Here, the king's homoerotic desire for the boy is the original, and the princess's heteroerotic desire the copy.

The princess's desire ought not to be immediately coded as heteroerotic, however.[77] She falls in love with Zigao believing he is a woman. What is interesting is the way in which the princess's defiant protest that no man could compare quickly gives way to recognition of the practicalities as she forces Zigao into a sexual relationship with her by threatening to blackmail him. Her confirmed antipathy toward the opposite sex suddenly gives ground to an opportunistic consumption of whichever gender presents itself. She seems more interested in Zigao's hyperfemininity than concerned about what lies beneath his feminine exterior.

---

75. This phrase is drawn from Cao Zhi's "Luoshen fu" 洛神賦, where it refers to the spirits who accompany the goddess of the Luo river (*Wen xuan*, 2: 899).

76. Here the princess compares Zigao to Shangyuan furen 上元夫人, a Daoist deity (*Shaoshi xianshu zhuan* 少室先姝傳, p. 5).

77. For an analysis of the play that describes the princess as 'ambiguously heterosexual' in a 'highly flexible sexual system," see Siu Leung Li, *Cross-Dressing in Chinese Opera*, pp. 186-89.

What the princess learns from Zigao, what she is infected by, is not simply the sexual licentiousness of the actor but his rhetorical dexterity, and in particular, his use of allusion to encode himself.

> If he had a silk cap covering his head, or were wearing purple official's robes,
> I'd take a husband like that.
> I would do justice to his lying naked to the waist on the eastern bed;[78]
> I'd gladly content myself with raising
>   his tray to my forehead to show my respect. (16a)[79]

The princess's encoding of her own gender through allusive citation mimics Zigao's claims to supersede all predecessors, claims which are shortly undermined. Zigao enters full of bravado:

> So, how do I look in golden hairpins and a gauze official's cap?
> I laugh myself silly thinking of the female collator of texts Xue Tao 薛濤.[80]
> In murky waters you can't tell carp from bass;
> Only when the water's clear can you finally tell the two apart. (16b–17a)

---

78. "Lying naked to the waist on the eastern bed" 袒腹東床 is an epithet for a good son-in-law. The phrase refers to the story of how the famed Six Dynasties calligrapher Wang Xizhi 王羲之 was selected as a son-in-law by Chi Jian 郗鑒. Chi Jian sent a messenger to Xizhi's uncle Wang Dao 王導 requesting him to select a son-in-law. The messenger came back saying that all the Wang sons were admirable men. "'When they heard that someone had come to spy out a son-in-law, all of them conducted themselves with circumspection. There was just one son who was lying sprawled out on the eastern bed as though he hadn't heard about it.' Chi said, 'He's just the one I want.' When he went to visit him, it turned out to be Wang Xizhi" (Liu Yiqing 劉義慶, *Shishuo xinyu jiaojian* 世說新語校箋, pp. 361–62; Mather, *Shih-shuo hsin-yü: A New Account of Tales of the World*, pp. 186–87). The same story is repeated in Wang Xizhi's biography in the *Jin shu* (pp. 2093–102) with a slight variation—Wang Xizhi was lying on the bed eating.

79. The Han dynasty figures Meng Guang 孟光 and Liang Hong 梁鴻 are traditionally viewed as the ideally respectful wife and husband. Their biography in the *Hou Han shu* relates that every night when Liang Hong arrived home, Meng Guang would have prepared his supper and would raise the tray to the level of her eyebrows to show her respect (Fan Ye, *Hou Han shu, juan* 83, pp. 2765–69).

80. Collator of texts was a conventional first position for students who had done well in the examinations; various anecdotes suggest that the Tang dynasty courtesan Xue Tao 薛濤 (768–831) was so admired by the governor of Sichuan that he considered nominating her for the post. As Wilt Idema and Beata Grant (*The Red Brush*, pp. 182–183) note, however, none of the anecdotes are reliable.

Zigao mocks his presumed predecessor, the Tang woman poet Xue Tao, of whom it was said that she should be awarded the official title "female collator of the classics" (*nü jiao shu* 女校書) in recognition of her learning. Once again, the indeterminacy of his gender renders him superior: "In murky waters you can't tell carp from bass." That confidence in his indeterminacy, however, is quickly dismantled by the Princess's interrogation:

> Princess: Just now, sister-in-law, you were in the palace. Did you make any flowers?
> Zigao: None. I've just read a few lines of a book.
> Princess: Reading books is men's business. Why are you imitating them?
> Zigao (aside): That's odd. Why does she keep staring at me so? My replies were wrong again. I almost let it show.
> Princess: Sister, why have you gone red all of a sudden?
> Zigao: I was drinking, so my face reddened.
> Princess: As a woman, you are not supposed to go round drinking wine. Let's stroll beyond the veranda by the garden. (They walk). (17a)

The natural world provides a number of motifs of gender inversion that the princess uses to probe Zigao. As they walk by the pond, Zigao asks why there are only female ducks. The princess answers that these birds are strange, for all the males have become females. Zigao blunders on, asking why one tree has two kinds of flowers on it. The princess replies that the tree has been "grafted." Here in miniature the text replicates that structure of imitation and inversion noted elsewhere. Contrary to expectation, it is not the human world that mirrors the natural world, but the natural world that reflects the human world—the ultimate inversion.

The princess moves to unmask Zigao, asking if she might try on his slippers to compare the size of their feet, and then demanding:

> (Sings:) Who's to say we shouldn't be able to see a bit of budding breast?
> I'm just afraid that when you stand on the fragrant steps a wind will lift your skirts,
> Or perhaps there will be a time when bathing in the hot springs, you won't put your shirt on in time.
> And when that happens, will you not fail in pretending to have light and radiant lotus petal footsteps and soft moist nipples?

(Speaks:) Sister, don't try to fool me. Tell me the truth. (18b)

It is precisely by evoking the specter of the future revelation of Zigao's "soft moist nipples" and "light and radiant lotus" feet that the princess punctures the illusory play of presence and absence that Zigao created in his initial challenge to the spectator. That earlier play allowed the spectator to enjoy the possibility of belief even while knowing that what he witnessed was a simulation. Like Zigao himself, the princess ironically deploys the notion of disavowal. Once defined by his witty repartee, Zigao is now reduced to a stammer. He confides to the audience that he can no longer play his part: "My replies were wrong again. I almost let it show." Ultimately, the princess shuts down the polysemous play of crossed genders in which Zigao had engaged:

> You are not the female ghost of the Cui 崔 family, who gave a golden bowl.[81]
> You are not Zheng Yingtao 鄭櫻桃, the demon clad in red robes....[82]
> You need not be like Zhu Yingtai 祝英台, disguising her glamour,[83]
> You should not copy the man of Lu, who locked his vermilion doors.[84]
> Why not show a little mercy?
> Save yourself the need for the pretenses of a hypocrite.
> You might end up with some merit in Heaven's eyes....
> You're as charming as Zhuo Wenjun 卓文君; don't blame me for pestering you.[85]

---

81. A reference to an anecdote in the *Soushen ji*, in which a young man on a hunting trip enters the underworld and engages in a romance with the daughter of the Cui family. She becomes pregnant. He leaves to return to his previous life; four years pass, and she appears and presents him with a son, giving him a golden bowl as well. See Gan Bao, *Soushen ji, juan* 16, pp. 203–5.

82. Zheng Yingtao was a boy actor who was the favorite of the Zhao emperor Shi Jilong 石季龍 (r. 335–48). At Zheng's behest, Shi murdered both his wives (*Jin shu, juan* 106, p. 2761).

83. According to popular legend, Zhu Yingtai and Liang Shanbo 梁山伯 were a pair of star-crossed lovers. Zhu Yingtai disguised herself as a man in order to study and take the examinations and fell in love with her schoolmate Liang Shanbo. Later, Liang went to visit her and found out that she was a woman; he wanted to marry her, but she was already betrothed. He died of grief, as did she on visiting his tomb.

84. The man of Lu 魯男子 refers to an anecdote related in the Mao commentary to the *Classic of Poetry* about a man whose adherence to principles of propriety supplanted human feeling. One night when there was a terrible storm, his female neighbor, whose roof was leaking, rushed over and beseeched him to let her in, but he refused. Later, "the man of Lu" became an epithet for a man who avoids relations with women ("Xiangbo" 巷伯, *Shi Mao shi zhuan shu, juan* 19, pp. 48–49).

Who told you to look so much like Pan Yue?[86]
The angrier you get, the cuter you become,
And I match your dark looks with a smile. (19b–20a)

The princess mimics Zigao's technique of self-definition through negation, divesting him of his allusive role models. If Zigao used definition
through negation to enlarge the scope of his potential gender, the princess
employs it to close down possibilities—all with the aim of reducing his
polymorphousness. Zigao is not a female ghost seducing a man, nor the
cross-dressed Zheng Yingtao seducing the future emperor of the Zhao,
Shi Jilong 石季龍, nor the man of Lu, who had no interest in women.
The king and the princess, then, model different modes of spectatorship.
The king takes great pleasure both in Zigao's illusory femininity and in
the plenitude or seeming totality of his gender attributes. In contrast, the
princess divests the cross-dresser of his capacity to cast illusion, stripping
him of his indeterminacy and omnipotentiality.

Act IV

The princess's foreclosure of the play of gender is only temporary. But it
enables the plot to double in on itself, so that the homoerotic marriage of
the first half of the play is mirrored by a heteroerotic marriage in the second. Zigao's second marriage is somewhat different from the first. The
wedding between Zigao and the king was a public affair accompanied by
much fanfare. The marriage between Zigao and the princess, by contrast,
is a clandestine matter, performed entirely by the princess.

If the third act begins with the unmasking of Zigao as "queen," the
fourth begins with the unmasking of the affair between Zigao and the
princess. The king's cross-examination of the lovers recalls the princess's
exposure of Zigao. In this act, however, Zigao regains the singing role, and
it is his turn to define the positions the various actors assume. When the

---

85. Zhuo Wenjun 卓文君 was the wife of the first-century poet Sima Xiangru 司馬
相如; here the princess alludes to the scandal caused by Zhuo Wenjun's elopement with
Sima Xiangru (see *Han shu, juan* 57, pp. 2529–31).

86. Pan Yue was an author of the Jin Dynasty famed for his good looks (*Shishuo xinyu
jiaojian*, pp. 326–27; Fang Xuanling, *Jin shu, juan* 55, p. 1500).

king interrogates him as to his clandestine relationship with the princess, he spins a vision of the princess as the unattainable goddess of Chu:

> I remember that day by the trellis of roseleaf raspberry.
> I recall that time beside the curtain of kingfisher jade.
> I spied her face like a flower.
> Just as I had made several delicate and deep bows.
> I was separated as far from her as though she were in the hermit's cave on the south side of Wu Mountain.
> Naturally, it was hard for me to ask whether the passing clouds were far or near.
> (25a)

The goddess of Chu is one of the many roles Zigao assumed (and rejected) for himself earlier. When the princess first spied Zigao, she described him as the goddess. Now Zigao re-envisions the princess as the goddess. The use of the same allusive reference to serve not only the king's and the princess's desire for the cross-dressed boy but the boy's desire for the princess links these various types of desire. It also points to the capaciousness of allusive reference, in a way that suggests that any notion of an authentic relation between the historical icon and its contemporary incarnation is as ludicrous as the madcap plot.

Incensed at the transgression of his sister and his lover, the king initially orders them both to hang themselves. But he hastily relents, reasoning that by marrying the boy to his sister, he can preserve his access to him. He directs that the boy wear women's clothes for the wedding, but in a way that divests the gesture of significance by depicting it as provisional and utilitarian:

My beauty, let's have you make your vows to each other. Today you will be a bridegroom. You ought to return to your original garb. However, a gauze cap and black boots would simply be too ordinary. Don't change—we'll just keep you in women's dress. (28a)

This wedding becomes Zigao's third wedding in as many acts. Wang Jide played on the conventional grand reunion (*da tuanyuan* 大團圓) in which scholar and beauty are united in marriage: here the marriage is open-ended, and all three principals are in effect wedded to one another. Rather than providing the conventional closure, the wedding is one of a series, no more permanent than the serial impersonations of the cross-dresser. This last wedding codifies the betwixt and between status of the cross-dresser as the site of both heteroerotic and homoerotic desire. The king's decision that he and his sister will share the boy achieves the combination of seemingly incompatible perspectives that the cross-dresser had challenged us to hold in tension at the beginning of the play. But the unsatisfying and unconvincing nature of this ending suggests that correctly pairing the actor is as impossible as correctly seeing him.

At the conclusion of the play, Zigao taunts the audience with his triumphant mastery of illusion:

> When I was the queen, you never saw my golden lotus feet.
> As the husband of a princess, I cover myself with an embroidered stole.
> It's this kind of pretending and costuming that make true and false hard to tell apart.
> In these two types of marriage
> I was heedless from start to finish, and all turned out as I wished. (28b)

"When I was the Queen, you never saw my golden lotus feet." With this taunt, Zigao momentarily creates the fiction that he had bound (golden lotus) feet. Yet his feet were never bound. As he declared at the opening of the play, "All I would need is bound feet of three inches, and my charms would never be second to those in red skirts." His claim, however, effectively creates the illusion of presence. We momentarily believe that we missed seeing his bound feet because he tells us that we never saw them. The optical illusion that Zigao rhetorically produces points to the way in which the performance of gender has throughout the play been discursive as much as visual. We have witnessed a rhetorical shell game.

In the closing lines, Zigao and the king similarly confuse the audience's temporal perception, reversing the relation between past and future so that the characters become points of origin instead of derivation:

The king: "Such a strange thing has happened today. Will not the historians of tomorrow record this in *The Compilation of the Glamorous and Strange*, and expect those who come after us to think it an amusing story?"
Zigao (Sings to the tune "Dianqian huan"):

This wedding, casually noted with a vermillion brush on red paper,
Will stand out as a new oddity in the history books.
A thousand years from now people will joke about it as they trim their silver
    lamps.[87]
Who ever saw the face of the Dowager Empress Bo 薄 on the cloud steps?[88]
Even though one ought to write literature in a spirit of jest,
How could we merely have said whatever came to mind? (29a)

The king's question invokes *Yanyi bian* 艷異編 (The compilation of the glamorous and strange), the anthology of fiction that contains the classical tale on which *Nan wanghou* is based. [89] As the king and Zigao project themselves as characters in a tale to be recorded in the future, they reverse the actual sequence of authorship. The play is based on the tale, but according to the characters, the tale will be based on the play. The original becomes a copy, the past seems to emulate the present, and the present begins to become the cultural past. When Zigao argues that, outside the world of the play, he will become "a new oddity . . . in the history books," the onstage present, the historical past, and the fictional narrative that are the play's source wind together, twisting round and round as though on a Möbius strip. The play does to its sources what Zigao did to the female sex; it divests its origins of their originary status, inverting the natural hierarchy between original and copy. The simulacrum becomes more highly valued than the original; in fact, it becomes an original.

87. "As they trim their silver lamps" refers to the telling of stories. The phrase is found in the title of the collection of stories *Jiandeng xinhua* 剪燈新話 (New stories written while trimming the wick of the lamp), compiled by Qu You 瞿佑 (preface dated 1378).

88. The Dowager Empress Bo, the consort of the first emperor of the Han and mother of Emperor Wen, is mentioned twice in the *Hou Han shu*, although not in such a way as to clarify the reference to her here (see Fan Ye, *Hou Han shu, juan* 1 *xia*, p. 33, and *zhi* 8, p. 1405). The Tang poet Niu Sengru 牛僧儒 wrote a fabulous tale concerning the Dowager Empress Bo; the implication is that this play, like Niu Sengru's tale, takes wild liberties with historical facts (Niu Sengru, *Zhouqin xingji* 周秦行記).

89. *Yanyi bian*, p. 137. The *Yanyi bian* is conventionally attributed to Wang Shizhen, but this attribution is likely spurious.

Conclusion

The final aria is, like the opening lines of the play, an invitation to herme-neutic activity that taunts us with our inability to settle on a final inter-pretation. When Zigao asks, "Whoever saw the face of the Dowager Em-press Bo on the cloud steps?" we realize that allusive reference depends on a structure of perception in which a single element stands in for a lost plenitude. In claiming to supersede one historical model after another, Zigao ruptures the illusion that allows allusion to function. His quick permutations as he frenetically adopts and discards allusive models belie the notion that the models of the past can be immanent in the figures of the present. Zigao implies that the auratic power that we bestow on allu-sive reference protects us from the knowledge of the chasm that divides us from the past, and thus from a sense of lack with regard to the past. Thus, this campy spoof momentarily engages in a serious critique of the way in which allusive reference structures our relation to the past.

In a last address, the king mocks the audience, "I reckon that he who wrote this play only borrowed our story to manifest his talents and in-scribe his satire. Those of you in the audience today should not take this too seriously." Even as we are given an invitation to interpretation, we are told that we will never be able to decode, or master, the text. In this sense, the reader's relation to the play resembles the spectator's relation to the boy actor. Just as the actor achieves power over the spectator through his employment of visual paradox, the text asserts its mastery over the reader through its employment of temporal paradox.

The closing lyrics of *Nan wanghou* feature the actors as authors of their own literary destinies. We should not forget, however, that the figure of the actor—indeed, the hyperfemininity of the male actor—is the fantasy of the literati author. Indeed, the very rivalry that we have noted for the ground of femininity is a construction of the literati author. The author enables the actor to make a claim to a superior femininity by scripting the words that the actor recites as he makes that claim. In this sense, a drama such as *Nan wanghou* is not just a comment on, but an aid to, the male ac-tor's self-fashioning as an icon of femininity.

When Zigao declares that he will become an icon that future genera-tions will imitate, the ways of the stage move beyond the theater and into the world. Half a century later, the actor Xu Ziyun, like Zigao, was praised by literati authors as more charming than Dongxian of the Han and was commemorated in a portrait whose title positions him as a cross-dressed Yang Guifei. The poems in praise of Ziyun, which are examined in the next chapter, echo the themes of Zigao's lyrics in praise of himself. In those poems, we see how the character Zigao might well have achieved his wish and become a cultural icon emulated by future generations.

FIVE

The Literary Consumption of Actors in Seventeenth-Century China

In this chapter, I discuss the social circulation of actors, asking how a highly social form of theatrical spectatorship may have served to strengthen ties among a rarified stratum of the mid-seventeenth century elite. We saw in the previous chapter that Wang Jide's drama *The Male Queen* took as its theme a play of illusion and disillusion that was quintessentially theatrical, and showed how that play might characterize not only the spectator's reception of the gender of the cross-dressed actor but also the literatus's understanding of allusion. This chapter builds upon that analysis by asking how this tension between illusion and disillusion might have been significant to a distinguished coterie among the mid-seventeenth century literary elite as they employed a homoerotic discourse in praising the charms of the cross-dressed actor. If, in the previous chapter, it was the gender of the actor that became ambiguous as the tension between illusion and disillusion was strategically employed, in these poems, how might a similar dynamic create ambiguity in the poet's articulation of homoerotic sentiments? How might the perspective characteristic of the social spectator habituated to the perceptual challenges of the theater be applied to an understanding of the poems' phrasing of homoerotic sentiments?

My analysis focuses on poems in praise of the actor Xu Ziyun written by a number of high-ranking officials and literary luminaries, such as Gong Dingzi, Wang Shizhen, and Mao Xiang.[1] Xu Ziyun, a servant in the home of Mao Xiang, was for seventeen years romantically involved with the poet Chen Weisong, one of the most famed lyricists of the Qing.[2] Chen's privileged status contrasted sharply with Xu's, for Xu was quite possibly not even a commoner under Qing law, but a "base person" (*jianmin*).[3] Yet their romantic attachment was celebrated by some of the most eminent statesmen and literary luminaries of the early Qing, whose poems in praise of Xu declared both their desire to emulate Chen and the impossibility of fulfilling that desire. The poems of Chen's circle liken him to the Tang poet Du Mu 杜牧 (803–52), whom they view as the last of the romantics; his nonchalant disdain for social propriety becomes a way of understanding the love of a literatus for an actor.

The men who frequented the salon of Mao Xiang were from the highest stratum of the national elite, in terms of both their political and their literary status. Wu Weiye, for example, was *primus* in the metropolitan

---

1. Many of these poems are found in a collection entitled *Jiuqing tuyong* 九青圖詠 (Poems on the portrait of Jiuqing), which consists of over 150 poems inscribed as colophons for a portrait of Ziyun. Poems in tribute to Ziyun by Chen Weisong's and Mao Xiang's contemporaries are also reprinted in an early Republican collection, *Yunlang xiaoshi* 雲郎小史 (A brief history of Yunlang), compiled by Mao Xiang's late nineteenth-century descendant Mao Heting 冒鶴亭. A noted bibliophile, Mao Heting collected the extant works of his ancestors and published them under the title *Maoshi congshu* 冒氏叢書 in 1911–17. *Yunlang xiaoshi* includes letters and prefaces by contemporaries of Mao Xiang as well as a number of poems written to commemorate Ziyun's performances, bid him farewell, and mourn his death. Both collections are reprinted in Zhang Cixi, *Qingdai yandu liyuan shiliao zheng xubian*, pp. 958–1001. Some of these poems also appear in *Xu benshi shi* 續本事詩 (Sequel to affairs that inspired poems), edited by the seventeenth-century literatus Xu Qiu 徐釚 (1636–1708), a friend of Chen Weisong's who was a colleague of his in compiling the official Ming history. See, e.g., Xu Qiu, *Ciyan congtan*, pp. 245, 367, 370.

2. Chen was the leader of the Yangxian 陽羨 school of song lyric (*ci* 詞). One of the three dominant schools of the Qing, the Yangxian school modeled itself after the "virile" (*haofang* 豪放) lyrics of Su Shi and Xin Qiji 辛棄疾 (1140–1207); see Chia-ying Yeh, "The Ch'ang-chou School of Tz'u Criticism," p. 439.

3. We do not know enough about Xu Ziyun's status prior to entering Mao Xiang's household to know whether he was a base person or a commoner; if he were bought as a musician or actor, he was likely of hereditary base status, whereas if he were bought as a servant and then trained to sing and act, he may have been a commoner.

examinations of 1631 and one of the most famous men of letters of his day.[4] Gong Dingzi was successively president of the Board of Punishments in 1664–66, of the Board of War in 1666–69, and of the Board of Ceremonies in 1669–73.[5] The famed poet and literary critic Wang Shizhen served as police magistrate of Yangzhou in 1659 and was a frequent guest at Mao's estate at Rugao 如皋 during his tenure in Yangzhou; he later became president of the Censorate and of the Board of Punishments.[6] Although the liaisons of such authors as Mao Xiang, Gong Dingzi, and Wu Weiye with the famed courtesans of the age have been much discussed, the circulation of actors among them has received little attention.[7]

This occlusion reflects in part the paucity of sources beyond the corpus of poems on Xu Ziyun. These poems represent the most substantial body of texts on any seventeenth-century actor, indeed any actor prior to the mid-Qing. Numerous poems in tribute to actors through the ages survive, and in the case of a well-known actor such as Gong Dingzi's traveling companion Wang Zijia 王紫稼 (1622–57), several sets of poems are still extant.[8] Members of Mao's circle also wrote poems on the occasions of

---

4. Hummel, *Eminent Chinese of the Ch'ing Period*, pp. 882–883; Wakeman, *The Great Enterprise*, pp. 821–72.

5. Hummel, *Eminent Chinese of the Ch'ing Period*, p. 431.

6. Ibid., pp. 831–32; Wakeman, *The Great Enterprise*, p. 1002.

7. Indeed, Mao Xiang, Gong Dingzi, Wu Weiye, and their circle were the architects of the courtesan cult of the late Ming and early Qing. Mao Xiang's biography of the former courtesan Dong Bai 董白, who became his concubine; Hou Fangyu's 侯方域 (1618–55) biography of the courtesan Li Xiangjun 李香君, with whom he was romantically involved; Gong Dingzi's poems in tribute to the courtesan Gu Mei 顧媚, whom he also married; and Wu Weiye's songs in tribute to the courtesan Bian Yujing 卞玉京, who once proposed to him, contributed to a literature that romanticized the courtesan as a figure of nostalgia and an emblem of loyalism. For further discussion of the relationships between these literati and courtesans, see Kang-i Sun Chang, *The Late-Ming Poet Ch'en Tzu-lung*; and Wai-yee Li, "Heroic Women in Qing Literature."

8. The same poets who celebrated Xu Ziyun also exchanged a number of poems written to or about the actor Wang Zijia. Wang, who was originally from Suzhou, is commemorated in Wu Weiye's "Wanglang qu" 王郎曲 (Song of Master Wang) as a wily trickster who mesmerizes a new generation of youths after the fall of the Ming, continuing to perform as though the dynasty had not succumbed; see Wu, *Wu Meicun quanji*, pp. 283–85. Meng Sen (*Xinshi congkan*, p. 89) believes Wu to have written "Wanglang qu" for Wang in 1656 as a poem on parting. Qian Qianyi 錢謙益 (1582–1664) also presented Wang with a set of fourteen quatrains to mark their parting when Wang traveled to Beijing in 1652. Three years later, when Wang left Beijing for the south, Gong Dingzi wrote a

birthdays and partings to three other actors in Mao's troupe, Qinxiao 秦
簫, Lingchu 靈雛, and Yangzhi 楊枝.[9] However, no other set of poems in
tribute to an actor is comparable to the Ziyun corpus in terms of its detailed documentation of the relationship between an actor and a literatus.[10] In most poems in praise of actors from this period, the actors are
identified only by a surname to which the suffix *lang* 郎 (master or boy) is
added, and little more is known about them than the troupe with which
they performed.[11]

　　These poems in praise of Xu Ziyun, then, offer a rare opportunity to
discuss the social significance of the circulation of actors among literati
during the early Qing.[12] In elucidating the significance of these poems, I

---

set of fourteen matching quatrains that rhymed with Qian Qianyi's. Gong also wrote
twelve quatrains mourning Wang's untimely death at the hands of the censor Lin Senxian
林森先. Xu Qiu, *Ciyan congtan*, p. 276. These sources are collected in Meng Sen, *Xinshi
congkan*, pp. 85–98.

　　9. Xu Qiu, *Ciyan congtan*, pp. 271, 320; Zhang Cixi, *Qingdai yandu liyuan shiliao zheng
xubian*, "Yunlang xiaoshi," pp. 958–59.

　　10. See Zhao Shanlin, *Lidai yongju shige xuanzhu*, for a comprehensive collection of
poems concerning the theater.

　　11. Very few actors are identified by more than their surname; the use of the given
names of Wang Zijia and Xu Ziyun by their patrons indicates they were both more respected and more intimate with the literati who wrote about them than the ordinary actor. However, the three different sets of characters used to transcribe Wang Zijia's given
name suggest that the name was seldom written and that he likely did not engage in poetic
correspondence. Xu Ziyun, in contrast, had a literary pseudonym (*hao* 號), Jiuqing 九青,
and a style name (*zi* 字), Manshu 曼殊, in the manner of a literatus.

　　12. Wu Cuncun treats the Xu Ziyun corpus in *Homoerotic Sensibilities in Late-
Imperial China*, pp. 67–80. She analyzes the poems to claim that there was a "change in
romantic fashion from courtesan to boy actor among the early Qing elite" (p. 78). However, as I observe in note 7 to this chapter, the most famed of the poets included in the Ziyun corpus also authored the poems constitutive of the courtesan cult of the late Ming and
early Qing. This suggests that these authors wrote in various modes rather than that the
fashion had swung to boy actors. Gong Dingzi and Mao Xiang memorialized their relationships with courtesans in poetry and prose. But in their poems on actors, if courtesans
are mentioned, it is in the abstract and in service of the assertion that the charms of the actor are superior. A poem entitled "Quatrains by Qu Youzhong on Watching a Performance" (Zhang Cixi, *Qingdai yandu liyuan shiliao zheng xubian*, "Yunlang xiaoshi," p. 961)
describes the courtesans of Nanjing as "muck and shit" in comparison to the beautiful
boys of Mao's theatricals: "Qinxiao 秦簫 sings and Yangzhi 楊枝 dances / In their mist
Ziyun is dangerously alluring / Hong'er 紅兒 and Xue'er 雪兒 are not worthy of being
named / And Taoye 桃葉 and Taogen 桃根 are like muck and shit." The poems in tribute

employ two different approaches. First, I draw on the anthropological literature on the gift to speculate about the ways in which the circulation of the poems created or strengthened bonds among their authors and show how individual poets map themselves into these social relations by professing their passion for the boy. In the pages that follow, I not only examine Mao Xiang's gift of Xu Ziyun to Chen Weisong but also discuss the more abstract exchanges that take place as the body of the actor circulates implicitly through these poems. The extensive literature on the gift has focused largely on the ways in which the circulation of gifts creates social networks that may be deployed instrumentally. But a less prominently developed path of argument has illuminated the ways in which the circulation of gifts establishes emotional connections.[13] These poems of longing and desire allow us to examine how the exchange of poems as gifts establishes a topography of emotional indebtedness among the poets of Chen's circle. The implicit gift of the actor creates such bonds, but, on a more immediate level, the poem is a material object whose exchange contributes to the instantiation of sociality. As the poems circulate among the members of this circle, so do the poets, enchained by their inalienable relation to the poems. These poems become, like the body of the actor, the site of concealed social relations; in them are inscribed the ties among their authors, Chen, and Ziyun.

Second, I examine the implications of these poets' claims to be "crazed with passion" (*qingchi* 情痴) in the context of the concealed social relations of these poems. The poems are generated in empathic resonance to Chen Weisong's passion for the actor; in this circle, he is considered the last of the romantics. How, then, should we understand the desire for the actor expressed in these poems? *Qing* is itself a paradoxical concept; the term eludes definition and often functions metaphorically, seeming to point to something else. I argue that this metaphorical operation of *qing* takes several forms: not only do the emotions professed by the speakers often seem to index other sorts of emotions, but the speaker's emotions

---

to boy actors should be read in the context of the literature on male love, in which arguments regarding the superiority of the love of boys plays a strong role, as we saw in the outrageous claims made in *Nan wanghou*.

13. Yan, *The Flow of Gifts*, pp. 141–46.

often seem to exist only as analogues of Chen Weisong's own emotions. The poets dramatize their own *qing* by likening it to that of Chen Weisong and writing in empathic resonance with him. One consequence of *qing*'s metaphorical operation is that it is difficult to say whether the desire expressed in these poems is homoerotic or, to use Eve Sedgwick's term, homosocial—that is, to determine which is more important: the expression of desire or the creation of social relations through the expression of shared desire.[14] These poems play with the assumption that they record genuine sentiment. In a nutshell, they make use of the tension between the lyric and the dramatic; their effectiveness as dramatic declarations of a homoerotic longing that echoes Chen Weisong's depends upon the premise that they are lyric utterances. The success of these poems as dramatic and resonant utterances is dependent in part on the reader's capacity to enter the illusion that they are expressions of personal sentiment. Like such metatheatrical texts as *Nan wanghou*, they demand that the reader keep illusion and disillusion in tension.

Although these texts are part of the seventeenth-century vogue for male love that scholars such as Vivien Ng, Bret Hinsch, and Giovanni Vitiello have discussed, the significance of the expression of homoerotic desire in this context needs to be carefully weighed.[15] Hinsch, Ng, and Vitiello view the new prevalence of texts that touch on male love as an indication that it was more widely and openly practiced during the late Ming than before. However, there may be reasons for the greater *discursive* visibility of male love other than more widespread practice. The ubiquity of *qing* as a theme in seventeenth-century literature and the strong interest in *qi qing* 奇情 (extraordinary *qing*) may in part account for the increased attention to *qing* between men in the literature of the period. In this regard, Michel Foucault's "repressive hypothesis" (his suggestion that "the steady proliferation of discourses concerned with sex" that began in eighteenth-century Europe marked the onset of a degree of

---

14. Sedgwick, *Between Men*, pp. 1–5.

15. Vivien W. Ng speaks of a "discursive explosion" in "Homosexuality and the State in Late-Imperial China," p. 76. Bret Hinsch (*Passions of the Cut Sleeve*, p. 119) notes a more intense awareness in the late Ming of a "homosexual tradition." On the proliferation of late Ming sources on male love, see also Vitiello, "The Dragon's Whim," pp. 341–73.

sexual repression previously unknown) counters the assumption that discussion *per se* is evidence of practice.[16]

Moreover, it is difficult to ascertain the degree to which these poems
attest to their author's desire for the actor as opposed to the extent to
which they fulfill the social obligation of flattering Chen's desire by echoing it. Did the authors of these poems intend to act on the desires expressed in them, or were they merely cultivating a shared bond with Chen
Weisong? The currency of these poems was not necessarily tied to the
gold standard of having experienced the actor's performance. Some of the
poems were penned by intimates of Chen Weisong's who had long acquaintance with the actor, others were likely written by men who had
seen only the actor's portrait.

The moralists whose warnings against liaisons with actors are strewn
across the pages of notation books would certainly have condemned such
declarations of desire for the actor.[17] Among those who sojourned at Mao
Xiang's estate in Rugao, however, connoisseurship of the theater—and of
actors—was a mark of sophistication, even cultivation. In the paradoxical
literary culture of the late Ming and early Qing, the transgression of
boundaries of status and of conventional heteroerotic norms lent extra
cachet. To the degree that a form of desire was considered unconventional (*qi* 奇) and opposed to traditional orthodoxies, it was potentially
authentic (*zhen* 真). Indeed, authentic passion (*zhenqing*) was the most
prized term in seventeenth-century literary culture.[18]

In these poems, Chen Weisong is frequently depicted as an incarnation of *zhenqing* through comparison to the Tang poet Du Mu, who was
often invoked during the late imperial period (and even during his own
time) as the last of the romantics, a figure with a great disregard for social
convention. Xu Ziyun was named after the Tang courtesan Ziyun, with
whom Du Mu was said to be smitten.[19] In likening Chen to Du Mu, the

---

16. Foucault, *The History of Sexuality*, pp. 18–49.

17. See, e.g., Lu Rong, *Shuyuan zaji*, p. 124; Shen Defu, *Wanli yehuo bian*, 2: 621; Xie
Zhaozhe, *Wuzazu*, p. 305, and Zhang Han, *Songchuang mengyu*, pp. 122–23.

18. Epstein, *Competing Discourses*, p. 8.

19. The Tang dynasty author Meng Qi 孟啓 related that when Du Mu was a censor in
Luoyang, his infatuation with Ziyun occasioned a legendary violation of social decorum.
Du Mu was not invited to a banquet attended by the luminaries of Luoyang society at
which Ziyun was to perform. Because Du Mu's duty as a censor was to discipline other of-

men in Chen Weisong's coterie deftly legitimated Chen's relationship with Xu Ziyun. Chen's eccentricity in engaging in a serious romance (as opposed to an evening's dalliance) with an actor was rendered socially acceptable by portraying him as "crazed with *qing*" (*qingchi*). The members of Mao's salon affirmed their common understanding not just through mutual appreciation of the boy's charms and the shared expression of desire for him but through a collective indulgence of Chen's passion for a servant. At the same time, the poets aspired to demonstrate that they, too, were fools for love by declaring their desire to enter into Chen and Ziyun's relationship.[20]

Theatricals at Mao Xiang's Estate

When Mao Xiang followed his father in refusing to serve the Qing dynasty, they retired to a country estate, the Shuihui yuan 水繪園, northeast of Rugao and only a hundred miles from Nanjing. There Mao entertained the cultural magnates and political notables of the age. Jiang Jingqi 蔣景祁 (1646–95?) wrote that Mao Xiang and Chen Weisong's father, Chen Zhenhui 陳貞慧 (1605–56), spent their entire family fortunes entertaining men of reputation (*mingshi* 名士).[21] This is no doubt an exag-

---

ficials, the host had been afraid that his presence might dampen the party. When Du Mu made it known that he wished to attend, the host had no choice but to express him an invitation. In the event, Du Mu did hinder the conviviality of the gathering, not so much because he imposed restraint on others as because he imposed none on himself. When he received the last-minute invitation, Du Mu was already drunk. Arriving at the party, he alienated the guests by simply staring at them. Du then asked the host to point out the courtesan Xu Ziyun, enraging the other courtesans. Having offended everyone present, Du Mu then composed a poem commemorating his own discourteousness. See Meng Qi, *Benshi shi*, pp. 18–19.

20. As Vitiello writes, "For a man of *qing* the common laws, the relative rules of society and of its pragmatic ethic, mean very little" ("The Dragon's Whim," p. 370).

21. "Chen Weisong was a guest at Rugao for ten years, where Mao Xiang was his host. At the end of the Ming, his father Zhenhui of Jialing 迦陵, and Mao Xiang of Rugao, Hou Fangyu of Shangqiu 商丘, and Fang Yizhi 方以智 of Tongcheng 桐城 . . . spent their entire families' wealth in getting to know the famed men of the age, and they were universally known as the 'Four Lords'" (Jiang Jingqi, "Jialing xiansheng waizhuan" 迦陵先生外傳 [An unofficial biography of Chen Weisong], quoted in Zhang Cixi, *Qingdai yandu liyuan shiliao zheng xubian*, p. 959). Jiang Jingqi (*zi* Jingshao 京少) was a noted *ci* poet from Yixing in Jiangsu.

geration, but it points to the importance of such activities in fostering political connections. Since both Mao and his father claimed to be in reclusion, the Shuihui Gardens is represented in these poems as a rustic retreat divorced from political concerns, a refuge from the vicissitudes of political life for the cosmopolitan libertines of Nanjing.[22] Contemporary politics are not mentioned in these poems about private theatricals. Yet, given the cast of characters who attended such entertainments, they could not by definition be so isolated.

Mao's entertainment of prominent members of the political and cultural elite featured his prized troupe of actors. His descendant Mao Heting 冒鶴亭 (1873–1959) wrote:

From every direction, the guests arrived as though they were returning home, men such as the sons and brothers of members of the Donglin 東林, Jishe 幾社, and Fushe 復社 parties. . . . Mao Xiang would earnestly detain his guests, bringing out his actors to entertain them. The actors included Xu Ziyun, Yangzhi, Lingchu, and Qinxiao, but Yunlang's [Xu Ziyun's] artistry and looks were superior to his peers, and people today still praise the everlasting love that he shared with Chen Qinian 陳其年 [Weisong].[23]

The members of the Donglin party and its successors, the Jishe and Fushe, were repeatedly subjected to political purges.[24] Chen Weisong's paternal grandfather, Chen Yuting 陳于廷 (1565–1635), an influential member of the Donglin, and his father Zhenhui, a key member of the Fushe, were victims of the periodic mass dismissals of adherents of these organizations from the bureaucracy. His grandfather, a censor noted for his frankness, lost his post after displeasing Ruan Dacheng, the notorious

---

22. Mao Xiang left Nanjing and Suzhou to return to Rugao because of pressure to join literary cliques in those urban centers. Mao's family had lived in Rugao since the end of the Yuan. His father and grandfather were both high officials, and he had considerable social advantages, becoming a friend of the artist Dong Qichang at age fourteen. Although he never passed the provincial examinations, he was active in politics as a member of the Restoration Society (Fushe 復社). For more on Mao Xiang, see Wakeman, *The Great Enterprise*, p. 139.

23. Zhang Cixi, *Qingdai yandu liyuan shiliao zheng xubian*, "*Yunlang xiaoshi*," p. 958.

24. The Donglin, or Eastern Forest Party, had for its base an academy of the same name founded in Wuxi in 1604. A loosely organized political coalition, it was formed in part for the advancement of civil service examination candidates. See Wakeman, "The Price of Autonomy."

henchman of the eunuch Wei Zhongxian 魏忠賢 (1568–1627).[25] His father was thrown into prison after denouncing Ruan's corruption, and according to Mao Heting, Mao Xiang spent several thousand taels to have him released.[26] In stating that the men of the Donglin, Jishe, and Fushe were frequent guests in Rugao, Mao Heting indicates that at Rugao, his ancestor regaled all the men of note on the "right side" of the factional politics of the period—the side that initially suffered at the hands of Wei Zhongxian but won in the courts of public opinion.

As Mao Heting suggests, the social and sexual circulation of actors in this world of private theatricals helped Mao Xiang affirm his connections with the members of these political societies. The Xu Ziyun poems owe their genesis in part to Mao Xiang's and Chen Weisong's position at the center of the most rarified stratum of the mid-seventeenth-century elite, a status that made the men of the age anxious to establish social connection with them. These poems not only testify to the social pleasure of expressing desire for the actor, but also bear witness to the pleasure of expressing membership in a community centered around Chen Weisong and, perhaps more important, his powerful patron, Mao Xiang.

Chen Weisong was the son of one of the most privileged aristocrats of Jiangnan. His father, Zhenhui, was known as one of Jiangnan's Four Lords (*si gongzi* 四公子; the others were Mao Xiang, Fang Yizhi 方以智 [?–1671?], and Hou Fangyu 侯方域 [1618–55]). The Four Lords were distinguished not only by their aristocratic birth and literary talent but also by a combination of political loyalism and romantic dissipation unique to the last decades of the Ming. Among the loyalists gathered in the southern capital of Nanjing, they were eminent and active within the Donglin party; they set the tone in the pleasure quarters of Qinhuai, where they found sanctuary among the most famous courtesans and actors of the age.[27]

---

25. Hummel, *Eminent Chinese of the Ch'ing Period*, p. 82.

26. Zhang Cixi, *Qingdai yandu liyuan shiliao zheng xubian*, "*Yunlang xiaoshi*," p. 959.

27. Chen noted in a poem that his father and Mao Xiang were "brothers" in the Qinhuai pleasure quarters (*Qinhuai jiu xiongdi* 秦淮舊兄弟) (Zhang Cixi, *Qingdai yandu liyuan shiliao zheng xubian*, "*Yunlang xiaoshi*," p. 967).

Chen Weisong was eminently poised for an illustrious literary career because of his father's friendships with such men as Mao Xiang and Wu Weiye. Wu Weiye tutored the young Weisong in poetry and did much to publicize his talent, calling him one of the rising poets of the southeast.[28] When Chen Zhenhui died, Mao Xiang invited Chen Weisong to live at his estate while he studied for the examinations.[29] The backing of this powerful patron positioned Chen among men of great influence. Yet despite Mao's patronage, Chen encountered great difficulty in obtaining a civil service position. Like his father before him, Chen passed only the *shengyuan* examinations and repeatedly failed subsequent attempts at the provincial examinations, although he tried until the age of 52.[30] Until the age of 53, his only government employment was a post in Nanyang, provided for him in 1669 by Mao Xiang's friend Gong Dingzi.

In 1679, when Chen was 53 years old, he sat for the *boxue hongci* 博學鴻詞, a special set of examinations sponsored by the Kangxi emperor as a means of recruiting talented Han Chinese literati and, in particular, of co-opting southern intellectuals into the Qing government in Beijing.[31] Although a number of eminent scholars declined the opportunity to participate in these examinations because of their continuing sentiments of loyalty to the Ming, it was primarily the men of Chen's father's generation that resisted most strongly. The calligrapher Fu Shan 傅山 (1607–84), in his seventies at the time of the examination, journeyed to Beijing so as not to offend a powerful patron, yet, once there, claimed to be too ill to sit the examinations.[32] Members of Chen's circle such as Deng Hanyi

---

28. In later life, Chen became close to the poets Nalan Xingde 納蘭性德 (1655–85) and Zhu Yizun as well as to Cao Xueqin's grandfather Cao Yin 曹寅, a confidant of the Kangxi emperor (Spence, *Ts'ao Yin and the K'ang-hsi Emperor*, pp. 51–56).

29. According to Mao Heting, Chen Weisong required three taels (*san jin* 三金) per month for his expenses at Rugao; Mao Xiang was surprised at his extravagance but permitted it because he cherished Chen's talent (Zhang Cixi, *Qingdai yandu liyuan shiliao zheng xubian*, "Yunlang xiaoshi," p. 967; Mao Heting gives no source).

30. Hummel, *Eminent Chinese of the Qing Period*, p. 103.

31. Some 180 candidates were summoned to take the *boxue hongci* examinations offered on April 11, 1679. Of these, 36 declined, feigned ill health, or died before the examination took place; 102 failed, and 50 candidates passed (Kessler, *K'ang-hsi and the Consolidation of Ch'ing Rule*, p. 159). See also Bai, "Turning Point."

32. Bai, *Fu Shan's World*, p. 215.

and Sun Zhiwei, who were only slightly younger, did participate.[33] Chen's generation could not ignore the fact that the examinations constituted a test of loyalism, but they were enticed by the examination's prestige as a cultural event, for the *boxue hongci* drew scholars from all over the nation together to exchange ideas and provided the first large-scale occasion for literary gathering and scholarly exchange since the Qing conquest.[34] Chen had not yet begun his career, and the examinations offered him an excellent opportunity. After passing the examinations, Chen was appointed a compiler of the history of the Ming dynasty, a project that had stalled until successful candidates in the *boxue hongci* were assigned to the project. Chen died four years later, when his career as an official had just begun.

Chen's repeated failures in the examinations prior to the *boxue hongci* left him without means but with plenty of leisure, and he became a permanent house guest at Mao Xiang's estate at Rugao, spending years there preparing for the examinations. Not daring to venture home to Yixing after each failure, he returned to Rugao, where he benefited from Mao's indulgence. The size of Chen's corpus of song lyrics testifies not only to his talent but to a life spent at leisure in the world of private theatricals; he was one of the most prolific writers of *ci* during the late imperial period.[35]

More important for our story, Mao also gave Chen Weisong the actor Xu Ziyun as his personal servant during his sojourns at Rugao. Ziyun was in his teens, some fifteen years younger than Chen, when he met Chen in 1658.[36] One of the most cherished performers within the acting troupe

---

33. Meyer-Fong, "Site and Sentiment," p. 135. Bai Qianshen ("Turning Point") points out that the expectation of loyalism did not extend to the sons of loyalists; five of Gu Yanwu's 顧炎武 (1613–82) nephews, for example, obtained *jinshi* degrees under the Qing.

34. Bai Qianshen ("Turning Point") notes that "large-scale gatherings like those held by one of the major societies, the Fu She, which had had as many as several thousand attendees and exerted tremendous influence nationwide" had not taken place since the fall of the Ming; the excitement that surrounded the *boxue hongci* was in part a response to the renewal of such opportunities.

35. Chen's collected works, the *Huhailou ji* 湖海樓集 (published in 1721), contains six volumes of prose, ten volumes of parallel prose, eight volumes of *shi* poetry, and thirty volumes of *ci*. Chen was well known both for his parallel prose and song lyrics. He published three collections of *ci*: the *Wusi ci* 烏絲詞, *Jialing ci* 迦陵詞, and the *Zhu Chen cun ci* 朱陳村詞, a collaboration with Zhu Yizun that made him nationally famous.

36. The date of Xu Ziyun's birth is unclear. Mao Heting gives it as 1644 because of a poem written by Chen Weisong in 1658 that seems to commemorate a first meeting with

Mao kept to entertain his friends, Ziyun was famed for his singing and his playing of the flute. He was already an actor before he entered Mao's service, although it is not clear where he performed. Nor is it known how Ziyun came to be in Mao's possession.

Chen did not own Ziyun, and the relationship was permitted to continue, it seems, only at Mao's pleasure. When in 1668 Chen and Ziyun left Rugao for Beijing without daring to inform Mao, the elopement caused a small scandal. On the way to Beijing, to make matters more awkward, the couple accidentally met Mao's son Danshu 丹書 (b. 1639). When the pair reached Beijing, Gong Dingzi, at the time President of the Board of War, wrote to Mao to intercede on their behalf:

Xu Ziyun followed Chen, and they are very happy together, but he feels uneasy because he did not inform you when he left. On the way they met Qingruo 青若 [Danshu]; Qingruo must have informed you of his contrition. My old friend, I know that because of your capacity for deep feeling you have cared for others more deeply than for yourself your whole life long. You must care for (*lian* 憐) Qinian [Weisong] more than you care for Xu Ziyun; one certainly will not want to punish him after the fact.[37]

This episode is often cited as proof of Mao's largesse toward Chen and Ziyun. Han Tan 韓菼 (1637–1704), a friend of Mao's who later became chancellor of the Hanlin academy and president of the Board of Ceremonies, added in a note to his poem "Lamenting the Death of Zheng Jun 徵 君 [Mao Xiang]" that Mao "had a servant whom he loved who was led away by a guest, but he never asked about it and treated him [the guest] even better afterward."[38] Gong Dingzi's reasoning, "You must love Qinian

---

Ziyun. It begins with the lines "A Yun at age fifteen / Stands charmingly beside the screen. / He asks smiling from whence the traveler hails / His pure, elegant beauty emanating from his shining eyes" (Zhang Cixi, *Qingdai yandu liyuan shiliao zheng xubian*, "Yunlang xiaoshi," p. 960). If the poem accurately described Xu Ziyun's age, he would have been fourteen by western count. It is conventional, however, to begin with the phrase " . . . at age 15" in writing poems about entertainers; Chen Weisong uses it as well in a poem to an actor named Yuanlang (Master Yuan). The phrase hearkens back to a poem by Zhang Han, "Zhou xiaoshi shi" (Poem on the little page by the name of Zhou). See Lu Qinli, *Xian Qin Han Wei Jin Nanbei chao shi*, 1: 737. For this reason, we cannot take it too literally. Still, we might surmise that Ziyun was in his teens at the time the poem was written.

37. Lu Qinli, *Xian Qin Han Wei Jin Nanbei chao shi*, 1: 968–69.
38. Ibid., p. 969.

more than you love Xu Ziyun; so you certainly will not want to punish him after the fact," is especially striking. Gong's reference to punishing Chen rather than Ziyun suggests that Ziyun, since he was of base status— indeed, the property of the Mao household—was not held responsible for the elopement. Yet Gong also spoke of Mao's affection for the actor in the same breath that he spoke of his affection for his best friend's son. Ziyun was not simply a plaything. He was a beloved member of the household.

Ziyun married, but his marriage seems to have had little impact on his relationship with Chen—at least so far as the poems by Chen's friends attest. Chen took a concubine several years after his wife died. At the time, Chen was with Ziyun in Zhongzhou. The concubine gave birth to a son in 1676, but when the son died two years later, her relationship with Chen ended.

Ziyun died in Yixing, Chen's ancestral home. Mao Heting suspects that he died at the beginning of the fourth month of 1675. Among the original drafts of Chen's poems, one mourning Ziyun, "Moved by Thoughts of the Past on Tomb-Sweeping Day" ("Qingming gan jiu" 清明感舊), had a note attached to it in Chen's hand: "At this time Yun had recently passed away." Chen appended twenty poems by his friends on the subject of Yun's death. Chen's brother, the editor of the printed edition of Chen's works, removed the note about Yun's death; perhaps Chen's family was not as accepting of the relationship as were Chen's friends.[39] In 1682 Chen died in the capital, mourned by Mao Xiang, who had buried Chen's father as well.

The Practice of Private Theatricals

During the late Jiajing and the Wanli periods, the practice of owning acting troupes and sponsoring performances at one's home became fashionable among members of the gentry.[40] The practice dates at least as far back

---

39. Ibid., p. 971.

40. For information on private acting troupes, see Lu Eting, *Kunju yanchu shigao*; Sun Chongtao and Xu Hongtu, *Xiqu youling shi*; and Wang An-Chi, *Mingdai chuanqi zhi juchang ji qi yishu*. One of the most renowned owners of such private troupes was Ruan Dacheng. Ruan became infamous as the adopted son of the eunuch Wei Zhongxian, but he was also much respected as a playwright, and his actors were known for their high levels of musicianship. Wu Weiye, in a piece written for Mao Xiang's fiftieth birthday, recalled

as the Southern Song. During the mid-Ming, it had enjoyed some popularity among aficionados of the theater such as the dramatist Li Kaixian and the connoisseur He Liangjun. However, it was around the turn of the seventeenth century that the fashion took hold, according to the memoirist Zhang Dai. Zhang Dai, whose family later owned not one but six acting troupes, including an all-female troupe, gave credit to his grandfather and his grandfather's friends for starting the craze:[41] "As for my family's musicians, we had none in generations past, but during the Wanli period my grandfather and his friends Fan Changbai 范長白, Zou Yugong 鄒愚公, Huang Zhenfu 黃貞父, and Bao Hansuo were connoisseurs and pioneered this virgin territory."[42]

As the theater historian Lu Eting has observed, as housing one's own actors became the norm for the gentleman of means, men of the gentry owned actors simply to fulfill a social obligation; possessing a troupe no longer testified to a deep interest in the theater.[43] However, many of Mao's closest friends were true connoisseurs. Gong Dingzi had his own troupe. Hou Fangyu's family owned a famed troupe that his father had purchased in Wuchang and brought back to Henan, where the ancestral home was located. A renowned musician hired especially for the purpose

---

that Mao, Chen Zhenhui, and Fang Yizhi were once drinking at the Crowing Cock Inn in Nanjing when they sent for Ruan's players and had them perform selections from Ruan's play *The Swallow Letter*. Ruan hoped that this was a signal that the three men no longer despised him, but his hopes were dashed when they lamented the immorality of the author even as they praised the opera's novel lyrics and scorned his efforts to redeem himself by offering his play (Wu, *Wu Meicun quanji*, p. 773). Kong Shangren used this anecdote as the basis for Scene 4 of *Taohua shan* (pp. 31–33).

41. See Wang An-Chi, *Mingdai chuanqi zhi juchang ji qi yishu*, pp. 97–98.

42. Zhang Dai, *Tao'an mengyi*, p. 37.

43. For information on private acting troupes, see Lu Eting, *Kunju yanchu shigao*, pp. 116–33; Sun Chongtao and Xu Hongtu, *Xiqu youling shi*, pp. 226–32; Wang An-Chi, *Mingdai chuanqi zhi juchang ji qi yishu*, pp. 94–115; and Zhang Faying, *Zhongguo xiban shi*, pp. 165–90. Lu Eting lists some thirty-two owners of private troupes from the mid-Ming to early Qing that we know by name. The list includes the prime minister Shen Shixing 申時行 (1535–1614) and wealthy connoisseurs of the arts such as Wen Zhengming 文徵明 (1470–1559) and He Liangjun, as well as playwrights such as Li Kaixian and Li Yu. The list of names is surprisingly small, considering that it spans some hundred years; one wonders if the practice of housing actors was as widespread as theater historians believe. It may be that the prominence of private troupes in the records of those connoisseurs whose writings define seventeenth-century theatrical culture has skewed our understanding.

trained Hou's troupe, but Hou's father also personally coached them.[44] Mao Xiang's own troupe was much acclaimed. A musician named Chen Jiu 陳九, whose son was Ziyun's peer, trained Mao's actors, and Mao and Chen Weisong also instructed them.[45] Such troupes might be composed of musicians bought specifically for the purpose of forming a troupe, who were then asked to perform menial tasks within the household, or of servants who originally belonged to the household and were then trained to act.[46] A page who was trained as a musician would be an especially valued companion for a literatus away from home; he could function as a secretary, entertainer, or sexual partner. Chen Weisong's poems suggest that Xu Ziyun had just such a range of functions.

At Mao Xiang's estate, celebrated courtesans and actors mingled with the highest-ranking statesmen and literary talents of the period. An eminent stratum of the elite feigned ignorance of caste distinctions, displaying their social confidence as they privileged talent over social status. The extreme privilege enjoyed by members of Mao Xiang's circle most likely helped to insulate them from the social opprobrium that could be attached to fraternization with actors, an opprobrium to which the death of the actor Wang Zijia in 1657 at the hands of the censor Lin Senxian 林森先 (n.d.) attests.[47] In the empyrean realm of Chen's circle, the trans-

---

44. Ibid., pp. 128–29.

45. Zhang Cixi, *Qingdai yandu liyuan shiliao zheng xubian*, "*Yunlang xiaoshi*," pp. 961, 976.

46. The abundance of the terms used to refer to these servants suggests the flexibility of their services. They were referred to as *jiayue* 家樂 (household musicians), *jiayou* 家優 (household actors), *jialing* 家伶 (household actors), *jia tong* 家童 (household servants), *sheng ji* 生伎 (musical performers), and *si er* 司兒 (servants).

47. Lin was originally not only a friend of Gong Dingzi, who was Wang's patron, but himself an admirer of the actor. However, the rumors swirling around the actor's corruption of officials and gentry women were such that he could not ignore them. Lin had Wang flogged and then forced him to stand in the cangue until he died. In another example of the censure of relations between literati and actors, Gong Dingzi's impeachment from his position as superintendent of the Northern Beijing Police in 1646 was in part due to his flagrantly conspicuous relations with actors and courtesans. The impeachment noted his affairs with cross-dressed male actors as well as his devotion to his concubine Gu Mei (a distinguished courtesan for whom he had paid 1,000 pieces of silver [Clunas, *Superfluous Things*, p. 118]) to the neglect of his parents, wife, and children (Wakeman, *The Great Enterprise*, p. 871). As the simultaneous mention of actors and courtesans would

gressive expression of desire for the actor—transgressive in that it violated boundaries of both gender and status—became in itself a form of social currency. As the historian Timothy Brook has remarked, "Public exposure was essential to the social purpose of homoeroticism in the late Ming. Like the buying of rare displayable artifacts, it marked off the truly rarefied at the pinnacle of elite status."[48] The libertines of Chen's coterie were so secure in their positions that they could risk their social capital by consorting with actors. This ability to assume risk allowed them to leverage that social capital by making fraternization with those of low status a mark of distinction that signaled their membership in a cosmopolitan stratum of the mid-century elite.

The transgression inherent in Chen's relationship with a servant was mitigated by the universal acknowledgment of Ziyun's talents as an actor. Yet, even if the disparity in social status between Chen and Ziyun was not a cause of apprehension in Chen's circle, it was still not insignificant. It heightened Mao's largesse in permitting the relationship to take place, emphasized the extraordinary nature of Chen's passion and devotion, and gave Mao's and Chen's friends an opportunity to display their liberality in applauding the relationship. In a quatrain from a series written in 1662 entitled *Chao chang ci* 怊悵詞 (Lyrics of sorrow in loss), Chen revealed his self-consciousness about the difference in his and Xu Ziyun's social status:

> As soon as I saw you at the banquet, I immediately felt close to you,
> All this life I will cherish our predestined love.
> Don't say that you as an actor are base from birth,
> You are [as talented as] the men described by Jiang Yan 江淹.[49]

In the first couplet, Chen justified his flouting of social convention by stating that their affinity was ineluctable. Suggesting not birth but talent should determine social status, Chen spoke of Ziyun as one of the literati

---

suggest, it was likely that it was not only Gong's fraternization with actors but the broader notion of dalliance during a period of mourning that was offensive.

48. Brook, *The Confusions of Pleasure*, p. 232.

49. Zhang Cixi, *Qingdai yandu liyuan shiliao zheng xubian*, "*Yunlang xiaoshi*," p. 962.

who populate the writings of the Southern Dynasties author Jiang Yan.[50] In another quatrain from the same collection, Chen wrote of Ziyun:

> Though the magpie's brain is about to run out, I still pour the wine,[51]
> How can I repay my soulmate (*zhiyin* 知音) in this life?
> On scraps of silk, a few splashes of ink; I will say no more.
> Please cherish the heart of this man of letters.[52]

Here Chen describes the actor as his soulmate (*zhiyin*). The usage of this term is particularly striking, for the mutuality inscribed in the trope of the "ideal listener" suggests a certain degree of interchangeability. Read in tandem, the two poems simultaneously acknowledge and attempt to disavow the gulf in social status between Chen and Ziyun.

As the sensitivity to status in these two poems indicates, it was the dramatic distinction in social status between the two lovers that made their passion noteworthy. These poems may seem a celebration of Ziyun's gifts, but they also celebrate the extraordinary and singular quality of Chen's passion. Dramatizing themselves as enraptured spectators, the poets who celebrated Chen's romance affect an ignorance of the gulf in social status between themselves and the actor, as Chen did in the poem above. This ignorance amplifies their passion by making it seem as though it knows no social strictures. The poets document their own capacity for feeling as they echo Chen's presumed sentiments.

Actors and Poems as Gifts

Many of the poems quoted in this chapter were written when Chen Weisong recruited his friends and acquaintances to pen poetic colophons for a portrait of Xu Ziyun (see Fig. 3). These poems were subsequently collected in a compilation entitled *Jiuqing tuyong* 九青圖詠 (Poems on the

---

50. The instant and wordless recognition that Chen invoked was often used to describe love matches in seventeenth-century sources, as well as to characterize the relation between the connoisseur and the object of his affection; see Zeitlin, *Historian of the Strange*, pp. 69–97.

51. Magpie's brain (*que nao* 鵲腦) was said to increase longing for a loved one when steeped in wine.

52. Zhang Cixi, *Qingdai yandu liyuan shiliao zheng xubian*, "*Yunlang xiaoshi*," p. 963.

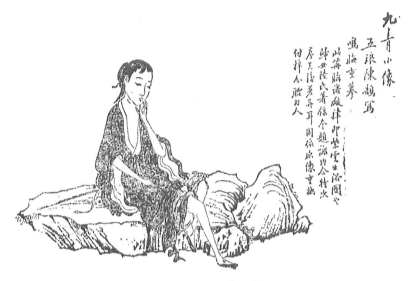

Fig. 3. Portrait of Yunlang

portrait of Jiuqing [Xu Ziyun]).[53] The collection features over 150 poems by seventy-odd poets, a veritable Who's Who of mid-seventeenth-century Jiangnan, with works by, among others, Du Jun 杜濬 (1611–87),

---

53. A reproduction of a woodblock print made of the portrait is appended here (see Fig. 3). The title of the painting, *Portrait on Leaving the Baths*, cross-dresses Ziyun as the consort of the Emperor Xuanzong, Yang Guifei. Despite the title, Xu Ziyun is not depicted as the curvaceous Yang Guifei emerging seductively from the baths of the Huaqing pools. He is, however, portrayed in a coy and seductive pose: dressed in an elaborately figured robe that falls open loosely at the neck, he sits with one hand on chin, a bare leg extended. A flute is placed next to him. It is unclear whether the portrait was painted by Chen Weisong himself or whether he commissioned an artist named Chen Hu 陳鵠 to paint it. The subtitle of a poem by Mao Xiang informs us that "Qinian [Chen Weisong] painted (*hua* 畫) a small silhouette of Ziyun and sought lyrics to inscribe on it from everyone" (Xu Qiu, *Ciyan congtan*, p. 245). However, mid-Qing inscriptions by owners of the portrait state that it was painted by Chen Hu of Wulang 五琅陳鵠. Writing during the Yongzheng reign period, Wu Qing 吳綮 stated that he had bought the portrait in a market and that Chen Hu of Wulang had painted it; this information is inscribed on the facsimile reproduction of the portrait in Zhang Cixi, *Qingdai yandu liyuan shiliao zheng xubian*, "*Jiuqing tuyong*," p. 999. A copy of the portrait was made during the Qianlong period by Luo Liangfeng 羅兩峰. Mao Guangsheng saw this copy in his youth (Zhang Cixi, *Qingdai yandu liyuan shiliao zheng xubian*, "*Yunlang xiaoshi*," p. 964).

Sun Zhiwei, You Tong 尤侗 (1618–1704), Mao Xiang, Mao's son Qingruo, Wang Shizhen, Wang's brother Shilu 王士祿 (1626–73), Han Tan, Wu Zhaokuan 吳兆寬 (?–1680), Deng Hanyi, and Chen Hu 陳瑚 (1613–75). The poets commemorate the great passion between Chen and Ziyun, flattering Chen as they express their desire to emulate him.

Many of these poets would probably have had no interest in praising Ziyun were it not for his relation with Chen Weisong. If Ziyun was the purported addressee, Chen Weisong was the primary one. The two formed two points of a triangle, the author inscribing himself as the third point as the three sides of the triangle became vectors of desire. The primary example of the exchange of the actor between elite men—Mao Xiang's gift of the actor to Chen Weisong—elucidates this geography.

Mao Xiang supposedly detected the budding romance between Chen and Xu Ziyun when he spied them flirting beneath the plum trees of his gardens. Niu Xiu 鈕琇 (?–1704), a friend of Chen's, described Mao's discovery of the affair:

Mao Xiang cherished (*ai* 愛) his [Chen Weisong's] talent and invited him to come to his country villa amidst the plum blossoms. There was a servant named Xu Ziyun, who was fetching in looks and had an excellent voice, and Mao Xiang commanded him to serve Chen in his study. As soon as Chen Weisong saw him, his spirit was moved. At that time the plum trees at the villa were in full blossom, and Chen Weisong and Xu Ziyun strolled beneath the trees in their light fragrance and scattered shadows.

Mao Xiang saw them. He feigned anger, had Xu Ziyun bound, and pretended that he would have him beaten. Chen Weisong was at a loss as to what to do but then realized that a word from Mao Xiang's mother was all that was needed to release Ziyun. It was approaching dusk. He went and knelt for a long time outside her door. When her maid opened it, he said, "I have an urgent matter. I ask that your Ladyship utter one jade-like word. Unless her Ladyship agrees, I will not rise." Then he related the matter of Ziyun.

After a while, a maid emerged and said, "You may stop kneeling now. Mao Xiang has received his mother's order and has already agreed not to punish Ziyun. But he must receive 100 poems on the subject of the plum blossom from you, to be completed this night, and then he will send Ziyun to be your personal servant." Chen Weisong was greatly pleased, and gathered his robes and returned to his quarters, where he lit a lamp, moistened his ink, and worked chanting poems (*kuyin* 苦吟) until the dawn. When the 100 quatrains were finished, he sent them to Mao Xiang. Mao Xiang read them aloud, beating out the rhythm. Then he laughed and sent Ziyun to Chen Weisong.[54]

The threat of violent punishment of Ziyun clearly frightened Chen Weisong, who immediately sought the aid of the one person in the household whose word Mao Xiang would have no choice but to heed: his mother. Although Niu Xiu wrote that Mao merely feigned anger, we cannot know whether Mao acted simply to obtain the forfeit of poems or whether this was a later interpretation intended to make light of the situation. Certainly, Mao's request that Chen compose 100 poems on the plum blossom was not innocent. The penalty required Chen to lyricize the scene of his transgression. Moreover, by demanding that Chen Weisong work through the night to send him the poems by dawn, Mao Xiang reminded him that their relation was that of patron and poet. Mao simultaneously assigned Chen a schoolboy's punishment and challenged him not to succumb to doggerel as he repeatedly revisited the same theme. At the same time, the forfeit of poems allowed Mao Xiang to make light of the gravity of his gift of the actor to Chen Weisong. It elegantly eased Chen's indebtedness, granting him dignity by allowing him to win the actor back.

Mao's refined wit emerges not only in the supposed frivolity of his request but in the pretense of equivalence between actor and poems. The poems became an initiatory gift that allowed Mao to make a counter-gift. Chen's sending of the poems to Mao created a path for the circulation of the actor, who traveled toward Chen in a direction counter to the poems. The potential exchange of the actor for a poem—that is, of the attentions of the actor for a poem—is a current that runs through all these works. In this regard, the poems unwittingly echo the initiatory exchange between Chen and Mao.

---

54. Niu Xiu, *Gu sheng*, pp. 40–41. The account is reprinted in Zhang Cixi, *Qingdai yandu liyuan shiliao zheng xubian*, "*Yunlang xiaoshi*," pp. 959–60. Niu Xiu's rendition seems to form the basis for later versions of this story. For a partial compilation of prose sources regarding Chen and Ziyun, see *Qingci jishi huiping*, pp. 164–65. Ye Gongchuo's 葉恭綽 (1881–1968) version conforms most closely to the stereotypical story of the wily actor seducing the literatus, perhaps because it was written long after the others; see Ye, *Qingdai xuezhe xiangzhuan heji*, p. 86.

If the poets of Chen's circle write in emulation of him, they also register sentiments of loss and longing, anticipating the generous deferral of their own desire. Mao gave his beloved servant Xu Ziyun to one whom he believed needed him more. His subsequent poems to Chen articulate longing for both Chen and Xu. By granting Xu to Chen, he created a pair who functioned as a unit without him. In Mao's poems, he attempts to re-insert himself as the third corner in a triangle. Wittingly or not, the poets of this coterie empathically recreate this geometry, registering *their* sentiments of loss as they assert their desire to become Chen's rivals. The presumed sentiments of the two men upon the exchange of the actor are conflated as the poets model themselves after both parties simultaneously.

In these poems, the experience of reading about the actor is often compared to that of meeting him. The poets repeatedly complain that literary representations of the actor stir their desire but do not satisfy it. The ensuing longing inspires poems in tribute to the actor—as though putting poems of desire into circulation might induce the actor to travel to the poet along the path traversed by the poems. If the experience of reading about the boy is not enough to satiate the poet's professed desire, neither is the experience of seeing the boy in person. Both literary and visual consumption only fuel the circulation of more poems. If the poet could possess the actor, the actor would no longer need to circulate, and the poet would no longer be connected to the other poets through the reciprocal exchange of representations of the object of desire. At a more elemental level, if his desire could be satisfied, it would no longer be *qing*.

It was because Xu Ziyun was so cherished that Mao's gift of him to Chen established him as a channel for the flow of sentiment between Mao and Chen themselves.[55] Mao's sacrifice of his beloved actor not only testified to his love for Weisong but created a path for future expressions of sentiment. The other members of Mao's circle may have viewed Ziyun only as an object of connoisseurship. But given their empathic resonance

---

55. Various anthropologists who have studied the gift have spoken of how transactions in persons—for example, the gift of one's child to a sister—allow the person who has been given away to become a channel for the flow of future gifts. Indeed, the person who has been exchanged becomes a channel not only for the transport of goods but for the flow of sentiment between donor and recipient. See, e.g., Mauss, *The Gift*, p. 7. We could view Mao Xiang's gift of Xu Ziyun to Chen Weisong in this light.

with Mao's and Chen's sentiments for the actor, the actor became a channel of emotional connection among the men of this coterie as well. In a sequence of poems written by Mao to Chen, Mao reminded Chen of his love for him by recalling his gift of the actor. Ziyun became the third point of the triangle. His insertion into the relations between Mao and Chen alters the character of the bond between them:

> At night I sent the servant boy to accompany you as you studied,
> I cherished my guest more than the most beautiful jade.
> When for six years you departed, my feeling was vast as the sea,
> When you meet him in the painting, he will ask after me.[56]

> Chen's rare talent makes riot of the classics,
> Chen's a fool in love, as much of a fool as Yunlang.
> There is none on earth who knows you as I do,
> I gave him to you instead of sending him away.[57]

Mao loved Chen and therefore sent him the beloved Ziyun, setting in motion a merry-go-round of displacement. Longing or desire is triangulated through the actor: "When you meet him in the painting, he will ask after me." Ziyun becomes an alternative route for a current of sentiment between Mao and Chen. But Chen can also be seen as the alternative route for a current between Mao and Ziyun. If the object of desire were Chen, we would assume that Mao's love was not eroticized; if it were Ziyun, we would assume that it might have been.

In the second poem, Mao declared: "I gave him to you instead of sending him away." Ziyun was Mao's property; in this poem he reminded Chen that the transfer created bonds of obligation and shared interest. Mao's gift to Chen bound Chen closer to Mao, just as a wife's selection of a concubine for her husband might help cement a sense of partnership between husband and wife. The triangular vectors between poet, actor, and Chen do not simply describe the paths the actor as gift might travel. The nostalgic longing that these poets expressed suggests that these social relations are also mapped within the poet himself.[58]

---

56. Ibid., "*Yunlang xiaoshi*," pp. 970, and "*Jiuqing tuyong*," p. 985.

57. Ibid., "*Jiuqing tuyong*," p. 985.

58. The incurable wistfulness of these poems recalls the endless mourning of Freud's melancholic subject, who is doomed to interject the lost object of affection and carry it

The Materiality of Poems:
The Metonymic Circulation of People and Thing

The community of poets defined by *Jiuqing tuyong* is delineated by the flow of poems as gifts, gifts that create networks of social relations. The poem, however, is not simply an object; rather, it is an artifact of a person, an extension of the author that circulates in his or her stead. This metonymic relation between persons and poems accounts for the peculiar status of poems among other types of artistic production. The poem is an archetypal example of the distinction Bronislaw Malinowski made long ago between ordinary commodities and valuables that can be exchanged only for other valuables and only in specifically encoded contexts.[59] We might consider for a moment the obvious and yet suggestive fact that individual poems were not meant to be sold.[60] Although there are indications that individual poems, like paintings, were sold for "brush-wetting silver" and then circulated as the work of the purchaser, the exchange of poems for money was certainly covert. Poems were meant only to be exchanged with other poems.

These distinctive features of the poem as an object of exchange stem from the governing assumption of Chinese poetics: the poem is a spontaneous emanation of what is "intensely on the mind," an overflow of powerful emotion.[61] Not only the poem but also the landscape that the poet wit-

---

within in an attempt to recuperate the loss. The occlusion that Mao felt on stumbling across Xu Ziyun and Chen resurfaces in the insistence of these poets on *inclusion*, in the fraught relationship between longing and belonging in these poems.

59. Malinowski, *Argonauts of the Western Pacific*, p. 184.

60. A possible exception would be the sale of poems by women poets in order to support themselves. The woman poet Shen Shanbao 沈善寶 (1807–62) mentioned in her poems that she sold her own poems and paintings to eke out a living; it is unclear from the text whether she sold individual poems or a collection, although it would be more likely that she sold a collection (Fong, "Writing Self and Writing Lives," pp. 274–75). The seventeenth-century poet Huang Yuanjie 黃媛介 also sold her own poems and paintings to support herself; Shen may have taken her as a model (ibid., p. 275). Another exception to the taboo on the sale of poems would be the sale of anthologies of poems, and it is a telling exception, for in an anthology, the poem is no longer a metonymic extension of an individual person but, rather, an example of the literary production of a group. The anthology then becomes a *thing*, which can be used instrumentally for educational or other purposes.

61. See Owen, *Omen of the World*, p. 58.

nesses and inscribes in the poem are viewed as metonymic extensions of the poet; the poem becomes a material artifact of the poet's state of mind. These suppositions may not describe the actual circumstances under which poems were composed. They did, however, govern traditional Chinese codes of reading, which assumed a metonymic relation between poet and poem that rendered the social circulation of poems equivalent to the social circulation of people.[62] It is not merely the body of the actor that implicitly travels the networks established by these poems; the poets themselves do.

These poems in tribute to actors, like the actors themselves, possess a singular sociability; neither is meant to be enjoyed by one man alone. The poem's relation to the poet is, in fact, analogous to the relation of the actor to his patron—although intimately attached to his patron, the actor by definition must circulate socially. The actor Xu Ziyun and the poems in tribute to him became channels for the flow of sentiment among Chen Weisong, Mao Xiang, and the members of their literary community. This flow of sentiment is expressed as an empathic resonance among the poets, a resonance that leads to the composition of more poems as a poet is moved to write about Chen and Xu Ziyun's relationship by the poems he reads about it. The representations of the actor become fruitful and multiply, as each poem acts as a magnet that draws more poems into the network. Mao's and Chen's sentiments ripple through the community like circles widening in water. The poems of their friends send the sentiments of the principals back to the center, and the expression of Mao's and Chen's longing for the actor is echoed by the poets in a kind of call and response. This empathic resonance between Mao's and Chen's sentiments of loss and longing and those voiced by the poets underscores the sense of lack of fulfillment so central to the self-dramatizing expressions of *qing* prominent in the literary culture of this period.[63]

---

62. Ibid., pp. 39–40.

63. As Wai-yee Li has remarked, "The infinitude of *qing* is best expressed through unfulfillment, the representation of how the desires of the self find no place in the scheme of things" (*Enchantment and Disenchantment*, p. 54). This empathic resonance (empathic rather than directly inspired by desire for Xu Ziyun) is characteristic of poems composed at parties and other gatherings.

Empathic Resonance: Fools for Love

There is a tantalizing lack of clarity about the nature of Chen and Xu Zi-yun's relationship, given the highly allusive language employed in the sources. A glance at a description of the relationship written by a fellow guest of Mao Xiang's at Rugao, the renowned poet Jiang Pingjie 蔣平階 (n.d.), illustrates the difficulties for the modern reader of pinpointing its nature. The description below is drawn from Jiang's preface to Chen's *Lyrics of Sorrow in Loss*, written when Chen and Xu Ziyun were separated in 1662.

Their affair of "the shared peach" and "the rent sleeve" has lasted four years,[64] but although they have moved each other with subtle words, they have never gone astray.[65] In this way Weisong cast off previous lovers and shed no tears[66] and still loved Yunlang [Xu Ziyun] increasingly, even though he commandeered the duke's chariot.[67] This can truly be called a level of favor deeper than that given consorts and palace ladies, or enjoyment greater than one has in a beautiful woman.[68]

The multiple allusions Jiang employed seem to work at cross-purposes, some suggesting physical consummation and others implying simply an emotional attachment. Such phrases as "the shared peach," "the rent

---

64. "The shared peach" refers to the love of Duke Ling 靈 of Wei 衛 for his male favorite, Mizi Xia 彌子瑕; the duke's besotted love was such that he did not see it as a violation of etiquette when Mizi Xia offered him the remainder of a peach he had been eating; rather, he viewed it as touching evidence of Mizi Xia's consideration for him (Han Feizi, *Han Feizi jishi*, pp. 223–24). "The rent sleeve" refers to the tenderness of the Emperor Ai 哀 of the Han toward his male favorite, Dongxian 董賢. When the emperor was called from an afternoon nap to attend court duties, he had the sleeve of his robe cut rather than disturb Han Dongxian sleeping beside him (Ban Gu, *Han shu, juan* 93, p. 3733).

65. In the Tang tale "Yingying zhuan" 鶯鶯傳 (The story of Yingying), the phrase "they have never gone astray" indicates that the two lovers have not yet consummated their passion. It is unclear whether by this point in time the meaning of the phrase was still so narrowly defined.

66. See Chapter 4, note 62, p. 156.

67. This allusion refers to a violation of sumptuary laws by a male favorite and is taken from the same story as the phrase "the shared peach" (see note 64 above). Mi Zixia forged an order from the ruler in order to use his chariot to see his sick mother. Instead of punishing him, the ruler praised his filiality, but after Mi Zixia lost favor, the ruler criticized him for having stolen his chariot (Han Feizi, *Han Feizi*, pp. 223–24).

68. Zhang Cixi, *Qingdai yandu liyuan shiliao zheng xubian*, p. 962.

sleeve," and "cast off previous lovers and shed no tears" clearly filiate Chen and Ziyun to historical precedents that describe the love of emperors and aristocrats for male favorites. They suggest that Weisong abandoned his previous favorites (whether male or female, we do not know) to engage in a monogamous relationship with Ziyun, that he ignored conventional boundaries of status in his consideration for him, and that even though Ziyun took advantage of Chen's besotted affection to demand greater and greater privileges, Chen paid no mind, but only increased his devotion to the actor. Yet the phrase "they have never gone astray," an allusion to the Tang dynasty tale "Yingying zhuan" 鶯鶯傳 (The Story of Yingying), suggests that Chen and Ziyun, despite their love for each other, had never had sex. This seeming contradiction may or may not have posed a problem for the original readers of this text. It is easier for us as modern readers to know how such terms functioned in the original sources than to decipher what seventeenth-century authors meant when they deployed them as allusions.[69]

The elusive quality of the term *qing*, which seventeenth-century authors used to describe sentiments of desire, love, and affection, compounds the problem of how we ought to understand the relationship between Chen and Ziyun. The term *qing* is omnipresent in the literature of the late Ming. The early seventeenth-century author Feng Menglong wrote in the preface to his massive compendium of tales about *qing*, *Qingshi leilüe* 情史類略 (A topical outline of the history of *qing*): "Would that all those who have *qing* could gather together to speak of its Dharma."[70] As Anthony Yu has quipped, the efflorescence of seventeenth-century literature about *qing* seems to have been written in answer to Feng's call.[71]

---

69. Contemporaries of Chen's used other allusions that described Ziyun as a sexual companion of Chen's; Deng Hanyi wrote in a poem after Ziyun's death that "Ziyun is already gone and Yangzhi has withered [a pun on the actor Yangzhi's name, "Willow Branch"]; / Master Chen has buried Yingtao in the shallow earth" (Zhang Cixi, *Qingdai yandu liyuan shiliao zheng xubian*, p. 976). An entertainer who became the male favorite of Shi Hu [who later became Emperor Wu of the Zhao (295–349)], Zheng Yingtao came to represent the stereotype of the actor as *femme fatale*; Shi Hu supposedly murdered two wives at Zheng Yingtao's behest.

70. Feng, *Qingshi leilüe*, 20.2a.

71. For an extensive investigation of the Confucian discourse on *qing*, see Anthony Yu, *Rereading the Stone*, esp. pp. 53–109.

The unstable and euphemistic quality of the term *qing* partially accounts for its titillating quality.[72] Simple claims to affection contain within them the possibility of being interpreted as lust.[73] An enigmatic term, *qing* can be translated as emotion, affect, feeling, disposition, or sentiment—or as love, longing, lust, passion, or desire. *Qing* is quintessentially metaphorical; it always points to something else.[74] This is true even of the range of emotions that the term incorporates. The way in which the term seems always to indicate absence in presence is also characteristic of *qing*'s relation to its object, for the object is often so undeserving as to seem a placeholder or a metaphor for something else. The expression of *qing* ultimately speaks not so much to the desirability of the object as to the passion of the desiring subject. This structure points to the self-reflexive, self-consuming quality of *qing*. More than anything else, *qing* desires its own perpetuation, and so it remains perennially unsatisfied. The term speaks more of the feeling subject than the object of desire or affection.

The capacity of *qing* to confer social distinction was in direct proportion to its elusiveness, and it became the most sought after quality among the seventeenth-century literary elite. In the context of these poems, the elusiveness of *qing* itself contributes to a sense of the elusiveness of the actor as the beloved. The poems pay tribute to Chen's relation with Ziyun by expressing desire for the actor, but at the same time they acknowledge that the actor is bound to Chen and can never be theirs. The poets, then, are nostalgic for the lost object of desire even in advance of the articulation of desire for him.[75]

---

72. If *qing* could be stably identified as lust or love, the most influential literary work of the seventeenth century, the southern drama *Mudan ting* would not have caused the furor it did; it was in part the suggestiveness of its valorization of *qing* that made the play such a phenomenon.

73. Conversely, seventeenth-century authors who wished to elevate the term relied on its ambiguities, defining it as the fellow feeling that forms the basis of social relations rather than as passion, which leads individuals to act in antisocial ways (Martin Huang, *Desire and Fictional Narrative*, pp. 46–47).

74. Maram Epstein (*Competing Discourses*, p. 62) observes that *qing*'s multiple meanings have led it to be used in contradictory ways, even by the same author.

75. Although the possible translations for the term are legion, in translating and discussing these poems, I favor "desire" because it incorporates a sense of the insatiability of *qing*.

Maram Epstein, Martin Huang, Wong Siu-kit, Wai-yee Li, and Anthony Yu among many others have engaged in extensive historical overviews of the polyvalent significances of *qing*.[76] My intention in this chapter is to illuminate a quality of the term that is often noted but seldom explicitly discussed: empathy. Empathy is in fact at the heart of the self-proclaimed "historian of *qing*" Feng Menglong's own definition of the term. In his first preface to *The Anatomy of Qing*, Feng described his own *qing* in terms of his capacity for empathy:

Since I was a young man, I have been burdened by being crazed with *qing* (*qing-chi*). To my friends and acquaintances, I gave all I had. I would be concerned about them through times of good fortune and bad. If I heard that someone was unusually destitute or suffering grave injustice, even if I didn't know him, I would seek to provide for him. Sometimes my efforts would not be sufficient, and then I would sigh for days on end, tossing and turning in the middle of the night, unable to sleep.[77]

A Buddhist saying Feng cited in this preface also points to the centrality of empathy in his understanding of *qing*: "With *qing*, the distant become intimate; without *qing*, the intimate become distant."[78]

The empathic quality of the *qing* described in the Ziyun poems is brilliantly encapsulated in the preface to Chen's *Lyrics of Sorrow in Loss* by Jiang Pingjie. The poems describe Chen's despair on being parted from Xu Ziyun in 1662. Jiang depicted his own grief on reading them:

At this time the autumn waters were about to be moved by winter winds, and the cicadas of the New Year would soon begin to hum. So Chen quit the farewell banquet and said that he would return home. He left his seat and prepared to depart. The winds on the river blow for over a thousand miles. How could they [Chen and Xu Ziyun] be expected to meet again? Thus we have these poems on parting, tunes that exhaustively describe the feelings of troubled hearts about to part. How could I not respond with emotion—and how could I possibly over-

---

76. Epstein, *Competing Discourses*, pp. 61–119; Martin Huang, *Desire and Fictional Narrative*, pp. 23–56; Wai-yee Li, *Enchantment and Disenchantment*; Wong, "Ch'ing in Chinese Literature"; Yu, *Rereading the Stone*, pp. 53–109.

77. Feng Menglong, *Qingshi leilüe*, 20.1b-2a. For translations of and commentaries on this passage, see Wai-yee Li, *Enchantment and Disenchantment*, p. 91; and Epstein, *Competing Discourses*, pp. 114–15.

78. Feng Menglong, *Qingshi leilüe*, p. 7.

come such emotions? My heart grieved as I read these poems, and there was no way to relieve my sorrow. I beat the rhythm of these poems and composed poems in response, but the poems I wrote only increased my sorrow.[79]

Moved by Chen's poems describing his despair at being parted from Zi-yun, Jiang was inspired to write his own. In so doing, he amplifies Chen's sentiments and empathically echoes them. But rather than bringing about a catharsis, his poems only increase his sorrow.

Jiang dramatized his own capacity to feel passion (*qing*) in part by suggesting that his passion had been evoked by Chen's. The object of that passion, Xu Ziyun, is largely occluded. Given that many of the poets writing colophons for the painting indicate that they had never met the actor, the pervasive sentiments of loss and longing in these poems are striking. The poems often speak more to the poets' relationship with Chen than to their desire for the actor. The poets' desire echoes Chen's; their empathic resonance with Chen's desire is another instance of the metaphorical nature or operation of *qing*. Although the poems are ostensibly stimulated by desire for the actor, since they are generated by empathic resonance with Chen's sentiments, the actor himself becomes insignificant. The primary emotional connection is not between author and actor but between the author and the poets who have inspired him.

But if the poets' nostalgia regarding the loss of an actor they have never met is expressed in empathy with and emulation of Chen, it is also expressed in *rivalry* with him. This rivalry is, however, quite companionable. Its primary motivation seems to be to compliment Chen Weisong rather than truly to contest his place. The poems might be compared to the poems men wrote to their friends congratulating them on the purchase of a concubine or lamenting the death of one. They play with the confusion caused by the mixed sentiments of empathy and rivalry.

Mao and his friends teased Chen by suggesting they wished to enter his relationship with Xu Ziyun. Wang Shizhen, for example, wrote a poem to Xu Ziyun subtitled "Written as Qinian [Weisong] in Jest" ("Xi dai Qinian" 戲代其年). Wang Shizhen also baited Chen by asking if he would lend Xu Ziyun to him "to hold his inkstand."[80] (The phrase implies

---

79. Zhang Cixi, *Qingdai yandu liyuan shiliao zheng xubian*, "*Yunlang xiaoshi*," p. 962.
80. Ibid., "*Yunlang xiaoshi*," p. 967.

that Ziyun would function as a "servant in the study," a well-known syn-
onym for a sexual plaything.) Wang Shizhen's elder brother, Shilu, posed
as Chen's rival as he reproached Chen for being unworthy of his primary
claim on the actor:

> As my dream fades and I wake from a drunken night, I ache with longing,
> Yet what can I do but stand before his portrait in hopes of seeing him?
> On the day we parted at the banquet, I could not find him,
> I am surprised that you are not as outrageous as the censor Du.[81]

Wang Shilu indicated his chagrin at having to settle for a representation
of the actor rather than the actor himself. Both the dream and the painting incite his longing but do nothing to satisfy it. At the moment of greatest promise, Wang claims, he could not find Ziyun. He has inevitably
been defeated in his rivalry with Chen—and thus chides Chen for not being as unfettered in his passion as the poet Du Mu.

Wang Shilu and Chen Weisong participated in a poetry circle in
Yangzhou during the 1660s that included the editor Deng Hanyi. (Deng
also lived at Mao Xiang's home in 1670 and served on Gong Dingzi's staff
as a secretary from time to time.)[82] Like Wang Shilu, Deng depicted the
banquet as a site of contestation for the actor's favors. He, too, declined to
compete with Chen, declaring that he dared not admit his desire for Ziyun in public:

> I listen to his clear song the whole night long,
> Dressed in red sleeves, he is even more pleasing.
> I've been beguiled by him since that time of confusion among the flowers in
>   the mist,
> But dare not call to him at the banquet.[83]

Although something transpired at a previous entertainment between
Deng and "the flowers in the mist" (Ziyun and the other entertainers),
Deng dared not signal to Ziyun publicly. This lyric may function as a
means of communication with Ziyun, the ultimate recipient of the collection. But more likely, the poem provided a means of flattering Chen, the

---

81. Xu Qiu, *Ciyan congtan*, p. 366; Zhang Cixi, *Qingdai yandu liyuan shiliao zheng
xubian*, "*Yunlang xiaoshi*," p. 965, and "*Jiuqing tuyong*," p. 988.

82. Meyer-Fong, "Site and Sentiment," pp. 147–53.

83. Zhang Cixi, *Qingdai yandu liyuan shiliao zheng xubian*, "Yunlang xiaoshi," p. 961.

compiler, as the author conceded his defeat in advance. Deng's admission of failure fashions a bond between himself and Chen. His admission of a desire that is doomed to unfulfillment and thus nostalgic even in advance of its expression is phrased as though it were private, but it is in fact a public and sociable act.

Friends of Chen's who had likely never seen Ziyun participated in this social circulation of polite admissions of unfulfilled desire. Wu Zhao-kuan's poem, like Deng Hanyi's, registers a wistful longing for Ziyun. His is a longing doubly deferred, however, for he seems to have known Ziyun only through his portrait and the lyrics in tribute to him:

> I love to light the lamp and read the songs about Jiuqing.
> The sounds of his song ripple through the air, stirring the figured gauze of his robe.
> Unfurling the painting in the spring breeze, I see his face for the first time.
> He is so far away—and what am I to do, separated from him by the dense clouds of Chu?[84]

The first line tells us that Chen circulated the painting and the previously submitted poems to Wu for comment, a comment that took poetic form. Wu wryly registered the fulfillment of a social duty. The redundancy of the expressions of desire for Ziyun recorded in this collection indicates that they were polite concessions to social and poetic convention (although such politesse might not have precluded stronger emotions). Although he had never seen Ziyun in person, Wu constructed a ground of shared interest with Chen and Mao by posing as a rival; he formed a bond with them by envying their possession.[85] One belongs to this community by expressing longing for the actor, by voicing a desire that is inevitably already deferred. On one level, this deference is simply polite. The temporal deferral of one's approach toward the object of desire is a form of defer-

---

84. Ibid., p. 965, and "Jiuqing tuyong," p. 984.

85. Wu's last line may refer to Ziyun's sexual involvement with Chen Weisong. (The phrase "the clouds of Chu" refers to the sensual pleasures of "clouds and rain" that, according to literary tradition, King Xiang of Chu took with the goddess of Wu mountain.) The line may also hint at Mao Xiang's proprietary rights to Ziyun, given the identity between the character "Xiang" in Mao Xiang's name and that of King Xiang of Chu. The *Shen nü fu* 神女賦 (Rhymeprose on the divine goddess) attributed to Song Yu describes the tryst of King Xiang of Chu with the goddess of Wu mountain; see Xiao Tong, *Wenxuan*, pp. 135–36.

ence to Chen's privileged relation to the actor. On another level, this deference emulates Mao and Chen's own deferral of their desires. As we have noted, it was not only Chen's sentiments of loss as he gave Ziyun up to marriage but also Mao's sense of bereavement after he gave his beloved actor to Chen that inspired these poets' empathic expression of loss and longing. Mao's poems repeatedly spiral back to the moment of his gift, speaking of the pain inherent in his own largesse, the cost to himself of his radical generosity. If these poets write in emulation of Mao's longing, they refer implicitly to their own largesse in allowing Chen to keep the actor. Their defeat in their rivalry with Chen, then, becomes re-encoded as an act of generosity. Once again, we are reminded that the object of desire is secondary. What is primary is the empathic resonance between elite men.

Homosocial Homoerotics

Empathic resonance points to the ways in which the desire *to be* another and the desire *for* another may often become confused. Building on the arguments of Claude Lévi-Strauss and Gayle Rubin regarding the "traffic in women," feminist theorist Eve Sedgwick has argued that although the exchange of a woman between two men serves to instantiate sociality through the common expression of heteroerotic desire, the bonds between men created by this exchange also open channels for the circulation of desire between the men themselves.[86] Under the aegis of the homophobia that Sedgwick sees as constitutive of modern patriarchy, this desire is social rather than sexual; for this reason, Sedgwick labels it "homosocial."[87]

These bonds are formed not simply through the expression of mutual desire for the boy but through the communal indulgence of Chen's extraordinary passion for a servant. The flouting of conventional boundaries of status is as important as the transgression of heteroerotic norms in

---

86. Sedgwick, *Between Men*, pp. 21–27; see also Lévi-Strauss, *The Elementary Structures of Kinship*, pp. 61–68; and Rubin, "The Traffic in Women."

87. The Ziyun poems provide an interesting contrast to Sedgwick's model, for in them, homoerotic desire is not suppressed. There was no shame in expressing desire for a boy who was a social inferior. The prohibition was not on expressing homoerotic desire *per se*, but on the expression of desire for someone of the same status rather than an inferior.

fashioning these homosocial bonds. The two gestures need not, of course, be defined as mutually exclusive; the transgression of boundaries of status may itself have been eroticized.

The expression of desire for the actor in these poems was a particularly encoded discursive practice. This becomes clear when we contrast it to the sentiments for actors registered in other genres. In their letters, Mao and his friends exchanged news of the actors' families and health. In a letter to Gong Dingzi, for example, Mao wrote: "Qinxiao is ill-fated and is already useless. This past spring, his face was thin as a needle. He repeatedly lay down and could not get up."[88] We would never find such sentiments in a poem about an actor. The contrast suggests that the expression of emotions of desire and rivalry within the poems constituted a kind of literary game.

Mao's son Qingruo composed a poem to accompany Ziyun's portrait that can be read as a comment on that game:

> My passion (*qing*) dies and rises again, though I myself am unaware.
> Occasionally this passion ties me to thoughts of you.
> If you want to understand my sorrow without end,
> Just look at that wisp of light cloud (*yun* 雲).[89]

The poet's passion is independent of the object, and even independent of the subject; the poet states that he himself is unaware (*bu zizhi* 不自知) of its rise and fall. It oscillates with a rhythm of its own, alighting on the boy only casually. Qingruo blames the actor for his heartbreak, but in a sophisticated twist, his description of Ziyun (literally, "purple cloud") as a "wisp of light cloud" renders the actor trivial and insignificant in comparison to the "sorrow without end" that he has inspired.

The seventeenth-century cult of *qing* made the expression of intense feeling a literary necessity; excess became the norm. The expression of desire in these poems is clearly indebted to a discourse of connoisseurship anchored in poetic convention. The poems play games with the potential confusion of expression of desire for the actor and response to the expression of other's desire. They voice homoerotic sentiments, flirting with the possibility of winning the actor's favors, but it is impossible to know the degree to which they seek simply to identify themselves as members of a

---

88. Zhang Cixi, *Qingdai yandu liyuan shiliao zheng xubian*, "Yunlang xiaoshi," p. 976.
89. Ibid., p. 970.

community by speaking in this mode. Chen's poems were written in compensation for a transgression. But the other poets simply played with the notion of transgression. This was not a community of men united by sexual congress with the actor, or even a community of men linked by desire for the actor. It was a community defined by the shared expression of disappointment at *not* being able to consummate longing for the actor. Although these poets employed a discourse of homoeroticism, since their expressions of desire always inscribed the impossibility of their satisfaction, they could rest comfortably in the knowledge of that impossibility.

Self-Dramatizing Spectators

The album *Poems on the Portrait of Jiuqing* gained more verses as it circulated, its readers submitting testimonies to the charms of Ziyun's portrait and to their own capacity for *qing*. In submitting these poems to the regard and consumption of the group, the poets allowed their *qing* to become an object of connoisseurship. As they did so, they themselves became actors on a public stage. Ironically, they signaled their cognizance of this position by dramatizing themselves as spectators. In the following excerpt from a lyric subtitled "to show to Mao Xiang" (*shi* Mao Pijiang 示冒辟疆), Chen Hu cynically observed that in dramatizing themselves as spectators they emulated Chen Weisong himself:

> Chaste Master Xu, aged fifteen or sixteen,[90]
> Wisps of black hair falling over his forehead, face like jade.
> I'm afraid that the Ziyun of yore could not equal you,
> All in the audience (*manzuo* 滿座) model themselves after Du Mu in their
>   lack of restraint.[91]

---

90. There is certainly an irony in Chen's vision of Xu Ziyun as "chaste." Not only was Ziyun, as an actor, inherently considered unchaste, but the term used here for "chaste" (*yaotiao* 窈窕) is drawn from the first poem of *The Classic of Poetry*, which, according to Han commentary, describes the courtship of the Duke of Zhou and his consort. (In fact, the term *yaotiao* did not have the connotation of "chaste" before the Mao commentary of the Han dynasty; this is an example of the power of commentary to change the significance of the terms it glosses.)

91. Zhang Cixi, *Qingdai yandu liyuan shiliao zheng xubian*, "Yunlang xiaoshi," p. 961; Xu Qiu, *Ciyan congtan*, p. 292.

Chen Hu portrayed Chen Weisong's rivals as engaged in a mass mimicry of Du Mu. But since Chen Weisong is frequently referred to as Du Mu in these poems, it is in fact he whom they seek to emulate, Chen, rather than Xu Ziyun, who is the true focus of their attention. Chen's passion becomes the object of the spectators' connoisseurship and the focus of their desire: their desire is not to be with Chen, but to *be* him.

Chen Hu inscribed a chain of viewing pleasure: as the audience watches the boy, the poet watches the spectators. The first three lines quoted above are devoted to connoisseurship of the boy; the last subjects the spectators themselves to evaluation. If the spectator usually believes himself unseen, Chen let the poets of this coterie know that they are seen. And indeed, they seem to crave a witness. It is the desire for a witness that leads them to draw attention to their lack of restraint.

Although these spectators desire to stand, like the actor, on a public stage, they mimic not the actor but the missing ideal spectator. Dramatizing themselves as spectators, the poets of Chen's coterie simultaneously watch the performance of Xu Ziyun (and Chen) on the main stage as they perform spectatorship on a side stage. As the film critic Miriam Hansen observes, mimesis is one of the spectatorial pleasures, for it allows the spectator to stand on his or her own stage.[92] Mimesis, then, is inherently histrionic. As noted above, many of these poems are written in emulation of Chen and in empathic resonance with his desire for the actor. Mimesis leads the poet to dramatize himself in his empathic response to Chen's Weisong's sentiments. Chen Hu placed these spectators in a double bind: they measure up neither to the model of the past, the Tang dynasty poet Du Mu, nor to the present incarnation of Du Mu, Chen Weisong himself. In both cases, the spectators are caught in the paradox of studied spontaneity. All parties vie to be the primary spectator, the man of unbridled passion (*zhenqing*). Once unbridled passion comes to function as a sign of distinction, however, it becomes impossible to express without self-consciousness.

The social importance of dramatizing oneself as spontaneously impassioned helps explain the prevalence of empathic longing in these poems. For empathy is by definition spontaneous, as evidenced in the words of Chen's friend Jiang Pingjie quoted earlier, "How could I not respond with emotion—and how could I possibly overcome such emotions?" Em-

---

92. Hansen, *Babel and Babylon*, p. 26.

pathy allows the sidelined spectator to overcome the hurdle of self-consciousness, to gain a sense of belonging: Jiang Pingjie's preface describes how he began to beat the rhythm of Chen's poems and spontaneously chanted his own poems in response to Chen's. It is the empathic quality of the response that renders it lyrical rather than merely histrionic. The sentiments expressed in these poems, because they are empathic, are both mimetic and expressive, at once staged and authentic. We saw in *Nan wanghou* that the challenge issued to the spectator was to preserve illusion and disillusion in tension simultaneously. The equivalent in these poems is the challenge issued to us as readers to perceive the co-existence of two seemingly incompatible types of utterance—the expressive and the mimetic. Otherwise put, rather than viewing these poems as genuine expressions of homoerotic sentiment toward the actor, or as responses to a social obligation, we need to keep in mind that the poems themselves prescribe a more sophisticated approach, asking us once again to hold illusion and disillusion in tension.

This poem comments on the motivations that shape the entire collection. It is the desire to be seen (but to be seen as one in a crowd) that emerges most clearly in these poems. That is why they yield so persuasively to an analysis that considers questions of social distinction. Ironically, however, one could say that to a certain degree these poets also desire to remain unseen, in that the self-inscription of these poets is highly generic, lacking in particularity. In modeling themselves after Chen Weisong, for example, the poets ensure that whatever might be unique or specific to themselves or their desire for the boy remains unknown. This is why we shall never be able to locate the desire expressed in them on the continuum between the homosocial and homoerotic; the importance of empathic resonance in the generation of these poems renders it impossible to isolate a single author's desire from that of the collective.

Xu Ziyun's Wedding

Ziyun married around 1675, when he likely would have been close to thirty years old. As a wedding gift for Ziyun, Chen wrote a song lyric to the tune "He xinlang" 賀新郎 (Congratulating the bridegroom). Niu Xiu noted that at the time of its composition, "Ziyun had been betrothed, and a date had been set for the wedding; Chen was dazed, as though he had suffered a loss." Niu concluded by saying, "This lyric circulated quickly from one mouth to another, and those who heard it were bowled over by it."[93]

> I sip a little *tumi* wine
> Pleased that this morning,
> Hairpins gleam in the silhouette of your tresses,
> Bobbing before the lanterns.
> On the other side of the screen, laughter and chatter,
> As they announce that the sparrow hairpins have just appeared.[94]
> Once again I stealthily cast
> A glance at Pan Yue.[95]
> I can't tell whether you are cock or hen,
> But when the wind lifts your robes,
> I furtively measure your feet.
> I send you off,
> To raise the bridal curtains on the marriage bed.

> For six years, staying in lonely haunts, you were my intimate companion.
> Hardest to forget,
> Is my companion of the red-fringed pillow,
> The tears like flowers that you gently shed.
> Today, you will be wed,
> Wife follows husband in sinuous chant.
> Try your best
> To act the role of a good husband.
> It's just that my gauze quilt is cold as iron,
> As I clutch my bamboo mat (*tao sheng* 桃笙),
> It is as though dawn will never come.[96]
> On my account,
> You must grieve no more.[97]

---

93. Niu, *Gu sheng*, p. 41. Xu Qiu's *Ciyan congtan* similarly states that "everyone was bowled over by it" (p. 205).

94. The sparrow hairpins refer to the bride's headdress.

95. Pan Yue was a famous male beauty of the Six Dynasties.

96. A *tao sheng* was a mat woven of a type of bamboo called "peachwood bamboo" (*tao zhi zhu* 桃之竹).

97. Chen Weisong, *Huhailou ciji*, pp. 327–28; Zhang Cixi, *Qingdai yandu liyuan shiliao zheng xubian*, "Yunlang xiaoshi," p. 966.

In this poem, Chen addressed the relation between role-playing and intimacy. He opens with his sentiments on viewing Xu Ziyun dressed in his wedding finery and genially adopts the detached voice of a benevolent patron calmly sipping his wine and looking with pleasure on the actor. A screen partitions Chen and Xu Ziyun from the bridal party. The bride and the feminine Xu Ziyun form mirror-images of each other, their shadows simultaneously cast from opposite sides of the screen. A palimpsest of shadow plays forms on the single screen.

At first, the bridal party seems a histrionic space, and Chen's moment with Xu Ziyun on the other side of the screen an intimate space. To state that the bride is about to appear, Chen employed a phrase that could describe the entrance of an actor on a stage. But somehow, although Xu Ziyun's side of the screen is quiet, it is lacking in the kind of intimacy we would expect. The man whom we thought was Chen Weisong now seems a spectator in a theater, bedazzled by Xu Ziyun, the cross-dressed actor. The spectator's knowledge of Xu Ziyun is suddenly so limited that he cannot even discern whether he is man or woman. Moreover, his access to Xu Ziyun is so circumscribed that he can only cast glances at him stealthily: "I furtively measure your feet."[98] The imminent separation between Chen and Xu Ziyun is evoked by Chen's lack of recognition of Xu Ziyun. His comment, "I can't tell whether you are cock or hen," is a phrase commonly used to praise an actor's ability to impersonate a woman. Chen reverses the normal usage of the phrase. Xu Ziyun today impersonates a man; originally Chen's bride, he now plays the role of groom. Duly inspected, Xu Ziyun is sent off by his patron to "raise the bridal curtains on the marriage bed," a phrase that suggests the marriage bed is yet another theatrical space.

There is a quick turn in mood between the first and second stanzas, a shift prized among connoisseurs of the song lyric. The second stanza abruptly veers to the deep intimacy Chen and Xu Ziyun shared in days past. Chen's voice suddenly grows maudlin as he recalls how Xu Ziyun was his most intimate companion when they traveled far from home "staying in lonely haunts." His vision quickly telescopes to the pillow he and Xu Ziyun shared; as he speaks of the "red-fringed pillow, the tears like flowers

---

98. Actors never bound their feet; Chen was merely employing a common index of gender.

that you gently shed," he leaves no doubt that theirs was a romantic intimacy. The declaration "Today, you will be wed" ruptures this moment. Unexpectedly, with the recollection that the wedding is at hand, we are back in the realm of the staged, as "wife follows husband in sinuous chant." Chen's admonition, "Try your best to act as a model husband," sounds as though he were merely coaching the actor in one more role. In Chen's final lines, he himself strikes a histrionic pose, depicting himself lying alone in bed, a martyr to his quixotic devotion to the actor.

Conclusion

> Like dust or dreams or silk floss,
> Who knows of my tacit affection?
> I regret coming home so late,
> No need to rattle the latch,
> Just knock slowly upon the screen.
>
> A shower of rain in the blue emptiness outside the window,
> By the third watch you have long been gone.
> In vain you left your beautiful lines,
> Pale clustered flowers on the paper,
> The phoenix-leg lamp aslant.[99]

Chen Weisong wrote this poem in response to one by Xu Ziyun that has long been lost. Ziyun had paid a call upon Chen; not finding him in, he had left a poem to that effect. Returning around midnight, Chen answered the poem, praising the actor's "beautiful lines" like "pale clustered flowers on the paper." This rather mundane poem—and the absence of the poem that inspired it—point to the tantalizing mysteries that trouble the reader of these occasional poems. The regret regarding the actor's absence that Chen registered in this poem is emblematic of the absence of the actor in the collections of poems discussed above. The poets complain of unsatisfied desire, speaking through a haze of longing even as they sit before the actor at a performance. Like Chen in this poem, they have always "just missed" the actor. All that is left are traces of the actor as these authors wake from dreams of him or sit before his portrait lost in reverie.

---

99. Zhang Cixi, *Qingdai yandu liyuan shiliao zheng xubian*, "Yunlang xiaoshi," p. 962.

The empathic resonance I have set forth as the generating principle of the collection explains only the ways in which these poems resonate with the sentiments of Mao and Chen Weisong. My analysis does not examine what it was like to be the object of exchange, so much as investigate the concerns of the men who performed the exchanges.[100] Their sentiments may have resonated with Ziyun's thoughts as well; we cannot know, for his poems have not survived. Ziyun's poems might have told us what it was like to be an object that confers distinction, the gift whose circulation reinforces networks of patronage and obligation. But we can only echo Chen Weisong's sentiments of regret at having arrived too late.

---

100. This is a problem endemic to the theoretical literature that has inspired my readings. Arguments regarding social distinction seldom explore what it is like to be the object that confers distinction. The literature on the gift seldom has an opportunity to interrogate the sentiments or subjectivity of the gift itself. Arguments regarding the traffic in women, even Gayle Rubin's and Eve Sedgwick's feminist reformulations of them, give far less consideration to the women exchanged than to the quality of the bonds formed between the men who exchange them.

SIX

The Theatricality of the Vernacular

in Taohua shan

Kong Shangren's historical drama *Taohua shan* is the seventeenth-century play that scholars most readily associate with the metatheatrical. As mentioned at the end of Chapter 2, it begins with a prologue that features an ur-spectator called the Keeper of Rites, who regales the audience with his experience of watching the play. An offstage audience in the wings asks this onstage spectator for his guidance. Ultimately it is not the play itself, but the events it depicts, that the play seeks to teach its audience how to regard: Kong Shangren brings the waning days of the Ming to life on stage in order to suggest the means by which the literatus might become a discerning spectator of historical tragedy. The play alternates between promoting Confucian loyalty and Daoist reclusion, modeling for the spectator the movement from attachment to detachment.

The characters within the play who have a privileged understanding of detachment are an array of historical actors, musicians, and courtesans, primary among them the mid-seventeenth-century storyteller Liu Jingting. I focus on Liu Jingting in this chapter because he incarnates the tension between illusion and disillusion so central to seventeenth-century conceptions of theatrical and social spectatorship. Liu's storytelling grants him a mobile and panoramic perspective. His quick shifts among registers are reminiscent of the linguistic dexterity of the male queen Chen Zigao. Kong drew on a number of historical sources in rendering his portrait of Liu Jingting, among which Wu Weiye's biography of Liu figures prominently. In these biographies, we find a familiar concern regarding the confluence of theatrical and social imposture. Wu registered a distinct ambivalence about the storyteller's dazzling rhetoric and his capacity to create illusion. Kong Shangren recasts that ambivalence, suggesting that the rhetorical dexterity of the storyteller is symptomatic of an ideological versatility that is necessary if the literatus is to come to terms with the fall of the Ming. It is precisely that ideological versatility, predicated on a cold detachment that results from an understanding of the transience of all things, which Kong holds up as a corrective for the literatus overwhelmed by nostalgia for the late Ming. Thus the storyteller's ability to play any role is what the literatus needs in order to adapt himself to the vicissitudes of the waning days of the Ming.

I begin this chapter by examining the mid-seventeenth-century sources used by Kong Shangren in developing his portrayal of the storyteller, and then engage in a reading of the play that focuses on the storyteller's significance. Liu Jingting is presented in both the mid-seventeenth-century sources and in *Taohua shan* as a trickster, a shape-shifter who, like Chen Zigao, possesses a linguistic facility and ideological plasticity. In this regard, he, like Zigao, is linked to anxieties regarding the duplicity and presumed social aspirations of actors. At the same time, Liu Jingting's verbal dexterity and mental resourcefulness serve as a reproach for the literatus's narrow band of understanding. The storyteller's gift of mimicry and his capacity for self-transformation are thus not deplorable but exemplary, for they reveal his privileged understanding of the arts of illusion.

Liu Jingting

Liu Jingting's career began in the markets and ended in them. In between, he fraternized with many of the major late Ming political players. He was on familiar terms with such literary luminaries as Qian Qianyi and served as the trusted assistant of General Zuo Ningnan 左寧南. The abundant sources regarding Liu detail the complexity of his relationship with the literary elite of his day.[1] Because of his friendships with literary and politi-

---

1. These biographical sources are described in Hong Shiliang, *Liu Jingting pingzhuan*, pp. 9–16; Chen Ruheng, *Quyi lunwen xuan*; and Wai-yee Li, "The Representation of History in *The Peach Blossom Fan*," p. 424.

cal leaders, men of national prominence such as Zhang Dai, Wu Weiye, Qian Qianyi, and Huang Zongxi 黃宗羲 (1610–95) wrote biographical sketches of him and poems in tribute to him. May Fourth–era scholars canonized Liu Jingting as the founder of premodern storytelling precisely because these eminent literary men wrote of his art.[2] Yet the seventeenth-century biographies by no means voice unconditional praise. The ambivalences of Liu's literati biographers recall the complex set of resonances that accrue to the figure of the actor.

I focus below on biographies by Wu Weiye and Huang Zongxi. The most substantial of the portrayals, they represent two polarities in the depiction of the storyteller. Both Wu and Huang worried about Liu Jingting's protean mutability, a concern that hearkens back to the traditional equation of theatricality with inauthenticity. Wu warned that the storyteller was a wily trickster, but he obviously delighted in Liu's ability to infiltrate boundaries of status and romanticized his liminal position at the threshold of two worlds. Huang Zongxi sought to contain this transgression of social hierarchies, voicing his outrage at Wu's celebration of the storyteller's art and warning that the rogue storyteller would manipulate those under his thrall.

A member of a cosmopolitan circle of men of national prominence, Wu Weiye was *primus* in the civil service examinations of 1631 and had a distinguished political career.[3] He socialized with courtesans, actors, and musicians and is well known for his ballads about the courtesans Bian Yujing 卞玉京 and Chen Yuanyuan 陳圓圓. Like Gong Dingzi and Mao Xiang, Wu flouted traditional boundaries of status by publicly celebrating his relationships with the denizens of the entertainment quarters. His romanticization of the courtesan exerted a great influence on depictions of the demimonde up through the nineteenth century. Wu Weiye knew Liu personally and wrote the biography at Liu's request. His work forms

---

2. As the literary historian Lu Eting observes, Liu became a "hero of the people" in the mid-twentieth century, in part because of the eminence of his seventeenth-century biographers. Lu Eting, *Qingdai xiqujia congkao*, p. 33.

3. In later years, however, Wu adopted the pose of an apolitical aesthete, perhaps because of his regret at having collaborated with the Qing. On his deathbed, he asked that his tombstone be engraved only with the words, "The poet Wu Meicun" (*Wu Meicun shiren* 吳梅村詩人) (Wakeman, *The Great Enterprise*, p. 1078).

the template for all later biographies, which, as is typical, suture together long quotations from Wu's text.

Huang Zongxi quoted extensively from Wu Weiye but, through the judicious use of ellipses and the addition of a few anecdotes, flattened the ambivalences of Wu's biography into a monovalent warning against the storyteller's incantatory rhetoric. Although Huang shared with Wu Weiye such friends as Qian Qianyi, he was far more conservative. Huang Zongxi viewed moral laxity as a primary reason for the fall of the Ming. His perspective presaged the reaffirmation of status boundaries that historians regard as characteristic of the early Qing. An advocate of textual purism who sought to excise Buddhist and Daoist influences from the Confucian classics, Huang was one of the most prominent men of his time in promoting the kind of *kaozheng* 考証 (evidential) scholarship and philological purism that would become the dominant trend in eighteenth-century thought.[4] Without drawing too close a connection between Huang's interest in philological purism and his rectification of Wu's biography, with his intellectual interests it is not surprising that he sought to demystify Wu's romanticization of the storyteller's art.

In *Taohua shan*, Kong Shangren celebrated Liu's rhetorical dexterity and capacity to navigate hierarchies of status. He overrode the traditional equation of linguistic plasticity with inauthenticity by showing how Liu's verbal abilities enabled him to serve Ming loyalists. Kong, himself a descendant of Confucius in the sixty-fourth generation, granted Liu a genealogy in the *Analects*, whitewashing the shadier aspects of Liu's past. His gentrification of the storyteller is paralleled in his systematic erasure of vernacularity in his suggestions regarding the performance of his play. Within the play itself, Kong celebrated the storyteller's capacity for improvisation, which he portrayed as characteristic of the vernacular. In the prefaces to the play, however, he demonstrated a dramatically different attitude toward improvisation. The preservation of the purity of his text became his primary concern as he attempted to circumvent potential linguistic innovations by actors performing his text. In the movement from the play to the prefaces, then, Kong recapitulated the movement from

---

4. Huang was the editor of the Ming *Shilu* 實錄 (Veritable records) and the author of the first detailed history of Chinese philosophy, the *Mingru xue'an* 明儒學案 (The records of Ming scholars).

Wu's position to that of Huang Zongxi, from delight in boundary cross-ing to an attempt to contain unruly transgressions. Like the storyteller himself, he is in this respect versatile.

Wu Weiye

Wu and Huang's biographies elucidate the relationship of Liu to men of cultivation (*ru* 儒). Both repeatedly voice the same anxiety: could the ed-ucated elite control the storyteller, or would the storyteller instead usurp the privileges of his literati patrons? That the storyteller's art dazzles his audience—that it is crowd-pleasing—is itself cause for concern. The ver-nacular storyteller can enthrall an audience in a way that the Confucian scholar, whose language is allusive and highly refined, cannot. Although the storyteller's incantatory orality worried both Wu and Huang, Wu was delighted by its power but feared its irresponsibility, whereas Huang sought to demystify it, to demonstrate its many errors.

Most biographies of Liu Jingting question the reliability of his self-presentation in various ways, sometimes seemingly inadvertently.[5] With the exception of Huang Zongxi, the authors aimed to praise him, yet they could not avoid the vexed question of his origins. Given that Wu Weiye's biography, the earliest account, formed the basis for later versions, we can get no closer to the historical Liu Jingting, yet Wu's account thematizes the impossibility of pinning down the storyteller's origins. It begins in typical fashion, with the information we would expect to find in the first lines of a biography: ancestral place of origin, pseudonyms, and evidence of early precocity. Each piece of information, however, becomes an occa-sion for the biographer to issue a warning:

Liu Jingting, a man from Taizhou 泰州 in Yangzhou prefecture, was probably surnamed Cao 曹. When he was fifteen, he was a fearless rogue whose name was already in the police files. He fled to Xuyi 盱眙 [Jiangsu], where he had no means of making a living. He took with him a volume of tales tucked under his arm. Al-though he had never been exposed to storytellers, after listening to them for a

---

5. Zhang Dai's sketch of Liu Jingting may be an exception. He shared none of Wu's and Huang's anxieties and ambivalences regarding Liu's ascension among the ranks of the elite. Rather, Zhang's respect for Liu is clear as he emphasizes Liu's sense of self-worth as a virtuoso of his craft. See Zhang Dai, *Tao'an mengyi / Xihu mengxun*, p. 45.

while, he could duplicate what he heard. He told stories in the markets of Xuyi, making things up as he pleased, and this was already enough to amaze the people of the markets.[6]

Wu was not even certain of Liu's original surname; his Liu is purely self-invented, a man without a lineage. He has committed an unnamed crime so grievous that he fled rather than accept responsibility. During his life on the lam, he refashions himself as a storyteller. His total exposure to storytelling consists of a single volume of tales. But he is able to mimic the storytellers he has heard and even to invent his own tales. Neither an apprenticeship nor book learning is behind his practice, a point Huang Zongxi will make much of.

The question of whether Liu is purely self-invented or a creation of the cultivated elite forms an undercurrent of Wu's biography. A man of classical learning (*ruzhe* 儒者) takes this vagrant under his wing and trains him to astound and manipulate his audiences. When asked who his teacher was, Liu replies:

I have no teacher. My only teacher was a man of cultivation, Master Mo Houguang 莫後光 of Yunjian. Master Mo said, "Although storytelling is a lesser craft (*xiaoji* 小技), in that it is used to discern human nature, to investigate local customs, and to give shape and form to the ten thousand things, it is not a different path from that of the man of cultivation (*bu yu ruzhe yi dao* 不與儒者 異道)."[7]

The story of Mo's tutelage of Liu has an allegorical quality. Wu Weiye suggests that in encouraging Liu, the gentry has unleashed this force upon itself.[8] Whether the educated elite can control their creation or whether the storyteller will usurp their privilege is a troubling concern, for the storyteller can enthrall an audience in a way that the man of cultivation cannot. Wu's account of the scholar's transformation of the storyteller is structured as a fable: Mo's instruction consists of a series of three lessons that resemble ritualized tests. His aim is to bring Liu's art to such a peak

---

6. Wu Weiye, "Liu Jingting zhuan" 柳敬亭傳, in *Wu Meicun quanji*, p. 1055.

7. Ibid.

8. Although scholars have taken this account at face value, even speculating as to the regional accent Mo may have had, we should not omit the possibility that Liu might have fabricated this story, inventing a literati mentor to account for a commoner's otherwise inexplicable skills.

that his audiences lose control over their own comportment. After their initial meeting, Liu retreats and concentrates for a month on refining his art. When he returns, Mo tells him that it has not yet reached a certain level. "Your audience will chuckle, but this [skill] was easy for you to attain." On his next visit, Mo praises Liu's ability to make his audience lose control of their bodies: "You are almost there. Those who hear you tell stories will sit on the edges of their seats, and their complexions will change. Their hair will stand on end, and their tongues will cleave to the roofs of their mouths and not be able to come down." After Liu's final visit, Mo states that Liu's art has reached such a peak that his audience will lose control of their minds: "You've got it! The look in your eyes, the gestures of your hands and of your feet—before you begin to speak, feelings of sorrow and joy are already in the atmosphere; this is the utmost in the art of storytelling."

Thereupon those in his audience lost themselves as though they were in a trance, and at the end of his tales, they were as mournful as though they had suffered a loss. Master Mo said, "Wherever you go in the world, no one will be able to cause difficulties for you." Then Liu bade him farewell and left, traveling to Yangzhou, Hangzhou, and Suzhou. He spent the longest time in Suzhou. Afterward, he traveled to Nanjing. Wherever he went, he associated with the local worthies, who all were very fond of him.[9]

The elite sorcerer has taught his apprentice how to enchant his audiences, how to manipulate and control them. Once trained by Mo, Liu embarks on a series of social conquests in the major cultural capitals of southern China.

Wu structured his biography of Liu by describing Liu's increasing command over a series of audiences; those of Liu's own social status are the least taken in by his self-invention. During his flight from justice, he stops beneath a willow tree after managing to cross the Yangzi river. With tears streaming down his face, he declares, "From now on, I will be surnamed 'Liu' 柳 (Willow)." Liu's companions refuse to take him seriously: "Because those who heard him knew that he was full of tricks, some of them laughed loudly and left."[10] As Liu's audiences increase in social status, they grow less discerning. "Twenty years later in Nanjing, there was a

---

9. Wu Weiye, *Wu Meicun quanji*, p. 1056.
10. Ibid., p. 1055.

Master Liu who excelled at conversation." He is celebrated by the local elite who cherish him as one of themselves. "Wherever he went, all those among his audience were amazed," but "there were some who knew that this was the man who rested beneath the willow tree after crossing the Yangzi all those years ago." As the skeptical bystanders of Liu's announcement below the willow tree observe the elite making fools of themselves over him, Liu's elite audience becomes a secondary spectacle.

In Nanjing, Liu is feted by officials of the highest rank, including the Ministers of War Wu Qiao 吳橋 and Fan Jingwen 范景文, who consider him an esteemed guest. What they value is Liu's knowledge of the desperadoes in the marshes, although, of course, he knows of them only through his storytelling. The guests at Wu's and Fan's banquets tell Liu that they had once thought his stories fiction but now recognize them to be true:

"Before, when there was no civil unrest, when the likes of us heard you tell of chivalrous knights or of bandits who fled to the marshes, we laughed and said that such things could not exist, and that you were certainly good at making things up. Who would have thought that now, unfortunately, we have come to see them with our own eyes!" When Liu heard this, he was quite moved.[11]

Liu's stories have been authenticated as political and social crises have revealed the gentry's narrow band of understanding. The storyteller's profession grants him a privileged level of insight.

Even as Wu praised Liu's ability to mediate between individuals and social strata, he also implicitly warned against the storyteller's arts of enchantment. The word he repeatedly used to describe Liu's effect on his audience, "to topple" (*qing* 傾), recalls the frequent warnings of poets and historians against "city-toppling" beauties before whom rulers lose their heads. If Master Mo, the mysterious figure who trains Liu to manipulate his elite audiences, can be read as a figure for the elite advocate of vernacular literature, he has unleashed a powerful force that cannot quite be trusted. In part because it is not grounded in self-cultivation, Liu's rhetoric is considered untrustworthy. His language is not an emanation of his own self in the manner of the poetic tradition. Instead, it mimics the language of others; the vernacular is cast as theatrical and therefore viewed as unmoored.

---

11. Ibid., p. 1056.

Even as Wu cautioned against the storyteller's power to mesmerize, his biography enhanced the storyteller's mystique. Written at Liu's request, ultimately it aided Liu in his self-invention. Wu added a commentary to the biography that sought to reassure his readers that if Liu transgressed boundaries of status, such transgressions were not motivated by social aspiration. Wu noted that General Zuo was also the patron of a physician named Yang Jiheng; Zuo wrote a memorial to suggest that Yang Jiheng receive the position of magistrate of Wucheng, which Yang accepted, only to leave the post shortly thereafter to reassume his former profession. In contrast, General Zuo offered to memorialize the emperor in order to gain an official position for Liu, but Liu "laughed and refused."[12] Wu romanticized Liu as a remonstrator who seeks justice for others but has no desire for personal gain. The mixture of pleasure and concern we find in Wu's biography regarding the storyteller's mastery over his audience is the governing trope of the seventeenth-century literature on actors. On one hand, the literatus is fascinated by the actor's mastery over his audience. On the other hand, the literatus fears losing mastery over the self, fears being manipulated by the actor. Even as such depictions applaud the art of the actor or storyteller, they attempt to police the boundaries between social strata, to ensure that the performer cannot use his mastery over the elite spectator to cross boundaries of status.

Huang Zongxi

Ignoring the deft ambivalences of Wu's text, Huang Zongxi explicitly wrote his biography of Liu Jingting as a corrective to Wu's seeming celebration of the storyteller's art. Huang Zongxi's revision of Wu's biography is reminiscent of his interest in textual purism, his desire to excise heterodox interpretations from the classical texts. For example, his *Yixue xiangshu lun* 易學象數論 (A discussion of the images and numbers associated with the study of the *Book of Changes*; published in 1661) sought to expunge interpretations of the classic in which a Daoist influence could be detected.[13] Huang's mission to ferret out non-Confucian readings long

---

12. Here Wu likened Liu to the jester Meng 孟 immortalized by the Han dynasty historian Sima Qian.

13. See Kai-wing Chow, *The Rise of Confucian Ritualism*, p. 57.

identified as orthodox helps explain not only his correction of Wu's biography but also his antipathy to Liu. The storyteller's capacity to mimic makes him particularly threatening, because the spurious origins of his reproductions of elite speech easily go undetected. Wu Weiye delighted in Liu's mimicry and punning; Huang instead seemed threatened by it.

Scandalized that Wu Weiye should have lent his prestige to this storyteller and dismayed by Wu's romanticization of a vernacular artist, Huang could not understand how a man of the elite could possibly laud a performer of a vernacular art. He comments dryly: "When I read *Dongjing meng hua lu* and *Wulin jiushi*, [I noted that] they record dozens of storytellers. From then till now, no one has ever heard their names. Now, these days, everyone praises the storytelling of Liu Jingting."[14] Insisting that a mere storyteller was not worthy of a biography, Huang complained that one might as well compare an engraver of woodblock illustrations to the great literati painters Tang Bohu 唐伯虎 and Wen Zhengming 文徵明. He claimed that he had rewritten Wu's biography of Liu only so that posterity might know the proper interpretation of the facts. Huang all but equated Wu Weiye with Master Mo, who, in Huang's telling of the narrative, becomes a sinister figure, a traitor to his caste. It is not simply Liu's transgression of boundaries of status, then, that Huang sought to undo, but also Wu's reinscription of that transgression in his celebration of a practitioner of a vernacular art.

Given this bias, it is to be expected that Huang's revision of Wu's biography focuses almost entirely on Liu's wrongful assumption of an undeserved social status. Each of Huang's additions or omissions is calibrated to add to our distrust of the storyteller. Wu, for example, had merely told us that Liu got into trouble with the law; Huang states that Liu's crime was punishable by death, and it was in fleeing the law that he changed his name. "Liu Jingting is from Taizhou in the Yang region. Originally he was surnamed Cao. When he was fifteen, he was a ruthless rascal and was sentenced to death. He changed his surname to Liu and went to the markets of Xuyi to tell stories. He was already able to dazzle the people of the marketplace." Nor, in Huang's version, is Mo Houguang a benign advocate of the storyteller. Instead, Huang's more sinister version of Mo first notes to himself, "This boy is clever and knows how to adapt to circumstances. I can

---

14. Huang Zongxi, *Huang Lizhou wen ji*, p. 86.

make him famed for his art." Mo then encourages Liu by telling him, "You will make your audience unable to control themselves" (*shi ren zhi xingqing buneng zizhu* 使人之性情不能自主).[15] By underscoring that Liu is only the apprentice of the sinister and ill-defined Master Mo, Huang attempts to neutralize Liu's hold over his audiences; ultimately, it is not a lowly storyteller, but a man of the gentry who is in control.

Wu romanticized Liu's freedom from the constraints of traditional boundaries of status; Huang criticized him for not knowing his place. Wu's portrait of Liu made much of the fact that the storyteller was not unduly impressed by wealth and power; he was never obsequious to those high in rank and treated those low in status with respect. In contrast, Huang was outraged that Liu should socialize so easily with those of higher status. If Wu had attributed Liu's instant celebrity at court to his social savvy, Huang claimed that it was because the elite of Nanjing feared General Zuo that they took pains to express respect for his protégé.

Huang's most scathing comment is that Zuo preferred Liu's language to that of the Confucian scholars in his employ, for Zuo was illiterate and could not appreciate the allusive prose of the scholars hired to compose military propaganda. Wu Weiye had mentioned in passing that Huang embellished the anecdote to emphasize the way in which Liu's verbal agility enabled him to con the unlettered general.

The scholarly gentlemen in Zuo's office made their arguments with polished phrases. They sought examples from the past to prove their points regarding the present. They expended the utmost energy in this. General Zuo was displeased with all of them. But Jingting picked up their language. His was the lively banter of the alleyways. And everything was to General Zuo's satisfaction.[16]

Liu learns to mimic the language of Confucian scholars in the same way that he learned storytelling. He teaches himself to duplicate their rhetoric by eavesdropping on their conversations and then rephrases the requisite sentiments in the bantering language of the streets.[17] Huang was particularly outraged that Zuo entrusted Liu with the composition of military documents, ignoring the Confucian scholars he employed for this pur-

---

15. Ibid., p. 87.
16. Ibid.
17. Ibid.

pose. The appeal of the storyteller's vernacular orality to the illiterate general enables Liu to usurp the place of the literatus.

As Liu supplants the Confucian scholars in Zuo's employ, the vernacular language of the streets becomes the language of governance. The classical language, which has policed boundaries of status and serves as a passport into the ranks of the governing class, is in danger of being replaced by a language that is crowd-pleasing and meretricious. Huang blamed the fall of the Ming on General Zuo's blindness to proper class distinctions. "Alas, General Zuo was a great general, and yet he took a jester to be his trusted companion; all those in his employ were petty men of the streets. How could he not be defeated in battle?"[18] Huang praised Liu's art only once: when the fall of the dynasty leaves Liu penniless, he returns to the markets to perform. The vernacular belongs in the markets; it is when the elite give it a national rather than a local platform that hierarchies of status crumble and chaos ensues.

The popularity of the storyteller's vernacular art enables Liu's social overreaching. The extension of his social aspirations beyond his station is clear, however, in his inability to write. According to Huang Zongxi, the eminent poet Qian Qianyi, a friend of both Wu and Huang's, once praised Liu by saying that Liu's true skill lay not in storytelling but in composing letters.[19] Huang claimed that Qian's "praise" was a snide reference to the fact that Liu's letters were full of *bai zi*, the mistaken use of homophonous characters. (English equivalents would be the use of "hear" for "here" or "buy" for "bye.") Such mistakes can only be seen and not heard. In Liu's hands, the language of the elite is bastardized, but his mistakes cannot be detected orally. Only those who obtain his written words can know. Illiterate himself, General Zuo cannot discern Liu's blunders. Without the written word, it is impossible to catch and punish Liu's transgression. Huang blamed General Zuo's defeat on his blindness to the storyteller's linguistic imposture.

---

18. Ibid. Both Huang and Wu compare Liu to a jester, to radically different ends. For Huang, the term is a disparagement, whereas Wu compared Liu to the famed jester You in order to praise Liu's integrity.

19. Anne McLaren (*Chinese Popular Culture and Ming Chantefables*, p. 46) notes that storytellers would be even less likely than actors to be literate, for they learned their texts orally.

As I mentioned above, Huang Zongxi was one of the foremost scholars in the nascent evidential scholarship movement that revived philological studies. Like others in this movement, Huang thought that the cure for the social decadence that he and others believed had led to the fall of the Ming lay in the correct understanding of Confucian texts.[20] This philological research sought to recover Han dynasty scholarship on the classics as a basis for reconstructing the wisdom of antiquity. Benjamin Elman, in his account of the seventeenth-century movement toward philological studies, emphasizes the connection between social order and orderly language.[21] Liu's replacement of the classical language of governance with the vernacular, then, would register as profoundly destabilizing. Indeed, for Huang Zongxi as well as later generations of scholars, the insouciant transgression of social boundaries that characterized the last days of the Ming could not be isolated from the dynasty's fall.

Taohua shan

Like Huang Zongxi, Kong Shangren, the author of *Taohua shan*, had a deep interest in ritual and in textual purism. Those interests, however, did not influence his romanticization of the verbal skills of the storyteller and of the linguistic heterogeneity of the vernacular. Kong Shangren's celebration of Liu's destabilization of language, of his puns and tricks of rhetoric, recalls a different lineage of the school of names. If Huang's notion of

---

20. Early Confucian thought viewed the rectification of names—the creation of an accord between "name" (*ming* 名) and "actuality" (*shi* 實)—as the primary task of governance. Huang's fear that transgression of linguistic boundaries leads to the erosion of social hierarchies recalls the belief of the Confucian school of names that right naming and social order are correlated. Benjamin Schwartz observes that in Confucian thought, "Language carries its own imbedded reflection of the true order. . . . The word 'father' carries the implication that the father will 'act like a father' as well as the assumption that the language will provide information on how to do so. Thus when Duke Ching of Chi asks Confucius about government he simply says, 'Let the prince be a prince, the minister a minister, and the son a son'" (*The World of Thought in Ancient China*, p. 92; the quotation is from *The Analects*, 12.11).

21. "The Confucian doctrine of 'rectification of names' (*zhengming* 正名) pointed to a social order in which human behavior must correspond to clearly defined names of social functions. . . . Social order demanded orderly language" (Elman, *From Philosophy to Philology*, p. 45).

right-naming seems arch-Confucian, Kong's observations on the relationship between language and knowledge in *Taohua shan* seem to have more in common with Zhuangzi's games with language, which often reveal how point of view is dependent on a naturalized perspective.

Kong's exploration of the importance of perspective in his portrayal of the storyteller's linguistic dexterity is closely allied with *Taohua shan*'s technique for granting its audience a sense of catharsis regarding the fall of the Ming. Through sudden and alienating shifts in perspective, Kong sought to enlighten the spectator as to the conditional nature of all worldly pleasures. He deployed the conceit of the "play within a play" to remind us that the entire world is a stage. The interludes that preface each half of the play are set forty years after the events depicted in it; the temporal shifts dislocate the spectator, so that what a moment ago was "here" is now "there."

With these quick shifts of perspective, the play aspires to rupture not only the illusion that the phenomenal world constitutes reality but also the spectator's ideological illusions as well. If Confucian loyalism is "this," and Buddhist-Daoist lack of attachment is "that," one can realize the contingent nature of the one only from the perspective of the other. Complete ideological freedom is, of course, ultimately an impossibility, since any movement toward "freedom" from ideology reinforces the ascendance of Buddhist-Daoist detachment. The triumph of such detachment over Confucian attachment is not only foreordained but a further inscription of ideological mystification.

Taohua shan's primary concern is with the antithesis between Confucian loyalism and Buddhist-Daoist lack of attachment, in both the romantic and the political spheres. It sets the romantic entanglement of its protagonist Hou Fangyu with the courtesan Li Xiangjun against the backdrop of the perilous last days of the Ming. Liu the storyteller introduces Hou Fangyu to Li Xiangjun as he tutors Hou Fangyu in the mores of the pleasure quarters. Hou, although the son of the president of the Board of Revenue, is destitute, and even though he wishes to "marry" Li and deflower her, he cannot afford the purchase price. The villainous and corrupt politician Ruan Dacheng seeks to curry favor with him by financing Li Xiangjun's wedding. When Li Xiangjun discovers that Ruan provided her trousseau, she angrily rejects it, modeling for Hou a sense of principle in social association that he as yet lacks. Spurned by Hou and his clique, Ruan gains power in the Southern Ming government, which has placed the Prince of Fu (福王) on the throne as the Hongguang 弘光 emperor. Ruan then begins a persecution of Hou and those associated with him, including Liu and Li Xiangjun.

Meanwhile, in a military subplot, the general Zuo Liangyu 左良玉 threatens to move his starving troops on Nanjing to obtain provisions for them. General Zuo was greatly indebted to Hou's father, and so Hou forges a letter from his father asking Zuo to stay his troops. Safe delivery of the letter is of the utmost consequence, but none of the men among the literary elite is willing to take on the task. Liu volunteers and, with his repertoire of jests and jokes, manages to penetrate the barrier of guards surrounding Zuo's headquarters. Once he has gained an audience with Zuo, Liu quickly becomes his favorite, acting as court jester and remonstrator.

The fortunes of Hou's clique quickly fall as Ruan ascends in the new government in Nanjing. Ruan orders Hou and his friends Chen Zhenhui 陳貞慧 and Wu Yingji 吳應箕 arrested. Zuo writes a denunciation of Ruan and entrusts it to Liu, asking him to take it to Nanjing.[22] In Nanjing, Liu is arrested and joins Hou Fangyu in prison. When Manchu troops conquer Nanjing, the two escape from prison and flee to the mountains, where many of the lesser characters in the play are already gathered in a Daoist monastery. Hou Fangyu and Li Xiangjun are reunited by chance at the monastery, where the presiding abbot, Zhang Wei 張薇, a former commander of the Imperial Guard in Beijing, has forsaken his Confucian studies to don Daoist robes. In the midst of their rejoicing, the abbot interrupts them and lectures them as to the folly of all Confucian bonds of human relation. Immediately, they renounce their ties to each other and proclaim cultivation of the Dao to be their only aim.

In the penultimate scene, the play gestures toward but then transcends the convention of the "grand reunion" (*datuanyuan* 大團圓) of the *chuanqi* drama, in which family members and romantic partners long separated typically gather on stage. As Li and Hou are reunited, the Daoist abbot states that such Confucian bonds as those between ruler and subject or husband and wife are no longer relevant now that the dynasty has

---

22. Chen Zhenhui was Chen Weisong's father, as we noted briefly in Chapter 4; like Mao Xiang, he was a close friend of Hou Fangyu.

fallen. An epilogue once more gestures toward reunion and lingering attachment toward the dynasty before negating these values for the last time. Liu Jingting, who has become a fisherman, meets with the musician Su Kunsheng 蘇崑生 and the anonymous master of ritual called the Keeper of Rites in the woods. They are drinking and singing ballads when a representative of the Qing government comes seeking Ming loyalist recluses, ostensibly to entice them to join the new government. The three quickly scatter, fleeing into the hills without a trace as Hou and Li did before them. Thus all the characters that emblematize loyalty have by play's end dispersed.

The Storyteller's Commentary on the Analects

The significance of Li Xiangjun as an emblem of constancy, an exemplar not only of romantic but of political loyalism, has been much discussed.[23] My focus here, however, is the way in which the dialectics of attachment and detachment also play themselves out among the "low" characters, the actors and musicians of the pleasure quarters. These are the very characters that represent the vernacular, not only in that they are performers of vernacular literary forms but also in that they are socially and corporeally of a lower strata, associated as they are with promiscuity and profit. Kong altered such conventional valuations so that the low characters' privileged understanding of performance now grants them a precocious understanding of detachment. It is the rude mechanicals who have a privileged understanding of illusion. If, as we saw in Wu's and Huang's biographies, performers have traditionally been suspect in part because of their powers to enchant, the performers whom Kong lauded strive to disenchant. Kong claimed for the theater the power to rupture illusion. He attempted to teach his audience to "break the paper window pane" (打破紙窗看世界), as Liu Jingting puts it in the first act of the play, and look beyond the phenomenal world.[24]

Taohua shan forms the capstone in the seventeenth-century gentrification of the southern drama. The language of the lyrics is more closely

---

23. See, e.g., Strassberg, *The World of K'ung Shang-jen*; Ho, "Cultural Transformation and the Chinese Idea of a Historical Play"; and Lu, *Persons, Roles, and Minds*.

24. Kong Shangren, *Taohua shan*, p. 9.

filiated to poetic genres associated with elite registers of speech (that is, *shi* and *ci*) than to the lyrics of Yuan drama or *sanqu*. Kong sought to grant the drama a classical heritage, as becomes evident in the prefaces to *Taohua shan*. His portrayal of the storyteller was certainly influenced by this gentrification through classicism. He portrayed Liu as a modern-day incarnation of the Han dynasty jester Dongfang Shuo 東方朔, in this way creating a classical genealogy for the storyteller. Kong also made the storyteller an honorary literatus, whitewashing Liu's dubious past. Wu romanticized the inclusion of the storyteller in the ranks of the governing elite but was troubled by it; Huang warned against it; Kong aided and abetted it. But although Kong's position seems far more pluralistic than Wu and Huang's, in fact his gentrification of the storyteller subtly concurs with their aims. It, too, contributes to the erasure of the popular.

As the play begins, Hou Fangyu and his friends Chen Zhenhui and Wu Yingqi consider their options for an afternoon's entertainment. Wu suggests that the trio pay a visit to the renowned storyteller Liu Jingting. Hou scornfully replies that Liu was employed by Ruan Dacheng, the "adopted son" of the eunuch Wei Zhongxian, and that he has no intention of associating with him. Wu retorts that Liu is, in fact, a man of principle; Liu walked out on Ruan in mid-performance when he found out that Ruan was a member of Wei Zhongxian's circle. Hou replies in astonishment, "I should never have expected to find such principles in a man of that sort." (Kong is writing in defiance of the facts; the historical Liu preserved good ties with Ruan, and this was one reason that Zuo was particularly anxious to take Liu into his employ.) As this discussion of Liu's principled adjudication of the problem of serving an undeserving master might suggest, Kong makes the storyteller an honorary literatus who confronts the same moral dilemmas as did the literati of the late Ming.

However, Kong allows the lesser characters to debunk the elite character's romanticization of the storyteller. When Hou Fangyu and his friends arrive at Liu's door, their servant shouts out, "Is pock-marked Liu at home?" Chen rebukes him, telling him to elevate his language: "He is a celebrity (*mingshi* 名士); you should address him as Master Liu" (Liu *xianggong* 柳相公). The servant does as he is told, but comically, becomes no more deferential, shouting: "Master Liu, open the door!"[25] The elite,

---

25. Ibid., p. 7.

who have adopted Liu Jingting as one of their own, delight in their willful transgression of boundaries of status. But the servant deflates their romantic affectations. As noted in Chapter 3, *chuanqi* drama commonly engages in this sort of ironic undercutting of the more refined registers of elite speech. The juxtaposition of high and low social and linguistic registers creates a reality effect, in which the vernacular, because it is practical, earthy, and materially grounded, seems more real. That this ironic deflation only works in one direction—the high never subverts the low—makes the realm of the elite seem illusory and abstracted or, as here, affected and theatrical.

Liu welcomes the scholars by saying, "You masters are all scholars and men of virtue (*dushu junzi* 讀書君子). You are so familiar with the *Shiji* and *Zizhi tongjian* 資治通鑑 [The comprehensive mirror of aid in government]; yet you have come to hear my vulgar performance (*sutan* 俗談)." He then declaims a poem, a lamentation on the past in regulated verse:

> In the deserted garden, a withered pine tree leans against a crumbling wall,
> The spring rain falls like silk threads over the fragrant grass covering the palace ruins,
> I dare not recall the rise and fall of the Six Dynasties.
> I lightly set my drums and clappers aside, and weep tears as I spin tales of broken hearts.[26]

The storyteller's mocking pretension to elite sensibility here is underscored by the incongruity of hearing these elegiac sentiments and refined language issue from the mouth of the clown (*chou*), the role-type of the actor who plays Liu's part. Liu continues, "I am only afraid that my historical tales and blindman's songs will be hard on your august ears (*zun er* 尊耳). What can I do but narrate a chapter of the *Analects* that you masters study?" Hou replies, "This is curious (*qi* 奇). How can you narrate the *Analects*?" Liu answers, "You masters speak of the *Analects*, why shouldn't I? Today I want to put on a cultivated air (*pian yao jia siwen* 偏要假斯文) and narrate a chapter of it."[27]

---

26. Ibid.

27. Ibid. The rhetorical flexibility and versatility Liu calls on here are inherent not only in his role as storyteller but in the role-type of the clown. The clown arguably encapsulates the features that characterize the vernacular itself; like the vernacular, he represents a lower stratum linguistically, socially, and corporeally, and he easily traverses boundaries.

In this first act, Kong elevates the status of the storyteller and of the theater by granting both a classical heritage, a genealogy in the *Analects*.[28] Although the chapter of the *Analects* on which Liu comments is in fact a later interpolation, commentators believed that it described how Confucius had enlightened the musicians of the court of Lu with his teachings. (It is ironic that the very section of the classical text Liu quotes to legitimate himself is itself apocryphal; although perhaps not an intended irony, this is in keeping with the way that ideological sources of legitimation quickly reveal their insubstantiality in this play.) The musicians, realizing that their masters were corrupt hegemons, deserted them to seek other masters or to enter reclusion.[29] Liu's recitation of this chapter is a tidy bit of self-promotion; he not only refers obliquely to his rejection of his erstwhile master, Ruan Dacheng, but implicitly places himself in the lineage of Confucius.

Liu's recitation is such a success that the scholars adopt the storyteller as an honorary literatus. As Liu concludes, the scholars praise the storyteller, saying that his remarks on the *Analects* are more satisfying than those of the commentators on the classics employed by the court. Chen applauds, "Wonderful! Wonderful! None of the writers of imperial proclamations and commentators on the classics we have today is this poignant and to the point (*tongkuai* 痛快). This indeed is the highest craft!"[30] The vernacular creates a space for itself by challenging the language of officialdom. In contrast to the language of the bureaucrat, it is emotionally unrestrained and therefore authentic.[31]

---

28. Kong had in fact a deep and professional interest in genealogy; he was the editor of the genealogy of the Kong clan, perhaps the most extensive genealogy of any Chinese family (Strassberg, *The World of K'ung Shang-jen*, pp. 72–73).

29. Wai-yee Li (*Enchantment and Disenchantment*, p. 424) has noted that in this performance, "Liu affirms his own freedom and also presages his transformation into a fisherman in the last scene, when the time for heroic action is over. . . . Liu implicitly compares himself to Confucius and defines his own action as a moral-political statement that restores efficacy and moral urgency to story telling and, by extension, drama."

30. Kong Shangren, *Taohua shan*, p. 9.

31. It is possible that Kong is creating a parallel between himself and Liu here. The Kangxi emperor sent emissaries to Kong's home in Qufu to obtain his commentaries on the *Daxue* 大學 (The great learning) and *Yijing* (The book of changes), and personally corrected them. Kong also spoke on the *Daxue* at court before the emperor. Kong wrote an account of these experiences that included a text of the oration on the *Daxue* he gave at

There is a definite irony here: although Liu's seeming transgression in commenting on the *Analects* delights his elite audience, it is now thought that Liu Jingting's lyrics in this act were composed not by the historical Liu but by a Confucian bureaucrat who aspired to be a storyteller. The vernacular ballad Liu chants in this scene is believed to have been penned by a retired official, a friend of Kong Shangren's named Jia Fuxi 賈鳧西 (1589–ca. 1670), who wrote drum songs (*guci* 鼓词) under the pseudonym "The Wood and Leather Wanderer" (Mu pi sanke 木皮散客).[32] Like Kong a native of Qu, Jia Fuxi passed the *jinshi* examinations in 1624 and became director of the Jiangxi bureau of the Board of Punishments in 1641. He resigned in protest over its policies and returned home to Qufu where he devoted himself to the composition and recitation of ballads. The trajectory of Jia Fuxi's career as a storyteller was the opposite of Liu's. Liu ascended from the markets to the highest echelons of the elite; Jia left his official position to tell stories in the marketplace. Kong modeled Liu on Jia Fuxi; the character of the storyteller who becomes an honorary literatus was based on a literatus who wanted to be a storyteller.

When performed by Liu in Act 1, Jia's ballad forms an extended self-introduction, giving an account of why Liu left Ruan's employ. In Jia Fuxi's repertoire, the ballad was also autobiographical; it described his resignation from office to enter reclusion as a storyteller.[33] With Liu's performance of Jia's ballad, Kong inscribed a palimpsest not of different texts but of different performances of the same words. The performance context of the lyrics alters as Liu chants them, and they gain a new significance.

Kong wrote a short biography of Jia, in which he described how Jia requested that his superiors impeach him after he resigned from office, but his superiors refused. When they asked on what grounds he should be im-

---

court (*Kong Shangren shiwenji*, pp. 425–37). For a translation of the entire account, see Strassberg, *The World of K'ung Shang-jen*, pp. 75–116. Interestingly, Strassberg records Kangxi's praise of Kong as being similar to Chen's praise of Liu: "Our official lecturers cannot compare with this one" (p. 87).

32. Interestingly, Jia is not cited as a source in Kong's prefatory list of sources (*kao ju* 考據). The ballads Liu recites are commonly attributed to Jia Fuxi, but there is some question as to whether this attribution is correct.

33. Jia's ballads were reprinted by the late Qing enthusiasts Ye Dehui 葉德輝 (1864–1927), Wu Woyao 吳沃堯 (1866–1910), and Wang Yirong 王懿榮 (1845–1900). This ballad is, however, not among them.

peached, he replied, "I engage in storytelling to the neglect of my official duties—that would be a good charge."[34] Cultivating an air of eccentricity, he made storytelling the obsession that defined him, and his avocation became his vocation. Kong's portrayal of Jia's rigid, almost laughably solemn advocacy of vernacular forms could not be further from his depiction of the storyteller Liu as an emblem of versatility, equally at home in a variety of linguistic registers and social strata.

Jia's dogged single-mindedness points to his employment of literary iconoclasm as an instrument of social distinction.[35] His iconoclasm consisted of no more than a simple inversion of norms. Visiting his neighbors, for example, he dressed in his official robes; calling on old colleagues, he wore casual clothes. Similarly, he recited the *Analects* in the marketplace and engaged in storytelling in the offices of officials. Wu's biography of Liu told how all delighted in the way he confounded social expectations by treating the elite of the capital with no ceremony. In contrast, Kong reported that when Jia performed his ballads before ministers and officials in their offices, "his listeners were aghast and thought him a weird eccentric." And when Jia recited the *Analects* in the marketplace, because "his style mixed elegance and vulgarity, the serious and the satirical, much like Li Zhi, Xu Wei, and Yuan Hongdao of the late Ming, hardly anyone among the local people understood it."[36]

Kong's comparison of Jia to Li Zhi, Xu Wei, and Yuan Hongdao compliments him by likening him to these early aficionados of vernacular literary forms. The association suggests that, like them, Jia engaged in a contrapuntal play with linguistic registers that only the most refined sensibilities could appreciate. Yet in some ways, Jia seems susceptible to the Gong'an school's caricature of the archaists. Yuan Zhongdao wrote that inappropriate citation of the ancients in the archaist manner was

34. Kong Shangren, "Jia Fuxi zhuan," 貴鬼西傳, in *Kong Shangren shiwenji*, pp. 495–97. The translation cited here is from Strassberg, *The World of K'ung Shang-jen*, p. 36–40.

35. As noted in Chapter 3 above, the seventeenth-century "invention" of a vernacular literary tradition permitted a small sector of the elite to define itself as cosmopolitan by creating a culturally sophisticated hybrid language that is both intensely allusive and peppered with local idiom. Their advocacy of the vernacular was not simply an aesthetic act; it was also a subversion of boundaries of status that conferred social distinction.

36. Kong Shangren, "Jia Fuxi zhuan," in *Kong Shangren shiwenji*, pp. 495–97. See also Strassberg, *The World of K'ung Shang-jen*, pp. 36–40.

reminiscent of clothing oneself in summer hemp in the cold of winter.[37] Jia Fuxi's stilted affectation of vernacular speech could be similarly described as lacking sensitivity to context. In contrast to the storyteller's deft identification of the appropriate linguistic register for any situation, Jia seems linguistically and socially tone-deaf. His didactic pedantry recalls Kong Shangren's own in his prefaces to *Taohua shan*, where, as we shall see, Kong railed against any improvisatory addition or deletion to his crystalline work of art.

The Letter

Huang Zongxi decried Liu's recasting of the sentiments of Confucian bureaucrats in the language of the streets. When, in *Taohua shan*, Liu commits an equivalent heresy, elucidating the *Analects* in the vernacular, Kong seems to suggest that the vernacular language not only supports and aids the classical but also may supersede it. In Scene 10, Hou and his friends enlist Liu's help in delivering a letter to General Zuo's camp. The letter asks that Zuo not move his armies east, for fear that his soldiers will lay waste to Nanjing. At the opening of the scene, they make it clear that they consider Liu a mere entertainer. Soon, however, they have not only embraced him as one of their own but find themselves relying on his aid.

As the scene opens, Hou discovers Liu alone at home chanting to himself and expresses his amazement that Liu should be performing in the absence of an audience. Liu replies, "Storytelling is my vocation (*benye* 本業). I am like a gentleman (*xianggong*) sitting leisurely in his study playing the *qin* 琴 and chanting poems. Do *you* need someone to listen?"[38] Rebuking Hou for his assumptions, Liu insists that, like many of the gentry, the storyteller chants to amuse himself, untainted by consideration of profit. This exchange prefaces the storyteller's gradual assumption of the functions of the literati in the next scenes. As the conversation between Hou and Liu ends, an acquaintance of Hou's father, the literati painter Yang Wencong, arrives to summon Hou to draft a letter in his father's name to

---

37. Yuan Hongdao, *Yuan Hongdao ji jianjiao*, p. 709.
38. Kong Shangren, *Taohua shan*, pp. 70–71. On the significance of the term *benye*, see Lu, *Persons, Roles, and Minds*, p. 233; Lu suggests that Liu here likens himself to those engaged in agricultural cultivation, an occupation considered primary in classical thought.

General Zuo. Seeing Hou listening to the storyteller, Yang asks impatiently, "In times like these, how can anyone listen to stories?" By the scene's end, however, it is clear that the storyteller's rhetorical skills are more critical to the survival of the dynasty than Hou's letter, which will never reach Zuo unless Liu manages to penetrate Zuo's encampment.

Pressured by starving troops, the general is about to sack Nanjing. Hou's father was General Zuo's beloved patron, and so at Yang Wencong's suggestion, Hou forges a letter from his father, asking Zuo not to move on Nanjing.[39] The refined sentiments of the letter are useless unless it is delivered, and the elite characters are helpless in the face of this practical consideration. Liu volunteers, telling Hou and Yang that he will have no difficulty penetrating the encampment because he is familiar with such intrigues from his storytelling.

When Hou Fangyu asks Liu to take the letter to General Zuo's camp, a contest between classical writing and vernacular orality ensues, and it becomes clear that although the vernacular begins by supporting the classical, it may soon usurp its place. Liu turns the scene into a competition between oral improvisation and classical text. In a long song suite, he compares the relative utility of the literatus's writing brush and the storyteller's tongue. He concludes by informing Hou that the letter is in fact not necessary, for his verbal dexterity alone suffices:

> "I don't need to explain carefully what is in the letter.
> Why need they understand it further?
> It's a waste of my breath,
> If I went empty-handed,
> the outcome would be no different,
> I'd still have my bag of tricks.
> I'll depend on the sharpness of my tongue to scold the men and horses into
>   withdrawing.
> They'll retreat 800 miles."[40]

---

39. It is noteworthy that he forges the letter at Yang Wencong's urging; Yang is here, as in Hou's decision to take Ruan's money to buy Li Xiangjun's trousseau, a corrupting influence. Viewed in this light, Liu's rejection of the letter is not simply an aggressive statement of the superiority of colloquial over elite writing, but a rejection of Hou's falsification; see Kong Shangren, *Taohua shan*, p. 71.

40. Ibid., p. 72.

Liu praises his own nimbleness of wit, his rhetorical flexibility and adaptability in the face of changing situations (*suiji yingbian de koutou* 隨機應變的口頭). (The language here echoes that of Wu Weiye and Huang Zongxi's biographies.) Hou's calcified rhetoric, which is merely an imitation of his father's prose, is unnecessary; Liu's improvisation supersedes it. In the last line, Liu's speech becomes aggressively vernacular, leaving his elite audience effectively tongue-tied. After Liu has left, Hou says blandly, "I have always said he's as good as any of us. Storytelling is only a hobby of his" (*shuoshu nai qi yuji er* 説書乃其餘技耳).[41] The elite is blind to the threat or the aggression of the colloquial language, even when it defines itself as that which makes elite language obsolete. As the storyteller declares the scholar's refined compositions unnecessary, the scholar, ignoring the threat, praises Liu as an honorary literatus. This is precisely the scenario that Huang Zongxi most feared.

In the early scenes of the play, Kong displayed the storyteller's adept acculturation to the world of the elite. Once he has established Liu's ability to inhabit that world, he showed how Liu exceeds it. Liu's capacity for improvisation allows him to function as a mediator among different social strata, to facilitate communication between literati and general, between general and troops. The storyteller's linguistic ingenuity is more helpful than the literatus's linguistic refinement, his capacity for improvisation socially more useful than the literatus's single persona.[42] The literatus is relatively paralyzed, for he can act and speak only one role. No matter how circumstances change, he is pinned in place by the language of the Confucian elite and by Confucian expectations of the behavior appropriate to a certain social stratum. The performer's protean mutability is more valuable than the literatus's constancy in these parlous times.

Versatility and the Marketplace

Liu Jingting's linguistic plasticity enables him to fake his way past the barriers to General Zuo's camp. It also enables him to infiltrate more abstract boundaries of status and gain acceptance among the capital's elite (here Kong Shangren is clearly drawing on Wu's biography). The storyteller's

---

41. Ibid., p. 73.
42. Ibid. p. 72.

ideological versatility is closely allied with the play's juxtaposition of competing Confucian and Daoist visions as to how one might come to terms with the fall of the Ming.

Kong begins the play by introducing the storyteller as a man who incarnates principles of Confucian loyalty. As noted above, Liu leaves the employ of Ruan Dacheng when he discovers Ruan's treacherous nature and later risks his life to save the capital from a siege. As the play continues, however, Liu becomes an exemplar of Buddhist-Daoist detachment as well. His storytelling gives him a unique understanding of the rise and fall of dynasties, of flux and change, and that grants him a detachment particularly valuable to the political elite on the eve of the Qing conquest. By the play's end, the dynasty has fallen, and Liu leads Hou Fangyu to a Daoist monastery, where Hou abandons his Confucian attachments to family and country to don Daoist robes.

Liu defines himself through a juxtaposition of terms that are rarely placed in proximity to each other, invoking a kind of category crisis that renders him tantalizingly elusive and yet paradoxically ubiquitous. For the storyteller seems strangely of nowhere and yet at home everywhere. The mysteries of Liu's origins further his capacity to claim any social space as his own. Scene 10 constitutes the storyteller's second self-introduction. In Scene 1, he demonstrated his ease with the classical heritage. Here, he introduces himself as a man of the marketplace:

> I, old man Liu, roam the river and lakes full of boasts about myself.
> Buying up the present and selling the past is how I make my way.[43]
> For years I've feared becoming a retainer of the wealthy,
> I leisurely sit on the street and drink cold tea.[44]

If, in Scene 1, he described himself as an inheritor of the classical past, here he presents himself as an entrepreneur; he buys up the present and sells the past. The vernacular language is invested in the present, the classical language in the past. Liu is a modern man, whose relation to the sacrosanct classical past is unabashedly instrumental. His ideological versatility grants him a certain independence—he is not a retainer of the wealthy, but instead oversees others' fates.

---

43. In other words, by telling tales of the past.
44. Kong Shangren, *Taohua shan*, p. 70.

What do you think I'm like? I'm like King Yama, holding in my palm a hefty book of accounts, in which is written the names of countless ghostly souls. I'm also like the Milo Buddha, thrusting out my great belly in which are stuffed limitless ephemera, the ups and downs of this world. When I lightly beat my drum and clappers, thunder and rain, wind and dew issue forth; my tongue and lips have only to move, and days turn and seasons change.[45]

Like King Yama and the Milo Buddha, the storyteller is a constant governing the changes of the universes of which he tells. But he speaks irresponsibly, without basis; there is nothing to govern the constant itself. Liu quickly shifts metaphors, in a way that is reminiscent of the cascades of allusion in which the cross-dressed boy Zigao cloaked himself. He concludes the speech above, "I, pock-marked Liu, say whatever comes to mind, but it makes people happy."[46] His irresponsibility grants him the versatility that renders him so indispensable to the elite; his plasticity is also the source of his detachment.

Although, on one hand, Liu's constant mutation makes him seem capricious and even unreliable, on the other, it fosters in him a dispassion that the literatus needs to cultivate. Hou, paying a visit to Liu, requests to hear any tale told in an "exciting (*renao* 熱鬧) and straightforward (*shuangkuai* 爽快) manner." Liu rebukes him, "Master, do you not know that exciting scenarios give rise to depression, and straightforward affairs become complicated ones?"

In the closing scenes of *Taohua shan*, Liu's understanding of the ephemeral nature of all worldly phenomena is finally brought home to the literatus. *Taohua shan* functions as a eulogy for the loyalism of the courtesan and, by implication, for the loyalism of the literati of the Southern Ming. But their steadfast allegiance is not only commemorated but also overwritten. In the final scene, the courtesan must learn the lesson that the storyteller repeatedly imparts in his narration of the rise and fall of dynasties. Loyalty is simply a form of attachment, and understanding this is a condition of enlightenment.

---

45. Ibid.
46. Ibid.

From Confucian Attachment to Daoist Detachment

In the penultimate scene, Liu Jingting escorts Hou Fangyu to a Daoist temple. The abbot, Zhang Wei, opens the scene by describing his conversion from careworn civil servant to carefree Daoist priest:

> The affairs of this world are many and confused.
> I spent half a life in this dusty world and my ruddy face has grown old,
> I retired none too soon,
> For I had had enough of the clamor of the puppet theater.
> Moved to tears along the empty road, I pause and cry out[47]
> And then burst into laughter.
> All has come to rest,
> Where immortals dwell, those with furrowed brows have been few.[48]

The lines "Moved to tears along the empty road, I pause and cry out / And then burst into laughter" suggest the cathartic movement from passion to dispassion we find in these final scenes. The enlightened spectator of the "clamor of the puppet theater," of the changing governments of the war years, will not mourn with "furrowed brows."

In the first half of the scene, Zhang leads a chorus in a ritual that commemorates the last emperor of the Ming. The ritual evokes a play in miniature, and Zhang, for an instant, becomes reminiscent of the playwright. Zhang visualizes for his audience the fates of the key characters in the play, conjuring up the figures of the dead. As he closes his eyes and summons them, they appear on stage as ghosts, briefly introducing themselves and then announcing whether they have received new posts in Heaven or met their doom. Zhang's vision provides a semblance of the "grand reunion" (*da tuanyuan* 大團圓) with which the *chuanqi* typically ends.

This closure accomplished, the scene abruptly shifts focus. The scene is, in essence, two scenes in one; the participants in the ritual exit, and the major and minor characters reassemble on stage to listen to the abbot's sermon at the Daoist monastery. The remaining characters become Daoist adepts. Confucian loyalism has no significance once the ghosts of the past have been put to rest. Hou Fangyu is reunited with Li Xiangjun;

---

47. An allusion to the Six Dynasties poet Ruan Ji 阮籍.
48. Kong, *Taohua shan*, p. 252.

both have been led by the "low" characters to listen to the abbot. Hou and Li immediately express their gratitude at the loyalty of the minstrels Su and Liu who have brought them thus far, Hou stating, "When we are home once more as man and wife, we shall endeavor to repay their kindness." Abbot Zhang interrupts their musings:

Zhang: What are you whispering about? Earth and heaven have been turned upside down, and you still cling to the roots of passion and the sprouts of lust! How laughable!

Hou: You miss the mark. Since time immemorial men and women have married; this is one of the primary bonds of human relationship. Sorrow and joy in separation and reunion are the natural outgrowth of love. How can you interfere with them?

Zhang: [angrily] Hmmph! Two fools for love, no more than bugs! Where are nation, home, ruler, or father now? Can you not then cut off the root of this lustful passion? [sings]

> I sigh in desperation over you spoiled children,
> heedless of the rise and fall of dynasties . . .
> coyly making such fools of yourselves upon the stage that bystanders laugh.
> I urge you to flee quickly upon the clear bright path before you.

Hou: [bows] As you speak these words, I wake from my dream, a cold sweat pouring from me.

Zhang: Have you understood then?

Hou: Your disciple understands.

Zhang: Since you understand, make your obeisances to Ding Jizhi, your tutor. [Hou makes his obeisances].

Li Xiangjun: Your disciple also understands.

Zhang: Then make your obeisances to Bian Yujing, your tutor. [She makes her obeisances.]

Zhang [to Ding and Bian]: Give them Daoist robes.[49]

Now that nation and family, prince and father, are all gone, Zhang states, there is no longer a place for romantic attachment. Zhang subjects the passionate sentiments of Li and Hou to mockery by invoking the figure of the worldly stage, on which they are rendering themselves such fools "that

---

49. Ibid., p. 258.

bystanders laugh." The only way to exit this worldly stage, his words imply, is to flee toward the "clear bright path" of Daoist self-cultivation.

Hou is immediately enlightened. Li Xiangjun follows, "When I look back, all is illusion, who is this man before me?" If *Mudan ting* unleashed the term *qing* on seventeenth-century literary discourse, *Taohua shan* laid it to rest.[50] It is not that the bands between sovereign and subject, husband and wife are now illusory. Rather, the realization that enlightens Hou Fangyu and Li Xiangjun is that illusion inevitably *structures* social relations. The Confucian bonds of human relation and the loyalty that are their foundation are all premised in illusion.

Although the play proper ends with the shattering of the romantic illusions of the protagonists, it continues with an epilogue (*yuyun* 餘韻) in which Su Kunsheng, Liu, and the Keeper of Rites meet high in the mountains to sing ballads they have composed in commemoration of the lost world of the Ming. The epilogue complicates the trajectory from attachment to detachment, passion to dispassion. The previous scene had seemed a fitting place to end the play. In the scene's coda, Zhang concluded, "Thanks to me, the peach blossom fan was torn to shreds. No longer shall these foolish insects be allowed to spit forth soft strands and ensnare each other in myriad ways." Li Xiangjun's loyalty to Hou, which the play has done so much to commemorate, was from Zhang's perspective no more than an attachment motivated by desire.

The epilogue, however, retreats from this vision of utter disillusion. Having led Li Xiangjun and Hou Fangyu to the Daoist establishments where they will practice self-cultivation, Su Kunsheng and Liu Jingting have become woodcutter and fisherman, fulfilling the ancient ideal of agrarian reclusion. As performers, they have a privileged understanding of the simultaneous experience of illusion and disillusion. For this reason, it is particularly fitting that they appear for one final time in the epilogue, which occupies a liminal status both within and without the illusory realm that constitutes the play proper. They are joined by the other character who best understands liminality, the Keeper of Rites, whose soliloquies form the prologue as well as the interstitial act that separates the two halves of the play.

---

50. Ibid., p. 259.

Of all the characters in the play, only the three who appear in the epilogue, Liu, Su, and the Keeper of Rites, have not undergone a conversion and abandoned their former identities by play's end. They are distinguished from the others in part because they have had no significant attachments. Rather, they served as tutors and exemplars. It is particularly interesting that Liu, Su, and the Keeper of Rites survive unchanged, for they are the characters in the play most linked to the playwright himself.

All three sing laments for the lost dynasty. Liu's is a historical ballad, which the Keeper of Rites praises by likening it to the compositions of the eminent poet Wu Weiye. Su Kunsheng's contribution, a song sequence that is a nostalgic meditation on the past, bemoans the destruction of the pleasure quarters of Nanjing. This song sequence, like the ballad with which Liu opened the play, was in fact penned by the literatus Jia Fuxi. Both explicitly and implicitly, then, the musicians are likened to literati; they exhibit the historical consciousness and sentiments of loyalism expected of a literatus. The sudden rupturing of attachment in the previous scene gives way to the nostalgia of the epilogue; disillusionment cedes to willful illusionment.[51]

However, in the final lines of the epilogue these lamentations of the loyalists are abruptly contained. A runner serving the Manchu court comes upon the three. Feigning sleep, he overhears their conversation and deduces that they must be loyalist recluses. As he makes to arrest them, the tone quickly shifts from the poetic to an almost comic slapstick. The three protest that they are not famous or learned enough to qualify as loyalist recluses. The Keeper of Rites says, "I'm merely a Keeper of Rites who puts on a cultivated air (*jia siwen* 假斯文)"; Liu and Su similarly protest that they are simply a storyteller and a ballad singer. The runner remarks: "Don't you know? Those famous scholar-officials and literati, they were all heroes who understood their duty in these times. Starting three years ago, they all came out of the mountains. Now we want to round up exactly your sort."[52] Nostalgia for the lost dynasty is once again punctured, as we discover that the famous scholar-officials who gave it its grandeur

---

51. As Wai-yee Li ("The Representation of the History in the *Peach Blossom Fan*," p. 431) observes, "Here historical reflection leads not to philosophical acceptance but to a deepening sense of loss and sadness."

52. Ibid., p. 269.

have joined the Qing government. These three last loyalists to the Ming suddenly scurry off into the hills.

In this last scene and epilogue, the play displays an ideological versatility reminiscent of that of Liu Jingting himself. Beginning in a Confucian mode, it veers abruptly toward a Daoist conclusion, then retrenches, engaging momentarily in Confucian nostalgia for the lost Ming before ultimately adopting a perspective of alienation toward Confucian loyalism. The play's ideological versatility makes the spectator more conscious of the contingency of any lens through which one might view the world of forms.[53]

The Author as Actor: Kong's Appropriation of the Vernacular

Although *Taohua shan* celebrates the improvisatory wit of the storyteller, an entirely different attitude toward actors and improvisation appears in the prefaces Kong appended to the play. In these prefaces, Kong sought to rob the actor of the ability to improvise, warning actors against amending his lyrics in any way. Struggling for primacy with the actors who will present his play, he aggressively proclaimed his mastery over this vernacular literary form.

The play is packaged in a series of six prefaces that guide the reader in appreciating the author's intentions in writing the play. In any preface, the author becomes a figure on a public stage; Kong's prefaces cast him as the exemplary playwright. He functions as a connoisseur of the marvels of his own work, describing its strengths to the reader. Kong is the only premodern playwright known to me to have attached to his own drama the type of preface entitled "comprehensive regulations" (*fanli* 凡例), which announces the guidelines behind a composition in a certain genre or provides information regarding principles of selection. Editors who compiled collections of essays often appended a *fanli*; playwrights who

---

53. The paratactical juxtaposition of different ideological positions and different emotional modalities reminds us that the play itself is illusion; this recalls the way in which the heteroglossic juxtaposition of different registers of speech and different genres in seventeenth-century fiction highlights its fictionality.

assembled collections of plays or wrote commentaries on them often prefaced such editions with a *fanli*. Wang Jide, for example, appended one to his edition of *Xixiang ji*. But to introduce one's own play with a *fanli* was an innovative act and, given that Kong was not an established playwright, a bold one.

The preface's general statement of the principles of dramatic composition suggests that the play to follow models such principles. It begins with the lines: "*Taohua shan* is a pearl, and the brush that composed *Taohua shan* is a dragon. Piercing through clouds and entering mists, the dragon's eyes and claws never leave the pearl, whether coming at it straight on or from the side. The spectator (*guanzhe* 觀者) should use discerning eyes (*juyan* 巨眼)."[54] The dragon toying with the pearl in his claws represents the author playing with the text; the spectacle Kong describes is the movement of the author's brush. The reader's amusement lies in watching the movements of the author's mind.

In Kong's prefaces, it becomes clear that he saw himself in competition with the actors who would one day recite his lines for control over the text:

In the scripts of older days, only 30 percent of dialogue was written down; the actors would add the other 70 percent when they took to the stage. Their vulgar demeanor and déclassé jests turned gold into iron, becoming a hindrance to the literary text. In this play, I have completed all the dialogue, and I will not allow the addition of another word. If the chapters are a bit long, it is for this reason.... The structure of each act ought not to be altered in any way. Mine is not like the plays of an earlier era.... When actors cut songs to make the acts shorter, what is left is never appropriate and betrays the painstaking labors of the author.[55]

The actors are to be mere instruments of the author's design. Kong's approach on the prefaces is quite at odds with his promotion in the play itself of the storyteller's capacity for improvisation (which as we remember, rendered Hou's letter superfluous).

---

54. Kong Shangren, *Fanli*, in *Taohua shan*, p. 11. Here Kong drew on Jin Shengtan's commentary to the *Xixiang ji*, in which Jin described the author's mastery of his subject in similar terms.

55. Ibid., pp. 11–12.

Kong was certainly not alone among seventeenth-century dramatists in fearing that actors would vulgarize the script. Wang Jide, the author of *Nan wanghou*, wrote in *Qulü*:

> When actors, being of a lower class (*yongxia youren* 庸下優人), come across the compositions of literati, not only do they not understand them but it is not easy for them to pronounce the words. The colloquial plays of the villages (*cunsu xi-ben* 村俗戲本) are perfectly suited to their level of knowledge, and their base and rustic tunes can be taught orally to illiterates. For these reasons, there is competition among them to perform them; their suitability follows from their convenience.[56]

Kong's contemporary Hong Sheng complained bitterly that actors had bastardized his play, lamenting, for example, that one troupe had been costumed entirely in red in a mourning scene (the scene "Kuxiang" 哭像).[57] It was Kong Shangren, however, who took the most dramatic measures to contain the improvisatory and vernacular speech of the actors when his play was performed, despite his exaltation of the improvisatory nature of the vernacular within the play.

In one preface, Kong noted that since he was a novice at musical composition, a friend notated the score. "As I finished each lyric, I would have him beat the time while singing it, and if there were minor awkwardnesses, he would immediately make adjustments, so that the entire score had no infelicities." In other words, there is no need for actors who perform his play to modify it in any way.[58] The exemplary actor of Kong's prefaces, then, is a far cry from his portrayal of the actor (and the storyteller) as tutor and guide of the literatus in *Taohua shan*. Moreover, although in *Taohua shan* Kong lionized the storyteller who thrusts various social groups and discursive worlds in tension, in the prefaces the elite reader forms the sole legitimate audience. This disjunction between prefaces and play points to the codification of the values of the late-Ming in the play itself.

---

56. Wang Jide, *Qulü*, in *Zhongguo gudian xiqu lunzhu jicheng*, p. 154. Wang sounds quite a bit like Huang Zongxi; the "vulgar" status of the actors ought to correspond with the vulgarity of the texts they perform.

57. Hong Sheng, "Liyan" 例言, in *Changsheng dian*, p. 2. See also Ho, "Cultural Transformation and the Chinese Idea of the Historical Play," p. 295.

58. Kong Shangren, "Ben mo," *Taohua shan*, p. 5.

In all of the depictions we have considered, Liu Jingting is distinguished not by a set of characteristics or even by a single speech register but by his versatility. It is his nimbleness in infiltrating boundaries that sets him apart. He evades definition, being both indefinable and omnipresent. Just as he described himself with a series of negations, his biographers seemed able to describe the storyteller only by telling us what he was not: not sur-named Liu, not a bona fide storyteller. His protean mutability aroused the suspicion of anti-theatricalists such as Huang Zongxi, whose warnings against Liu's mimicry of the language of Confucian scholars resonated with the anti-theatricalist writings examined in Chapter 1. But it is pre-cisely this mutability that allows the trickster Liu to demonstrate a kind of ideological versatility that *Taohua shan* intimates the literatus needs if he is to come to terms with the fall of the Ming. Huang's conception of Liu engages the anti-theatricalist concern with discerning dissimulation; Huang aspires to educate the reader to see through Liu's imposture. In contrast, *Taohua shan* offers a more sophisticated tension between illu-sion and disillusion.

In *Taohua shan*, Kong Shangren aspired to do more than use the paral-lel between world and stage to demonstrate the illusory nature of the phenomenal world. *Taohua shan* shows us that the ideological constructs through which we perceive the events of the phenomenal world are them-selves structured by illusion. The play lauds Confucian loyalism, holding up performers such as Liu Jingting as principled incarnations of this ideal. Yet by play's end, the objects of Confucian loyalism, the family and the nation, are revealed to be mere ephemera, and the characters become Daoist recluses. The epilogue once more turns to Confucian loyalism, however, suggesting that the recluse is haunted by nostalgia. The play, then, advocates an ideological versatility that is modeled in the storyteller Liu Jingting himself. This versatility is the only way to escape the illusion of attachment without succumbing to the ideological mystification of de-tachment; freedom lies not in escaping one for the other, but in alternat-ing between the two.

We should not forget, however, that by Kong's time, the crossing of registers and the transgression of boundaries that entranced the literati aficionado of the storyteller were historical artifacts. Even the tension between illusion and disillusion, which Zhang Dai so beautifully articulated, is here codified. The Keeper of Rites speaks in the prologue and interlude of the past, identifying the year in which he speaks as 1684, and then inviting us to view a historical drama. This structure neatly allies the past with illusion, so that there is nothing demanding or difficult about the quality of perception required of the spectator. *Nan wanghou* sought to challenge the theatrical spectator with tricks of perception that trained the spectator to hold illusion and disillusion in tension; the Yunlang poems showed us how that capacity might influence an understanding of the homoerotic sentiments they expressed; *Taohua shan* educates the spectator by holding Liu Jingting up as an example of a privileged understanding of the illusory nature of all worldly forms—an example that emanates from a time and place now securely past.

Conclusion

In Wang Heng's northern drama *The Real Puppet* (*Zhen kuilei*), a retired official traveling incognito in the countryside stops to watch the puppet theater. This puppet theater is of a special sort: the puppets are human actors dressed as puppets. During the performance, a messenger arrives with an imperial commendation for the retired official. The official and the messenger agree that the official must don court robes to thank the emperor for his grace. But where in the countryside are such robes to be found? The retired official, to the onstage audience's shocked surprise, borrows the robes of a human puppet dressed as a prime minister. As the official declares in the play's concluding remarks:

> Those who act in plays are half-real and half-false.
> Among those who watch plays, who is false and who is real?[1]

The couplet challenges the spectator to consider the question of his own authenticity. As we conclude, I would like to linger over this question— What is an authentic (*zhen*) spectator?

The investigation of seventeenth-century conceptions of theatrical and social spectatorship I have presented in the preceding chapters could serve as an extended refutation of the romanticization of the classical Chinese

---

1. Wang Heng, *Zhen kuilei*, p. 424. The play is in the tradition of the Daoist deliverance play. The official who receives the imperial commendation, we ultimately learn, is in fact one of the Eight Immortals, and so the commendation means no more to him than it would have had he received it in an actual puppet theater.

stage as a type of theater that in the very conditions of its performance cultivates alienation in the spectator. If my elucidation of Chinese conceptions of theatricality during the heyday of literati interest in the classical theater—the period during which Chinese authors have indulged most deeply in philosophical speculation about the theater and theatricality—has relevance to contemporary writing on western theater, it is because classical Chinese theater has long furnished a vision of an alternative tradition in which Platonic illusions of presence could be replaced by an effortlessly self-critical theater. From the writings of Bertolt Brecht to the more recent criticism of Samuel Weber, the classical Chinese theater has held out the promise of a mode of spectatorship that would critique naturalistic representation and sympathetic response.[2] Weber, in the mode of Brecht, engages in a discussion of a performance of Peking opera he has viewed that focuses on the sense of "hollowness" and "separation" he ascertains in this form of art. This hollowness, he states, is quintessentially theatrical, and is detectable even in the sounds of the wood blocks and cymbals of the Peking opera. Its effortless theatricality forms a reproach to a western anti-theatrical tradition that in its "desire for self-identity informs the condemnation of the theater."[3] He uncritically quotes Brecht ("What appears particularly important for us in Chinese theater is its efforts to produce a true art of beholding [*eine wahre Zuschaukunst*]")[4] and goes on to state that "the aim of such art is self-dissimulation," for the

---

2. Min Tian ("Alienation-Effect for Whom") has engaged in a lucid and thorough critique of Brecht's writing on the alienation effect to show where Brecht was mistaken in his reading of Mei Lanfang's performance. Tian notes that Brecht's sense that the Chinese actor "achieves the A-effect by being seen to observe his own movements" derived from the fact that he witnessed a demonstration, rather than actual performance. For this reason, Brecht believed that the Chinese actor was extremely self-conscious regarding the technical aspects of his art. As Tian intimates, Brecht's misinterpretation of the classical Chinese theater influenced Mei Lanfang's conception of the Chinese theater and has had a strong influence on contemporary Chinese theater's conception of its own history.

3. "The scene begins with a brief musical prelude, in which the timbre of the instruments—wood blocks and cymbals being struck in rhythmic patterns—almost seem to "embody" the separation itself, in the very "hollowness" of the sounds.... Such hollowness marks separation as a kind of inner space rather than an interval in-between. Theater takes place in the hollow of this separation, which it deploys and to which it responds" (Samuel Weber, *Theatricality as Medium*, p. 27).

4. Bertolt Brecht, *Schriften zum Theater*, 4: 38, as cited in Samuel Weber, *Theatricality as Medium*, pp. 24–25.

classical Chinese theater provides "an unforgettable exhibition of theatricality" in its staging of "separation."[5] As we have seen, the notions of theatricality associated with the seventeenth-century Chinese theater suggest that the most refined form of spectatorship is not estranged or alienated. Rather, the distinction between external verisimilitude and an internal understanding inherited from earlier theories of the arts permitted the seventeenth-century spectator to cultivate a simultaneous absorption in and disengagement from the world of forms.

I would like to further investigate that notion of absorption with a reading of a short story from the early seventeenth-century collection *Bian er chai* (Hairpins beneath a cap) entitled "Qinglie ji" 情烈記 (A tale of a martyr for passion). The story speaks to a radical attachment between spectator and actor, one reminiscent of the sympathetic identification that readers and viewers of *Mudan ting* felt with its protagonist Du Liniang. This notion of radical attachment between spectator and spectacle is quite distinct from either of the primary modes of spectatorship investigated in the preceding chapters, from the unmasking of imposture found in *Naihe tian* and *Mudan ting* or the sophisticated play on perception of Zhang Dai, *Nan wanghou*, and *Taohua shan*. It is more readily found in anecdotal writing on the theater than in the texts of plays, as the wealth of anecdotes after publication of *Mudan ting* regarding the impassioned response of spectators and readers attest. In concluding, then, I am turning to a fictional text clearly influenced by this response to *Mudan ting* to illuminate an alternative to those notions of authentic spectatorship we have already explored. Li Yu and many of the authors we have considered equated authentic spectatorship with the ability to see through social imposture. In the text we examine below, the authentic spectator is one who so identifies with the spectacle that he is willing to lose himself in it.

Bian er chai is a set of four variations on the theme of *qing* written by an anonymous author using the pseudonym "Master Moonheart Drunk by West Lake" (Zui Xihu xinyue zhuren 醉西湖心月主人). In comparison to the other texts discussed in this book, we know little about the circumstances in which this collection came into circulation. We have no information about the writer other than his authorship of a collection of

---

short stories entitled *Fragrance of the Pleasant Spring* (*Yichun xiangzhi* 宜
春香質). Similarly, nothing is known of the commentator who styled
himself "The Daoist Master Haha What Can You Do About Fate" (*Naihetian he he daoren* 奈何天呵呵道人).[6] This lack of knowledge about
the author or commentator suggests the text's humble origins, as does the
poor quality of the typography and the author's somewhat naïve literary
style. Yet *Bian er chai* speaks to a number of the other texts we have considered in suggesting a model of social spectatorship drawn from a portrait of the relationships between literati and actors.

"Qinglie" suggests that authentic passion (*zhenqing*) is a valued quality
in the theatrical spectator not only because it helps overcome the distance
between spectator and actor but also because it allows the spectator to
discern unrecognized virtue or talent (which we might view as the con-
verse of unmasking social imposture). The story describes a young literatus reduced by poverty to joining an acting troupe, where he cross-dresses
to play the female lead. The influence of *Mudan ting* is clear in the lyrics
that preface the narrative, which recall Du Liniang's death and return
from the grave: "Both life and death stem from *qing* and *qing* alone; / He
whose *qing* is authentic will always be exemplary in life and death." In the
mode of Wang Jide's *Nan wanghou*, however, "Qinglie" is determined to
go *Mudan ting* one better, arguing that this boy actor is a more loyal partner than any woman could be because his capacity for emotional attachment is of a higher order. Thus "Qinglie" presages *Taohua shan*'s rehabili-
tation of the actor or courtesan, overriding the conventional association
of the actor with promiscuity and profit and re-envisioning him as an emblem of loyalty.[7]

---

6. The two collections were published during the Chongzhen reign period by the
"Plowing the Mountain with a Brush Studio," but we do not know if this studio was a
publishing house or another pseudonym of the author. For discussions of these stories, see
Martin Huang, *Desire and Fictional Narrative*, pp. 176–84; and Vitiello, "Exemplary Sodomites," pp. 88–132. For information on the surviving editions of *Bian er chai*, see Wang
Ch'iu-kuei and Chen Ch'inghao, *Siwuxie huibao* series, pp. 17–20; and *Mingdai xiaoshuo
jikan* 明代小説集刊, vol. 6, no. 2, 3: 525–76. There are two extant editions of *Bian er chai*:
one held in the Beijing Municipal Library as well as in the Tenri Library in Japan, upon
which the *Mingdai xiaoshuo jikan* version is based; the other is in the National Palace Museum in Taipei and was the basis for the *Siwuxie huibao* edition.

7. The stories of *Bian er chai* proselytize for male love by attempting to show that a relationship between two men can simultaneously fulfill four of the five Confucian bonds of

"Qinglie" argues for the respectability of passion (*qing*) between literati and boy actors, emphasizing the deep affective bonds between male lovers. At the same time, it suggests that the reader may himself attain a similarly heightened level of identification with the protagonists. What makes this text unique among other seventeenth-century short stories that treat male love is the presence of a commentary that exhorts the reader to sympathize with the protagonists and understand their plight. "Qinglie" is didactic both in that the reader is exhorted to follow the example of the protagonists and in that the commentator furnishes a model of impassioned admiration and deep empathy.

The title places this story in the tradition of biographies of virtuous women (*lie nü*) 烈女 who sacrifice themselves for others, a genre that flourished in the late Ming.[8] The virtuous woman in question, the martyr for *qing*, is a young boy named Wen Yaquan 文雅全 who kills himself in order to preserve his chastity—here defined as sexual loyalty—toward his male lover, Yun Han 雲漢. A son of a magistrate from Fujian, Wen Yaquan falls in with a rough crowd after his father dies, beginning a life of carousing, drinking, and acting on the stage. He naturally excels at acting and gradually "sinks into the floating world of the theater."[9] Upon learning that Wen has taken to the stage, his fiancée's father is determined to break off the engagement. He has Wen's elder brother, a scholar, thrown into prison on false charges of receiving stolen goods. Wen is also implicated and jailed. When Wen's betrothed refuses to renounce her love for him, her father bribes the jailor to kill him. But the jailor takes pity on

---

human relationship: lord and retainer; elder and younger brother, friends, and husband and wife. (The cross-dressing of the junior partner enables the fulfillment of the last dyad.) Each of these relationships has a specific type of loyalty associated with it: loyalty to one's lord (*zhong* 忠), between brothers (*ti* 悌), between friends (*yi* 義), and to one's husband (*jie* 節). As Gregory Pflugfelder (*Cartographies of Desire*, p. 103) has observed, the presumed age difference between lord and retainer, or elder and younger brother, conveniently maps onto the social stratification of senior and junior partners in a same-sex relationship. The relationship between friends is an exception, but the same-sex relationship modeled after this Confucian bond calls upon the age-old notion of the ideal friend (*zhiyin* 知音).

8. See Carlitz, "Desire, Danger and the Body"; *idem*, "The Social Uses of Female Virtue in Late Ming Editions of *Lienü zhuan*"; Elvin, "Female Virtue and the State in China"; and T'ien, *Male Anxiety and Female Chastity*.

9. *Bian er chai*, p. 182.

him and helps him escape. He flees to an inn, resolving to continue his studies, but his purse is soon empty. One day the innkeeper overhears Wen singing of his despair. Mistakenly, he believes that Wen is singing because he is happy and compliments him on his fine voice. When he learns of Wen's destitution, he suggests Wen join a *Kunqu* acting troupe that he is sponsoring and take the role of female lead.

One day, a scholar named Yun Han sees Wen performing and immediately recognizes that he is a literatus. They become friends, and Yun subsequently rescues Wen from the clutches of a patron of the theater who has sexual designs on him. Wen decides that, since he is penniless, he has nothing with which to repay Yun but his body and determines to seduce him wearing his feminine stage costume. Although Yun initially resists accepting the sacrifice of Wen's body, ultimately he succumbs to temptation. After a graphically described love scene, they pledge their faithfulness to each other for eternity.

The new couple runs short of money, and Wen joins another acting troupe to support his lover's studies. A powerful and rapacious official engaged in the salt trade sees him performing and concocts a scheme to abduct him and keep him as his catamite. Once again sacrificing himself for his lover, Wen negotiates a price for himself that will grant Yun funds for his journey to the capital to take the examinations. After Yun is safely on his way, Wen commits suicide in order to demonstrate his everlasting fidelity, cutting off his own head with a sword. Wen's ghost then finds Yun and journeys with him toward the capital, Yun never once suspecting that his lover is a ghost. When the pair discovers that their purse is again empty, Wen devises a new plot to fund Yun's studies: he suggests that Yun pose as his elder brother and sell him as a concubine. Later, Wen engineers Yun's marriage to the daughter of the magistrate whose concubine he had been. His duty done now that Yun is married and well established in his career, Wen finally reveals to Yun that he is a ghost and takes his leave to assume a position in the official bureaucracy of the netherworld.

The tale's structure plays on the misrecognition and revelation of Wen's true status.[10] The capacity or incapacity of others for sympathetic

---

10. Behind such recognition scenes lies the story of Yu Rang 豫讓, a retainer of the Warring States period whose biography is first recounted in *Zhanguo ce* (Stratagems of the Warring States). Yu Rang becomes a canonical example of the retainer motivated by a

identification rests in their ability to discern that Wen is a literatus (*wen ren* 文人). A series of tests prove that the discerning spectator—always a man of cultivation—will label Wen a literatus despite the fact that he has so fallen in the world as to become an actor (the text provides the reader with a broad hint in the name Wen Yaquan, which could be translated as "the utmost in literary elegance"). When Yun first spies Wen, Wen is acting women's roles on the stage. Immediately recognizing that Wen is a literatus, Yun wonders aloud why a literatus should be performing onstage, how he has "fallen among these apes." His discernment contrasts with the blindness of the audience, who argue that Wen cannot possibly be a literatus, for how could a literatus have so fallen as to enter an acting troupe? The recognition between Wen and Yun is mutual: as Wen performs, he sees Yun staring at him, and thinks, "Here among the base crowds is a minister who could save the age." When Yun comes to visit Wen, Wen tearfully thanks him for recognizing his status. "Today you saw me on a stage full of actors and recognized that I was a literatus. You are the only friend who understands me."[11] Yun's instantaneous recognition of Wen as another literatus contrasts with the blindness of the vulgar spectator to Wen's true worth.

In an episode that presages the salt merchant's designs on Wen, a theatergoer named Shi Gandang 石敢當 presumes that Wen, because he is an actor, is sexually available. The narrative establishes in multiple ways that

---

pure allegiance to his lord. He embarks on a tragic mission to murder Lord Xiang 襄 of Zhao 趙 in order to avenge a master who truly understood him, the Earl of Zhi 知伯. Yu Rang explains that "a man must be willing to die for the one who understands him" just as "a woman pretties herself for the man who takes pleasure in her" (*shi wei zhiji zhe si, nü wei yueji zhe rong* 士爲知己者死, 女爲悦己者容). In order to gain proximity to Lord Xiang, Yu Rang must disguise himself; he scars his face, paints it with lacquer and brands himself a prisoner with a hot iron, so deforming his features that even his wife does not recognize him until she hears his voice. When he realizes that his voice may betray him, he swallows charcoal to alter it. Lord Xiang recognizes him each time, and ultimately must have him killed (see Lau, *A Concordance to the Zhanguoce,* p. 106). The tragic irony is that the tale gives more evidence of Lord Xiang's understanding of Yu Rang than of the Earl of Zhi, for Lord Xiang anticipates Yu Rang's intentions and sees through his disguises each time. Following the model of Yu Rang, Wen's sacrifice of his body to Yun is justified by the fact that only Yun truly understands him—understanding here being refigured as a recognition of status.

11. "Qinglie," 1.13a.

Shi Gandang is *su* 俗 (vulgar), but perhaps the most important aspect of Shi's vulgarity is his assumption that Wen is sexually available to him. When Wen refuses his advances, Shi attempts to force him into an embrace. Wen angrily rejects him, and Shi slaps him, exclaiming, "Prostitutes, actors, lictors, and soldiers (*chang you li zu* 娼優隸卒) are the basest strata of society. How dare you give offense to a literatus?" The next day, Shi files a complaint against Wen at the district magistrate's office, and Wen is bound and brought before the magistrate. The magistrate orders a mock civil service examination in which Wen and Shi are both ordered to compose eight-legged essays (*baguwen*). The test reveals that the "actor" is in fact a literatus, and Shi, the presumed scholar, merely a pretender. By the time Wen has effortlessly finished his eight-legged essay, Shi has not written a word. The test both confirms Wen's true status and exposes Shi's imposture.[12] Of Shi, the commentator remarks dryly, "Unfortunately these types are often in the schools," reminding us of the mockery of the glut of aspiring licentiates in *Mudan ting*.[13] The "sorting" of status performed by Yun and the magistrate aligns them with the reader, who has a privileged understanding of Wen's status from the beginning.[14] In effect, the reader of this melodramatic text becomes the *zhiji* 知己 or *zhiyin* 知音 of the characters, the "ideal listener" who understands all.[15]

The author of *Bian er chai* wrote in his other collection of stories, *Yichun xiangzhi*: "Never has there been a manual of *qing*. I would like to

---

12. The text exhibits this extraordinary concern with Wen's status as a literatus in part because it enhances the sacrifice inherent in his assuming the penetrated position. Since Wen is a literatus, his willingness to be penetrated is a sacrifice of the highest order, a loss not only of his gender but his status. Martin Huang (*Desire and Fictional Narrative in Late-Imperial China*, p. 183) makes a similar point in his analysis of this text: "A passive partner is able to demonstrate his devotion or *qing* to his lover by giving up his rights as a man and becoming a woman, a sacrifice unavailable to a 'real' woman in a heterosexual relationship since she is already in the inferior position."

13. *Bian er chai*, p. 202.

14. The narrative's concern with establishing Wen's status as a man of cultivation is, in a somewhat vulgar manner, evident from the start; his first name, "Yaquan," literally means "complete elegance."

15. Maram Epstein (*Competing Discourses*, p. 91) describes the relationship between *zhiji* as one "in which genuine intellectual and spiritual communion occurs. These relationships connote a willingness to defy social custom and place affective bonds above career or the more conventional orthodox loyalties to family and state."

provide a manual of *qing*." The two commentaries to *Bian er chai*—that of the author and that of the anonymous commentator who styled himself Daoist Master Haha What Can You Do About Fate—enhance the sense that *Bian er chai* is such a manual, instructing the reader as to how to respond to such exemplars as Wen with pity and compassion. The commentaries actively promote the reader's understanding of the characters by providing insight into their emotional states. When Wen's elder brother sighs, "Right now the ways of Heaven are not clear. Unfortunately, those who do evil things are blessed," the commentator writes, "This is what one says when one's heart is grieved" (*shangshi yu* 傷時語).

The commentator exhorts the reader to empathize with the characters, both by modeling empathy and by shaming the reader into the proper response. At numerous points—for example, when Wen begs the jailor to kill him—the commentator exclaims, "How pitiable!" (*kelian* 可憐). When the brothers are about to be parted, never to see each other again, the narrator states, "Every one of those in the jail with them sighed in grief," and the commentator exclaims, "Whoever reads this and does not shed tears must have no brotherly feeling" (*ti*). Similarly, when Wen's mother comes to take him home after his imprisonment and, exclaiming in dismay at his wretched state, faints to the floor, the commentator writes, "Whoever reads this and does not shed tears must have no human kindness" (*ci* 慈).[16] It is not that we are supposed to fashion ourselves after these characters so much as that we are meant to feel for them, and to feel in their image. The commentary proselytizes for same-sex love by encouraging, even demanding, the sympathy of the reader. The commentators resemble a first rung of spectators whose heightened response provides an emotional template on which the reader can map himself. The model for such sympathetic spectatorship within the text itself is Yun's initial recognition of Wen on the stage, which blends an acute discernment of status with the sympathetic overflow of feeling between actor and spectator. Thus the relation of radical attachment and passionate devo-

---

16. Similarly, in the story "Qinglie," a son sells himself into prostitution to provide his father with the 100 taels he needs to be released from jail. Upon hearing this, the father falls into a faint. The interlineal commentary states, "Whoever reads and does not shed tears must have no *ci*." Later, he exclaims, "I can't bear to read this" (*bu ren du* 不忍讀; *Bian er zhai*, pp. 276–77).

tion between actor and spectator describes not only the relation between fictional characters, but the relation between readers and fictional characters.

Texts such as *Taohua shan* ultimately suggest that detachment is a prerequisite for authentic perception. But almost paradoxically, the notion of radical emotional attachment between reader and character proposed in *Bian er chai* is allied with authenticity of perception as well, for at the height of sympathetic identification between actor and character or between spectator and actor, the self disappears, becoming a channel for another. In this way, extremes of attachment become a way of reaching detachment. *Bian er chai*, then, adds another dimension to the notions of theatrical spectatorship we have elucidated above. The radical attachment of the spectator proposed in *Bian er chai* is the polar opposite of the mandate to see through social imposture explored in the opening chapters of this book.

&

The essential argument of this book is that theatrical modes of spectatorship furnished models for modes of social spectatorship in seventeenth-century China. We began with the question of why the theater achieves such figurative power in seventeenth-century literary culture, why it comes to be seen as a metaphor for both the problems and the solutions of the age. Traditional Confucian thought had no means of responding to the rise of the mercantile—it could neither explain nor contain it. Nor was it particularly suited to conceptualizing the plight of the tutors and schoolmasters who had pursued the traditional means of advancement, study for the examinations, only to be trapped in the burgeoning pool of licentiates who would never achieve the *juren* degree. These changes in the traditional constitution of the elite made unsatisfied aspiration and undeserved success one of the primary concerns of the age. The notion of theatrical performance became a conventional metaphor for the misalignment of the nominal and "real," for false valuation and false devaluation. Actors, acting, and the theater became associated with the empty spectacle of social pretension, as we saw most tellingly in Tang Xianzu's skewering of archaism, in which poetic allusion became the social script of the aspiring.

The notion of the world as stage had long referred to the vanity of earthly riches, the spiritual impoverishment of worldly fame. This conception of the worldly stage never dropped out of sight—it furnished a sort of consolation, for example, in Pu Songling's story of the actor who emerged from licentiate Zhang's heart. However, it was joined by the two conceptions of theatricality we have elucidated in the pages above. The first, which required that the social spectator limit the capacity of the theatrical to transform the social by seeing through the imposture of social aspiration, was the far simpler notion. It lay beneath the strident claims of the anti-theatricalist writings we examined in Chapter 1, and perhaps comically, adhered in the equally strident tone of the anti-archaists whose writings we discussed in Chapter 3. The second, an inherently mobile and participatory perspective that asked the spectator to maintain illusion and disillusion in tension, was more complex. This social spectatorship was most brilliantly modeled by Zhang Dai, in whose work the question of authenticity was displaced from the relation of theatrical spectacle to its referents; authenticity became a judgment of the spectator's capacity for perception instead. Theatrical spectatorship became allied with a particular relation between illusion and disillusion—the ability to hold the two in tension. If a more vulgar notion of theatricality was concerned that illusion might be mistaken for authenticity, in this more sophisticated notion of theatrical and social spectatorship, one engaged with illusion while understanding it to be such.

These two notions of theatricality were often paired, so that the second became a rebuttal of sorts to the first. In Chapter 1, the writings of partisans of the theater, who suggested that the most refined observer might enter illusion *after* recognizing it as such, answered the diatribes of anti-theatricalists who believed they could simply alert the social spectator to the faddishness and fallaciousness of the theater. My pairing of *Mudan ting* and *Nan wanghou* in Chapters 3 and 4 follows this logic; *Mudan ting*'s concern with the scripted and staged quality of archaist literary discourse is put in perspective by *Nan wanghou*'s insight that allusive reference is premised in illusion. *Nan wanghou* showed us that the form of spectatorship in which illusion and disillusion were held in tension was predicated in the perspectival challenges the actor issued to the spectator. My reading of the poems in tribute to the actor Yunlang illustrated how this notion of spectatorship, which took shape in the world of private theatricals, elucidates the complex referential status of the homoerotic sentiments articulated by the poets of Chen Weisong's circle. The analysis of *Taohua shan*, the late-seventeenth century play that provides the most developed conceptualization of the relation between theatrical and social spectatorship, argues that Kong Shangren eulogizes the mobile and panoramic quality of perspective that allowed Liu to move deftly among disparate social and linguistic registers. That aesthetic enabled the cultivation of an ideological versatility that Liu Jingting models for the literatus seeking to come to terms with the fall of the Ming, an ideological versatility that informs the structure of the play itself.

The most sophisticated seventeenth-century commentators explored the capacity to hold illusion and disillusion in tension as they surveyed the topography of social spectacle. As they showed how the tension between reality and illusion quintessential to the theater might map onto social spectacle, they relocated the question of authenticity from the spectacle to the spectator. Ultimately, the display of sophisticated structures of perception itself signaled discernment. A type of social spectatorship modeled on theatrical spectatorship, in which the discriminating spectator engages with illusion while understanding it to be such, became a new source of social distinction. A refined capacity for perception became a more subtle means of displaying rank than the purchase of emblems of literati cultivation. The vulgar concerned themselves with being seen; the more refined with ways of seeing.

Appendix

APPENDIX

The Male Queen

Composed by The Unofficial Historian of the Towers of Qin

Commentary by the Man of Leisure from Yang Terrace[1]

Dramatis Personae (in order of appearance)
Note: The *dan*, *mo*, *jing*, *tiedan*, and *xiaodan* role-types play the same characters throughout. The *chou*, however, plays several characters.
Dan (female lead): Chen Zigao, a penniless boy who finds favor with the king of Linchuan
Chou (clown): Soldier of the king of Linchuan
Mo (subordinate male role): Soldier of the king of Linchuan

---

1. Since both "Towers of Qin" (Qinlou 秦樓) and "Yang Terrace" (Yangtai 陽台) refer to trysting places, a reader would know immediately on seeing the pseudonyms that this is an erotic text. "The Towers of Qin" refers to the love affair between Nongyu 弄玉, the daughter of Duke Mu 穆 of Qin 秦, and a musician who could make the sound of the phoenix on his flute. He taught Nongyu to play so beautifully that the couple's playing attracted phoenixes; Duke Mu built the pair a "Phoenix Tower" and they lived among the phoenixes who alighted there. The pair eventually rode the phoenixes into the sky (Liu Xiang, *Liexian zhuan,* p. 29). "Yang Terrace" refers to the place on Wu 巫 Mountain where King Xiang of Chu dreamed he encountered a goddess, according to the "Rhymeprose on Gaotang" 高唐賦 attributed to the poet Song Yu 宋玉 (see Xiao Tong, *Wen xuan,* pp. 875–86).

Jing (secondary male role): Chen Qian, King of Linchuan, later Emperor
    Wen of the Chen dynasty[2]
Chou (clown): Palace woman
Tiedan (lesser female role): Palace woman
Chou (clown): Princess's maid
Xiaodan (auxiliary female lead): Princess Yuhua, the king's sister

> The king of Linchuan cared not to distinguish male and female.
> The Princess Yuhua falsely married a husband in skirts and hairpins.
> The maid Nongtao mistakenly acted as their go-between.
> Here is the story of how Chen Zigao changed his garb
> and became "The Male Queen."[3]

ACT I

[Zigao played by the *dan* (female lead) enters dressed as a young boy in black and recites:]

Luscious clouds of hair, black tunic so feminine that I myself am surprised,

---

2. Chen Qian 陳蒨 (527–66) was a historical personage. The nephew of Emperor Wu 武 of the Chen, he was enfeoffed as Prince of Linchuan (臨川王). Linchuan, in the northeastern part of Jiangxi, was an important stronghold, and Emperor Wu entrusted Chen Qian with its defense because of his military prowess. Upon Emperor Wu's death, Chen Qian succeeded him as Emperor Wen (r. 560–67). When he became ill, he entrusted military affairs to his general Han Zigao 韓子高. Han Zigao was originally of a poor family. According to his biography in the *Chen shu*, he met the Emperor Wen at the age of sixteen, at a time when he was seeking to return home after finding refuge in the capital during Hou Jing's rebellion. Emperor Wen saw him, and asked if he would be willing to serve him. Han Zigao began as a personal servant, but as he grew older, the emperor made him a military commander. The biography emphasizes the intimacy of the relationship, stating that Emperor Wen favored Zigao immensely. Zigao's martial prowess and his feminine appearance are prominent features of the account, in which he is described as "beautiful of countenance, in appearance like a woman" (see Yao Silian, *Chen shu, juan* 20, pp. 269–70).

3. Neither "prince" nor "king" is an adequate translation for the Chinese "wang" 王 here. "Prince" does not convey the degree of power Chen Qian had as head of a fiefdom. "King" sounds as though he were an independent ruler, which was not the case. I chose to use "King" and "Queen" to avoid confusion between the Princess Yuhua, younger sister of the king, and Zigao, who would become "The Male Princess" were Chen Qian "Prince of Linchuan."

I fear that you won't be able to distinguish when you cast your eyes.[4]
In the East the sun shines, in the West the rain falls,
People say they have no feelings, but surely they do.[5]

My name is Chen Zigao,[6] my nickname Qionghua.[7] My family is from the area of Jiangnan.[8] When Hou Jing rebelled, I was still young and followed my father to the capital to escape the chaos of war.[9] There I wove and sold reed sandals to survive. Now I've grown to sixteen years of age. Recently I heard that the king of Linchuan has slaughtered the traitors and that the roads are open again. I would like to look for a companion, and to plead with him to make the journey home with me. I just need to make this one trip.

Even though my body is that of a man, my features are like those of a woman. I was born with a beauty most tempting. A painting could not capture the beauty of my face when my makeup is freshly applied. Come to think of it, if I am not the Dragon Girl who scatters flowers before the

---

4. The phrase "won't be able to distinguish (不分明)" draws on Chen Shidao's (陳師道, 1053–1102) "Fangge xing 放歌行" (see Chen Shidao, *Houshan jushi wenji* 後山居士文集, 4.23a).

5. This last line quotes the concluding lines of Liu Yuxi's 劉禹錫 "Zhuzhi ci" 竹枝詞 (Bamboo branch poem): "Green the willows, level the river waters. / I hear the sound of my love singing above the waters. / In the East the sun rises, in the West the rain falls, / People say they have no feelings, but surely they do" (*Yuefu shiji*, ed. Guo Maoqian, 4: 1141). As noted in Chapter 4, the line "People say they have no feelings, but surely they do" puns on two characters that are both pronounced *qing*, "clear" 晴 and "feeling" 情 (although the two characters have different tonal inflections, the difference would be masked as the actor sang the lines). The character for "passion" or "feeling" is used in the "Zhuzhi ci" and in the play. In the context of the previous line, "In the East the sun rises, in the West the rain falls," the audience would presumably hear not "feeling" but "clear," and the last line would be understood as, "People say the skies are not clear, but surely they are."

6. The character Chen Zigao is based on the historical figure Han Zigao; the first instance in which Han acquires the surname Chen is the classical tale "Chen Zigao zhuan" 陳子高傳 by the Ming author Li Xu 李詡, collected in *Lüchuang nüshi* 綠窗女史, *juan* 5.

7. *Qionghua* 瓊花: literally, "Red jade flower;" a rare flower, believed to bestow immortality if eaten. This is a feminine name that matches his girlish looks.

8. Jiangnan 江南 refers to the area south of the Yangzi river, and in particular, a delta circumscribed by Suzhou, Hangzhou, and Nanjing.

9. Hou Jing 侯景, style name Wan Jing 萬景, became prince of Henan in 547. He later claimed to be an emperor of the Han dynasty. Han Zigao's biography in the *Chen shu* states that Han Zigao took shelter in the capital during Hou Jing's rebellion (Yao Silian, *Chen shu*, *juan* 20, p. 269).

throne of the bodhisattva Guanyin, mistakenly reincarnated on Earth,[10] then I must be a reincarnation of the Golden Boy clasping a tray from the Jade Emperor's palace, now descended to earth.[11] Yesterday a physiognomer told me that I had the face of a dragon and the neck of a phoenix.[12] If I were a woman, I could certainly make a match with a king. [Sighs.] Had I only been born a girl, I could depend on my talent and beauty. I wouldn't need to be competitive with others in the harem. I'd be so foxy I would bewitch the king.[13] Even if he were a man of iron, I could make half his body go so limp it couldn't move. What a pity I was made a boy by mistake!

[Xianlü mode] "Shanghua shi" (Zigao sings:)

No one can distinguish the peacock from the peahen.
I've passed sixteen springs of my youth for naught.
I have the same brows of kingfisher green as those of a beauty.
All I would need is bound feet of three inches,
And my charms would never be second to those in red skirts.

Reprise:

Newly dressed in embroidered sleeves of scented gauze,
With a smile I gently flirt beside the flowers.
If you could lend me a woman's body,
I would need neither powders nor creams,

---

10. The Dragon Girl who scatters flowers (San hua long nü 散花龍女) is one of the servants by the side of the bodhisattva Guanyin 觀音 and is said to be responsible for bringing the flowers of spring.

11. The Golden Boy 金童 and the Jade Maiden 玉女 are scribes of the Jade Emperor, the head of the Daoist pantheon. According to legend, the Golden Boy and the Jade Maiden had a secret affair, which the emperor punished by sending them to earth. They needed to go through seven generations of marriage on earth before returning to Heaven. Here Zigao suggests that he is a doomed lover of one of those seven reincarnations.

12. The dragon refers to an emperor, the phoenix to an empress.

13. These lines allude to the description of the future Empress Wu Zetian by Luo Binwang 駱賓王 (ca. 640–84), "Entering the harem, she feels jealous; being a beauty she is unwilling to yield to another. / She hides her face with her sleeves, and excels at flattery; so foxy she can bewitch an Emperor." 入門見嫉, 蛾眉不肯讓人; 掩袖工讒, 狐媚偏能惑主 (see Liu Xu, 劉昫, *Jiu Tang shu* 舊唐書, juan 67, pp. 2490–91).

But I guarantee my charms would completely entangle a man of feeling.[14]

(Soldiers enter and recite:)

> Outside the city the war has ceased,
> In the camps the drums and horns press on.
> Whips snap and golden stirrups sound,
> People return singing songs of victory.

We are foot soldiers in the service of the king of Linchuan.[15] Our great master has been victorious in battle, and the troops are withdrawing after victory. We have been ordered to patrol in advance of the troops. In the distance there walks a young boy. Let's capture him! (Offstage brass and drum sound; soldiers follow in pursuit.)

(Zigao enters in panic, screaming:) Before me brass and drums sound continuously. I don't know whose troops are advancing. Now that I'm here, there's no place to run. What shall I do?

(Soldiers enter in pursuit:) In pursuit of you we'd run all the way to Heaven.[16] We shall catch up with you, for we have clouds flying beneath our feet. Got him! (Tie him up.)

First Soldier: So, boy, whose spy are you? You've been in the way of my horse. (To second soldier:) Let's take him and cut off his head as a sacrifice for our triumphant return.

Second Soldier: Brother, look at this lad. His face is like a flower. I don't know if I have the heart to kill him.

(Zigao kowtows:) Generals, spare my life.

---

14. The tune titles used suggest that the text of the play up to this point forms a prologue of sorts. "Shanghua shi" is usually the first tune in the Xianlü mode.

15. As mentioned above, Chen Qian was enfeoffed as Prince of Linchuan 臨川. Linchuan had a strategic position in defending the northern and southern empires during the Six Dynasties, and Emperor Wu trusted Chen Qian with this position because of his military prowess.

16. Literally, to *Yanmo tian* 焰摩天, the third level of heaven in Buddhist cosmology.

(First Soldier:) All right. Brother, you and I will spare his life, and keep him among the troops. During the daytime he can collect hay for the horses, and at night he will be our plaything. Each of us can take a turn at him.

(Second Soldier:) Brother, I don't think this seductive thing was meant for us.[17] Our great king loves the "Southern Mode" more than anything. We'll offer him as a present and thus render a meritorious service. Then we will be heavily rewarded.

(First Soldier:) That makes sense. Our great king has arrived. Let's take the boy to the king's tent.

(Zigao begs for mercy:) Please, generals, take pity on me.

(Soldiers escort him to exit.)

(Jing, costumed as the king of Linchuan, leads his troops on stage:)

> The Central Plain is still dark; the murderous vapors have not dispersed.
> The blade hanging from my waist stinks of foul blood.
> Where is the general's battle steed now?
> Wild grasses and idle flowers cover the ground with sorrow.[18]

I am the king of Linchuan, Chen Qian. Recently, I extinguished Hou Jing, slaughtering his family. I am moving my troops back to my command

---

17. Seductive thing (*yao wu* 妖物). Feng Menglong gives an etymology for *yao* at the beginning of the section of his *Qingshi leilüe* entitled "Qingyao" 情妖 that suggests that young men as well as women may be called *yao wu.* "The character *yao* is composed of the characters *nü* (female, woman) and *yao* (young). Thus a beautiful young girl is described as *yao.* Now, the spirits of birds, beasts, plants, the five material elements, and such things frequently take the forms of young persons in order to bewitch men, with those who manifest themselves as young men, however, numbering but one out of every ten" (Feng Menglong, *Qingshi leilüe,* vol. II, 21: 86; cited and translated in Mowry, *Chinese Love Stories,* p. 134.

18. The expression 野草閑花 "wild grasses and idle flowers" refers to pretty women of dubious virtue; here the expression paves the way for the king's introduction to a pretty boy of questionable morals.

post at Wuxing.[19] Soldiers, send out the orders to move ahead. (The troops hail the king in response.)

(First Soldier and Second Soldier escort Zigao to the fore:)
For the king's ears:
Today in advance of the troops we captured a young boy. We ask our great King to command us as to what to do.

(King:) Bind him and take him before the camp to cut off his head. Sacrifice him before the flag.

(Zigao cries out:) My King, have pity on me!

King: What a lovely, feminine voice this lad has! Raise your head so that I can take a look.

(Zigao raises his head.)

(King glances at him and makes a gesture of surprise:) Goodness. His lips are so red, his teeth so white! His eyes are lively and his brows clear. He looks as though he has stepped out of a painting. What family could have given birth to such a beautiful child? Soldiers, release his bonds quickly. Don't frighten him. (Troops undo the bonds.)
(King:) My lad, let me just ask who you are. Why did you come here? Tell the truth.

(Zigao:) My Lord, please lend me your ears and take pity on your humble servant.

[Xianlü mode] "Dian jiangchun" (Zigao sings:)
Fleeing the chaos of war, I came to the capital,
And have lived like an orphan for several years.
Quaking with terror and dread, I have been endlessly longing for home,
And so I have offended my lord by impeding his way.

---

19. Chen Qian 陳蒨 was the future Emperor Wen 文 of the Chen. Wuxing 吳興 was an area located in present-day Zhejiang.

(King sighs:) So you are on the road home, fleeing the chaos of war. Where are you from? What is your name?

"Hunjiang long" (Zigao sings:)

I'm from the Tiantai Mountains;
The third family from the mouth of Taoyuan creek is mine.[20]

(King:) No wonder he seems like an immortal sent to earth.

(Zigao sings:) I have the same surname as my lord.

(King:) So you are also a Chen. Even your surname is a good surname.

(Zigao sings:) My name is Qionghua.

(King:) And a good name for you too. In truth, you look like a jade flower.

(Zigao sings:) I weave green rushes and white hemp fibers to make my living.[21]

(King:) So you are the child of a humble family—that won't be any hindrance.[22]

(Zigao sings:) I lament that I'm merely a wren, and in marriage may not compare with mandarin ducks and drakes.[23]
I hope my lord will have mercy on me.
Think of me as an ant and spare me.

---

20. The Tiantai 天台 mountains in Eastern Zhejiang were well known as a haven for Daoist hermits during the Han and Six Dynasties. The name Taoyuan 桃源, "Peach Spring," calls to mind the poet Tao Yuanming's portrayal of a timeless idyll in his "Peach Blossom Spring." See Tao Yuanming, "Taohuayuan ji," *Tao Yuanming ji jiaojian*, p. 275.

21. Such rushes were used to make mats; white hemp fiber was used to make rope or clothing.

22. The king suggests that Zigao's being of a family of menial laborers should be no hindrance to their union; he is already considering having Zigao enter the harem.

23. The phrasing refers to Zhuangzi's statement that the wren (*jiaoliao* 鷦鷯) seeks no more than a branch to be content. Zhuangzi, *Zhuangzi jishi*, vol. 1, p. 24. Mandarin ducks and drakes are a traditional symbol of marital bliss.

(King intones:) Lad, I won't hurt you. Don't panic. It would be a pity if we were to scare you silly. How old are you this year?

"You hulu" (Zigao sings:)

You ask how many fragrant years has this Blue Jade? I'm at the age at which a girl has yet to lose her maidenhead, for I'm just sixteen.[24]
Look at my double hairknots, bound with bright red thread.[25]

(King:) What abilities have you?

(Zigao sings:)

My charming figure is used to straddling a horse.
My soft waist knows how to pull a bow of the most flexible wood.[26]
I can with great care hold your precious sword.
With patience I'll accompany you as you drink from your jade cup.
And when you are bored,
I'll be the puppet with which you play.
(He speaks:) My lord, I don't dare tell you that I am the most delightful little lover.

(King sighs:) Today I've met a real little lover in you. Tell me, who are your family members? Would you be willing to leave them behind?

"Tianxia le" (Zigao sings:)

I am like flowers blown from a tree that float on the east wind.
If you ask about my roots,
I have only father and mother at the opposite end of the sky.[27]

----

24. "Blue Jade" refers to a young woman of humble origin. The term derives from a set of six songs ostensibly written by Prince Runan of the Song (420–78) that include the lines: "When Blue Jade broke her gourd / her lover was toppled by passion." *Yuefu shiji*, ed. Guo Maoqian, pp. 663–664.

25. "Double hairknots"雙鬟 refers to a child's hairstyle.

26. *Wu hao jia* 烏號架: the *wu hao* is a kind of bird that makes its nest in a tree of very flexible wood.

Other than that, I have no sisters who are close to me, and lack even
more brothers to depend on.
But if a benefactor should appear, I would willingly allow myself to be seduced.

(King:) My lad, we were destined to meet. Rise and stand as we speak. Do you want to be rich and noble? Would you enter my service?

(Zigao kowtows:) I shall serve you faithfully to the end of my life. I'm just afraid that my lord will abandon me.

(King:) Rise and speak.

(Zigao rises and stands.)

"Cunli ya gu" (Zigao sings:)

I was born and grew up among thorny bushes;[28]
I'm afraid that my sort ought not to approach the peony steps.
If I can prepare to take your orders,
Do some household chores,
And wait upon you,
Then I shall certainly gain some peace and ease, feel looked after,
Be spared some beatings and curses.
Who dares expect
A red brocade silk cloak,
A white jade belt,
Yellow gold hanging?
(Kowtows.) Spare me from becoming an eunuch.

(King:) It would be a pity. How could I bear to castrate you? I think your figure is unexpectedly like a woman's, so I shall select you to enter my palace. Together with these women here you may serve me. Would you be willing?

(Zigao:) My lord.

---

27. It is unclear here whether he states that father and mother are at opposite ends from each other, or whether both are separated from himself; if the latter, they are deceased.

28. I.e., in a harsh environment.

"Yuan he ling" (Zigao sings:)

You say I'm as sweet and graceful as your female servants.
I would happily change my hair style to be like that of the inner palace.[29]
I bet that if I lightly brush on vermilion powder and peach blush, I can make
  myself as glamorous as can be.
It's just my arched feet and waist that are different in comparison.
But I'll tie on a long skirt, and then myself won't be able to tell what is real and
  what is false.

(King:) Your words agree with me. Attendants, fetch a brightly colored robe and my personal phoenix patterned belt with the white jade buckle, and give it to him to wear. (The attendants respond.)

(Zigao puts on the armor and ties on the belt.)

(King:) My lad, even though the consorts and ladies of my palace are many, there is none with a figure such as yours. If you are a match for my desires, tomorrow I will make you the queen of my court. What do you think of that?

(Zigao kowtows:) Long live the King. In the past there have been women rulers; there ought also to be a male queen. I'm just afraid that your wife's background is so humble that I won't be able to satisfy your wishes.

"Shang ma jiao" (Zigao sings:)

If you think I compare to Xi Shi,[30]
And could pair with the son of the ninth Heaven,
I will give up my man's shirt for a gauze skirt,
And will spare you ten vessels of powder for guarding the inner chambers (*shou
  gong sha*).[31]

---

29. "The inner palace" refers to the quarters of the palace women.

30. Xi Shi 西施 is thought to have been a famed beauty of the kingdom of Yue 越 during the Spring and Autumn period.

31. In other words, in contrast to the king's consorts, Zigao, as a male, could not possibly give birth to a bastard son, and thus the king need not worry about his potential infidelity. *Shou gong sha* was a legendary powder used to maintain the chastity of the king's consorts. It was made by feeding geckos cinnabar (硃砂) and then grinding the geckos to a paste. When

(King:) It's just as you say. The only thing is that one may object that you and I have the same surname. What shall we do?

(Zigao:) As long as my lord stands behind this, who will criticize it? In ancient times, the rulers of Lu and Wu were of the same surname but still there was marriage between the two families. If my lord were to bestow your extraordinary favor upon me, could I not be such a wife as Wu Mengzi?[32]

"Sheng hulu" (Zigao sings:)

Since olden times, the Zhus and the Chens were of one family.[33]
As lotus leaves nestle the lotus flowers,
They are better matched with each other than with shoots from other trees,
I am just worried that in the golden palace,
Behind the pearl curtain,
My feminine beauty may be different from what you expect when I perform
    my rituals as wife.

(King:) Attendants, give this child a red horse and a coral whip. He will be a part of my entourage. Send the orders to the generals and officials to ride forward.

(Attendants respond.)

(Zigao makes a gesture of mounting a horse and rides with them.)

"Houting hua" (Zigao sings:)

Look at how the redness of this horse reflects the glow in my cheeks.
A coral riding whip bobs next to my raven tresses.

---

the paste was smeared on the bodies of the King's consorts, it could not be washed off, and would not disappear unless they had sex. See Zhang Hua 張華, *Bo wu zhi* 博物志, 4.7b–8a.

32. Wu Mengzi was the wife of Duke Zhao of Lu 魯. They were both of the lineage of the Duke of Zhou, and thus both shared the surname Ji 姬. In the *Analects*, Confucius is accused of showing favor to Duke Zhao for not criticizing him on this point. See *Lunyu jishi, juan* 14, p. 496.

33. The Zhus 朱 and the Chens 陳 referred originally to an ancient village in Xuzhou in which everyone was surnamed either Zhu or Chen, and the two families intermarried for generations. Later it came to refer to the repeated intermarriage of two families.

As I gather my green sleeves, they brush the painted banners.
Clutching red gauze, I send off sparkles from my sword.
I'm not used to these layers of purple tufted chain mail hanging from my
    shoulders.
Its great brilliance is too much for this little cutie.

"Liu ye'er" (Zigao sings:)

Look at the brightly gleaming lances and spears arrayed,
The teeming web of banners and pennants displayed.
I am the immortal Zitong descending to earth surrounded by a troop from
    heaven.[34]
Now with this light yellow kerchief of gold-speckled gauze,
My nice little body is all decked out, worthy of boast.

"Jisheng cao" (Zigao sings:)

What luck that I, a foolish lad,
Have had the good fortune to land in an aristocratic home.
When it comes to shedding tears for cast-off fish, I will make Longyang
    astonished,[35]
When it comes to holding golden pellets, I'll leave Han Yan to gape in
    surprise.[36]
When it comes to snatching phoenix combs, I'll let Qin Gong curse me.[37]
Who says that daughters bring honor to a family?[38]

---

34. Zitong 梓童 was a Daoist deity thought to be of aid in finding success in one's career and worldly prosperity. There is a pun inscribed here, as the same term could be used by the emperor to address his consorts.

35. The king of Wei 魏 was fishing with his male favorite, Longyang 龍陽, when Longyang started to weep, comparing his own situation to that of a fish who would be rejected once a bigger fish were caught (Liu Xiang, *Zhanguo ce*, Wei 4; *juan* 25, p. 917).

36. Han Yan 韓嫣: a reference to a male favorite of Emperor Wu of the Han who was so confident of the king's favor that he used pellets of gold in his slingshot. Han Yan's biography in the *Shi ji* (*juan* 125, p.3194) does not mention the story of the golden pellets; it appears in later sources such as Feng Menglong's *Qingshi leilüe*. Feng Menglong, *Qingshi leilüe, juan* 22, pp. 15b-16b.

37. Qin Gong 秦宮 was a favorite of the Eastern Han general Liang Ji 梁冀. Li's wife, Sun Shou 孫壽, was also enamored of Qin Gong, and so Qin Gong was allowed free access to Sun Shou's bedchamber as well (Fan Ye, *Hou Han shu, juan* 34, pp. 1180-81). In referring to Longyang, Han Yan, and Qin Gong, Zigao is saying he will supersede history's most celebrated male favorites.

I tell you, a boy now rides in the chariot of the monarch's first wife.

(Attendants:) We inform the king that we have already arrived at Wuxing.

(King:) Hold the horses. (Enters the palace.)

(King:) Generals and officers are given leave to attend their business in their own barracks.

(Attendants hail and leave the stage.)

(King:) My lad. Follow me into the palace, and change into women's dress. Tonight you will wait upon me in my bedchamber.

(Zigao kowtows:) Long live the king.

"Zhuan sha" (Zigao sings:)

> I'll change my hairstyle from a child's,
> Were I to pretend to be a palace woman for awhile,
> I would just be afraid that when I see the consorts and women of the palace I
>   should be ashamed.
> I steel myself to part the crimson gauze bed curtains with tightly furrowed brows.
> Don't talk about how I should enjoy this luxury,
> I merely worry that the tender pistle and charming blossom,
> Will not be in a position to complain of exhaustion,
> I'll just have to bite as hard as I can through the sunset-red bed covers.
> Now I'll lightly rouge my cherry lips and delicately draw my eyebrows in the
>   shape of distant mountains.
> The god of spring has been mistakenly rouged like a crab apple flower.

(Exit)

---

38. The phrase that I have translated as "bring honor to a family" reads literally "are the lintel of a family's gate." Once the daughter of a house received imperial favor, the characters on the lintel of the entrance to a family's home would be changed. Chen Hong's 陳鴻 "Changhen ge zhuan" 長恨歌傳 (Account of the "Song of Eternal Regret") quotes a ditty popular during the An Lushan rebellion. "Men are not enfeoffed, but women become consorts, / I see that women, surprisingly, are the lintel of a family's gate" 男不封侯女作妃，看女卻爲門上楣 (Bai Juyi, *Bai Juyi ji jianjiao*, p. 23).

ACT II

(*Chou* and *tiedan* actors enter costumed as palace women:)

(First Palace Woman:) Falling rain, rolling clouds, it's always the same story. Peach flowers are mistakenly thought to be almond blossoms.[39]

(Second Palace Woman:) If I had known earlier that I would not find favor, I'd have bought a little more rouge and gloss to paint my peony.[40]

(First Palace Woman:) We are the serving women Nongtao and Meiliu from the palace of the king of Linchuan.[41] What an oddly beautiful thing our king brought back the other day from his campaign! The king had him change to women's dress and has bestowed upon him much favor.[42] This morning the king commanded that he be crowned mistress of the palace and ordered us to attend to him at his toilette. So all we can do is to wait upon him. (Laughs:) Sister Meiliu, it is so laughable. We entered the palace so many years ago, but never found favor with the king. He's only just married into the household, and already they're up to this strange business. How could such a queen with a "handle" exist!

---

39. Here the text plays with language from Song Yu's "Rhymeprose on Gaotang." The poem's description of sexual encounter as "rolling clouds and falling rain" 翻雲覆雨 became a frequently invoked epithet for sexual relations.

40. The lines ironically suggest that they would have applied more rouge had they realized earlier that the King would lose interest in them once Zigao appeared. This phrasing is drawn from a poem by the landscape painter Li Tang 李唐 (1066–1150) in which he complains of his contemporaries' lack of appreciation for his majestic style, stating "Had I known earlier that my work would not find favor, I would have bought more red to paint peonies." 早知不入時人眼，多賣胭脂畫牡丹. Li Tang, "Ti hua" 題畫, *Songshi jishi*, ed. Li E, p. 1116.

41. The name of the palace women may be translated as Blossoming Peach (Nongtao) and Beauteous Willow (Meiliu); both names suggest sensuality and sex.

42. In translating the play, I have been forced to choose pronouns to describe Chen Zigao, a problem not present in the original, which uses the non-gendered pronoun *ta* 他. I have chosen pronouns based on the information the character speaking has shown he or she possesses. Here, since the serving women show that they know that Zigao is a boy, I use "he."

(Second Palace Woman:) Sister Nongtao, you don't seem to know that our king is an eel. Of course he wants to look for a loach to be his mate.

(First Palace Woman:) Do you mean to say that you, a clam, might as well mate with my oyster?[43]

(Second Palace Woman:) Hah. No more idle chat. The queen is coming.

(Zigao enters in women's costume:)

Pale blush heavily applied also suits me.[44]
I need only to add some mountain flowers to be a woman.
Snow hides the egret; one sees it only as it flies.
The willows hide parrots; it's when they speak that you know their presence.[45]

Ever since I entered the palace, I have received great favor from the king; he has cherished me as no other. Today he made a decree that he wanted to establish me as queen. He told me to finish my toilette and wait for his orders. I see now that the affairs of this world are hard to predict. For instance, a scholar just needs luck at the right moment, and then what does it matter what his scholarly abilities are? He will succeed. There are so many beautiful concubines and servants in the Six Palaces, but none of them can compare with me.

(Palace women bow:) Nongtao and Meiliu kowtow.

(Zigao:) Rise. Bring me my hamper of cosmetics.

---

43. The second palace woman jokingly suggests that sexual desire should be based on anatomical similarity, leading to the innuendo in the first palace woman's rejoinder.

44. Here Zigao compares himself to the legendary beauty Xi Shi. The phrase "Pale blush heavily applied also suits me" is drawn from Su Shi's poem, "Yin hu shang chu qing hou yu er shou" 飲湖上初晴后雨二首, which contains the couplet, "If one were to compare the beauty of West Lake (Xihu) to that of Xi Shi, pale blush heavily applied will always suit." Su Shi, *Su Shi shi ji*, vol. 2, p. 1430.

45. This last couplet is a commonly used phrase that suggests that time is needed for the true nature of phenomena to be revealed.

(Palace women bring the cosmetics. Zigao applies cosmetics in front of the mirror.)

(Zhonglü mode:) "Fen die'er" (Zigao sings:)

I face the gauze-covered window speckled with gold,
Looking in the mirror and learning to do my hair in the palace style.
Palace maids, blow out the lamp before the painted screen.
Look! The embroidered curtain is raised high,
The vermilion balustrade so spacious.
The light of dawn begins to glow.
Suddenly the scent of perfume wafts by.
It's that sneaky east wind, traveling past the paulownia flowers for the
    first time.

(First Palace Woman:) My queen, put on this gold hair ornament inlaid with jade.

"Zui chunfeng" (Zigao sings:)

I put on a pair of gold hair ornaments inlaid with jade.

(Second Palace Woman:) Your highness, wear these two hairpins.

(Zigao sings:) Two gold hairpins.

(First Palace Woman:) Mistress, weave these flower blossoms in your hair.

(Zigao sings:) I take tender flower blossoms, and stick them charmingly in the dark clouds of my hair.

(Second Palace Woman:) Your highness, fasten these jade pendants at your waist so that they chime.

(Zigao sings:) Listen to the sound of these jade pendants, chiming as they hang.

(First Palace Woman:) Your highness, try on these clothes.

(Zigao sings:)

A slender brocade sash flutters like clouds at sunrise,
Brightly colored embroidered sleeves outshine the moon,
A long, rustling skirt of many colors blows about in the wind.

(First Palace Woman:) Your highness, your look today is even more stylish than usual.

(Zigao:) Silly girl.

"Tuo bushan" (Zigao sings:)

My beautiful face was originally like a woman's,
Do you mean to say that these days I am even more beautiful than usual?
Only recently have I become a bit used to a woman's toilette.
That's why I feel even more charming than I did when we first met.

(First Palace Woman:) You look so extraordinarily handsome; what woman could come close?

"Xiao Liangzhou" (Zigao sings:)

You women just streak on some rouge to mimic sweet blossoms,
If you don't use cosmetics, you don't stand out.
I, however, just lightly apply powder and kohl, thinly brush on yellow.
I need only glance flirtatiously,
And I become more charming than women in rouge.

(Second Palace Woman:) Your highness, today you have been made queen. I don't know which of the ancients could compare to you.

(Zigao:) You mean to ask which of the ancients might compare?

"Reprise" (Zigao sings:)

There was only Dongxian of the Han, who once because of the emperor's favor of the cut sleeve could lord it over grandees and ministers.[46]

---

46. Dongxian 董賢 was the male favorite of Emperor Ai 哀 of the Han (r. 7 bce–1 bce), and his relationship with Emperor Ai gave rise to the common epithet for male love, the passion of the cut sleeve (斷袖之愛) "Once they took a nap together during the day, and

But even he did not have the primary position in the harem.
Today I will be crowned and receive an official status that tops all other consorts and women of the court.
To have such high position and power as a woman,
Will render my name praised for a thousand years.

(Order is relayed from offstage:) His highness sends an order that her highness, having finished her toilette, should kindly proceed to the Palace of Eternal Autumn to pay her respects.

(First Palace Woman:) His highness requests that her highness go to present her respects. [All exit stage temporarily.]

(King, leading the palace women, enters:) The new beauty I've acquired is another Boy Zhang the Sixth.[47] I laugh at how ill his red sleeves fit.[48] When a large turtledove flies up into the paulownia tree, onlookers will comment.[49] (Sighs.) I, the king of Linchuan, am an eccentric when it comes to romance. A few days ago I brought a beauty home from the campaign. His figure is charming, and his mind is quick; with regard to that I have no complaints. Ordinarily my nature is extremely impatient. If the officials and palace women depart from my expectations even slightly, I don't know how many heads I hack off in a day. But whenever he is by my side, even affairs of the gravest consequence recede to the back of my mind. What an odd creature I am. This is an auspicious day. I have readied the imperial seal, crown, and stole and will crown him a proper Queen.

Dongxian lay on the emperor's sleeve. The emperor wanted to get up, and since Dongxian had not woken, he did not want to disturb him, so he had his sleeve cut and rose. Such was his love and favor for Dongxian." (Ban Gu, *Han shu* 漢書, *juan* 93, p. 3733).

47. Master Zhang the Sixth 張六兒 was a male favorite of the Tang dynasty empress Wu Zetian 武則天, as was his brother. Upon Wu Zetian's abdication, the two brothers were executed. See Liu Xu, *Jiu Tang shu*, *juan* 28, p. 2708.

48. The red sleeves may be a reference to the young male entertainer Zheng Yingtao 鄭櫻桃, who was the favorite of Shi Hu 石虎, the third Emperor of the Former Zhao (335–348). Zheng ordered Shi Hu to kill both his wives, and Shi Hu did as he asked. *Jin shu*, *juan* 106, pp. 2761.

49. This phrase is a re-writing of the common saying, "When the wind blows over a paulownia tree, naturally passersby will comment on its length." In other words, any extraordinary event will arouse gossip.

Attendants, deliver my proclamation for her highness to ascend to this
palace quickly. (Palace women relay the order.)

(Zigao leads First and Second Palace Woman onto the stage. Zigao kowtows:) Long live the king.

(King:) Rise. I thank you, my beauty. Ever since you entered the palace,
you have served me diligently. Among the thousands of my harem, there
is none who can surpass you. Today I crown you as Queen; you must carry out your responsibilities with circumspection.

(Zigao:) This servant has received excessive favor from your highness. To
be able to serve you in your bedchamber has already surpassed my expectations. If I am formally made the foremost among your consorts, I am
afraid that the consorts and palace women will be jealous. I'd rather die
than accept this favor.

(King:) You need not refuse so stubbornly. Who would dare to be jealous
of you? Eunuchs, take note. If anyone of the rank of consort or palace
woman and below is jealous of her highness, the person will be immediately beheaded, and her head displayed in warning to others.

(The attendants respond in concert.)

(King:) Bring over the the imperial seal, ribbon, and ceremonial robes.
Now pay your respects.

(Zigao dons his headdress and robe, paying his respects.)

"Shang xiaolou" (Zigao sings:)

I recall how your concubine was wandering like duckweed afloat,
I thank Your Majesty's billowing waves of grace.
You have mistaken Song Yu, whom women peeped at over his eastern wall,[50]

---

50. Song Yu, in his "Deng tuzi haose fu" 登徒子好色賦 (Rhapsody on licentious master Deng), defended himself from the accusation that he could not be trusted around the
royal harem, given his astounding good looks and persuasive wit. He argued that despite

For the goddess of Gaotang.[51]

I have been forced to become the consort Zhao Feiyan in the Zhaoyang palace.[52]

I am about to enter the wedding chamber, be regarded as a woman, and follow my wifely duties.

I only hope that I may bring you happiness and pleasure, and that I will be forever free from harm.

(King:) Tell them to begin the banquet.

(Zigao takes a cup.)

"Reprise" (Zigao sings:)

Tenderly I lift the hem of my embroidered skirt,

Smooth is the jade cup I raise.

Let me, a He Yan said to wear powder,[53]

Become the consort Zhang Lihua of the Jieqi palace.[54]

---

the fact that a comely neighbor had often peeped at him over the eastern wall of his garden, he had remained faithful to his ugly wife. Xiao Tong, *Wen xuan, juan* 19, p.892.

51. In other words, the king has mistaken Song Yu, the author of the "Rhymeprose on Gaotang," for the goddess immortalized in the rhymeprose. The implication is that the king should have made Zigao a minister like Song Yu, rather than dressed him as a woman.

52. Emperor Cheng 成 of the Han (r. 32 -6 bce) built the Zhaoyang 昭陽 palace for his consort Zhao Feiyan 趙飛燕.

53. He Yan 何晏 (?-249) was an important scholar of the school of metaphysical learning (*xuan xue* 玄學) and annotated the *Analects* and *Dao de jing*. He was a stepson of Cao Cao, and married one of his daughters. He was also famed for his beautifully white skin. Records conflict as to whether his complexion was dependent on artifice; the *Shishuo xinyu* suggests that because his skin was so white, he did not need powder. (Liu Yiqing 劉義慶, *Shishuo xinyu jiaojian*, p. 325; see Mather, *Shih-shuo hsin-yü: A New Account of Tales of the World*, p. 308). Richard Mather's notes to his translation of the *Shishuo xinyu* cites Yu Huan's 魚豢 *Wei lüe* 魏略: "He Yen was by nature egocentric, and whether active or at rest was never without a powder puff in his hand. When he walked anywhere, he looked back at his own shadow" Mather, *Shih-shuo hsin-yü: A New Account of Tales of the World*, p. 309.

54. The last emperor of the Chen dynasty built the Jieqi 結綺 palace for his consort Zhang Lihua 張麗華, an ostentatious structure with curtains made of pearls. The consort Zhang Lihua was viewed in the historical records as a femme fatale who contributed to the fall of the dynasty. Like the reference to Yang Guifei, this reference is anachronistic, yet carries ominous overtones. The King (Chen Qian) at the moment is fighting for the establishment of the Chen dynasty and himself has not yet ascended the throne. His nephew will one day be the last emperor.

My thanks to you, King Xiang of Chu, who encountered the goddess of the
    falling rain,[55]
Just face your powdered one and enter the land of drunkenness,
Wine splashing, music softly played,[56]
Sing a farewell to those polished gauze skirts.

(King:) Bring chairs over. Have a seat, my queen. My beauty, I see that
you have a pliant figure, delicate and radiant, your soft flesh charming and
tender. Last night I may have been less than respectful. Did I cause any serious injury?

(Zigao:) My body belongs to the king. Even if I were to die, how could I
dare to think of myself?

"Manting fang" (Zigao sings:)

You bees and butterflies have always been less than respectful.
What need to talk of charming flowers and favored willows,[57]
Or of those who are attracted to fragrant jade-like beauties?
Even if several layers of bedcovers were wet through by spring tides,[58]
I could only endure to my death.
Like Liang Lüzhu, who threw her body from a tower,[59]
Like the concubine of Xiang Yu of Chu, who slit her throat beside the lamp,[60]
I, too, would look death in the face.
I wouldn't care about the pain.

---

55. Here the text quotes from Song Yu's "Rhymeprose on Gaotang." See footnote 39.

56. The phrase is taken from Liu Yong's lyric "He chong tian." 鶴沖天, which contains the lines, "I could bear to exchange my ephemeral fame/ for wine splashing and music softly played." *Quan Song ci jian pian*, ed. Tang Guizhang, p. 38.

57. The phrase "charming flowers and favored willows" is drawn from Li Qingzhao's
song lyric "Nian nu jiao," though it is inverted here. *Li Qingzhao ji*, p. 36.

58. See Du Fu, "*Chun shui*" 春水, *Du shi xiang zhu*, vol. 2, p. 799.

59. Liang Lüzhu 梁綠珠 was the concubine of Shi Chong 石崇 (249– 300 A.D.). A
beauty who excelled at playing the flute, she was desired by Sun Xiu 孫秀, who managed
to have Shi Chong arrested when he refused to give up Lüzhu. When the soldiers came to
arrest Shi Chong, he said to Lüzhu, "It is because I have offended others on your behalf
that this is happening to me now." Lüzhu, crying, said, "Then I will die before your eyes."
She then threw her body from the tower to preserve her loyalty to Shi Chong. He and his
whole family were subsequently executed. (*Jin shu, juan* 33, p. 1008).

60. Legend has it that the concubine Yu 虞姬 of Xiang Yu 項羽, the hegemon of Chu,
slit her throat when it became clear that Xiang Yu's defeat was imminent.

If for the present I suffer some physical distress, what does it matter?

(King:) Well said. But still I am concerned for you. Bring the great goblet, so that I may drink a full cup. My beauty, I see that you may well accommodate my object, but your own object is indeed also very manly and robust. I am a great general, and you are my second in command. It would not be difficult for us to conquer all the women soldiers of the world.

(Zigao covers face with fan and smiles:) I was just thinking that the powdered ranks are full of able generals such as Sunzi and Wu Qi.[61] If it weren't for my iron-strapped spear, your highness's Jiangzhou could not help but be lost.[62]

"Kuaihuo san" (Zigao sings:)

You are one of the crack troops in the fields of willows and flowers,[63]
I lead the vanguard of the land of feminine beauties.[64]
With our pair of erect greenish black lances among the powdered brigades,
We could be like generals among the prostitutes.

(King:) Well said! I will drink another cup of wine. My beauty, last night I dreamed that I was riding a horse up a mountain. The road was steep, and I was about to fall. I relied on you to give me a hand and lift me up.[65] I am truly indebted to you. Today you are established as queen, and I will much rely on you.

---

61. Sunzi 孫子, the famous military strategist who allegedly composed the *Art of War*, served the ruler of Wu during the Spring and Autumn period. Wu Qi 吳起 was a general of first Lu and then Wei during the Warring States period.

62. The Jiangzhou 江州 referred to here was a territory not far from Chen Qian's base in Linchuan; it is within modern-day Jiangxi.

63. "Fields of willows and flowers" here refers to brothels and other such venues.

64. Literally, "the land of jade and red dresses."

65. Here the play quotes the account of the relationship between Zigao and the King of Linchuan (later Emperor Wen of the Chen) in the *Nan shi*. "The emperor once dreamed that he was ascending a mountain on horseback; the road was precipitous and he was about to fall. Zigao propelled him upward and he ascended into the sky." *Nan shi*, p. 1664. The brief anecdote presumably took place before the King of Linchuan became the Emperor Wen, and suggests that once he became Emperor, Chen Qian attributed his rise in part to the aid of Han Zigao.

(Zigao:) Your servant has received your deep favor, and this could not be repaid even with my death. I ought to serve you with all the means I possess until I die of exhaustion. How dare I not devote my whole heart to you?

"Chao tianzi" (Zigao sings:)

I could not dare forget that moment with the king in the shark's cloth tent.[66]
Even if in a dream I were one of the marching ants about to fall from a great hill,[67]
I would still have to hold the vermilion wheels of your carriage.
Were I one of those ladies who trails silk in the royal consort's chambers,
Or one who has been stripped of her jewelry, having lost the king's favor.
I would still assume women's garb.
But if I were to change my clothes and alter my voice,
I would be suited to a warrior's magnificent helmet.

(King:) Ah, my beauty, it's just as you say, the real women are all just ordinary, and no match for the rarity of you, the false one. Since I embarked upon a military career, I have long given up composing poems. But today, having met such a rare beauty, how can I fail to compose a poem for you? Eunuchs! Remove the banquet dishes. Bring over my royal brush and inkstone. My beauty, I'll just write on the surface of your robe. Palace women, hold out his sleeve. (Writes and reads aloud:)

In the past we heard of the little page by the name of Zhou.[68]
Today we will sing a song to the tune of "Mingxia tong."
His hands are as white as a jade duster.[69]

---

66. "Sharkman's silk" refers to an expensive silk. The *Taiping yulan* 太平御覽 writes of a "shark man" in the South Seas who wove cloth. "The *Bowu zhi* 博物志 relates: There is a shark man who lives in the South Seas. He lives in the water like a fish. . . . He does not waste effort in weaving. His eyes can cry pearls like tears" (*Taiping yulan*, 790, 10b).

67. This refers to the dream of Chen Qian's related in the *Nan shi*; see footnote 66.

68. These lines refer to a poem by Zhang Han 張翰, "Zhou xiaoshi shi" 周小史詩 (Poem on the little page by the name of Zhou) (Lu Qinli, *Xian Qin Han Wei Jin Nanbei chao shi*, 1: 737).

69. A reference to the Six Dynasties male beauty Wang Yan 王衍. "Wang Yan's face and appearance were symmetrical and beautiful, and he was subtle in conversing about the mysterious (*xuan* 玄). He constantly gripped a sambar-tail chowry (*zhuwei* 麈尾) with a

If he were to go out in his ram-drawn carriage, the streets would be as if
    empty.[70]
Who will look on with longing if two males stand side by side?
The royal guards shall give way to you.[71]

My beauty, what do you think of this poem. Does it please you? Put it
aside carefully, and think of it as one of my favors to you.

(Zigao kowtows:) The unsightly figure of your servant has received your
undeserved praise. My gratitude knows no bounds. I will store it as a
treasure with my clothing and will take it with me to the grave.

"Sibian jing" (Zigao sings:)

This is a new fashion in palace tunics,
The imperial ink still wet,
Inscribed for several lines,
The characters are pleasing to the utmost and have the energy of autumn wind,
They gleam like pearls of varying size and shape,
Are more valuable than countless embroidered pairs of mandarin ducks and
    mating phoenixes scattered riotously on cold white silk.

(From offstage drums of dawn sound)
(Attendants:) My lord, the drums have sounded at court. We ask the king
to proceed to the throne.

(King:) My beauty, I am going for a while to the morning session at court.
Consorts and palace women, respectfully present your congratulations to
Her Highness. Prepare the servants for the evening banquet.

---

white jade handle which was completely indistinguishable from his hand." Liu Yiqing,
Shishuo xinyu jiaojian, p. 327; translation from Mather, *Shih-shuo hsin-yü: A New Account
of Tales of the World*, p. 310.

70. Wei Jie 衛玠, grandson of Wei Guan 衛瓘, a grand courtier of the Western Jin
court, was known for his handsomeness. As a youth, when he went about in his ram-
drawn carriage, all who saw him thought him like a jade figure. He died in 311, forty-five
days after fleeing to the south; legend had it that he was "stared to death" by the rustic
southerners struck by his beauty (*Jin shu, juan* 36, p.1067; see also Mather, *Shih-shuo hsin-
yü: A New Account of Tales of the World*, p. 598n).

71. In other words, Zigao is both a feminine beauty and a great warrior.

(Zigao kowtows:) I pay my respects and send off His Highness.

(King:) Don't concern yourself with such formalities.

(The eunuchs follow the king offstage. The crowd of women attendants respectfully congratulates Zigao: Long live the queen.)

(Zigao:) Rise. Today I have been named to the primary position of the inner palace. All of you consorts and palace women must follow my rules. As for those who disobey, I will act according to the king's orders and behead the offenders. (The attendants respond, showing they heed.)

"Shua hai'er" (Zigao sings:)

I am the foremost amongst the young lotus flowers growing in the golden
    pond,
It embarrasses me terribly to be called Brother Zhang the Sixth.[72]
Now I have been transported by the god of the waves to the land of many-
    colored clouds,[73]
And am in charge of three hundred fragrant red blossoms.
Just as swallows and orioles become intimate by sharing a nest,
And bees and butterflies see no harm in occupying the same branch,
It's just perfect to nestle side by side.
This is what is meant when it is said that a gorgeous peony
Still requires green leaves to complement it.

(Zigao:) Women attendants, the king has ordered that the evening banquet be prepared.
We must have a troupe of dancers and singers offer entertainment.
You would not want to be unfamiliar with your routines. Let us rehearse.
(Attendants assent and play music.)

"Fourth from Coda" (Second Palace Woman sings:)

Lovely before the flames above the silver candlesticks,
Graceful beside the zither lacquered in brocade patterns,
She plucks delicately at the strings and softly sings:

---

72. Brother Zhang the Sixth: the lover of Empress Wu Zetian.
73. The land of many-colored clouds: a land of immortals.

They answer the call for entertainers, following the carved chariot,
She answers the call for songs and leaves her inner chambers to sing.[74]
Tonight the song I sing for them,
Is the tune "Fishhawk," the poem about the virtuous maiden.[75]

"Third from Coda" (A palace maid dances:)

My sleeves are like rose-colored clouds three feet long from shoulder to tip,
My waist is but a slip of fragrance to roll between your thumb and index fingers.
A quiet breeze through the willow branches, lingering on the red steps.
This light-footed dance is born of a love for the clear green of Qian creek.[76]
It matches these winding tunes sung out of pity for everlasting "Midnight."[77]
No doubt that once the phoenix curtains are closed,
Zhao Feiyan, the dancing queen, will be greatly pleased,[78]
And the Tang emperor Xuanzong, lover of the barbarian drums, will topple
  over laughing.

"Second from Coda" (Zigao sings:)

Look at the Milky Way that spans a thousand yards,
Its magpie bridge cuts a lengthy swath.
The Herd Boy and the Weaving Girl will descend tonight.[79]

---

74. The song cites Li Bai's "Gongzhong xingle ci," 宮中行樂詞. The carved chariot refers to that of the consort Zhao Feiyan as she leaves her inner chambers to sing. *Li Bai ji jiaozhu*, p. 379.

75. According to the Mao 毛 commentary, "*Guanju*" 關雎 (Fishhawk), the first poem in the *Shi jing* 詩經 (Classic of poetry), celebrates the marriage of the Duke of Zhou 周 to a virtuous consort. See Chapter 3, note 53.

76. The dance of Qianxi 前溪 was a dance that originated in the South and had become very popular by the Tang; *Qianxi* 前溪 thereafter became a common term for dance. See, for example, Li Shangyin 李商隱, "Hui zhong mudan wei yu suo bai" 回中牡丹爲雨所敗), in *Li Shangyin shige jijie*, 1: 271.

77. The "midnight" *Ziye* 子夜 songs are an anonymous set of songs linked to the figure of a courtesan named Ziye said to have lived during the Eastern Jin. *Ziye* became a common term for song in Tang and post-Tang verse.

78. A reference to Zhao Feiyan, consort of the Han emperor Cheng (see note 52); she was said to be so light on her feet she could dance on the Emperor's palm.

79. According to legend, the Herd Boy and the Weaving Girl are star-crossed lovers (linked to the stars Altair and Vega) permitted to meet only once a year, on the seventh day of the seventh month. Their mention here simply suggests that the wedding of the king and Zigao is a rare occasion.

Beautiful brows, gleaming white teeth, the bride pretty as jade.
Embroidered divan, gold screen, fragrance everywhere.
Who would have thought that you, the master of the orioles and flowers,[80]
Would make me the specially favored one among your harem?

(Zigao:) Women attendants, you are temporarily dismissed.
When the king returns to the palace, you will serve at the evening banquet.
You may not dodge your responsibilities or be late.

(The attendants say aye).

"Coda" (Zigao sings:)

Prepare the jade-ornamented toilette box to refresh my evening makeup,
   And the golden brazier for burning incense in the evening.
I predict that when you withdraw from court the moon will be astride the tops
   of the flowering trees.
You will hear only the sound of water dropping from the copper timepiece
   that hangs from the eaves.

(Exit.)

ACT III

(*Xiaodan* costumed as a princess leads the First and Second Palace Women, played by the *chou* and *tie*, on stage:)
Thick canopies, layers of curtains—in a hundred yards of fabric I'm stuck.
Pitying the flowers, I have simply wasted away.
The most beautiful women have the worst luck.
I should not blame the spring wind—I should lament my fate instead.
I am the younger sister of the king of Linchuan, Princess Yuhua. I'm just sixteen years old and have not yet been matched with a husband. My

---

80. "Orioles and flowers" refers to young women.

brother yesterday crowned a queen. She has such a countenance that fish would dive to the bottom of the stream when they saw her and geese would alight from the sky; the moon would hide itself and flowers would feel ashamed.[81] With such a heavenly figure, she is the most attractive woman in the kingdom. In this generation she has no peer. Forget about my brother, a man, falling in love with her. I am a girl, and I wouldn't mind swallowing her down like a drink of cold water. Oh, that there are such women in the world!

[Yuediao mode] "Dou anchun" (Princess sings:)

Just look at her charming beauty marks, shaped like flowers,
Pupils bright as clear water.
Her clouds of hair black as a pair of ravens.
Her lips look like a flower bud about to blossom.
She has such unique charms,
None could hold themselves back.
I find her incomparable.
I can't recall anyone who looks like her.
Perhaps the beautiful woman in the picture beside the eastern window,
Having a good time on a swing resembles you.[82]

(First Palace Woman:) Does her ladyship admire the beauty of her highness? If only I can bring you a husband of that sort tomorrow, you'll be fine.

(Princess:) You silly wench, she is a woman! How can a man compare to her?

---

81. Here Wang Jide plays with phrases used in *Zhuangzi* to emphasize the relativity of aesthetic values. The princess employs the phrases simply to praise the beauty of Zigao, but the original context of the phrases in *Zhuangzi* belie her words: "Men claim that Mao-ch'iang and Lady Li were beautiful, but if fish saw them they would dive to the bottom of the stream, if birds saw them they would fly away, and if deer saw them they would break into a run. Of these four, which knows how to fix the standard of beauty for the world?" Zhuangzi, "Qiwu lun," *Zhuangzi jishi*, p. 93; the translation is from Burton Watson, *The Complete Works of Chuang-tzu*, p. 46.

82. "Riding on a swing" is a common epithet for foreplay.

"Zihua'er xu" (Princess sings:)

She is a sprite on the riverbanks picking kingfisher feathers.[83]
An immortal beauty from Shao Shi gathering pinenuts.[84]
Pendants chiming, the goddess of the mountains of Chu.
How can you take some outsider, a *man*,
And compare him to this charming consort of the King's inner palace?
Don't mention that idea again!
If he had a silk cap covering his head, or were wearing purple official's robes,[85]
I'd take a husband like that.
I would do justice to his lying naked to the waist on the eastern bed.[86]
I'd gladly content myself with raising his tray to my forehead to show my
　　respect.[87]

(First Palace Woman:) Princess, do you really love the mistress? If you knew about her private parts, would you love her even more?

(Princess:) What is this all about? She isn't a man; why should I love her?

---

83. This phrase is drawn from Cao Zhi's "Luoshen fu" 洛神賦, where it refers to the spirits who accompany the goddess of the Luo river. *Wen xuan*, vol. 2, p. 899.

84. Here the princess compares Zigao to Shangyuan furen 上元夫人, a Daoist deity. *Shaoshi xianshu zhuan* 少室先姝傳, p. 5.

85. From the Tang, black silk caps and purple robes began to be formal wear for senior courtiers.

86. "Lying naked to the waist on the eastern bed" 袒腹東床 is an epithet for a good son-in-law. The phrase refers to the story of how Wang Xizhi 王羲之 was selected as a son-in-law by Chi Jian 郗鑒. Chi Jian sent a messenger to Wang Xizhi's uncle Wang Dao 王導 requesting him to select a son-in-law. The messenger came back saying that all the Wang sons were admirable men. "'When they heard that someone had come to spy out a son-in-law, all of them conducted themselves with circumspection. There was just one son who was lying sprawled out on the eastern bed as though he hadn't heard about it.' Chi said, 'He's just the one I want.' When he went to visit him, it turned out to be Wang Xizhi." (Liu Yiqing, *Shishuo xinyu jiaojian*, pp. 361–62; Mather, *Shih-shuo hsin-yü: A New Account of Tales of the World*, pp. 186–87). The same story is repeated in Wang Xizhi's biography in the *Jin shu* (pp. 2093–102) with a slight variation, in which Wang Xizhi was lying on the bed eating.

87. The Han dynasty figures Meng Guang 孟光 and Liang Hong 梁鴻 are traditionally viewed as the ideally respectful wife and husband. Their biography in the *Hou Han shu* relates that every night when Liang Hong came home, Meng Guang would have prepared his supper, and would raise the tray to the level of her eyebrows to show her respect (Fan Ye, *Hou Han shu, juan* 83, pp. 2765–69).

(First Palace Woman:) She isn't a man, but she has one more "toggle" than you do.[88]

(Princess:) This maid's gone mad. How can you say that?

(First Palace Woman:) You don't know? The mistress is a boy who's been transformed into a girl.

(Princess:) What nonsense. If he were a boy, what would the king want with him?

(First Palace Woman laughs:) Princess, you see only the Northern Mode inside the palace. You don't know about the Southern Mode outside.[89]

(Princess makes a startled gesture:) Are there really such things?

"Jin jiaoye" (Princess sings:)

She is not a pheasant or a red mandarin duck,
Why need she be decked out in gold and jade?
If she has transplanted her roots and grafted on a new bud,
Why doesn't she clue us in?
Nongtao, go quickly and ask her to come out. Let me have a close look at her.

(First Palace Woman faces the stage entrance and makes a gesture of invitation:) The princess invites our mistress to appear.

(Response from backstage:) The queen is coming.

(Zigao enters, leading maids.)
So, how do I look in golden hairpins and a gauze official's cap?
I laugh myself silly thinking of the female collator of texts Xue Tao.[90]

---

88. The word I have translated as "toggle" here is *niu* 紐.

89. The "Southern Mode" 南風 refers to erotic liaisons between men. The "Northern Mode" 北風 is not a common term, but here is used in counterpoint to the Southern Mode to refer to liaisons between men and women.

90. The term "female collator of texts" (*nü jiao shu* 女校書) alludes to the Tang dynasty courtesan Xue Tao 薛濤 (768–831). Collator of texts in the imperial library was a

In murky waters you can't tell carp from bass,
Only when the water's clear can you finally tell the two apart.

(They greet each other. The princess looks Zigao up and down. Both sit.)

(Princess:) Just now, sister-in-law, you were in the palace. Did you make any flowers?

(Zigao:) None. I've just read a few lines of a book.

(Princess:) Reading books is men's business. Why are you imitating them?

(Zigao turns aside:) That's odd. Why does she keep staring at me so? My replies were wrong again. I almost let it show.

(Princess:) Sister, why have you gone red all of a sudden?

(Zigao:) I was drinking, so my face reddened.

(Princess:) As a woman, you are not supposed to go round drinking wine. Let's stroll beyond the veranda by the garden. (They walk.)

(Zigao:) Miss, what kind of flower is that?

(Princess:) That is a tree peony.

(Zigao:) How is it that one tree has two kinds of flowers on it?

(Princess:) This peony tree has been grafted. Its root is still that of a bush peony.

(Zigao:) Miss, what kind of birds are those on the pond?

---

conventional first position for students who had done well in the examinations. Various anecdotes suggest that Xue Tao was so admired by the governor of Sichuan that he considered nominating her for the post, although, as Wilt Idema and Beata Grant note, none of the anecdotes are reliable. See Idema and Grant, *The Red Brush,* pp. 182–183.

(Princess:) Those are mandarin ducks and drakes.[91]

(Zigao:) Why are there only female ducks there?

(Princess:) Those birds are strange. The males have all become females.

(Zigao:) What kind of bird is that with the long tail?

(Princess:) It is a peacock, sister-in-law. The peacock has many feathers of gold and iridescent green. The peahen is less pleasing to the eye.

(Zigao:) Nongtao, will you catch that butterfly?

(Palace women try to catch the butterfly.)

(Princess:) Sister, this butterfly is a fool. Don't try to catch him.

(Zigao:) How do you know it is a fool?

(Princess:) Sister, if it were not a fool, having seen such pretty flowers, how could it not know to pick them?

(Zigao turns her back:) How is it that today the princess keeps teasing me with her remarks? It must be that I somehow let the secret slip. But what shall I do?

(Princess turns her back:) My servant Nongtao said that my sister-in-law was a man. But the queen covers well. One could easily be fooled.

"Tiaoxiao ling" (Princess sings:)

Is she in truth a man or not?
A Peach Leaf or Peach Root? One doesn't know in the end.[92]

---

91. Symbols of conjugal happiness.

92. Wang Xizhi ostensibly had two sisters as concubines, named "Peach Leaf" (*Taoye* 桃葉) and "Peach Root" (*Taogen* 桃根); later the names became common terms for a

Perhaps a man would be more bold and dashing,
Could not be so seductive and charming.
But if he were as handsome as Pan Yue and did not take advantage of the
     prime of his life,
It would leave me even more broken-hearted.

Enough. I have an idea. (Princess to Zigao:) Sister, let me try on your embroidered slippers. Let's see whose foot is smaller.

(Zigao:) There's no need for you to try them on. I'll send a pattern to you.

(Princess:) Sister, why is it that there isn't any bulging in your breasts?

(Zigao:) I haven't matured yet, so they haven't grown.

(Princess:) Oh sister, why do you conceal things from me?

"Gui santai" (Princess sings:)

You're just wearing a skirt trailing the ground,
To hide your feet delicate as hooks.
You are in your youth,
Wearing a gown of thin gauze.
Who's to say we shouldn't be able to see a bit of budding breast?
I'm just afraid that when you stand on the fragrant steps a wind will lift your
     skirts,
Or perhaps there will be a time when bathing in the hot springs, you won't put
     your shirt on in time.
And when that happens, will you not fail in pretending to have light and radiant lotus petal footsteps and soft moist nipples?

(Speaks:) Sister, don't try to fool me. Tell me the truth.

"Tusi'er" (Princess sings:)

You are not the female ghost of the Cui family, who gave a golden bowl.[93]

---

concubine or a beautiful woman. Here it seems as though the princess is making an anatomical joke as she refers to "Peach Root."

93. A reference to an anecdote in the *Soushen ji*, in which a young man on a hunting trip enters the underworld and engages in a romance with the daughter of the Cui family.

You are not Zheng Yingtao, the demon clad in red robes.[94]

You've done nothing more than temporarily taken lotus flowers to be flowers
of the roseleaf raspberry.

Why fear that spring will know the difference? Stop worrying!

(Zigao:) Miss, what are you saying? If I did not have a woman's body, why
would your elder brother desire me?

(Princess:) Sister, you need not deny it. I have some advice for you.

"Shengyao wang" (Princess sings:)

Stop clinging to your delusions.

You must act as soon as you can.

It happens that we are locked in the Bronze Sparrow Terrace amidst the spring
wind.[95]

Bees will not spy on us,

Butterflies won't know us.

Why do we need red leaves to be our matchmaker?[96]

(Speaks:) Sister. I am embarrassed to say this,

(Sings:) But it would be you who would be taking advantage of me.

She becomes pregnant, and he leaves to return to his previous life. Four years later, she appears and presents him with his son, giving him a golden bowl as well. See Gan Bao, *Soushen ji, juan* 16, pp. 203–205.

94. See note 48 above.

95. Here Wang Jide draws upon the Tang poet Du Mu's quatrain "Red Cliff" 赤壁, which contains the lines, "If the east wind had not given advantage to Zhou Yu, the two Qiao sisters would have been locked deep in the Bronze Sparrow Terrace that spring." *Fanchuan shi ji zhu*, p. 271. The Bronze Sparrow Terrace was a palace built by Cao Cao 曹操 after losing the famed Battle of Red Cliff to Zhou Yu 周瑜. The Qiao sisters were the most famed beauties of the south; the younger was Zhou Yu's wife. The princess suggests that she and Zigao suffer a confinement similar to that the Qiao sisters would have endured had Zhou Yu lost the battle of Red Cliff, and that they should thus engage in an affair.

96. A story from the *Taiping guangji* features a wedding between a former palace woman and a man who spied poems she had written on red leaves and thrown into the gutter; they floated to the exterior of the palace, where he spotted the red leaves and responded in similar fashion. On the occasion of their wedding, the palace woman wrote a poem that read 'A pair of fine lines flowing in the water, / Ten years of secret thoughts fill our pure hearts, / Today we have unexpectedly become phoenix mates, / So we know the red leaves are good matchmakers'" (*Taiping guangji, juan* 354, p. 2807).

(Zigao:) Miss, how could we do something like that? If your brother knew, it would be an unseemly mess.

(Princess:) Ah, sister.

"Ma lang'er" (Princess sings:)

It's not that I saw your money and formed this intention.
It's you who's monkeyed with what's right and wrong and so caused all this trouble.
I couldn't care less about the fact that he and I are sister and brother.
You must follow me in this urgent matter.
(She tugs at Zigao's hand; Zigao makes a fleeing motion.)

(Zigao:) Miss, I'm not feeling well. Let's go in.

(Princess holds her fast:) Sister, where are you going?

"Reprise" (Princess sings:)

This time you can't claim there is someone of whom you are afraid.
Before the others, we'll be sisters-in-law, each following the other.
Behind their backs we'll be husband and wife, a well-matched pair.
I guarantee you that no one will find anything offensive.

(Zigao:) Miss, we are sisters-in-law. How could we do that kind of thing?

(Princess:) Sister, don't be a hypocrite. Help me out a bit!

"Luosiniang" (Princess sings:)

You need not be like Zhu Yingtai, disguising her glamour.[97]
You should not copy the man of Lu, who locked his vermilion doors.[98]

---

97. According to popular legend, Zhu Yingtai 祝英台 and Liang Shanbo 梁山伯 were a pair of star-crossed lovers. Zhu Yingtai disguised herself as a man in order to study and take the examinations and studied with Liang Shanbo for three years without revealing her sex. Later, Liang went to visit his schoolmate and found out that she was a woman. He wanted to marry her, but she was already betrothed. He took ill and died. The next year, she visited his grave, and when she climbed the grave mound, the earth opened and swallowed her. Zhang Jin 張津, *Siming tujing shi'er juan* 四明圖經十二卷, *juan* 3, p. 528.

Why not show a little mercy?
Save yourself the need for the pretenses of a hypocrite.
You might end up with some merit in heaven's eyes.

(Zigao, making an angry gesture:) Miss, even if you haven't read the books of the sage Confucius, you ought to know the rites pased down by the Duke of Zhou. How can you trifle with me this way?

(Princess:) Sister, don't get yourself worked up.

"Xiaotao hong" (Princess sings:)

You're as charming as Zhuo Wenjun; don't blame me for pestering you.[99]
Who told you to look so much like Pan Yue?[100]
The angrier you get, the cuter you become.
And I match your dark looks with a smile.

(Princess kneels:) Gathering my red skirt, I fall to my knees before you.

(Zigao kneels and pulls the princess to her feet:) Sister, how can you do this?

(Princess:) Sister, if you really are not willing, I will not tell you of my feelings by playing on the Lüqi *qin*.[101] Nor need I lie sorrowing under embroidered covers. [Takes out a handkerchief and pantomimes hanging herself.] I will simply hang myself to the west of the boudoir window.

---

98. The man of Lu 魯男子 refers to an anecdote related in the Mao commentary to the *Classic of Poetry* about a man whose adherence to principles of propriety supplanted human feeling. One night when there was a terrible storm, his female neighbor, whose roof was leaking, rushed over and beseeched him to let her in, but he refused. Later, "the man of Lu" became an epithet for a man who avoids relations with women. "Xiangbo" 巷伯, *Shi Mao shi zhuan shu, juan* 19.48–49.

99. Zhuo Wenjun 卓文君 was the wife of the first-century poet Sima Xiangru 司馬相如; here the princess alludes to the scandal caused by Zhuo Wenjun's elopement with Sima Xiangru. See *Han shu, juan* 57, pp. 2529–2531.

100. Pan Yue 潘嶽 was a Jin Dynasty author famed for his handsomeness. Liu Yiqing, *Shishuo xinyu jiaojian*, pp. 326–27; see *Jin shu, juan* 55, p. 1500.

101. The *qin* of Lüqi 綠綺 refers to the zither that the poet Sima Xiangru used to seduce his future wife Zhuo Wenjun.

(Zigao makes a struggling motion:) Miss, why are you so hasty all of a sudden? How about letting me think it over for a few days? I'll get back to you.

(Princess:) Sister-in-law, I beg you in great earnest. Are you simply unyielding? I have no other recourse, then, than to go and tell my brother how *you've* been flirting with *me*.

"Tian zheng sha" (Princess sings:)

I was born and grew up in the depths of the women's quarters.
I've never thought much about spring romance.[102]
All of a sudden you take liberties with me.
I don't care if flowers wilt and jade shatters.
Both of us will have an equal share of the blame.

(Zigao makes a laughing motion:) Miss, you really are full of ruses. There's no way out for me. I'll just have to do what you say.

(Princess:) You servants, go to the rear. (Servants leave the stage. Princess holds Zigao's hand.)

"Dongyuan le" (Princess sings:)

I had thought that the dream of Yang terrace wouldn't return when called.
Who would have thought to see the day when an iron tree would bloom?
It makes it hard for me to distinguish sorrow from happiness.
I'm just afraid that behind the gauze curtains,
My cardamom bud won't be able to stand the spring wind that batters the
    flowers.[103]

Princess: Let's secretly take our marriage vows and swear an oath. (Together they make their obeisances.)

---

102. Literally, "I've never thought much about green leaves shriveling and red flowers fattening," a phrase which plays with the Song poet Li Qingzhao's 李清照 line "Red grows thin and green fattens" 紅瘦綠肥 "Ru meng ling" 如夢令. (*Li Qingzhao ji*, p. 1).
103. Here, the princess mimics the very words the queen used in Act II.

"Mian daxu" (Princess sings:)

Our host is the jade mirror,
And our go-between is a gold comb.
Our guarantor is a purple swallow,
Our master of ceremonies is a yellow oriole.
We'll just ask the old man in the temple of the Ocean Spirit to be our chief
    matchmaker.
A pinch of earth is the incense with which we pray to complete our ceremony.
Please protect these moth-browed beauties.
Let us secretly become husband and wife without danger or disaster.

Sister-in-law, you are a fairy man from the Jasper Island of immortals. By mistake you became a luscious woman of the golden palace. Now I am fortunate to be close to the powdered He Yan.[104] I certainly cherish the scented Han Shou.[105] I have a lustrous pearl. It has a value of ten thousand taels. Since I was young I have studied calligraphy and painting. On this white fan, I will paint a pair of birds flying and write a poem as a token of our longing for each other. Maids, bring brush and inkstone.

(First and Second Palace Women mount the stage and offer brush and inkstone. The princess paints.)

(First Palace Woman looks on:) Very interesting. You draw birds well. That pair of birds is also engaged in a bit of funny business.

(Princess takes the fan, writes a poem and reads it aloud:)

Others say a round fan is like the round moon,[106]

---

104. See He Yan, note 53 above.

105. Han Shou was a man of the Jin famous for his good looks, who seduced the daughter of Jia Chong, one of the most powerful men of the early Jin court. She gave him a rare perfume that lasted for weeks once applied, and it was because of this perfume that their affair was detected. (Liu Yiqing, *Shishuo xinyu jiaojian*, 35.5; Mather, *Shih-shuo hsin-yü: A New Account of Tales of the World*, p. 487).

106. The King's poem draws upon the song "Tuan shan lang" 團扇郎 (Boy with a round fan) by Emperor Wu 武 of the Liang 梁. "In his hand a fan round and white/pure as the full moon in autumn" (*Yuefu shiji*, ed. Guo Maoqian, 2: 661). It may also refer to Jiang Yan's "Ban Jieyu yong shan" 班婕妤詠扇 "A silk fan like the full moon/has its origin in the white silk of the weaver's shuttle-painted to resemble the daughter of the king of

I say the moon does not stay round for long.
I hope that in the warm South,[107] there will be no hint of frost,[108]
And that this fan will pass in and out of my lover's sleeves for hundreds and
  thousands of years.

(First Palace Woman looking on:) Hey, your characters are well written.

(Princess:) Tsk. My maid talks too much.

"Zhuolusu" (Princess sings:)

A moonlit pearl, round as a spoonful of water.
Is this raw silk fan,
Like a circle of jade, white and perfectly round.
This pair of green birds in flight accompanies
Two lines of precious characters.
In all these elements there is deep meaning,
Cherish this fan as though it were a pearl,
Carry it with you as though it were a round silk fan.
Be a pair with it as though you were *jian* birds.[109]
Follow each other as constantly as the bright moon follows those on earth.
Sister-in-law, you mustn't let this fan leave your sleeves.

(She makes a motion of giving it to Zigao.)

(Zigao:) Miss, originally I imitated Han Chong.[110] I served the girl of Qin
by playing the flute.[111] I am unworthy to receive such gifts of gold inlay,

---

Qin/who rode a phoenix into the mists/ The painting is esteemed by this age, but the new
cannot replace the old. . . ." Jiang Yan, "Zati sanshi shou" 雜體三十首, Lu Qinli, p. 1570.

107. Literally, "in the land of Yan 炎," which here refers to the south, or the Yangtze
delta where these events take place.

108. In other words, the weather will always be warm, and you will always need a fan.

109. The *jian* 鶼 was a mythical bird with one eye and one wing that needed to travel
in pairs in order to fly. *Er ya zhu shu*, p. 195.

110. Han Chong 韓重 was a young man who fell in love with the daughter of Fu Chai
夫差, the King of Wu. His parents' overture to Fu Chai was rejected, and Fu Chai's
daughter died broken-hearted. Later Han Chong visited her grave, and she emerged to
spend time with him, giving him a pearl as a token of her love. See Gan Bao, *Soushen ji*,
juan 16, p. 199–201.

111. See note 1 above.

and I am ashamed to requite you with jade and jasper.[112] How can I be worthy of such deep sentiments? Thank you, sister. (Thanks her.) This lustrous pearl will hang at my waist. Night and day, seeing it will be like looking upon you. Nongtao, take this round white fan. Put it away for me carefully. (Gives the fan to the First Palace Woman.)

(Palace Woman makes a comic gesture, saying:) Ahh. I thought the queen was pure as ice or jade. She is for our master the King's private enjoyment. We would not dare to offend her.[113] Now that she is having an affair with the princess, she's just like the Yangzi River, turbid and dirty. Why doesn't everyone have a go at her? (Teases Zigao:) Ah, Your Highness, I have a fan over here too. Let me give it to you as a proof of love.

(Princess making an angry gesture:) Ugh, you immodest slut! What kind of person are you? How could you be so rude! Let Meiliu drag her away. Give this immodest slut a beating.

(Second Palace Woman beats the First Palace Woman in response.)

(Princess:) If you are ever like this again, I will tell the King to cut off your head. (Holding Zigao's hand:) Sister, my brother has not come to the palace yet. Let's take advantage of the opportunity to enter my chambers and take a nap.

"Coda" (Princess sings:)

Let's take advantage of this flowery boudoir to shelter ourselves against the
  cold east wind.
I'll accompany the Jade Disk consort to a spring nap in the Huaqing hot
  springs.[114]
I'm just afraid that a passion-crazed butterfly will topple me.

---

112. A reference to one of the earliest and best-known poems on the exchange of love tokens, "Mugua" 木瓜 of the *Shi jing*. The poem includes the line: "She throws a quince, I requite her with jade and jasper" (*Shi jing zhuxi*, pp. 191–92).
113. Literally, "would not dare to brush against her dragon scales," dragons being the symbol of supreme authority.
114. Jade Disk (*yuhuan* 玉環) is an epithet for Yang Guifei. The Huaqing 華清 hot spring was the name of the baths the Tang emperor Xuanzong had built for Yang Guifei.

And the reckless peach flowers will give you more satisfaction than you had ever dreamed of.

(First Palace Woman and Second Palace Woman are left alone on stage. First Palace Woman faces the exit and points at the Princess:) Humph. Princess, you let the provincial officials set fires but won't even let the common people light a lamp.[115] If you've been up to those kinds of tricks, you had better relax a little, and let us have a go at her. Instead you had to get jealous. *Ai ya,* you gave me a good thrashing. I didn't even have a chance to eat the mutton, but still I smell as though I had.[116] The proof of your felony happens to have fallen into my very own hands. Sister Meiliu, tomorrow I am going to take this round white fan and inform the king about these goings-on. Princess, you will be in the same straits as a snake barbecued in a bamboo tube.[117] You will die straight away.

(Second Palace Woman:) Sister Nongtao, don't put our mistress in such an awkward position.

(First Palace Woman:) Sister Meiliu, she didn't even let us have a taste. We might as well make her walk the plank. Who told you, Princess, that you could beat up a wasp when you are just a butterfly? Your Highness, when this scandal touches you, spring won't last much longer.

(Second Palace Woman:) Since passions have reached such a point that no one can bear to turn back, we will let the east wind decide all.[118]

---

115. According to the Song author Lu You 陸游, an official named Tian Deng 田登 placed a taboo on the character for lamp (*deng* 燈) because the character was homophonous with his name. Lu You, *Lao xue'an biji,* 5.44. Over time the meaning of the anecdote changed to signify the abuse of power in allowing those of higher rank greater privilege than the common people.

116. In other words, I received no benefit and was still punished.

117. This is a folk saying. A snake usually curls when it is cooked; it would be cooked in a bamboo tube to maintain a straight shape. Here the phrase simply means that the princess will be as helpless as a snake being cooked in a bamboo tube, which can do nothing but wait for death.

118. The King has been repeatedly likened to the east wind, which blows the petals of the flower blossoms away and thus causes spring, the season of romance, to end.

(Exit.)

ACT IV

(King leads his palace servants on stage:) As long as they wear red sleeves, I don't ask who they are.[119] It has always been true that in the eyes of one dazzled by love, anyone can look like Xi Shi.[120] In a hundred years there are 36,000 days. If we amuse ourselves each day, how long will our pleasure last? Since I, the king of Linchuan, established the beauty Chen as my queen, even though I have dallied a bit, I have not stopped going to court to grant audience. He doesn't seem to take advantage of my favor over him, as would a Zheng Yingtao. I am just like Dongfang Shuo, who lived in defiance of convention![121] These past few days, because that Wang Sengbian fellow has the intention to annex us, I have been discussing military strategy, and haven't had any free time.[122] Today I've got a bit of leisure. I have no idea how my beauty is faring in the palace. Call the serving maids to come over.

(The house servants pass on the order:) The King summons the serving maids to come. (There is a response from backstage and the First Palace Woman enters holding the fan.)

(First Palace Woman:) The peaches and pears of the inner garden are fragrant just now, and no onlooker is allowed to break a branch. Good and evil will ultimately meet their just reward; it's only a matter of time. Your servant kowtows.

(King:) How has your mistress's health been these past two days?

---

119. In other words, I don't care whether my counterpart is male or female. The red sleeves may refer to Zheng Yingtao (see note 48 above), a male entertainer who was a favorite of the Zhao emperor Shi Hu.

120. See note 30.

121. Dongfang Shuo 東方朔 (193–54 bce) was a courtier who served Emperor Wu of the Han and was known for his wit and sagacity.

122. Wang Sengbian 王僧辯 (?–555 ce) was originally an ally of Chen Qian's uncle Chen Baqian, and then later his rival.

(First Palace Woman:) These past two days my mistress has become quite exhausted.

(King:) Why is your mistress exhausted?

(First Palace Woman:) Your slave dares not say.

(King:) What? What do you mean, you cannot say?

(First Palace Woman:) My mistress has been working hard to amuse the princess. She hasn't gotten up yet.

(King grunts angrily:) What kind of mouth have you got, you immodest slut? You must be jealous of your mistress, to stain her reputation so. Bind this slave and take her to be beheaded.

(First Palace Woman:) Sir, have pity on me. If you say I slander her, here is this white fan as proof.

(King:) Bring it here.

(King looks at the fan and reads the poem:) This is suspicious. Can it be that they have really done something like that? Call your mistress, quickly.

(First Palace Woman faces the stage entrance:) The king summons the mistress.

(Response from offstage:) The mistress is coming.

(Zigao enters followed by serving maids.)

[Shuangdiao mode:] "Xinshui ling" (Zigao sings:)

I heard an urgent summons at the Palace of Cloaked Fragrance.
I've come with such haste, and I can't help feeling exhausted.
This wasn't to watch a game of kickball in the South Palace;
Nor was it to play on the swing in the west garden.

(First Palace Woman:) Our king asks that the mistress come quickly.

(Zigao sings:) Why such an uproar? The cause of this disaster must be that round white fan.
(Sees the king:) Long live the king.

(King:) You needn't engage in formalities. My consort, what have you been up to in the palace these past two days?

(Zigao:) I haven't been up to anything.

"Zhuma ting" (Zigao sings:)

Spring on the embroidered couch is captivating.
I'm not accustomed to cutting and sewing, so the phoenix scissors have been idle.
By the carved window lattice, fragrant flowers flourish,
Occasionally when I finish my toilette I write on phoenix-patterned paper.
I listen to the orioles cry, but only in the Green Poplar Pavilion.
Watching the flowers fall, I don't go beyond the Green Moss Courtyard.
This past while, I have felt weak in the limbs.
I've been tired and listless,
And have been resting on a sleeping mat surrounded by red gauze netting.

(King:) Have you seen the princess or not?

"Chenzui dongfeng" (Zigao sings:)

I remember that day by the trellis of roseleaf raspberry.[123]
I recall that time beside the curtain of kingfisher jade.
I spied her face like a flower.

---

123. The *tu-mi* is the roseleaf raspberry.

Just as I had made several delicate and deep bows,
I was separated as far from her as though she were in the hermit's cave on the
     south side of Wu Mountain.[124]
Naturally, it was hard for me to ask whether the passing clouds were far or near.

(King:) Did you do anything with her or not?

"Yan'er luo" (Zigao sings:)

I hurriedly gathered my hair ornaments of kingfisher jade.
She slowly concealed herself with the white silk fan.
By what karmic affinity were we led to dally with each other?
Why did we tarry and linger?

(King:) You haven't much of an explanation, have you. Why have you
grown so gaunt?

"Desheng ling" (Zigao sings:)

Why have I lost my luster?
Yesterday I served you at a banquet.
Early in the morning I rose early to comb my hair and powder myself.
The spring morning was chill.
By chance I happened to stand before the lovely flowers.
For this reason my cheeks have hollowed before my beloved's eyes.
In front of these others,
Don't give me any trouble, you relentless King Xiang of Chu!

(King reveals the round fan:) So you haven't been up to anything. Take a
look at this thing. Where did it come from?

(Zigao:) I don't know where it came from.

(King:) You're still denying it? (Gestures to the First Palace Woman:)
Wasn't she a witness?

(First Palace Woman kneels:) It was really Nongtao who told on you.
Forgive me, mistress.

---

124. See note 1.

(Zigao kneels)

"Qiao pai'er" (Zigao sings:)

This is called having the culprit in hand as you seize an adulterer.
Catching a thief with the stolen goods in plain sight,
In such a case, one can't even employ the eloquence of the debaters Su Qin and
    Zhang Yi.[125]
Banish me to Chaoyang, eight thousand leagues away.[126]

King: You needn't stay on your knees. Rise. Nongtao, quickly call the princess here.

[First Palace Woman faces the stage exit and says:] The King calls for the princess. The affair of your round white fan has come to light.

[Princess enters:] Over in the palace I suddenly hear messengers hurrying me forth. Ashamed, I want to go forward but I keep hesitating. When the moon is full, soon dark clouds hide it. Once flowers have blossomed, storms quickly wreak havoc on them. Today my elder brother calls for me. It must be because that maid Nongtao has stirred up trouble. What should I do? There's no help for it. I have no choice other than to go and see my elder brother.
[Enters and sees him:] Long live my elder brother.

King: My sweet sister. A fine thing you've been up to!

Princess: Your little sister hasn't been up to anything.

Zigao: Miss, you needn't deny it. It was this servant, Nongtao, who took that fan and told your brother. [Kneels.] My lord, it had nothing to do with her. It's entirely my fault.

---

125. Su Qin 蘇秦 and Zhang Yi 張儀, debaters of the Warring States period.

126. Chaozhou 潮州 in Guangdong 廣東, supposedly an uninhabitable area. Wang Jide's phrasing here echoes Han Yu's 韓愈 poem "Qiuzi" 秋字 (Autumn words). *Han Changli quanji*, p. 163.

Sings to the tune of "Tianshui ling":

She is a stippled duck in the emerald water,
A many-hued phoenix in the cinnabar mountains.
A darling swallow of the Forbidden City.
She is simply so lovely.
I reason that my waiting for the moon to emerge,
The chance meeting with my phoenix mate,
The time I spent with her when stealing the incense,[127]
Are all determined by the karmic affinities of previous generations.

King: You're *still* offering excuses? I favored you so much, and you did this to me! [Points to the princess:] A fine princess. So young, and yet so reckless. Since you have done something like this, serving maids, give each of them a handkerchief. Let them hang themselves.

[Princess kneels and makes a crying gesture:] Older brother, have pity.

[Zigao kneels:] I have received such kindness from my lord. Now that I've done such a thing, who can I blame but myself? It's just that I've served you so long, and I'm worried that no one will cater to your needs as I do. Even in the underworld, your humble concubine will still be concerned about you.

Sings to the tune of "Zhegui ling":

My enticing figure kneels before the throne.
When I turn back and look at the Eternal Gate, my tears like rain fall.[128]
I will be in mortal pain as I twist my red tunic.
Snatch that belt of white silk several yards long.
Sadly I am approaching the underworld.
I will become a Wang Zhaojun, who quit the inner palace under duress.[129]

---

127. A reference to Han Shou; see note 105 above.
128. The Eternal Gate in the Han palace. Emperor Wu of the Han fell out of love with the Empress Chen. She had Sima Xiangru write the *Chang men fu* 長門賦 (Rhymeprose on the Eternal Gate), and gave it to the emperor.
129. Refers to the story of Wang Zhaojun 王昭君, told in the northern drama *Han gong qiu* 漢宮秋 (Autumn in the palace) by Ma Zhiyuan 馬致遠 (fl. c. 1280). Wang Zhaojun was recruited to join the emperor's harem by a minister named Mao Yanshou. See Ge Hong 葛洪, *Xijing zaji* 西京雜記, p. 9. Her family refused to give him the cus-

Or a Yang Guifei, who died and was buried in overgrown fields.
My king,
I'm just concerned that tonight you will sleep alone.
Who will be by your side?
You are in such a hurry to separate these two lovers,
But the pretty one whom you send off has everlasting regret.

[Cries] Master, after I, your concubine, die, you must take care of yourself from morn to night, in cold and in heat. Please do not think of me again.

[Princess cries:] Brother, have pity on us.

[King sighs tearfully, advances and stands at stage front. Zigao and the princess hold hands and cry. King turns his back:] Aah. How ought this affair to conclude? I must hold them responsible, for this offence is too grievous to be neglected. But if I have them both killed, not only would it be a pity to lose my sister, I'd never be able to find such an incomparable beauty again. I have a thought. . . . I've just been thinking of finding a husband for my little sister. Why not take this opportunity to make them husband and wife? What could be wrong with that? [Advances and sits down.] All right. Get up. The two of you deserve to die. But I can't bear to lose you. I'll make your wish come true, and make you husband and wife. [Zigao and Princess kowtow.]

Zigao: Long live his majesty.

Princess: Long live my elder brother.

"Yueshang haitang" (Zigao sings:)

Thank you, merciful god of spring, for your compassion.
That helped this private liaison of the Herd Boy and the Weaving Girl,
   our karmic destiny, bear fruit.[130]

---

tomary payoff, and so Mao ensured that the portrait of her that the emperor saw was flawed. She languished unknown in the harem until one day the emperor discovered her true beauty; Mao escaped to the Hun tribes bearing her true portrait, and the leader of the Huns demanded her in tribute, upon which she was sent to live among the Huns.

   130. See note 79 above.

A fragrant soul returning from death,
I am still trembling with fear,
We should unfurrow our brows,
And be as relaxed as Liu and Ruan at the Tiantai mountain.[131]

King: My beauty, let's have you make your vows to each other. Today you will be a bridegroom. You ought to return to your original garb. However, a gauze cap and black boots simply would be too ordinary. Don't change—we'll just keep you in women's dress. Nongtao, you're the maid who knew right from wrong. Come over here. We'll make you the maid of honor. Help the Queen and the Princess complete the rituals.

First Palace Woman [makes a gesture of assent]: In vain I was the enemy of their love. Unintentionally, I ended up helping them plead for mercy. [Recites aloud:]

Mistress, Heaven's gladness shines before you.
Princess, a red phoenix settles by your brow.[132]
The former brother-in-law becomes a husband.
And a bad marriage has been transformed into a good one.
Will the Mistress and the Princess please exchange their respects.

[Zigao and Princess bow.]

First Palace Woman: A moment of evening in spring is worth a thousand
  gold.[133]
Tonight, what need is there to probe any further?
Flowers grown with care often don't survive.

---

131. Liu Chen 劉晨 and Ruan Zhao 阮肇 were two men of the Eastern Han who went to the Tiantai 天臺 mountains to gather medicinal herbs and lost their way. They wandered without food for thirteen days, after which they found a peach tree. They ate of the fruit and then found magic cakes floating out of a grotto. Following the stream, they happened to meet two fairy women and were invited to their homes. After half a year they grew lonely for their homes and left. When they arrived home, they realized that seven generations had passed. See Liu Yiqing 劉義慶, *You ming lu* 幽明錄, p. 1.

132. Both "Heaven's gladness" and "red phoenix" refer to auspicious days for marriage. The "red phoenix" refers to a star that governs marriage.

133. The text echoes Su Shi 蘇軾's poem "Chun ye" 春夜 (Evening in spring). Su Shi, *Su Shi shi ji, juan* 48, p. 2592.

But if you casually stick a willow twig in the ground, its leaves grow thick
    and dense.
Will the Mistress and the Princess pay respects to his majesty?

[Zigao and Princess bow.]

First Palace Woman: Like Nongyu, the Princess has made an unusual
    match.[134]
She married a flute boy costumed as a palace lady.
If they hadn't experienced the penetrating cold,
Then how could the plum flowers blossom with such irresistible
    fragrance?[135]

King: My beauty, yesterday you were a queen. Today you are a husband of
a princess. Isn't this one of the strangest events the world has seen?

Zigao sings a reprise of "Yueshang haitang":

When I was the queen, you never saw my golden lotus feet.
As the husband of a princess, I cover myself with an embroidered stole.
It's this kind of pretending and costuming that make true and false hard to tell
    apart.
In these two types of marriage
I was heedless from start to finish, and all turned out as I wished.

King: Such a strange thing has happened today. Will not the historians of
tomorrow record this in *The Compilation of the Glamorous and Strange,*
and expect those who come after us to think it an amusing story?[136]

Zigao sings to the tune of "Dian qian huan":

This wedding, casually noted with a red brush on red paper,
Will stand out as a new oddity in the history books.

---

134. See note 1.
135. This couplet is from a poem by the Zen monk Huang Chai. See Puji, *Wudeng huiyuan, juan* 20, p. 14a.
136. The classical tale on which the play is based does in fact appear in the collection of
tales *Yanyi bian* 艷異編 (The compilation of the glamorous and strange). *Yanyi bian,* attrib. Wang Shizhen, p. 137.

A thousand years from now people will joke about it as they trim their silver
   lamps.
Who ever saw the face of the Dowager Empress Bo on the misty steps?[137]
Even though one ought to write literature in a spirit of jest,
How could we merely have said whatever came to mind?

King: I reckon that he who wrote this play only borrowed our story to
manifest his talents and inscribe his satire. Those of you in the audience
today should not take this too seriously.

All sing together to the tune of "Qingjiang yin":

We laugh that the flower on Jiang Yan's brush tip,
Has scattered into a thousand fragments of spring.[138]
Chill frost hastens the spittoon,[139]
A shower of red blossoms falls like sleet on the sandalwood clappers.[140]
A few sticks of rouge remain beneath the circling moon.[141]

---

137. The Dowager Empress Bo 薄 was the consort of the first emperor of the Han and
mother of Emperor Wen. (Fan Ye, *Hou Han shu, zhi* 志 8, p. 3177). The Tang poet Niu
Sengru 牛僧儒 wrote a fabulous tale concerning the Dowager Empress Bo. The implication is that this play, like Niu Sengru's tale, takes wild liberties with historical facts. Niu
Sengru, *Zhou Qin xingji* 周秦行記.
   138. The Liang 梁 dynasty poet Jiang Yan 江淹 dreamed that the Daoist Guo Pu 郭璞
came to him and asked him to surrender the brush he had lent him long ago. When he
woke from his dream, he found that his words no longer flowed, and people of the age said
that his talent had been exhausted. See Li Yanshou, *Nanshi*, p. 1451.
   139. "Chill frost" here may refer to the autumn years of one's life. The latter part of the
line may refer to an anecdote regarding the Eastern Jin aristocrat Wang Dun 王敦, who was
an aficionado of the poetry of Cao Cao, and loved the line "the old nag in the stable yearns to
go a thousand miles" 老驥伏櫪, 志在千里; he damaged his jade spittoon by beating on it
repeatedly as he chanted the line. The line above would then read, "In our hoary years, we are
inspired by Wang Dun, who broke his spittoon." See Fang Xuanling, *Jin shu, juan* 98, p. 2557.
   140. Clappers are a musical instrument used in the theater.
   141. The circling moon connotes the passing of time, the sticks of rouge transient
pleasure.

Reference Matter

Works Cited

Sources in Chinese

Aoki Masaru 青木正兒. *Zhongguo jinshi xiqu shi* 中國近世戲曲史. Ed. Wang Gulu 王古魯. Shanghai: Shangwu yinshuguan, 1936.

Bai Juyi 白居易. *Bai Juyi ji jianjiao* 白居易集箋校. Ed. Zhu Jincheng 朱金城. 6 vols. Shanghai: Shanghai guji chubanshe, 1988.

Ban Gu 班固. *Han shu* 漢書. 20 vols. Beijing: Zhonghua shuju, 1962.

Bian er chai 弁而釵 (Hairpins beneath a cap). Ed. Chen Ch'ing-hao 陳慶浩 and Wong Chiu-kuei 王秋桂. *Siwuxie huibao* 思無邪匯寶, vol. 6. Taipei: Taiwan daying baike, 1995.

Bian er chai. *Mingdai xiaoshuo jikan* 明代小説輯刊, series 2, vol. 2. Chengdu: Bashu shushe, 1955.

Cai Yi 蔡毅. *Zhongguo gudian xiqu xuba huibian* 中國古典戲曲序跋彙編. Ji'nan: Qilu shushe, 1989.

Cao Xueqin 曹雪芹. *Honglou meng sanjia pingben* 紅樓夢三家評本. Shanghai: Shanghai guji chubanshe, 1997.

Chen Duo 陳多 and Ye Changhai 葉長海, eds. *Zhongguo lidai julun xuanzhu* 中國歷代劇論選注. Changsha: Hunan wenyi chubanshe, 1987.

Chen Duo 陳多, Qi Senhua 齊森華, and Ye Changhai 葉長海, eds. *Zhongguo quxue da cidian* 中國曲學大辭典. Hangzhou: Zhejiang jiaoyu chubanshe, 1997.

Chen Fang 陳芳. *Qingchu zaju yanjiu* 清初雜劇研究. Taipei: Xuehai chubanshe, 1991.

Chen Hongmo 陳洪謨. *Zhishi yuwen* 治世餘聞. Beijing: Zhonghua shuju, 1985.

Chen Ruheng 陳汝衡. *Quyi wenxuan* 曲藝文選. Beijing: Zhongguo quyi chubanshe, 1985.

Chen Shidao 陳師道. *Houshanjushi wenji* 後山居士文集. Shanghai: Shanghai guji chubanshe, 1984.

Chen Weisong 陳維崧. *Huhailou ciji* 湖海樓詞集. In *Qing ba da mingjia ciji* 清八大名家詞集, ed. Qian Zhonglian 錢仲聯. Changsha: Yuelu shushe, 1992.

Cheng Zai 承載 and Qian Hang 錢杭. *Shiqi shiji Jiangnan shehui shenghuo* 十七世紀江南社會與生活. Hangzhou: Zhejiang renmin chubanshe, 1996.

Dai Bufan 戴不凡. *Xiaoshuo jianwen lu* 小說見聞錄. Hangzhou: Zhejiang renmin chubanshe, 1982.

Da Ming lü jijie 大明律集解. Beijing: Zhonghua shuju, 1991.

Duan Chengshi 段成式. *Youyang zazu* 酉陽雜俎. In *Yingyin Wenyuange Siku quanshu* 景印文淵閣四庫全書, vol. 1047. Taipei: Taiwan shangwu yinshuguan, 1983.

Du Fu 杜甫. *Dushi xiangzhu* 杜詩詳注. Ed. Qiu Zhao'ao 仇兆鰲. Beijing: Zhonghua shuju, 1989.

Du Mu 杜牧. *Fanchuan shiji zhu* 樊川詩集注. Ed. Feng Jiwu 馮集梧. Shanghai: Shanghai guji chubanshe, 1998.

Erya zhushu 爾雅注疏 in *Shisan jing zhushu* 十三經注疏. Ed. Li Xueqin 李學勤. Beijing: Beijing daxue chubanshe, 1999.

Fan Lian 范廉. *Yunjian jumu chao* 雲間據目鈔. In *Biji xiaoshuo daguan* 筆記小說大觀, vol. 6. Yangzhou: Jiangsu Guanglin guji keyinshe, 1984.

Fan Ye 範曄, ed. *Hou Han shu* 後漢書. 12 vols. Beijing: Zhonghua shuju, 1965.

Feng Menglong 馮夢龍. *Qingshi leilüe* 情史類略. In *Feng Menglong quanji* 馮夢龍全集, ed. Wei Tongxian 魏同賢, vols. 37–38. Shanghai: Shanghai guji chubanshe, 1993.

Feng Yuanjun 馮沅君. *Guju shuohui* 古劇說彙. Shanghai: Shangwu yinshuguan, 1947.

Fu Xihua 傅惜華. *Mingdai chuanqi quanmu* 明代傳奇全目. Shanghai: Renmin wenxue chubanshe, 1959.

———. *Mingdai zaju quanmu* 明代雜劇全目. Beijing: Zuojia chubanshe, 1958.

Gan Bao 甘寶. *Sou shen ji* 搜神記. Taipei: Liren shuju, 1982.

Ge Hong 葛洪. *Xijing zaji* 西京雜記. Beijing: Zhonghua shuju, 1985.

Gong Dingzi 龔鼎孳. *Dingshantang quanji* 定山堂全集. Hefei: Tingyi shuwu, 1883.

Gu Qiyuan 顧起元. *Kezuo zhuiyu* 客座贅語. Beijing: Zhonghua shuju, 1987.

Guan Hanqing 關漢卿. *Guan Hanqing ji* 關漢卿集. Ed. Ma Xinlai 馬欣來. Taiyuan: Shanxi renmin chubanshe, 1996.

Guo Yingde 郭英德. *Ming Qing chuanqi shi* 明清傳奇史. Nanjing: Jiangsu guji chubanshe, 1999.

———. *Ming Qing wenren chuanqi yanjiu* 明清文人傳奇研究. Beijing: Beijing shifan daxue chubanshe, 1994.

Han Feizi 韓非子. *Han Feizi jishi* 韓非子集釋. Ed. Chen Qiyou 陳奇猷. Shanghai: Shanghai renmin chubanshe, 1974.

Han Yu 韓愈. *Han Changli quanji* 韓昌黎全集. Ed. Yang Yi 楊義 and Jiang Yewei 蔣業偉. Beijing: Yanshan chubanshe, 1996.

———. *Han Changli shiji xinian jishi* 韓昌黎詩集繫年集釋. Ed. Qian Zhonglian 錢仲聯. Shanghai: Shanghai guji chubanshe, 1994.

Han Zhongli dutuo Lan Caihe 漢鍾離度脫藍彩和. In *Guben xiqu congkan* 古本戲曲叢刊, 4th series. Shanghai: Shangwu yinshuguan, 1958.

He Liangjun 何良俊. *Siyou zhai congshu* 四友齋叢書. Beijing: Zhonghua shuju, 1997.

Hong Sheng 洪昇. *Chang sheng dian* 長生殿. Ed. Xu Shuofang 徐朔方. Beijing: Renmin wenxue chubanshe, 1993.

Hong Shiliang 洪式良. *Liu Jingting pingzhuan* 柳敬亭評傳. Shanghai: Shanghai gudian wenxue chubanshe, 1956.

Hu Shi 胡適. *Hu Shi wencun* 胡適文存. Taipei: Yuandong chubanshe, 1971.

Hua Shu 華淑. *Pidian xiaoshi* 癖癲小史. In idem, *Xianqing xiaopin* 閒情小品. Wanli ed. Copy in the Harvard-Yenching Library, Cambridge, MA.

Hua Wei 華偉 and Wang Ayling 王瓊玲, eds. *Ming Qing xiqu guoji yantaohui lunwenji* 明清戲曲國際研討會論文集. Taipei: Zhongyang yanjiuyuan, Zhongguo wenzhe yanjiusuo choubeichu, 1998.

Huang An 黃安. *Xijin shixiao lu* 錫金識小錄. Preface dated 1752. Copy in Harvard-Yenching Library, Cambridge, MA.

Huang Wenyang 黃文暘, comp. *Quhai zongmu tiyao* 曲海總目提要. 2 vols. Beijing: Renmin chubanshe, 1959.

Huang Zongxi 黃宗羲. "Liu Jingting zhuan" 柳敬亭傳. In *Huang Lizhou wenji* 黃梨洲文集. Beijing: Zhonghua shuju, 1959.

Jiang Yingke 江盈科. *Jiang Yingke ji* 江盈科集. Ed. Huang Rensheng 黃仁生. Changsha: Yuelu shushe, 1997.

———. *Xuetao xieshi* 雪濤諧史 (Xuetao's history of jests). In *Ming Qing xiaohua shizhong* 明清笑話十種, ed. Li Xiao 李曉 and Ai Ping 愛平. Xi'an: Sanqin chubanshe, 1998.

Jiao Xun 焦循. *Jushuo* 劇說. Taipei: Shangwu yinshuguan, 1973.

Jin Ping Mei cihua 金瓶梅詞話. Hong Kong: Taiping shuju, 1993.

Jin shu 晉書. Ed. Fang Xuanling 房玄齡. Beijing: Zhonghua shuju, 1974.

Jing Junjian 經君健. *Qing dai shehui de jianmin dengji* 清代社會的賤民等級. Hangzhou: Zhejiang renmin chubanshe, 1993.

———. "Shilun Qingdai dengji zhidu" 試論清代等級制度. *Zhongguo shehui kexue* 中國社會科學, no. 6 (1980): 149–71.

Koake Takeshi (Xiaoming Xiong) 小明雄. *Zhongguo tongxing'ai shilu* 中國同性愛史錄. Hongkong: Fenhong sanjiao chubanshe, 1984.

Kong Decheng 孔德成. *Ming Qing sanwen xuanzhu* 明清散文選注. Taipei: Zhengzhong shuju, 1974.

Kong Shangren 孔尚任. *Kong Shangren shiwenji* 孔尚任詩文集. Ed. Wang Weilin 汪蔚林. Beijing: Zhonghua shuju, 1962.

———. *Taohua shan* 桃花扇. Ed. Wang Jisi 王季思 et al. Beijing: Renmin wenxue chubanshe, 1991.

Langxian 浪仙, pseud. *Shi dian tou* 石點頭. Shanghai: Shanghai guji chubanshe, 1935.

Li Bai 李白. *Li Bai ji jiaozhu* 李白集校註. Ed. Qu Tuiyuan 瞿蛻園 and Zhu Jincheng 朱金城. Shanghai: Shanghai guji chubanshe, 1998.

Li Huimian 李惠綿. "Wang Jide qulun yanjiu" 王驥德曲論研究. Master's thesis, National Taiwan University, 1992.

———. *Xiqu yaoji jieti* 戲曲要籍解題. Taipei: Zhengzhong shuju, 1991.

Li Qingzhao 李清照. *Li Qingzhao ji* 李清照集. Ed. Lin Yangci 林洋慈. Taipei: Guojia shudian, 1983.

Li Rihua 李日華. *Weishuixuan riji* 味水軒日記. Shanghai: Shanghai yuandong chubanshe, 1996.

Li Shangyin 李商隱. *Li Shangyin shige jijie* 李商隱詩歌集解. Ed. Liu Xuekai 劉學鍇 and Yu Shucheng 餘恕誠. Beijing: Zhonghua shuju, 1996.

Li Xiusheng 李修生, ed. *Guben xiqu jumu tiyao* 古本戲曲劇目提要. Beijing: Wenhua yishu chubanshe, 1997.

Li Yanshou 李延壽, ed. *Nan shi* 南史. 6 vols. Beijing: Zhonghua shuju, 1975.

Li Yu 李漁. *Li Yu quanji* 李漁全集. Ed. Guan Feimeng 關非蒙. Hangzhou: Zhejiang guji chubanshe, 1998.

Li Zhi 李贄. *Li shi fenshu / Xu fenshu* 李氏贄焚書續焚書. Kyoto: Chūbun shuppansha, 1971.

Liao Ben 廖奔. *Zhongguo gudai juchang shi* 中國古代劇場史. Henan: Zhongzhou guji chubanshe, 1997.

———. *Zhongguo xiqu tushi* 中國戲曲圖史. Henan: Henan jiaoyu chubanshe, 1996.

Liu Shide 劉世德. *Mingdai sanwen xuanzhu* 明代散文選注. Shanghai: Shanghai guji chubanshe, 1980.

Liu Xiang 劉向. *Liexian zhuan* 列仙傳. Shanghai: Shangwu yinshuguan, 1936.

———. *Zhanguo ce* 戰國策. Shanghai: Shanghai guji chubanshe, 1998.

Liu Xu 劉昫. *Jiu Tang shu* 舊唐書. Beijing: Zhonghua shuju, 1975.

Liu Yiqing 劉義慶. *Shishuo xinyu jiaojian* 世説新語校箋. Shanghai: Shanghai guji chubanshe, 1982.

———. *You ming lu* 幽明錄. Beijing: Wenhua yishu chubanshe, 1988.

Liu Zongyuan 柳宗元. *Liu Zongyuan quanji* 柳宗元全集. Ed. Cao Minggang 曹明綱. Shanghai: Shanghai guji chubanshe, 1997.

Liu Zongzhou 劉宗周. *Liuzi quanshu* 劉子全書. Taipei: Huawen shuju, 1968.

Luo Di 洛地. *Xiqu yu Zhejiang* 戲曲與浙江. Hangzhou: Zhejiang renmin chubanshe, 1991.

Lu Eting 陸萼庭. *Kunju yanchu shigao* 崑劇演出史稿. Shanghai: Shanghai wenyi chubanshe, 1980.

———. "Qingdai quanben xi yanchu shulun" 清代全本戲演出述論. In *Ming Qing xiqu guoji yantaohui lunwenji* 明清戲曲國際研討會論文集, ed. Hua Wei 華偉 and Wang Ayling 王瓊玲. Taipei: Zhongyang yanjiuyuan, Zhongguo wenzhe yanjiusuo choubeichu, 1998.

———. *Qingdai xiqujia congkao* 清代戲曲家叢考. Shanghai: Xuelin chubanshe, 1995.

Lu Qinli 逯欽立, ed. *Xian Qin Han Wei Jin Nanbei chao shi* 先秦漢魏晉南北朝詩. Beijing: Zhonghua shuju, 1982.

Lu Rong 陸容. *Shuyuan zaji* 菽園雜記. Beijing: Zhonghua shuju, 1985.

Lu You 陸游. *Lao xue'an biji* 老學庵筆記. Shanghai: Shangwu yinshuguan, 1936.

Lunyu jishi 論語集釋. Ed. Cheng Shude 程樹德, Cheng Junying 程俊英, and Jiang Jianyuan 蔣見元. Beijing: Zhonghua shuju, 1990.

Luo Jintang 羅錦堂. *Zhongguo sanqu shi* 中國散曲史. Taipei: Zhongguo wenhua daxue chubanbu, 1983.

Mao Xiang 冒襄. *Tong ren ji* 同人集. Late Ming. Reprinted in *Rugao Mao shi congshu* 如皋冒氏叢書, ed. Mao Guangsheng. N.p.: n.d. [1911–18].

Mao Xiaotong 毛效同, ed. *Tang Xianzu yanjiu ziliao huibian* 湯顯祖研究資料彙編. Shanghai: Shanghai guji chubanshe, 1986.

Meng Qi 孟棨. *Benshi shi* 本事詩. In *Benshi shi / Xu benshi shi / Benshi ci* 本事詩/續本事詩/本事詞. Shanghai: Shanghai guji chubanshe, 1991.

Meng Sen 孟森. *Xinshi congkan* 心史叢刊. Shenyang: Liaoning jiaoyu chubanshe, 1988.

Mingdai xiaoshuo jikan 明代小説集刊. Ed. Hou Zhongyi 侯忠義. Vol. 6, no. 2, 3: 525–76. Chengdu: Bashu shushe, 1993.

Niu Sengru 牛僧儒. *Zhou Qin xingji* 周秦行記. Taipei: Yiwen yinshuguan, 1965.

Niu Xiu 鈕秀. *Gu sheng* 觚賸. Taibei: Wenhai chubanshe, 1982.

Pan Zhiheng 潘之恒. *Pan Zhiheng quhua* 潘之恒曲話. Ed. Wang Xiaoyi 汪效倚. Beijing: Zhongguo xiju chubanshe, 1988.

Pu Songling 蒲松齡. *Liaozhai zhiyi* 聊齋誌異. Ed. Ren Duxing 任篤行. Ji'nan: Qilu shushe, 2000.

———. *Liaozhai zhiyi huijiao huizhu huiping ben* 聊齋誌異會校會注會評本. Ed. Zhang Youhe 張友鶴. Taipei: Liren shuju, 1991.

Qi Biaojia 祁彪佳. *Qi Zhongmin gong riji* 祁忠敏公日記. Beijing: Shumu wenxian chubanshe, 1987.

Qian Nanyang 錢南揚, ed. *Tang Xianzu xiqu ji* 湯顯祖戲曲集. Shanghai: Shanghai guji chubanshe, 1978.

Qian Qianyi 錢謙益. *Liechao shiji xiaozhuan* 列朝詩集小傳. Shanghai: Shanghai guji chubanshe, 1983.

———. *Muzhai you xue ji* 牧齋有學集. Shanghai: Shanghai guji chubanshe, 1996.

Qingci jishi huiping 清詞紀事會評. Ed. You Yiding 尤以丁 and You Zhenzhong 尤振中. Hefei: Huangshan shushe, 1995.

Qinhuai yuke 秦淮寓客, pseud. *Lüchuang nüshi* 綠窗女史. Facsimile reprint of late Ming edition. *Ming Qing shanben xiaoshuo congkan* 明清善本小説叢刊, 2nd series. Taipei: Tianyi chubanshe, 1985.

Quan Ming sanqu 全明散曲. Ed. Xie Boyang 謝伯陽. Ji'nan: Qilu shushe, 1994.

Quan Song ci jianbian 全宋詞簡編. Ed. Tang Guizhang 唐圭璋. Shanghai: Shanghai guji chubanshe, 1995.

Quan Tang shi 全唐詩. Beijing: Zhonghua shuju, 1985.

Shaoshi xianshu zhuan 少室先姝傳. Taipei: Yiwen yinshuguan, 1966.

Shen Defu 沈德符. *Wanli yehuo bian* 萬歷野獲編. 3 vols. Beijing: Zhonghua shuju, 1980.

Shen Jing 沈璟. *Bo xiao ji* 博笑記. Shanghai: Shangwu yinshuguan, 1954.

Shen Tai 沈泰, ed. *Shengming zaju* 盛明雜劇. 2 vols. Beijing: Zhongguo xiju chubanshe, 1958.

Shi Maoshi zhuanshu 詩毛氏傳疏. Ed. Chen Huan 陳奐. Beijing: Beijingshi Zhongguo shudian, 1984.

Shijing zhuxi 詩經注析. Ed. Cheng Junying 程俊英 and Jiang Jianyuan 蔣見元. Beijing: Zhonghua shuju, 1991.

Sima Qian 司馬遷. *Shiji* 史記. 10 vols. Beijing: Zhonghua shuju, 1985.

Shi Puji 釋普濟. *Wudeng huiyuan* 五燈會元. Taipei: Guangwen shuju, 1971.

Shisan jing zhushu 十三經注疏. Ed. Ye Shaojun 葉紹鈞. Beijing: Zhonghua shuju, 1987.

Song shi chao 宋詩鈔. Ed. Wu Zhizhen 吳之振, Lü Liuliang 呂留良, and Wu Zimu 吳自牧. Shanghai: Shanghai sanlian shudian, 1988.

Su Shi 蘇軾. *Su Shi shiji* 蘇軾詩集. Beijing: Zhonghua shuju, 1996.

———. *Su Shi wenji* 蘇軾文集. Beijing: Zhonghua shuju, 1996.

Sun Minji 孫民記. *Youling kaoshu* 優伶考述. Beijing: Zhongguo xiju chubanshe, 1995.

Sun Chongtao 孫崇濤 and Xu Hongtu 徐宏圖. *Xiqu youling shi* 戲曲優伶史. Beijing: Wenhua yishu chubanshe, 1995.

Taiping guangji 太平廣記. Ed. Li Fang 李昉. Beijing: Renmin wenxue chubanshe, 1959.

Taiping yulan 太平禦覽. Ed. Li Fang 李昉. 4 vols. Beijing: Zhonghua shuju, 1960.

Tan Zhengbi 譚正璧. *Sanyan Liangpai ziliao huibian* 三言兩拍資料彙編. 2 vols. Shanghai: Shanghai guji chubanshe, 1980.

Tang Song ba da jia wenzhang jinghua 唐宋八大家文章精華. Ed. Liu Yuchang 劉禹昌 and Xiong Lihui 熊禮匯. Wuhan: Hubei renmin chubanshe, 1997.

Tang Xianzu 湯顯祖. *Mudan ting* 牡丹亭. Ed. Xu Shuofang 徐朔方 and Yang Xiaomei 楊笑梅. Beijing: Renmin wenxue chubanshe, 1993.

———. *Tang Xianzu quanji* 湯顯祖全集. Ed. Xu Shuofang 徐朔方. Beijing: Beijing guji chubanshe, 1999.

———. *Tang Xianzu shiwen ji* 湯顯祖詩文集. Ed. Xu Shuofang 徐朔方. Shanghai: Shanghai guji chubanshe, 1979.

Tao Shiling 陶奭齡. *Xiaochaisang nannan lu* 小柴桑喃喃錄. Wuning: Li Weizhi, Chongzhen era (1628–44). Microform. 2 vols.

Tao Yuanming 陶淵明. *Tao Yuanming ji jiaojian* 陶淵明集校箋. Ed. Yang Yong 楊勇. Taipei: Zhengwen shuju, 1987.

Tian Shouzhen 田守真, ed. *Ming sanqu jishi* 明散曲紀事. Chengdu: Bashu shushe, 1996.

Wang An-Chi 王安祈. *Mingdai chuanqi zhi juchang ji qi yishu* 明代傳奇之劇場及其藝術. Taipei: Xuesheng shuju, 1986.

———. *Mingdai xiqu wulun* 明代戲曲五論. Taipei: Da'an chubanshe, 1990.

Wang Heng 王衡. *Zhen kuilei* 眞傀儡. In *Mingren zaju xuan* 明人雜劇選, ed. Mei Chu 梅初. Taipei: Xunxian chuban gongsi, 1973.

Wang Jide 王驥德. *Fangzhuguan yuefu* 方諸館樂府. Changsha: Shangwu yinshuguan, 1948.

———. *Nan wanghou* 男王后. In *Shengming zaju* 盛明雜劇, ed. Shen Tai 沈泰. 2 vols. Beijing: Zhongguo xiju chubanshe, 1958.

———. *Qulü* 曲律. Ed. Chen Duo 陳多 and Ye Changhai 葉長海. Hunan: Hunan renmin chubanshe, 1983.

———. *Qulü* 曲律. In *Zhongguo gudian xiqu lunzhu jicheng* 中國古典戲曲論著集成, vol. 4. Beijing: Zhongguo xiju chubanshe, 1959.

Wang Liqi 王利器. *Yuan Ming Qing sandai jinhui xiaoshuo xiqu shiliao* 元明清三代禁毀小說戲曲史料. Taipei: Heluo tushu chubanshe, 1980.

Wang Shifu 王實甫. *Xixiang ji* 西廂記. Ed. Wang Jisi 王季思. Shanghai: Shanghai guji chubanshe, 1996.

Wang Shizhen 王世禎. *Chibei outan* 池北偶談. Beijing: Zhonghua shuju, 1982.

Wang Shunu 王書奴. *Zhongguo changji shi* 中國娼妓史. Shanghai: Sanlian shudian, 1988.

Wu Weiye 吳偉業. *Wu Meicun quanji* 吳梅村全集. Shanghai: Shanghai guji chubanshe, 1990.

———. *Wu Meicun shiji jianzhu* 吳梅村詩集箋注. Shanghai: Shanghai guji chubanshe, 1983.

———. *Wu shi jilan* 吳詩集覽. Taipei: Zhonghua shuju, 1966.

Wu Zao 吳藻. *Yinjiu du "Li sao" tu: Qiao ying* 飲酒讀離騷圖喬影. In *Qingren zaju erji* 清人雜劇二集, ed. Zheng Zhenduo 鄭振鐸. Hong Kong: Kongmen shudian, 1969.

Wu Zimu 吳自牧. *Meng liang lu* 夢梁錄. In *Dongjing Menghualu wai sizhong* 東京夢華錄外四種. Beijing: Xinhua shudian, 1998.

Xiqu luncong 戲曲論叢. Ed. Zhao Jingshen 趙景深. Lanzhou: Gansu renmin chubanshe, 1986.

Xiangyan congshu 香豔叢書. Ed. Zhang Tinghua 張廷華. Beijing: Renmin wenxue chubanshe, 1990.

Xiao Tong 蕭統, comp. *Wenxuan* 文選. Shanghai: Shanghai guji chubanshe, 1997.

Xie Guozhen 謝國楨. *Ming Qing biji tancong* 明清筆記談叢. Kowloon: Huaxia chubanshe, 1967.

Xie Zhaozhe 謝肇淛. *Wuzazu* 五雜俎. Beijing: Zhonghua shuju, 1959.

Xu benshi shi 續本事詩. In *Benshi shi / Xu benshi shi / Benshi ci* 本事詩/續本事詩/本事詞. Shanghai: Shanghai guji chubanshe, 1991.

Xu Fuming 徐扶明. *"Mudan ting" yanjiu ziliao kaoshi* 牡丹亭研究資料考釋. Shanghai: Shanghai guji chubanshe, 1987.

———. *Yuan Ming Qing xiqu tansuo* 元明清戲曲探索. Hangzhou: Zhejiang guji chubanshe, 1986.

Xu Fuzuo 徐復祚. *"Qu lun fu lu"* 曲論附錄. *Sanjia cunlao qu tan* 三家村老曲談. Shanghai: Zhonghua, 1940.

Xu Ling 徐陵, comp. *Yutai xinyong* 玉台新詠. Annot. and trans. Uchida Sen-nosuke 內田泉之助. 2 vols. Tokyo: Meiji shoin, 1974.

Xu Qiu 徐釚. *Ciyuan congtan* 詞苑叢談. Ed. Tang Guizhang 唐圭璋. Shanghai guji chubanshe, 1981.

Xu Shuofang 徐朔方. *Lun Tang Xianzu ji qita* 論湯顯祖及其他. Shanghai: Shanghai guji chubanshe, 1983.

———. *Xu Shuofang ji* 徐朔方集. Hangzhou: Zhejiang guji chubanshe, 1993.

Xu Shupi 徐樹丕. *Shi xiao lu* 識小錄. Shanghai: Shanghai shudian, 1994.

Xu Wei 徐渭. *Sisheng yuan* 四聲猿. Ed. Zhou Zhongming 周中明. Shanghai: Shanghai guji chubanshe, 1984.

Yagisawa Hajime 八木澤元. *Mingdai juzuojia yanjiu* 明代劇作家研究. Trans. Luo Jintang 羅錦堂. Hong Kong: Longmen shudian, 1966.

Yanyi bian 豔異編. Comp. Wang Shizhen 王世貞 (attrib.). Yangzhou: Jiangsu guangling guji keyingshe, 1998.

Yang Bojun 楊柏峻, ed. *Mengzi shizhu* 孟子釋注. Beijing: Zhonghua shuju, 1990.

Yao Silian 姚思廉, ed. *Chen shu* 陳書. Beijing: Zhonghua shuju, 1972.

Ye Changhai 葉長海. *Qu xue yu xiju xue* 曲學與戲劇學. Shanghai: Xuelin chubanshe, 1999.

———. *Zhongguo xiju xue shigao* 中國戲劇學史稿. Shanghai: Shanghai wenyi chubanshe, 1987.

Ye Changhai 葉長海, ed. *Wang Jide Qulü yanjiu* 王驥德曲律研究. Shanghai: Zhongguo xiju chubanshe, 1983.

Ye Gongchuo 葉恭綽. *Qingdai xuezhe xiangzhuan heji* 清代學者象傳合集. Taipei: Wenhai shuju, 1969.

Yu Huai 餘懷. *Banqiao zayu* 板橋雜語. In *Yanshi congchao* 艷史叢鈔. Taipei: Guangwen shuju, 1976.

Yuan Hongdao 袁宏道. *Yuan Hongdao ji jianjiao* 袁宏道集箋校. Ed. Qian Bocheng 錢伯城. Shanghai: Shanghai guji chubanshe, 1979.

———. *Yuan Zhonglang suibi* 袁中郎隨筆. Beijing: Zuojia chubanshe, 1995.

Yuanqu xuan 元曲選. Ed. Zang Maoxun 臧懋循. Beijing: Zhonghua shuju, 1991.

Yuefu shiji 樂府詩集. Ed. Guo Maoqian 郭茂倩. Beijing: Zhonghua shuju, 1991.

Zeng Yongyi 曾永義. "Mingdai zaju yanjin de qingshi" 明代雜劇演進的情勢. In *Zhongguo gudian wenxue lunwen jingxuan congkan* 中國古典文學論文精選叢刊. Ed. Zeng Yongli. Taipei: Youshi wenhua shiye gongsi, 1980.

———. *Ming zaju gailun* 明雜劇概論. Taipei: Xuehai chubanshe, 1979.

———. *Shuo xiqu* 說戲曲. Taipei: Lianjing chuban shiye gongsi, 1997.

———. *Shuo su wenxue* 說俗文學. Taipei: Lianjing chubanshe, 1980.

Zhaijin qiyin 摘錦奇音. Ed. Gong Zhengwo 龔正我. In *Shanben xiqu congkan* 善本戲曲叢刊, ed. Wang Ch'iu-kuei 王秋桂. Taipei: Taiwan xuesheng shuju, 1984.

Zhang Cixi 張次溪. *Qingdai yandu liyuan shiliao zheng xubian* 清代燕都梨園史料正續編. Beijing: Zhongguo xiju chubanshe, 1988.

Zhang Dai 張岱. *Langhuan wenji* 瑯嬛文集. Changsha: Yuelu shushe, 1985.

———. *Tao'an mengyi / Xihu mengxun* 陶庵夢憶／西湖夢尋. Shanghai: Shanghai guji chubanshe, 1982.

Zhang Faying 張發穎. *Zhongguo xiban shi* 中國戲班史. Shenyang: Shenyang chubanshe, 1991.

Zhang Geng 張庚 and Guo Hancheng 郭漢城. *Zhongguo xiqu tongshi* 中國戲曲通史. 3 vols. Taipei: Danqing tushu, 1985.

Zhang Haipeng 張海鵬 et al., eds. *Ming Qing Huishang ziliao xuanbian* 明清徽商資料選編. Hefei: Huangshan shushe, 1985.

Zhang Han 張瀚. *Songchuang mengyu* 松窗夢語. Beijing: Zhonghua shuju, 1997.

Zhang Hua 張華. *Bo wu zhi* 博物志. In *Yingyin Wenyuange Siku quanshu* 景印文淵閣四庫全書, vol. 1047. Taipei: Taiwan shangwu yinshuguan, 1983.

Zhang Jin 張津. *Siming tujing shi'erjuan* 四明圖經十二卷. In *Xuxiu siku quanshu* 續修四庫全書, vol. 704. Shanghai: Shanghai guji chubanshe, 1995.

Zhao Nanxing 趙南星. *Xiao zan* 笑贊. In *Ming Qing xiaohua shizhong* 明清笑話十種, ed. Li Xiao 李曉 and Ai Ping 愛平. Xi'an: Sanqin chubanshe, 1998.

Zhao Shanlin 趙山林. *Lidai yongju shige xuanzhu* 歷代詠劇詩歌選注. Beijing: Shumu wenxian chubanshe, 1988.

———. *Zhongguo xiqu guanzhong xue* 中國戲曲觀眾學. Shanghai: Huadong shifan daxue chubanshe, 1990.

Zhongguo gudian xiqu lunzhu jicheng 中國古典戲曲論著集成. Beijing: Zhongguo xiju chubanshe, 1959.

Zheng Xuan 鄭玄. *Zhou li* 周禮. Shanghai: Shangwu yinshu guan, 1922.

Zhou Lianggong 周亮工 and Zhou Zaidu 周在都. *Laigu tang cangshu: jiaji shizhong* 賴古堂藏書：甲集十種. N.p.: Zhoushi Laigu tang 周氏賴古堂, 1829.

Zhou Mi 周密. *Wulin jiushi* 五林舊事. In *Dongjing menghua lu wai sizhong* 東京夢華錄外四種. Beijing: Xinhua shudian, 1998.

Zhou Yibai 周貽白. *Zhongguo xiqu lunji* 中國戲曲論集. Beijing: Zhongguo xiju chubanshe, 1960.

———. *Zhongguo xiqu shi* 中國戲曲史. 3 vols. Shanghai: Zhonghua shuju, 1953.

Zhu Jianming 朱建明. "Cong Yuhuatang riji kan Mingdai Shanghai de xiqu yanchu" 從玉華堂日記看明代上海的戲曲演出. In Zhao Jingshen 趙景深, ed., *Xiqu luncong di yi ji*, 戲曲論叢第一輯. Lanzhou: Gansu renmin chubanshe, 1986, pp. 130–49.

Zhu Yizun 朱彝尊. *Pu shu ting ji* 曝書亭集. Taipei: Shijie shuju, 1935.

Zhuang Yifu 莊一拂. *Gudian xiqu cunmu huikao* 古典戲曲存目彙考. 3 vols. Shanghai: Shanghai guji chubanshe, 1982.

Zhuangzi jishi 莊子集釋. Ed. Guo Qingfan 郭慶藩; comp. Wang Xiaoyu 王孝魚. Beijing: Zhonghua shuju, 1961.

Sources in Western Languages

Agnew, Jean-Christophe. *Worlds Apart: The Market and the Theater in Anglo-American Thought, 1550–1750*. Cambridge, Eng.: Cambridge University Press, 1986.

Appadurai, Arjun, ed. *The Social Life of Things: Commodities in Cultural Perspective*. Cambridge, Eng.: Cambridge University Press, 1986.

Auerbach, Nina. *Private Theatricals: The Lives of the Victorians*. Cambridge, MA: Harvard University Press, 1990.

Bai, Qianshen. "Fu Shan and the Transformation of Chinese Calligraphy in the Seventeenth Century." Ph.D. diss., Yale University, 1996.

———. *Fu Shan's World: The Transformation of Chinese Calligraphy in the Seventeenth Century*. Cambridge, MA: Harvard University Asia Center, 2003.

———. "Turning Point: Politics, Art and Intellectual Life During the *Boxue hongci* Examination (1678–1679)." Unpublished paper.

Bakthin, Mikhail. *The Dialogic Imagination*. Ed. Michael Holmquist; trans. Caryl Emerson and Michael Holmquist. Austin: University of Texas Press, 1981.

Barish, Jonas. *The Antitheatrical Prejudice*. Berkeley: University of California Press, 1981.

Barr, Allan. "Pu Songling and *Liaozhai zhiyi*: A Study of Textual Transmission, Biographical Background, and Literary Antecedents." Ph.D. diss., Oxford University, 1983.

Barthes, Roland. *The Fashion System*. Trans. Matthew Ward and Richard Howard. Berkeley: University of California Press, 1983.

Belsky, Richard. *Localities at the Center: Native Place, Space, and Power in Late Imperial Beijing*. Cambridge, MA: Harvard University Asia Center, 2005.

Bentley, Tamara Heimarck. "Authenticity in a New Key: Chen Hongshou's Figurative Oeuvre, 'Authentic Emotion,' and the Late Ming Market." Ph.D. diss., University of Michigan, 1996.

Berger, Henry. *Imaginary Audition: Shakespeare on Stage and Page*. Berkeley: University of California Press, 1989.

Billiter, Jean-François. *Li Zhi: philosophe maudit (1527–1602)*. Geneva: Librairie Droz, 1979.

Birch, Cyril. *Scenes for Mandarins: The Elite Theater of the Ming*. New York: Columbia University Press, 1995.

Birch, Cyril, ed. and trans. *Anthology of Chinese Literature from Early Times to the Fourteenth Century*, New York: Grove Press, 1965.

———. *The Peach Blossom Fan*. Berkeley: University of California Press, 1976.

———. *The Peony Pavilion*. Bloomington: Indiana University Press, 1980.

Blair, Ann. *The Theater of Nature: Jean Boudin and Renaissance Science*. Princeton: Princeton University Press, 1997.

Bourdieu, Pierre. *Distinction: A Social Critique of the Judgment of Taste*. Trans. Richard Nice. Cambridge, MA: Harvard University Press, 1984.

———. *Language and Symbolic Power*. Cambridge, MA: Harvard University Press, 1991.

———. *Outline of a Theory of Practice*. Trans. R. Nice. Cambridge, Eng.: Cambridge University Press, 1977.

Bray, Alan. "Homosexuality and the Signs of Male Friendship in Elizabethan England." In *Queering the Renaissance*, ed. Jonathan Goldberg. Durham: Duke University Press, 1994, pp. 40–61.

———. *Homosexuality in Renaissance England*. London: Gay Men's Press, 1982.

Brecht, Bertolt. *Brecht on Theatre: The Development of an Aesthetic*. Ed. and trans. John Willett. New York: Hill and Wang, 1964.

Brewer, John. *The Pleasures of the Imagination: English Culture in the Eighteenth Century*. New York: Farrar Straus & Giroux, 1997.

Brokaw, Cynthia. *The Ledgers of Merit and Demerit: Social Change and Moral Order in Late Imperial China*. Princeton: Princeton University Press, 1991.

Brook, Timothy. *The Confusions of Pleasure: Commerce and Culture in Ming China*. Berkeley: University of California Press, 1998.

———. *Praying for Power: Buddhism and the Formation of Gentry Society in Late-Ming China*. Cambridge, MA: Harvard University, Council on East Asian Studies, 1993.

Brooks, Peter. *The Melodramatic Imagination: Balzac, Henry James, and the Mode of Excess*. New York: Columbia University Press, 1985.

Brown, Steven T. *Theatricalities of Power: The Cultural Politics of Noh*. Stanford University Press, 2001.

Bruster, Douglas. *Drama and the Market in the Age of Shakespeare*. Cambridge, Eng.: Cambridge University Press, 1992.

Cady, Joseph. "Masculine Love: Renaissance Writing and the 'New Invention' of Homosexuality." *Journal of Homosexuality* 23, no. 1 (Jan.–Feb. 1992): 9–43.

Cahill, James. *The Compelling Image: Nature and Style in Seventeenth-Century Chinese Painting*. Cambridge, MA: Harvard University Press, 1982.

———. *The Distant Mountains: Chinese Painting in the Late Ming Dynasty, 1570–1644*. New York: Weatherhill, 1982.

———. *Fantastics and Eccentrics in Chinese Painting*. New York: Arno Press, 1976.

———. *The Painter's Practice: How Artists Lived and Worked in Traditional China.* New York: Columbia University Press, 1994.

———. *The Restless Landscape.* Berkeley: University Art Museum, 1971.

Carlitz, Katherine. "Desire, Danger, and the Body: Stories of Women's Virtue in Late Ming China." In *Engendering China: Women, Culture, and the State,* ed. Christine Gilmartin, Lisa Rofel, Gail Hershatter, and Tyrene White. Cambridge, MA: Harvard University Press, 1994.

———. *The Rhetoric of the "Chin P'ing-mei."* Bloomington: Indiana University Press, 1986.

———. "Printing as Performance: Literati Playwright-Publishers of the Late Ming." In *Printing and Book Culture in Late Imperial China,* ed. Cynthia J. Brokaw and Kai-wing Chow. Berkeley: University of California Press, 2005.

———. "The Social Uses of Female Virtue in Late Ming Editions of *Lienü zhuan.*" *Late Imperial China* 12, no. 2 (Dec. 1991): 117–52.

Chan, Wing-tsit, comp. and trans. *A Sourcebook in Chinese Philosophy.* Princeton: Princeton University Press, 1963.

Chang, Kang-I Sun. "The Idea of the Mask in Wu Wei-yeh (1609–1671)." *Harvard Journal of Asiatic Studies* 48 (1988): 289–320.

———. *The Late-Ming Poet Ch'en Tzu-lung: Crises of Love and Loyalism.* New Haven: Yale University Press, 1991.

Chaves, Jonathan. "The Panoply of Images: A Reconsideration of the Literary Theory of the Kong-an School." In *Theories of the Arts in China,* ed. Susan Bush and Christian Murck. Princeton: Princeton University Press, 1983, pp. 341–64.

———. *Pilgrim of the Clouds: Poems and Essays by Yuan Hongdao and His Brothers.* New York: Weatherhill, 1978.

Cheng P'ei-k'ai. "T'ang Hsien-tsu, Tung Ch'i-ch'ang, and the Search for Cultural Aesthetics in the Late Ming." *Proceedings of the Tung Ch'i-ch'ang International Symposium,* ed. Wai-ching Ho. Kansas City: Nelson-Atkins Museum of Art, 1991, 2: 1–12.

———. "Reality and Imagination: Li Chih and T'ang Hsien-tsu in Search of Authenticity." Ph.D. diss., Yale University, 1980.

Chou, Chih-p'ing. *Yüan Hung-tao and the Kung-an School.* New York: Cambridge University Press, 1988.

Chow, Kai-wing. *The Rise of Confucian Ritualism in Late Imperial China: Ethics, Classics, and Lineage Discourse.* Stanford: Stanford University Press, 1994.

Chow Tse-tung. *The May Fourth Movement.* Cambridge, MA: Harvard University Press, 1960.

Chu, Madeleine Men-li. "Ch'en Wei-sung, The Tz'u Poet." Ph.D. diss., University of Arizona, 1978.

Clunas, Craig. "'All in the Best Possible Taste': Ming Dynasty Material Culture in the Light of the Novel *Jin Ping Mei.*" *Bulletin of the Oriental Ceramic Society of Hong Kong* 11 (1994–97): 9–19.

———. "Connoisseurs and Aficionados: The Real and the Fake in Ming China (1369–1644)." *Why Fakes Matter: Essays on Problems of Authenticity,* ed. Mark Jones. London: British Museum Press, 1992, pp. 151–56.

———. "The Novel *Jin Ping Mei* as a Source for the Study of Ming Furniture." *Orientations* 23, no. 1 (Jan. 92): 60–68.

———. *Pictures and Visuality in Early Modern China.* London: Reaktion Books, 1997.

———. *Superfluous Things: Material Culture and Social Status in Early Modern China.* Urbana: University of Illinois Press, 1991.

Davis, Tracy C., and Postlewait, Thomas. "Theatricality: an Introduction." In *Theatricality,* ed. Tracy C. Davis and Thomas Postlewait. Cambridge, Eng.: Cambridge University Press, 2003, pp. 1–39.

de Bary, William Theodore. "Individualism and Humanitarianism in Late Ming Thought." In *Self and Society in Ming Thought,* ed. idem. New York: Columbia University Press, 1970, pp. 145–247.

Dolby, William. *A History of Chinese Drama.* London: Paul Elek, 1976.

Egan, Charles. "Reconsidering the Role of Folk Songs in Pre-T'ang Yüeh-fu Development." *T'oung Pao* 86 (2000): 47–99.

Egan, Ronald C. *Word, Image, and Deed in the Life of Su Shi.* Cambridge, MA: Harvard University Press, 1994.

Elman, Benjamin A. *A Cultural History of Civil Examinations in Late Imperial China.* Berkeley: University of California Press, 2000.

————. "The Formation of 'Dao Learning' as Imperial Ideology During the Early Ming Dynasty." In *Culture and State in Chinese History: Conventions, Accommodations, and Critiques*, ed. Theodore Huters, R. Bin Wong, and Pauline Yu. Stanford: Stanford University Press, 1997.

————. *From Philosophy to Philology: Intellectual and Social Aspects of Change in Late Imperial China*. Cambridge, MA: Harvard University, Council on East Asian Studies, 1990.

Elvin, Mark. "Female Virtue and the State in China." *Past and Present* 104 (1984): 111–52.

Epstein, Maram. *Competing Discourses: Orthodoxy, Authenticity, and Engendered Meanings in Late Imperial Chinese Fiction*. Cambridge, MA: Harvard University Asia Center, 2001.

Faure, Bernard. *The Red Thread: Buddhist Approaches to Sexuality*. Princeton: Princeton University Press, 1998.

Faurot, Jeannette. "*Four Cries of a Gibbon*: A *Tsa-chu* Cycle by the Ming Dramatist Hsu Wei (1521–1593)." Ph.D. diss., University of California, Berkeley, 1972.

Fei, Faye Chunfang, *Chinese Theories of Theater and Performance from Confucius to the Present*. Ann Arbor: University of Michigan Press, 1999.

Feldman, Martha. "Magic Mirrors and the *Seria* Stage: Thoughts Toward a Ritual View." *Journal of the American Musicological Society* 49, no. 3 (Fall 1995): 423–83.

————. *Opera and Sovereignty: Transforming Myths in Eighteenth-Century Italy*. Chicago: University of Chicago Press, 2007.

Fèral, Josette. "Theatricality: The Specificity of Theatrical Language." *SubStance* 31, no. 2&3 (2002): 94–108.

Ferguson, James. "The Cultural Topography of Wealth: Commodity Paths and the Structure of Property in Rural Lesotho." In *American Anthropologist* 94, no. 1 (1992): 55–73.

Ferris, Lesley, ed. *Crossing the Stage: Controversies on Cross-dressing*. New York: Routledge, Kegan, Paul, 1993.

Fong, Grace S. "Writing Self and Writing Lives: Shen Shanbao's (1808–1862) Gender Auto/Biographical Practices." *Nan nü: Men, Women and Gender in Early and Imperial China* 2, no. 2 (Dec. 2000): 259–303.

Foster, Susan Leigh. "Walking and Other Choreographic Tactics: Danced Inventions of Theatricality and Performativity." *SubStance* 31, no. 2&3 (2002): 125–46.

Foucault, Michel. *The History of Sexuality*. 3 vols. New York: Vintage Books, 1980.

Freedman, Barbara. *Staging the Gaze: Postmodernism, Psychoanalysis and Shakespearean Comedy*. Ithaca: Cornell University Press, 1991.

Freud, Sigmund. "Fetishism." In *The Standard Edition of the Complete Psychological Works of Sigmund Freud*, vol. 21. Trans. James Strachey. London: Hogarth Press, 1961.

Fried, Michael. *Absorption and Theatricality: Painting and the Beholder in the Age of Diderot*. Chicago: University of Chicago Press, 1980.

Furth, Charlotte. "Androgynous Males and Deficient Females: Biology and Gender Boundaries in Sixteenth- and Seventeenth-Century China." *Late Imperial China* 9, no. 2 (Dec. 1988): 1–31.

Fuss, Diana. *Essentially Speaking: Feminism, Nature, & Difference*. New York: Routledge, 1989.

Gallagher, Catherine, and Stephen Greenblatt. *Practicing New Historicism*. Chicago: University of Chicago Press, 2000.

Garber, Marjorie. "The Logic of the Transvestite: The Roaring Girl." In *Staging the Renaissance*, ed. David Scott Kastan and Peter Stallybrass. New York: Routledge, 1991, pp. 221–34.

———. *Vested Interests: Cross-Dressing and Cultural Anxiety*. New York: Routledge, 1992.

———. *Vice Versa: Bisexuality and the Eroticism of Everyday Life*. New York: Simon and Schuster, 1995.

Ginzburg, Carlo. *Myths, Emblems, and Clues*. Trans. John and Anne C. Tedeschi. London: Hutchinson Radius, 1990.

Girard, René. *Deceit, Desire, and the Novel: Self and Other in Literary Structure*. Trans. Yvonne Freccero. Baltimore: Johns Hopkins Press, 1965.

Goldberg, Jonathan. *Sodometries: Renaissance Texts, Modern Sexualities*. Stanford: Stanford University Press, 1992.

Goldman, Andrea. "Actors and Aficionados in Qing Dynasty Texts of Theatrical Connoisseurship." *Harvard Journal of Asiatic Studies* 68, no.1 (June 2008): 1–56.

Goldman, Andrea. "Opera in the City: Theatrical Performance and Urban Aesthetics in Beijing, 1770–1870." P.h.D. diss., University of California, Berkeley, 2003.

Goodrich, L. Carrington, and Chaoying Fang, eds. *Dictionary of Ming Biography, 1368–1644.* 4 vols. New York: Columbia University Press, 1976.

Gran, Anne-Britt. "The Fall of Theatricality in the Age of Modernity." *SubStance* 31, no. 2&3 (2002): 251–64.

Grant, Beata, and Idema, Wilt. *The Red Brush: Writing Women of Imperial China.* Cambridge, MA: Harvard University Asia Center, 2004.

Greenblatt, Stephen. *Renaissance Self-Fashioning: From More to Shakespeare.* Chicago: University of Chicago Press, 1980.

———. *Shakespearean Negotiations.* Berkeley: University of California Press, 1986.

Guo, Qitao. *Ritual Opera and Mercantile Lineage: The Confucian Transformation of Popular Culture in Late Imperial Huizhou.* Stanford: Stanford University Press, 2005.

Hall, John. *The Advancement of Learning.* Ed. A. K. Croston. Liverpool: University Press, 1953.

Halperin, David M. "Forgetting Foucault: Acts, Identities and the History of Sexuality." *Representations* 63 (Summer 1998): 93–120.

———. "Historicizing the Subject of Desire: Sexual Preferences and Erotic Identities in the Pseudo-Lucianic Erotes." In *Foucault and the Writing of History,* ed. Jan Goldstein. Oxford: Basil Blackwell, 1994, pp. 19–34.

———. *One Hundred Years of Homosexuality and Other Essays on Greek Love.* New York: Routledge, Kegan, Paul, 1990.

Halperin, David M.; John J. Winkler; and Froma I. Zeitlin, eds. *Before Sexuality: The Construction of Erotic Experience in the Ancient Greek World.* Princeton: Princeton University Press, 1989.

Halpern, Richard. *The Poetics of Primitive Accumulation: English Renaissance Culture and Genealogy of Capital.* Ithaca: Cornell University Press, 1991.

Hanan, Patrick. *The Chinese Short Story: Studies in Dating, Authorship and Composition*. Cambridge, MA: Harvard-Yenching Institute, 1973.

———. *The Chinese Vernacular Story*. Cambridge, MA: Harvard University Press, 1981.

———. *The Invention of Li Yu*. Cambridge, MA: Harvard University Press, 1988.

Hansen, Miriam. *Babel and Babylon: Spectatorship in American Silent Films*. Cambridge, MA: Harvard University Press, 1991.

Hansson, Anders. *Chinese Outcasts: Discrimination and Emancipation in Late Imperial China*. New York: Brill, 1996.

Hawkes, David, trans. *The Story of the Stone*. 5 vols. Harmondsworth, Eng.: Penguin, 1973.

Hay, Jonathan. *Shitao: Painting and Modernity in Early Qing China*. Cambridge, Eng.: Cambridge University Press, 2001.

Hay, John. "The Body Invisible in Chinese Art." In *Body, Subject and Power in China*, ed. Angela Zito and Tani E. Barlow. Chicago: Chicago University Press, 1994, pp. 42–77.

He, Yuming, "Productive Space: Performance Texts in the Late Ming." Ph.D. diss., University of Calfornia, Berkeley, 2002.

Hegel, George. *Phenomenology of Spirit*. Oxford: Clarendon, 1977.

Hegel, Robert E. *The Novel in Seventeenth-Century China*. New York: Columbia University Press, 1981.

———. *Reading Illustrated Fiction in Late Imperial China*. Stanford: Stanford University Press, 1998.

Henry, Eric. *Chinese Amusement: The Lively Plays of Li Yü*. Hamden, CT: Archon Books, 1980.

Hinsch, Bret. *Passions of the Cut Sleeve: The Male Homosexual Tradition in China*. Berkeley: University of California Press, 1990.

Ho, Lai Lin. "Cultural Transformation and the Chinese Idea of a Historical Play." Ph.D. diss., Princeton University, 1999.

Howard, Jean. "Cross-Dressing, the Theater, and Gender Struggle in Early Modern England." In *Crossing the Stage: Controversies on Cross-Dressing*, ed. Lesley Ferris. London: Routledge, Kegan, Paul, 1993, pp. 20–47.

Hsi, Angela Ning-jy Sun. "Social and Economic Status of the Merchant Class of the Ming Dynasty, 1368–1644." Ph.D. diss., University of Illinois at Urbana-Champaign, 1974.

Hsu, Pi-ching. "Feng Meng-lung's Treasury of Laughs: Humorous Satire on Seventeenth-Century Culture and Society." *Journal of Asian Studies* 57, no. 4 (Nov. 1998): 1042–68.

Hsu, Tao-ch'ing. *The Chinese Conception of the Theatre.* Seattle: University of Washington Press, 1985.

Hu, John. "Ming Dynasty Drama." In *Chinese Theater: From Its Origins to the Present Day*, ed. Colin Mackerras. Honolulu: University of Hawai'i Press, 1983, pp. 60–91.

Hu Ying. *Tales of Translation: Composing the New Woman in China, 1899–1918.* Stanford: Stanford University Press, 2000.

Huang Hung, Josephine. *Ming Drama.* Taipei: Heritage Press, 1966.

Huang, Martin W. *Desire and Fictional Narrative in Late Imperial China.* Cambridge, MA: Harvard University Asia Center. 2001.

———. *Literati and Self-Representation: Autobiographical Sensibility in the Eighteenth-Century Chinese Novel.* Stanford: Stanford University Press, 1995.

Hummel, Arthur, ed. *Eminent Chinese of the Ch'ing Period.* 2 vols. Washington, DC: U.S. Government Printing Office, 1943–44.

Hung, Ming-shui. *The Romantic Vision of Yüan Hung-tao, Late Ming Poet and Critic.* Taipei: Bookman Books, 1997.

———. "Yüan Hung-tao and the Late-Ming Literary and Intellectual Movement." Ph.D. diss., University of Wisconsin, 1974.

Idema, Wilt. *Chinese Vernacular Fiction: The Formative Period.* Leiden: Brill, 1974.

———. *The Dramatic Oeuvre of Chu Yu-tun (1379–1439).* Leiden: Brill, 1985.

Idema, Wilt, and Lloyd Haft. *A Guide to Chinese Literature.* Ann Arbor: University of Michigan, Center for Chinese Studies, 1997.

Idema, Wilt, and Stephen H. West. *Chinese Theater, 1100–1450: A Source Book.* Wiesbaden: Steiner, 1982.

Ihara Saikaku, *The Great Mirror of Male Love*. Trans. Paul Gordon Schalow. Stanford: Stanford University Press, 1990.

Jackson, Shannon. "Geneaologies of Performance and Gender Theory." In *Theatricality*, ed. Tracy C. Davis and Thomas Postlewait. Cambridge, Eng.: Cambridge University Press, 2003, pp. 186–213.

Jestrovic, Silvija. "Theatricality as Estrangement of Art and Life in the Russian Avant-garde." *SubStance* 31, no. 2&3 (2002): 42–56.

Jiang, Jin. "Heresy and Persecution in Late Ming Society: Reinterpreting the Case of Li Zhi." *Late Imperial China* 22, no. 2. (Dec. 2001): 1–34.

Jing, Shen. "Role Types in the Paired Fish, a *Chuanqi* Play." *Asian Theater Journal* 20, no. 2 (Fall 2003): 226–36.

Johnson, Barbara. *The Critical Difference*. Baltimore: Johns Hopkins University Press, 1981.

———. *A World of Difference*. Baltimore: Johns Hopkins University Press, 1987.

Johnson, David; Andrew Nathan; and Evelyn Rawski, eds. *Popular Culture in Late-Imperial China*. Berkeley: University of California Press, 1983.

Jones, Ann Rosalind, and Peter Stallybrass. *Renaissance Clothing and the Materials of Memory*. Cambridge, Eng.: Cambridge University Press, 2000.

Kastan, David, and Peter Stallybrass, eds. *Staging the Renaissance: Reinterpretations of Elizabethan and Jacobean Theater*. New York: Routledge, 1991.

Kessler, Lawrence. *K'ang-hsi and the Consolidation of Ch'ing Rule, 1661–1684*. Chicago: University of Chicago Press, 1976.

Ko, Dorothy. "Bondage in Time: Footbinding and Fashion Theory." In *Modern Chinese Literary and Cultural Studies in the Age of Theory: Reimagining a Field*, ed. Rey Chow. Durham: Duke University Press, 2000.

———. "The Complicity of Women in the Qing Good Woman Cult." In *Family Process and Political Process in Modern Chinese History*, pt. 1. 2 vols. Taipei: Academia Sinica, Institute of Modern History, 1992.

———. "Pursuing Talent and Virtue: Education and Women's Culture in Seventeenth- and Eighteenth-Century China." *Late Imperial China* 13, no. 1 (June 1992): 9–39.

———. *Teachers of the Inner Chambers: Women and Culture in Seventeenth-Century China*. Stanford: Stanford University Press, 1994.

Kopytoff, Igor. "The Cultural Biography of Things: Commoditization as Process." In *The Social Life of Things: Commodities in Cultural Perspective*, ed. Arjun Appadurai. Cambridge, Eng.: Cambridge University Press, 1986. pp. 64–91.

Lam, Ling Hon. "Emotional Indifference: Exploring Exteriority in Late Imperial Chinese Drama and Fiction," Ph.D. diss., University of Chicago, 2006.

———. "The Matriarch's Private Ears: Performance, Reading, Censorship, and the Fabrication of Interiority in *The Story of the Stone*." *Harvard Journal of Asiatic Studies* 65, no. 2 (December 2005): 357–415.

———. "What Is Wrong with *The Wrong Career*: The Archaeology of a Theater That Refutes the Metatheatrical." Unpublished paper.

Lau, D. C. *A Concordance to the Zhanguoce*. Taiwan: Commercial Press, 1993.

Leung, Kai-cheong. "Hsu Wei as Drama Critic: An Annotated Translation of *Nan-tzu hsu lu*, an Account of Southern Drama." Ph.D. diss., University of California, Berkeley, 1974.

Levy, André. "Un document sur la querelle des anciens et des modernes more sinico." *T'oung Pao* 54, no. 4–5 (1968): 251–74.

Levy, Howard. trans. *A Feast of Mists and Flowers: The Gay Quarters of Nanking at the End of the Ming*. Yokohama: Privately printed, 1966.

Lévi-Strauss, Claude. *The Elementary Structures of Kinship*. Boston: Beacon Press, 1969.

Li, Qiancheng. *Fictions of Enlightenment: "Journey to the West," "Tower of Myriad Mirrors," and "Dream of the Red Chamber."* Honolulu: University of Hawai'i Press, 2004.

Li, Siu Leung. *Cross-Dressing in Chinese Opera*. Hong Kong: Hong Kong University, 2003.

Li, Wai-yee. *Enchantment and Disenchantment: Love and Illusion in Chinese Literature*. Princeton: Princeton University Press, 1993.

———. "Heroic Women in Qing Literature." *Harvard Journal of Asiatic Studies* 50, no. 2. (Dec. 1999): 363–443.

———. "The Late Ming Courtesan: Invention of a Cultural Ideal." In *Writing Women in Late Imperial China*, ed. Ellen Widmer and Kang-I Sun Chang. Stanford: Stanford University Press, 1997, pp. 46–73.

———. "The Representation of History in *The Peach Blossom Fan*." *Journal of American Oriental Society* 115, no. 3 (1995): 421–33.

Lu, Tina. *Persons, Roles and Minds: Identity in "Peony Pavilion" and "Peach Blossom Fan."* Stanford: Stanford University Press, 2001.

Lynn, Richard John. "Alternate Routes to Self-Realization in Ming Theories of Poetry." In *Theories of Chinese Art*, ed. Susan Bush and Christian Murck. Princeton: Princeton University Press, 1983, pp. 317–41.

Mackerras, Colin. *Chinese Drama: A Historical Survey*. Beijing: New World Press, 1990.

———. "The Drama of the Qing Dynasty." In *Chinese Theater: From Its Origins to the Present Day*, ed. idem. Honolulu: University of Hawaii Press, 1983, pp. 92–117.

———. *The Rise of the Peking Opera, 1770–1870*. London: Oxford University Press, 1972.

Maclean, Marie. *Narrative as Performance*. New York: Routledge, Kegan, Paul, 1988.

Mahmood, Saba. *Politics of Piety: The Islamic Revival and the Feminist Subject*. Princeton: Princeton University Press, 2005.

Mair, Victor, ed. *The Columbia Anthology of Chinese Literature*. New York: Columbia University Press, 1994.

Malinowski, Bronislaw. *Argonauts of the Western Pacific*. Pacific Heights, IL: Waveland Press, 1984 [1922].

Mann, Susan. *Precious Records: Women in China's Long Eighteenth Century*. Stanford: Stanford University Press, 1997.

Mann, Susan, and Yu-Yin Cheng, eds. *Under Confucian Eyes: Writings on Gender in Chinese History*. Berkeley: University of California Press, 2001.

Mark, Lindy Li. "Kunju and Theatre in the Transvestite Novel *Pinhua baojian*." *Chinoperl Papers* 14 (1986): 37–59.

Marshall, David. *The Figure of the Theater: Shaftesbury, Adam Smith, Defoe and George Eliot*. New York: Columbia University Press, 1986.

Mather, Richard B., trans. *Shih-shuo hsin-yu: A New Account of Tales of the World*. Minneapolis: University of Minnesota Press, 1976.

Mauss, Marcel. *The Gift.* Trans. Ian Cunnisan. London: Cohen and West, 1954.

McClintock, Ann. *Imperial Leather: Race, Gender, and Sexuality in the Colonial Context.* New York: Routledge, 1995.

McCraw, John. *Chinese Lyricists of the Seventeenth Century.* Honolulu: University of Hawai'i Press, 1990.

McDermott, Joseph. *A Social History of the Chinese Book: Books and Literati Culture in Late-Imperial China.* Hong Kong: Hong Kong University Press, 2006.

McIntosh, Mary. "The Homosexual Role." In *Forms of Desire: Sexual Orientation and the Social-Constructionist Controversy,* ed. Edward Stein. New York: Routledge, 1992, pp. 465–67.

McLaren, Anne. *Chinese Popular Culture and Ming Chantefables.* Boston: Brill, 1998.

McMahon, Keith. *Causality and Containment in Seventeenth-Century Chinese Fiction.* Leiden: Brill, 1988.

McRae, John R. *The Northern School and the Formation of Early Ch'an Buddhism.* Honolulu: University of Hawai'i Press, 1986.

Meijer, M. J. "Homosexual Offenses in Ch'ing Law." *T'oung Pao* 71 (1985): 109–33.

Meyer-Fong, Tobie S. *Building Culture in Early Qing Yangzhou.* Stanford: Stanford University Press, 2003.

Montrose, Louis. *The Purpose of Playing: Shakespeare and the Cultural Politics of the Elizabethan Theatre.* Chicago: University of Chicago Press, 1996.

Mori, Mitsuya. "The Structure of Theatre: A Japanese View of Theatricality." *SubStance* 31, no. 2&3 (2002): 73–93.

Mowry, Hua-yuan Li. *Chinese Love Stories from Ch'ing-shih.* Hamden, CT: Archon Books, 1983.

Mullaney, Stephen. *The Place of the Stage: License, Play and Power in Renaissance England.* Chicago: University of Chicago Press, 1983.

Ng, Vivien. "Homosexuality and the State in Late-Imperial China." In *Hidden from History: Reclaiming the Gay and Lesbian Past,* ed. Martin Duberman, Martha Vicinus, and George Chauncey, Jr. New York: Penguin Books, 1989.

Nienhauser, William H., Jr., ed. *The Indiana Companion to Chinese Literature.* Bloomington: Indiana University Press, 1986.

Owen, Stephen. *An Anthology of Traditional Chinese Literature: Beginnings to 1911.* New York: Norton, 1998.

———. "The End of the Past: Rewriting Chinese Literary History in the Early Republic." In *The Appropriation of Cultural Capital: China's May Fourth Project,* ed. Milena Doleželová-Velingerová and Oldřich Král. Cambridge, MA: Harvard University Asia Center, 2001, pp. 167–92.

———. *Mi-lou: Poetry and the Labyrinth of Desire.* Cambridge, MA: Harvard University Press, 1989.

———. *Traditional Chinese Poetry and Poetics: Omen of the World.* Madison: University of Wisconsin Press, 1985.

———. "Place: Meditations on the Past at Jinling" *Harvard Journal of Asiatic Studies* 50, no. 2 (Dec. 1990): 447–58.

———. *Readings in Chinese Literary Thought.* Cambridge, MA: Harvard University, Council on East Asian Studies, 1992.

———. *Remembrances: The Experience of the Past in Classical Chinese Literature.* Cambridge, MA: Harvard University Press, 1985.

———. "Salvaging the Poetic in the Qing." In *Culture and State in Chinese History: Conventions, Accommodations and Critiques,* ed. Theodore Huters, R. Bin Wong, and Pauline Yu, pp. 105–29. Stanford: Stanford University Press, 1997.

———. *Traditional Chinese Poetry and Poetics: Omen of the World.* Madison: University of Wisconsin Press, 1985.

Pflugfelder, Gregory M. *Cartographies of Desire: Male-Male Sexuality in Japanese Discourse.* Berkeley: University of California Press, 1999.

Phelan, Peggy. *Unmarked: The Politics of Performance.* New York: Routledge, 1993.

Pietz, William. "The Problem of the Fetish, I." *Res* 9 (Spring 1985): 5–16.

———. "The Problem of the Fetish, II: The Origin of the Fetish." *Res* 13 (Spring 1987): 23–45.

———. "The Problem of the Fetish, IIIa: Bosman's Guinea and the Enlightenment Theory of Fetishism." *Res* 16 (Autumn 1988): 105–23.

Pollard, David. *A Chinese Look at Literature.* Berkeley: University of California Press, 1973.

Postelwait, Thomas. "Theatricality and Antitheatricality in Renaissance London." In *Theatricality*, ed. Tracy C. Davis and Thomas Postlewait. Cambridge, Eng.: Cambridge University Press, 2003, pp. 90–126.

Prosser, Jay. *Second Skins: The Body Narratives of Transsexuality.* New York: Columbia University Press, 1998.

Rawski, Evelyn. *Education and Popular Literacy in Ch'ing China.* Ann Arbor: University of Michigan Press, 1979.

Reinelt, Janelle. "The Politics of Discourse: Performativity Meets Theatricality." *SubStance* 31, no. 2&3 (2002): 201–15.

Robertson, Jennifer. *Takarazuka: Sexual Politics and Popular Culture in Modern Japan.* Berkeley: University of California Press, 1998.

Robertson, Maureen. "Voicing the Feminine: Constructions of the Gendered Subject in Lyric Poetry by Women of Medieval and Late Imperial China." *Late Imperial China* 13, no. 1 (June 1992): 63–110.

Rolston, David, ed. *How to Read the Chinese Novel.* Princeton: Princeton University Press, 1990.

Rosello, Mireille. *Infiltrating Culture: Power and Identity in Contemporary Women's Writing.* New York: Manchester University Press, 1996.

Roy, David T. "The Case for T'ang Hsien-tsu's Authorship of the *Jin Ping Mei*." *CLEAR* 8 (1986): 31–62.

Roy, David T., trans. *Ch'in P'ing Mei* (The Plum in the Golden Vase), vol. 1, *The Gathering*; vol. 2, *The Rivals*. Princeton: Princeton University Press, 1993, 2001.

Ruan Fang-fu and Tsai Yung-mei. "Male Homosexuality in Traditional Chinese Literature." *Journal of Homosexuality* 14 (1987): 21–33.

Rubin, Gayle. "The Traffic in Women: Notes Toward a Political Economy of Sex." In *Toward an Anthropology of Women*, ed. Rayna Reiter. New York: Monthly Review Press, 1975, pp. 157–210.

Schwartz, Benjamin. *The World of Thought in Ancient China.* Cambridge, MA: Harvard University Press, 1985.

Sedgwick, Eve Kosofsky. *Between Men: English Literature and Male Homosocial Desire.* New York: Columbia University Press, 1985.

————. *Epistemology of the Closet.* Berkeley: University of California Press, 1990.

Shen, Grant Guangren. *Elite Theatre in Ming China.* New York: Routledge, 2005.

Sieber, Patricia. *Theaters of Desire: Authors, Readers, and the Reproduction of Early Chinese Song-Drama, 1300–2000.* New York: Palgrave Macmillan, 2003.

Smith, Joanna F. Handlin. "Gardens in Ch'i Piao-chia's Social World: Wealth and Values in Late-Ming Kiangnan." *Journal of Asian Studies* 51, no. 1 (Feb. 1992): 55–81.

Sommer, Matthew H. "The Penetrated Male in Late Imperial China: Judicial Construction and Social Stigma." *Modern China* 23, no. 2 (Apr. 1997): 140–80.

————. *Sex, Law, and Society in Late Imperial China.* Stanford: Stanford University Press, 2000.

Spence, Jonathan. *The Memory Palaces of Matteo Ricci.* New York: Viking, 1984.

————. *Ts'ao Yin and the K'ang-hsi Emperor: Bondservant and Master.* New Haven: Yale University Press, 1966.

Stallybrass, Peter. "Transvestism and the 'Body Beneath': Speculating on the Boy Actor." In *Desire on the Renaissance Stage*, ed. Susan Zimmerman. New York: Routledge, 1992.

Stallybrass, Peter, and Allon White. *The Politics and Poetics of Transgression.* Ithaca: Cornell University Press, 1986.

Starr, Chloe. "Shifting Boundaries: Gender in *Pinhua baojian.*" *Nan nü: Men, Women, and Gender in Early Imperial China* 1, no. 2 (Oct. 1999): 268–302.

Strassberg, Richard E. "The Authentic Self in 17th-Century China." *Tamkang Review* 8, no. 2 (1977): 61–100.

————. *The World of K'ung Shang-jen: A Man of Letters in Early Ch'ing China.* New York: Columbia University Press, 1983.

Strathern, Marilyn. *The Gender of the Gift.* Berkeley: University of California Press, 1988.

Struve, Lynn. *Voices from the Ming-Qing Cataclysm: China in Tiger's Jaws.* New Haven: Yale University Press, 1993.

Swatek, Catherine C. "Feng Menglong's Romantic Dream: Strategies of Containment in His Revision of *The Peony Pavilion*." Ph.D. diss., Columbia University, 1990.

———. *The Peony Pavilion Onstage: Four Centuries in the Career of a Chinese Drama*. Ann Arbor: University of Michigan, Center for East Asian Studies, 2002.

Tanaka Issei. "The Social and Historical Context of Ming-Qing Local Drama." In *Popular Culture in Late Imperial China*, ed. David Johnson, Andrew J. Nathan, and Evelyn S. Rawski. Berkeley: University of California Press, 1985, pp. 143–60.

Teiser, Stephen A. *The Ghost Festival in Medieval China*. Princeton: Princeton University Press, 1988.

Tian, Min. "Male *Dan*: The Paradox of Sex, Acting, and Perception of Female Impersonation in Traditional Chinese Theatre." *Asian Theatre Journal* 17, no. 1 (Spring 2000): 78–97.

T'ien, Ju-k'ang. *Male Anxiety and Female Chastity: A Comparative Study of Chinese Ethical Values in Ming-Ch'ing Times*. Leiden: Brill, 1988.

Tomlinson, Gary. *Metaphysical Song: An Essay on Opera*. Princeton: Princeton University Press, 1999.

Traub, Valerie. *Desire and Anxiety: Circulations of Sexuality in Shakespearean Drama*. New York: Routledge, 1992.

Trilling, Lionel. *Sincerity and Authenticity*. Cambridge, MA: Harvard University Press, 1971.

Van Zoeren, Steven. *Poetry and Personality: Reading, Exegesis and Hermeneutics in Traditional China*. Stanford: Stanford University Press, 1991.

Vinograd, Richard. *Boundaries of the Self: Chinese Paintings, 1600–1900*. Cambridge, Eng.: Cambridge University Press, 1992.

———. "Vision and Revision in Seventeenth-Century Painting." In *Proceedings of the Tung Ch'i-ch'ang International Symposium*, ed. Wai-ching Ho. Kansas City: Nelson-Atkins Museum of Art, 1991, pp. 1–28.

Vitiello, Giovanni. "The Dragon's Whim: Ming and Qing Homoerotic Tales from *The Cut Sleeve*." *T'oung Pao* 78 (1992): 341–73.

———. "Exemplary Sodomites." Ph.D. diss. University of California, Berkeley, 1994.

von Glahn, Richard. "The Enchantment of Wealth: The God Wutong in the Social History of Jiangnan." *Harvard Journal of Asiatic Studies* 51, no. 2 (Dec. 1991): 651–714.

———. *Fountain of Fortune: Money and Monetary Policy in China, 1000–1700.* Berkeley: University of California Press, 1996.

———. "Municipal Reform and Urban Social Conflict in Late Ming Jiangnan." *Journal of Asian Studies* 50, no. 2 (May 1991): 280–307.

Wakeman, Frederic, Jr. "China and the Seventeenth-Century Crisis." *Late Imperial China* 7, no. 1 (June 1986): 7–26.

———. *The Great Enterprise: The Manchu Reconstruction of Imperial Order in Seventeenth-Century China.* 2 vols. Berkeley: University of California Press, 1985.

———. "The Price of Autonomy: Intellectuals in Ming and Ching Politics." *Daedalus* 101, no. 2 (Spring 1972): 35–70.

———. "Romantics, Stoics, and Martyrs in Seventeenth-Century China." *Journal of Asian Studies* 43, no. 4 (Aug. 1984): 661–65.

———. "The Shun Interregnum of 1644." In *From Ming to Ch'ing: Conquest, Region, and Continuity in Seventeenth-Century China*, ed. Jonathan D. Spence and John E. Wills, Jr. New Haven: Yale University Press, 1979.

Waley, Arthur. *Yuan Mei: Eighteenth-Century Chinese Poet.* London: George Allen and Unwin, 1956.

Wang, John. *Chin Sheng-t'an.* New York: Twayne Publishers, 1972.

Weber, Samuel. *Theatricality as Medium.* New York: Fordham University Press, 2004.

Weidner, Marsha, ed. *Views from Jade Terrace.* New York: Rizzoli, 1988.

West, Stephen H. "Part I, Essays: Drama." In *The Indiana Companion to Traditional Chinese Literature*, ed. William H. Nienhauser. Bloomington: Indiana University Press, 1986, pp. 13–30.

———. "Text and Ideology." In *Proceedings of the International Conference on Ming and Qing Drama*, ed. Hua Wei and Wang Ayling. Taipei: Academia Sinica. Institute for the Study of Literature and Philosophy, 1998, pp. 273–78.

West, Stephen, and Wilt Idema. "Introduction." In Wang Shifu, *The Moon and the Zither: The Story of the Western Wing.* Berkeley: University of California Press, 1991.

Widmer, Ellen. "The Epistolary World of Female Talent in Seventeenth-Century China." *Late Imperial China* 10, no. 2 (Dec. 1989): 1–43.

Wilshire, Bruce. *Role-playing and Identity: The Limits of Theatre as Metaphor.* Bloomington: Indiana University Press, 1991.

Wong, Siu-kit. "*Ch'ing* in Chinese Literature." Ph.D. diss., Oxford University, 1967.

Wu Cuncun. *Homoerotic Sensibilities in Late-Imperial China,* New York: Routledge, 2004.

Wu, Yenna. "The Inversion of Marital Hierarchy: Shrewish Wives and Henpecked Husbands in Seventeenth-Century Chinese Literature." *Harvard Journal of Asiatic Studies* 48, no. 2 (1988): 363–82.

Yan Haiping, "Theatricality in Classical Chinese Drama." In *Theatricality,* ed. Tracy C. Davis and Thomas Postlewait. Cambridge, Eng.: Cambridge University Press, 2003, pp. 65–89.

Yan, Yunxiang. *The Flow of Gifts: Reciprocity and Social Networks in a Chinese Village.* Stanford: Stanford University Press, 1996.

Yang, Mayfair Mei-hui. *Gifts, Favors and Banquets: The Art of Social Relationships in China.* Ithaca: Cornell University Press, 1994.

Yao Hsin-nung. "The Rise and Fall of the K'un Chü." *Tien-hsia Monthly* 2, no. 1 (1936): 63–84.

Ye, Yang. *Vignettes from the Late-Ming: A Hsiao-p'in Anthology.* Seattle: University of Washington Press, 1999.

Yee, Cordell D. K. "Chinese Cartography Among the Arts: Objectivity, Subjectivity, Representation." In *The History of Cartography,* vol. 2, ed. J. B. Harley and David Woodward. Chicago: University of Chicago Press, pp. 128–69.

Yeh, Catherine Vance. "Zeng Pu's *Niehai hua* as a Political Novel: A World Genre in Chinese Form." Ph.D. diss., Harvard University, 1990.

Yeh, Chia-ying. "The Ch'ang-chou School of Tz'u Criticism." In *Studies in Chinese Poetry,* by James R. Hightower and Florence Chia-ying Yeh. Cambridge, MA: Harvard University Asia Center, 1998, pp. 439–61.

Yu, Anthony. *Rereading the Stone: Desire and the Making of Fiction in "Dream of the Red Chamber."* Princeton: Princeton University Press, 1997.

Yung, Sai-shing. "A Critical Study of the *Han-tan chi.*" Ph.D. diss., Princeton University, 1990.

Yurchak, Alexei. "Soviet Hegemony of Form: Everything Was Forever, Until It Was No More." *Comparative Studies in Society and History* 45, no. 3 (2003): 480–510.

Zamperini, Paola. "Lost Bodies: Images and Representations of Prostitution in Late Qing Fiction." Ph.D. diss., University of California, Berkeley, 1999.

Zeitlin, Judith T. *Historian of the Strange: Pu Songling and the Chinese Classical Tale.* Stanford: Stanford University Press, 1993.

———. "The Petrified Heart: Obsession in Chinese Literature, Medicine and Art." *Late Imperial China* 12, no. 1 (June 1991): 1–25.

———. *The Phantom Heroine: Ghosts and Gender in Seventeenth-Century Chinese Literature.* Honolulu: University of Hawai'i Press, 2007.

———. "Shared Dreams: The Story of the Three Wives' Commentary on *The Peony Pavilion.*" *Harvard Journal of Asiatic Studies* 54, no. 1 (1994): 127–79.

Zhou Zuyan. *Androgyny in Late Ming and Early Qing Literature.* Honolulu: University of Hawai'i Press, 2003.

Zhuangzi. *The Complete Works of Chuang Tzu.* Trans. Burton Watson. New York: Columbia University Press, 1968.

Zimmerman, Susan, ed. *Erotic Politics: Desire on the Renaissance Stage.* New York: Routledge, 1992.

Index

Acting troupes: itinerant, 73; private, 59, 67n22, 73n36, 84n62, 88, 140n29, 186n40, 187n43; Juhe troupe, 80; Qinxiao, 176, 181, 206; Xiao nanya troupe, 85

Actors: base status of, 5–6, 14, 21, 43, 174, 186, 189, 255–56; boy actors, 14, 138, 140, 148, 166n82, 171, 176n12, 252; as gifts, 177, 190–95, 209, 213; promiscuity of, 41, 130, 139, 229, 252; as property, 3, 186, 195; as sexual plaything, 146, 160, 186, 203; sexual availability of, 86, 130, 143, 146–48, 160, 182, 186, 188, 203, 207, 255–56; as spies, 138

Actresses, 6n13, 140n29, 141–43, 187

Aesthetics, 23, 31, 32, 35, 56–58, 135–36, 291n81; aesthetic pleasure, 52, 56, 74–75; and vernacular, 234n35, 260; and *zhezi xi*, 66

Agnew, Jean-Christophe, 19n32, 122

Allegory, 219

Allusive citation, 13, 57, 90–92, 122, 164. *See also* Archaism; Citation

Anachronism, 62, 90n3, 283n54

Analects, 38, 100, 217, 226n20, 229–37, 274n32, 283n53

Androgyny, 147n49

Anthologies, 17, 92n4, 93, 196n60

Anti-archaism, 13, 57, 90–94, 104, 117–27, 131, 158, 234, 258–59. *See also* Archaism

Anti-theatricalists, 8, 28, 40–48, 56–57, 138, 247, 250, 259

Appearance: vs. reality, 8–9, 11, 15, 19, 29–30, 32–33, 36, 56, 58, 100, 133–36, 147, 227, 260; *ming*, 29, 33, 226n20. *See also* Illusion; Naming; Reputation

Archaism, 12–13, 57, 102, 104, 107, 112, 158; anti-archaism, 13, 57, 90–94, 104, 117–27, 131, 158, 234, 258–59. *See also* Allusive citation

Architecture: stage, 11–12, 59, 68, 71; temple, 9n16

Arias, 39, 66, 69–70, 132n12, 170; *sanqu*, 133, 152, 230

Artifice, 145–47, 151, 154, 283n53

Aspiration, social, 12, 36–37, 119, 138, 215, 225; and archaism, 13, 90–92,

98, 110, 112, 124, 158, 256, 258–59;
failed aspirations, 37, 39, 89, 94–95,
183, 258; and fashion, 43–44; freedom from, 51, 54–55. *See also* Careerism
Attachment: and detachment, 15–16,
86, 98, 214, 227, 229, 238–47; emotional, 197–98, 252, 257–58; radical,
251, 257–58; romantic, 174; and
spectatorship, 251; sympathetic, 15,
25, 150. *See also* Detachment; Romance; Sympathy
Audience, 18n26, 24, 67, 70–72, 74,
76, 79, 82–87, 97n20, 139, 207–8,
249, 255; and illusion, 14–15, 25, 30,
87, 169; instruction of, 15, 87, 229;
and *Mudan ting*, 101, 114, 119, 229;
and noise, 82, 84n60; and *Nan
wanghou*, 14, 145, 148–49, 152, 160,
166, 169, 171; and *Taohua shan*, 15,
25, 60, 214, 218–22, 224, 227, 229,
233, 235, 237, 240, 246; virtual, 86–
87; in *Male Queen* translation,
265n5, 314
Auspiciousness, 37, 67, 160, 281,
312n132
Authenticity, 8, 12–15, 19n32, 22, 35,
48, 58, 98, 132, 169; and archaism,
90–92, 95–96, 102, 115–17, 112n66,
119–21, 127, 132, 158; of illusion, 37;
and *Mudan ting*, 13–14, 90–92,
95–96, 102, 112n66, 115–17, 127, 132,
158, 251–52, 259; and *Nan wanghou*,
12–15, 58, 127, 132, 158, 168, 209,
251–52, 259; and passion (*zhenqing*), 21, 90, 127, 179, 208, 252; *qu*,
120; of spectatorship, 8, 13–15, 21–
23, 35, 249, 251–52, 258–60; and
Taohua shan, 12, 216–17, 232, 251–
52, 258–60; of vernacular, 90–92,

112, 115–16, 127, 158, 232; *zhen*, 22,
95–96, 120, 158, 179, 249
Authority, 14, 43, 100, 127–28, 157–58,
303n113; of texts, 107n51, 116
Autobiography, 233

Backstage, 86–87, 293, 305; offstage,
69–71, 86–87, 114, 143, 146, 214; in
Male Queen translation, 267, 281,
287, 288, 306. *See also* Screens
Baguwen, see under *Examinations*
Bai Pu, 49
Bai Qianshen, 184n33
Bakhtin, Mikhail, 92, 97
Ban Gu, 120
Banquets, 3, 42, 46, 55, 60n3, 61, 63–73
passim, 86, 104n39, 118, 130,
160n70, 179n18, 189, 201, 203, 221,
283, 286, 288, 290, 308
Bao Hansuo, 64, 73n36, 187
Baojian ji, 69
Bao Zhishui, 70
Barr, Alan, 38n21
Base status, *see under* Status
Behavior, social, 6, 42–44, 71, 107,
226n21, 237
Beijing, 60, 79–86, 117n79, 133, 140n31,
175n8, 183, 185, 188n47, 228
Bian er chai, 7, 251–52, 256–58
Bian Yujing, 175n7, 241
Biji (notation books), 20, 40–41, 78,
143, 179
Bin feng, 113
Birch, Cyril, 91, 95n15
Birthdays, 66–67, 84, 176, 186n40
Body, 10n19, 159; of actor, 130, 137, 145,
150–52, 154–55, 177, 197, 254,
255n10; female, 154, 297; in *Male
Queen* translation, 265, 266, 275,
284, 297. *See also* Cross-dressing

Harvard East Asian Monographs
(*out-of-print)

*83. Sang-Chul Suh, *Growth and Structural Changes in the Korean Economy, 1910–1940*

 84. J. W. Dower, *Empire and Aftermath: Yoshida Shigeru and the Japanese Experience, 1878–1954*

 85. Martin Collcutt, *Five Mountains: The Rinzai Zen Monastic Institution in Medieval Japan*

 86. Kwang Suk Kim and Michael Roemer, *Growth and Structural Transformation*

 87. Anne O. Krueger, *The Developmental Role of the Foreign Sector and Aid*

*88. Edwin S. Mills and Byung-Nak Song, *Urbanization and Urban Problems*

 89. Sung Hwan Ban, Pal Yong Moon, and Dwight H. Perkins, *Rural Development*

*90. Noel F. McGinn, Donald R. Snodgrass, Yung Bong Kim, Shin-Bok Kim, and Quee-Young Kim, *Education and Development in Korea*

*91. Leroy P. Jones and Il SaKong, *Government, Business, and Entrepreneurship in Economic Development: The Korean Case*

 92. Edward S. Mason, Dwight H. Perkins, Kwang Suk Kim, David C. Cole, Mahn Je Kim et al., *The Economic and Social Modernization of the Republic of Korea*

 93. Robert Repetto, Tai Hwan Kwon, Son-Ung Kim, Dae Young Kim, John E. Sloboda, and Peter J. Donaldson, *Economic Development, Population Policy, and Demographic Transition in the Republic of Korea*

 94. Parks M. Coble, Jr., *The Shanghai Capitalists and the Nationalist Government, 1927–1937*

 95. Noriko Kamachi, *Reform in China: Huang Tsun-hsien and the Japanese Model*

 96. Richard Wich, *Sino-Soviet Crisis Politics: A Study of Political Change and Communication*

 97. Lillian M. Li, *China's Silk Trade: Traditional Industry in the Modern World, 1842–1937*

 98. R. David Arkush, *Fei Xiaotong and Sociology in Revolutionary China*

*99. Kenneth Alan Grossberg, *Japan's Renaissance: The Politics of the Muromachi Bakufu*

100. James Reeve Pusey, *China and Charles Darwin*

101. Hoyt Cleveland Tillman, *Utilitarian Confucianism: Chen Liang's Challenge to Chu Hsi*

102. Thomas A. Stanley, *Ōsugi Sakae, Anarchist in Taishō Japan: The Creativity of the Ego*

103. Jonathan K. Ocko, *Bureaucratic Reform in Provincial China: Ting Jih-ch'ang in Restoration Kiangsu, 1867–1870*

104. James Reed, *The Missionary Mind and American East Asia Policy, 1911–1915*

105. Neil L. Waters, *Japan's Local Pragmatists: The Transition from Bakumatsu to Meiji in the Kawasaki Region*

106. David C. Cole and Yung Chul Park, *Financial Development in Korea, 1945–1978*

107. Roy Bahl, Chuk Kyo Kim, and Chong Kee Park, *Public Finances During the Korean Modernization Process*

108. William D. Wray, *Mitsubishi and the N.Y.K, 1870–1914: Business Strategy in the Japanese Shipping Industry*

109. Ralph William Huenemann, *The Dragon and the Iron Horse: The Economics of Railroads in China, 1876–1937*

*110. Benjamin A. Elman, *From Philosophy to Philology: Intellectual and Social Aspects of Change in Late Imperial China*

111. Jane Kate Leonard, *Wei Yüan and China's Rediscovery of the Maritime World*

170. Denise Potrzeba Lett, *In Pursuit of Status: The Making of South Korea's "New" Urban Middle Class*

171. Mimi Hall Yiengpruksawan, *Hiraizumi: Buddhist Art and Regional Politics in Twelfth-Century Japan*

172. Charles Shirō Inouye, *The Similitude of Blossoms: A Critical Biography of Izumi Kyōka (1873–1939), Japanese Novelist and Playwright*

173. Aviad E. Raz, *Riding the Black Ship: Japan and Tokyo Disneyland*

174. Deborah J. Milly, *Poverty, Equality, and Growth: The Politics of Economic Need in Postwar Japan*

175. See Heng Teow, *Japan's Cultural Policy Toward China, 1918–1931: A Comparative Perspective*

176. Michael A. Fuller, *An Introduction to Literary Chinese*

177. Frederick R. Dickinson, *War and National Reinvention: Japan in the Great War, 1914–1919*

178. John Solt, *Shredding the Tapestry of Meaning: The Poetry and Poetics of Kitasono Katue (1902–1978)*

179. Edward Pratt, *Japan's Protoindustrial Elite: The Economic Foundations of the Gōnō*

180. Atsuko Sakaki, *Recontextualizing Texts: Narrative Performance in Modern Japanese Fiction*

181. Soon-Won Park, *Colonial Industrialization and Labor in Korea: The Onoda Cement Factory*

182. JaHyun Kim Haboush and Martina Deuchler, *Culture and the State in Late Chosŏn Korea*

183. John W. Chaffee, *Branches of Heaven: A History of the Imperial Clan of Sung China*

184. Gi-Wook Shin and Michael Robinson, eds., *Colonial Modernity in Korea*

185. Nam-lin Hur, *Prayer and Play in Late Tokugawa Japan: Asakusa Sensōji and Edo Society*

186. Kristin Stapleton, *Civilizing Chengdu: Chinese Urban Reform, 1895–1937*

187. Hyung Il Pai, *Constructing "Korean" Origins: A Critical Review of Archaeology, Historiography, and Racial Myth in Korean State-Formation Theories*

188. Brian D. Ruppert, *Jewel in the Ashes: Buddha Relics and Power in Early Medieval Japan*

189. Susan Daruvala, *Zhou Zuoren and an Alternative Chinese Response to Modernity*

*190. James Z. Lee, *The Political Economy of a Frontier: Southwest China, 1250–1850*

191. Kerry Smith, *A Time of Crisis: Japan, the Great Depression, and Rural Revitalization*

192. Michael Lewis, *Becoming Apart: National Power and Local Politics in Toyama, 1868–1945*

193. William C. Kirby, Man-houng Lin, James Chin Shih, and David A. Pietz, eds., *State and Economy in Republican China: A Handbook for Scholars*

194. Timothy S. George, *Minamata: Pollution and the Struggle for Democracy in Postwar Japan*

195. Billy K. L. So, *Prosperity, Region, and Institutions in Maritime China: The South Fukien Pattern, 946–1368*

196. Yoshihisa Tak Matsusaka, *The Making of Japanese Manchuria, 1904–1932*

197. Maram Epstein, *Competing Discourses: Orthodoxy, Authenticity, and Engendered Meanings in Late Imperial Chinese Fiction*

198. Curtis J. Milhaupt, J. Mark Ramseyer, and Michael K. Young, eds. and comps., *Japanese Law in Context: Readings in Society, the Economy, and Politics*

199. Haruo Iguchi, *Unfinished Business: Ayukawa Yoshisuke and U.S.-Japan Relations, 1937–1952*

200. Scott Pearce, Audrey Spiro, and Patricia Ebrey, *Culture and Power in the Reconstitution of the Chinese Realm, 200–600*

201. Terry Kawashima, *Writing Margins: The Textual Construction of Gender in Heian and Kamakura Japan*

202. Martin W. Huang, *Desire and Fictional Narrative in Late Imperial China*

203. Robert S. Ross and Jiang Changbin, eds., *Re-examining the Cold War: U.S.-China Diplomacy, 1954–1973*

204. Guanhua Wang, *In Search of Justice: The 1905–1906 Chinese Anti-American Boycott*

205. David Schaberg, *A Patterned Past: Form and Thought in Early Chinese Historiography*

206. Christine Yano, *Tears of Longing: Nostalgia and the Nation in Japanese Popular Song*

207. Milena Doleželová-Velingerová and Oldřich Král, with Graham Sanders, eds., *The Appropriation of Cultural Capital: China's May Fourth Project*

208. Robert N. Huey, *The Making of 'Shinkokinshū'*

209. Lee Butler, *Emperor and Aristocracy in Japan, 1467–1680: Resilience and Renewal*

210. Suzanne Ogden, *Inklings of Democracy in China*

211. Kenneth J. Ruoff, *The People's Emperor: Democracy and the Japanese Monarchy, 1945–1995*

212. Haun Saussy, *Great Walls of Discourse and Other Adventures in Cultural China*

213. Aviad E. Raz, *Emotions at Work: Normative Control, Organizations, and Culture in Japan and America*

214. Rebecca E. Karl and Peter Zarrow, eds., *Rethinking the 1898 Reform Period: Political and Cultural Change in Late Qing China*

215. Kevin O'Rourke, *The Book of Korean Shijo*

216. Ezra F. Vogel, ed., *The Golden Age of the U.S.-China-Japan Triangle, 1972–1989*

217. Thomas A. Wilson, ed., *On Sacred Grounds: Culture, Society, Politics, and the Formation of the Cult of Confucius*

218. Donald S. Sutton, *Steps of Perfection: Exorcistic Performers and Chinese Religion in Twentieth-Century Taiwan*

219. Daqing Yang, *Technology of Empire: Telecommunications and Japanese Expansionism in Asia, 1883–1945*

220. Qianshen Bai, *Fu Shan's World: The Transformation of Chinese Calligraphy in the Seventeenth Century*

221. Paul Jakov Smith and Richard von Glahn, eds., *The Song-Yuan-Ming Transition in Chinese History*

222. Rania Huntington, *Alien Kind: Foxes and Late Imperial Chinese Narrative*

223. Jordan Sand, *House and Home in Modern Japan: Architecture, Domestic Space, and Bourgeois Culture, 1880–1930*

250. Wilt L. Idema, Wai-yee Li, and Ellen Widmer, eds., *Trauma and Transcendence in Early Qing Literature*

251. Barbara Molony and Kathleen Uno, eds., *Gendering Modern Japanese History*

252. Hiroshi Aoyagi, *Islands of Eight Million Smiles: Idol Performance and Symbolic Production in Contemporary Japan*

253. Wai-yee Li, *The Readability of the Past in Early Chinese Historiography*

254. William C. Kirby, Robert S. Ross, and Gong Li, eds., *Normalization of U.S.-China Relations: An International History*

255. Ellen Gardner Nakamura, *Practical Pursuits: Takano Chōei, Takahashi Keisaku, and Western Medicine in Nineteenth-Century Japan*

256. Jonathan W. Best, *A History of the Early Korean Kingdom of Paekche, together with an annotated translation of* The Paekche Annals *of the* Samguk sagi

257. Liang Pan, *The United Nations in Japan's Foreign and Security Policymaking, 1945–1992: National Security, Party Politics, and International Status*

258. Richard Belsky, *Localities at the Center: Native Place, Space, and Power in Late Imperial Beijing*

259. Zwia Lipkin, *"Useless to the State": "Social Problems" and Social Engineering in Nationalist Nanjing, 1927–1937*

260. William O. Gardner, *Advertising Tower: Japanese Modernism and Modernity in the 1920s*

261. Stephen Owen, *The Making of Early Chinese Classical Poetry*

262. Martin J. Powers, *Pattern and Person: Ornament, Society, and Self in Classical China*

263. Anna M. Shields, *Crafting a Collection: The Cultural Contexts and Poetic Practice of the* Huajian ji 花間集 *(Collection from Among the Flowers)*

264. Stephen Owen, *The Late Tang: Chinese Poetry of the Mid-Ninth Century (827–860)*

265. Sara L. Friedman, *Intimate Politics: Marriage, the Market, and State Power in Southeastern China*

266. Patricia Buckley Ebrey and Maggie Bickford, *Emperor Huizong and Late Northern Song China: The Politics of Culture and the Culture of Politics*

267. Sophie Volpp, *Worldly Stage: Theatricality in Seventeenth-Century China*